INCONVENIENT HISTORY

VOLUME IV: 2012

Numbers 1 through 4

A Quarterly Journal for Free Historical Inquiry
is published by History Behind Bars Press four times yearly in the
Spring, Summer, Fall, and Winter

EDITOR

RICHARD A. WIDMANN

ASSISTANT EDITOR

JETT RUCKER

EDITORIAL ADVISORY COMMITTEE

JOSEPH P. BELLINGER
ARTHUR R. BUTZ
ROBERT FAURISSON
JUERGEN GRAF
FRED A. LEUCHTER
CARLO MATTOGNO

PUBLISHER

HBB PRESS

Editorial and Subscription Inquiries

Inconvenient History
PO Box 439016
San Ysidro, CA 92143
USA

www.inconvenienthistory.com

Copyright 2013 History Behind Bars

All rights reserved. No part of this book may be reproduced in any manner whatsoever without written permission except in the case of reprints in the context of reviews. For information write: History Behind Bars Press, PO Box 439016, San Ysidro, CA 92143, USA.

ISBN 978-1-59148-991-7

ISSN 2324-7231

INCONVENIENT HISTORY, Volume IV, 2012

Table of Contents

Number 1, Spring 2012 1

Editorial
Bookburning in the Style of 2011
Richard A. Widmann 3

Resistance Is Obligatory
Germar Rudolf 9

Ritual Defamation: A Contemporary Academic Example
Daniel McGowan 32

Stephen F. Pinter: An Early Revisionist
Klaus Schwensen 46

A Postcard from Treblinka
Thomas Dalton 66

Review
The Wandering Who: A Study of Jewish Identity Politics *by Gilad Atzmon. Zero Books, Washington, D.C, 2011, 202 pp. US*
Ezra MacVie 78

The Palestinians as an "Invented People"
Rich Siegel 82

Comment
Relegation—A Formula for Blowback
Jett Rucker 88

Number 2, Summer 2012 93

Editorial
The Clash of the Nobelists
Jett Rucker 95

Historical Revisionism and 'Relativising the Holocaust'
K.R. Bolton 100

Christian Gerlach and the "Extermination Camp" at Mogilev
Carlo Mattogno.. 116

John Demjanjuk: The Man More Sinned Against
Nigel Jackson 128

A Postcard from Auschwitz
Thomas Dalton 173

On the Roads of Truth: Searching for Warwick Hester
Klaus Schwensen... 189

Review
Night *by Elie Wiesel. Bantam Books, New York, 1982, 109 pp.*
D.D. Desjardins 196

Review
Hitler's Austria 1938-1945: Popular Sentiment in the Nazi Era *by Evan Burr Bukey, University of North Carolina Press, Chapel Hill, N. C., 2000, 320 pp.*
Ezra MacVie... 220

Number 3, Fall 2012 225

Editorial
Imprisoned at Ellis Island
Richard A. Widmann.. 227

Count Potocki de Montalk and the Katyn Manifesto
K.R. Bolton 234

A Revisionist in Prison
Germar Rudolf... 247

Three Books on Treblinka
Thomas Kues... 254

The Number of Victims of Sachsenhausen Concentration Camp (1936-1945)
Klaus Schwensen...269

Review
The Black Swan (Revised Edition) *by Nassim Nicholas Taleb. Penguin Group, New York, 2010, 379 pp.*
Ezra MacVie...284

Review
The Gas Vans: A Critical Investigation *by Santiago Alvarez and Pierre Marais, The Barnes Review, Washington, D.C., 2011, 390 pp., illustrated, with notes, bibliography, indexed.*
Richard A. Widmann...289

Comment
Revisionism's Final Victories
Jett Rucker..293

Number 4, Winter 2012...297

Editorial
Uncle Sam, May I?
Jett Rucker..299

The Rumbula Massacre – A Critical Examination of the Facts, Part 1
Thomas Kues..303

And the War Came
Ralph Raico...357

Unholy Pursuit: the Charles Zentai Case in Australia
Nigel Jackson..367

Why They Said There Were Gas Chambers—or, Sing for Your Life!
Jett Rucker..409

From the Memoirs of a German Soldier: Auschwitz, Buchenwald and Alfred Hitchcock's First Horror Movie
Nemo Anonymous...418

Smoking Crematory Chimney at Auschwitz: A Correction
  Robert Bartec 425

Review
In the Garden of Beasts *by Erik Larson. Crown Publishing Group, New York, 2011, 448 pp.*
  Ezra MacVie 432

Volume IV

Number 1, Spring 2012

EDITORIAL

Bookburning in the Style of 2011

Richard A. Widmann

On Wednesday December 28th, print-on-demand publisher Lulu.com informed the staff at *Inconvenient History* that they had struck our two annual editions from availability. The so-called "Questionable Content team" tersely noted that our content was in violation of their membership agreement because it was "unlawful, obscene, defamatory, pornographic, indecent, lewd, harassing, threatening, harmful, invasive of privacy or publicity rights, abusive, inflammatory, or otherwise objectionable." With a bit more focus, they continued, "Lulu sells all over the world, including to France and Germany where revisionist books are illegal and anti-constitutional."

Immediately we wrote to Lulu to get additional information. Who issued a complaint about our materials? Was a formal complaint received from a representative of the French or German governments? What article in particular was found to be objectionable? Lulu did not see fit to respond to our inquiry. This leaves us only able to guess at the invisible hand behind the complaint.

The psychic intimidation employed by the complainant had its desired effect. The books are no longer available and a revenue stream was cut off, or at least temporarily interrupted.

In Ray Bradbury's prophetic science fiction novel, *Fahrenheit 451*, firemen are employed not to extinguish fires, but rather to burn offensive literature. The title is a reference to the temperature at which paper burns. In his novel, fire chief Captain Beatty explains the origins of the book burnings:

> "It didn't come from the Government down. There was no dictum, no declaration, no censorship, to start with, no! Technology, mass exploitation, and minority pressure carried the trick, thank God."[1]

In today's global economy, once-ironclad freedoms guaranteed by the First Amendment to the Constitution of the United States prohibiting laws which abridge freedom of speech or of the press apparently carry little weight. Lulu.com, an American company headquartered in

Raleigh, North Carolina, quickly sacrificed such freedoms on the altar of economic globalism. While Americans saw freedom of expression erode during the period of 'political correctness' ushered in throughout the 1990s, today's impulse not to "offend" has resulted in the censorship of thought and ideas that may be objectionable to one minority or another. Again, in the words of Captain Beatty:

> *"Colored people don't like Little Black Sambo. Burn it. White people don't feel good about Uncle Tom's Cabin. Burn it."* [2]

Contemporary bookburners have a long legacy preceding them of individuals and regimes who attempted to limit intellectual freedom. Here National Socialists are seen burning books deemed to oppose their ideology (11 May 1933) Bundesarchiv, Bild 102-14597 / Unknown / CC-BY-SA [CC-BY-SA-3.0-de (www.creativecommons.org/licenses/by-sa/3.0/de/deed.en)], via Wikimedia Commons

Bookburning unfortunately was not simply a fantastic idea of a science-fiction author. The history of bookburning dates back at least to the third century BC when China's Qin Dynasty burned books to suppress heretical views.[3] Many people think of the medieval period in Europe when many religious texts were burned from the Talmud to Tyndale's English language New Testament to Martin Luther's German translation of the Bible. In the years when such texts were meticulously scribed by hand, such burnings were quite effective in their impact. In more recent times, the German National Socialists burned many thousands of works deemed to be in opposition to Nazi ideology.

Today, some of the books most impacted by censorship and would-be "firemen" are revisionist titles. While organizations like the American Library Association are quick to complain about public burnings of best-sellers including J.K. Rowling's *Harry Potter* series, they refuse to even mention the burning of revisionist titles.[4]

One example of the burning of a revisionist title occurred in early 1995. After receiving several complaints from unspecified sources, a German publisher ordered the "recycling" of all existing copies of John Sack's *An Eye for an Eye*. Sack's book reported Jewish revenge against the Germans after World War II. Citing information from Germany's Federal Archives, Sack maintained that 60,000 to 80,000 ethnic Germans were killed or otherwise made to die between 1945 and 1948 in camps run by the Polish communist regime's Office of State Security.[5] Controllers of the German cultural establishment launched a bitter assault. Reviewers denounced it as a sensationalist, "vile docudrama" and a "gift to neo-Nazis." Soon, the book's publisher found itself deluged with complaints. Publisher Viktor Niemann ultimately ordered all 6,000 copies of the German edition to be destroyed. On February 13, 1995 he announced, "They will be recycled."[6]

In 1996, St. Martin's Press decided to publish David Irving's biography of Hitler's propaganda minister, Joseph Goebbels. Soon St. Martin's Press would receive dozens of complaints. St. Martin's Press publisher Thomas Dunne issued the following angry statement:

> *"A number of the calls we have received have expressed fury that we would publish a book by 'a man like David Irving' and have questioned our moral right to do so. I can only say that Joseph Goebbels must be laughing in hell. He, after all, was the man who loved nothing better than burning books, threatening publishers, suppressing ideas and judging the merits of ideas based not on their content but by their author's racial, ethnic or political purity. That is indeed a sad irony."*

Shadowy forces continued their campaign to ban the book. Initially, St. Martin's editors stood by their decision and insisted they found nothing wrong with Irving's book. The pressure increased – now including death threats. Finally, Thomas McCormack, Chief Executive Officer of St. Martin's gave in and reversed the company's earlier position. St. Martin's would not publish *Goebbels: Mastermind of the Third Reich*.[7]

One of the last books written by revisionist pioneer James J. Martin was *An American Adventure in Bookburning in the Style of 1918*. Here Martin, who coined the term, "inconvenient history" recounted how in late August 1918 President Woodrow Wilson's Secretary of War Newton Diehl Baker issued a directive ordering the removal from U.S. Army camp libraries of 31 publications that had been classified as "undesirable."[8] Included in this slender volume is Martin's article, "A Beginner's Manual for Apprentice Book Burners." Martin's satirical manual is a bibliographic record of works with unorthodox or unpopular viewpoints. He introduces for example a list of World War Two revisionist titles as follows:

> *"On the world events of 1933-47 your opinions were probably frozen into their current shape by the accounts of the virgin purity of the intentions and actions of the winners and the necessity and wisdom of everything done by them."*[9]

Today our bookburning is not in the style of 1918. It is not in the style of the twentieth century or earlier times at all. The technological advances of the 21st century have enriched our lives with almost unlimited possibilities. While the speed-of-light exchange of information may be used to topple totalitarian regimes and be used effectively to bring new light and freedoms to countries and nations that have only known the darkness of censorship and dictatorship, it has also empowered those who seek to silence all dissent and limit intellectual freedom and debate.

Today it is clear that Bradbury was correct that official government censorship is not needed to burn books. Technology and minority pressure will do the trick. Bradbury was wrong after all about the need for firemen. Bookburning will occur without smoke or fire at all. It will be done by removing content from the Internet. It will be done before the actual book is printed. It will be done without even a cry or a whimper from the so-called defenders of free speech.

For the books that are burned will only be those that are objectionable—or shall I say, *inconvenient*.

As a result of the apprentice bookburners and their efforts to burn two annual editions of *Inconvenient History*, we have decided to dedicate this Spring issue to the topic of Freedom of Speech. Make no mistake, those who side with the censors and the bookburners stand against intellectual freedom and liberty. Regardless of their motives, they are no different than the most repressive regimes and individuals in history who believe that they know better than you. As such, we have several important contributions. First, we are proud to present Germar Rudolf's "Resistance Is Obligation" a gripping account of his persecution for refusing to recant his scientific convictions. Dan McGowan recounts the story of his personal run-in with defamation on an American college campus. Jett Rucker describes one possible outcome of what he calls "reputational terrorism." We are also pleased to present Rich Siegel's timely commentary on the Palestinians as anything but an "invented" people. Thomas Dalton provides an interesting first-person look at the Treblinka concentration camp as it stands today in his "Postcard from Treblinka." Klaus Schwensen returns this issue with a detailed consideration of early revisionist Stephen F. Pinter. Finally Ezra MacVie is back with a fascinating look at Gilad Atzmon's *The Wandering Who: A Study of Jewish Identity Politics*.

If you stand with us against the apprentice bookburners, please support our work.

Notes:

1. Ray Bradbury, *Fahrenheit 451*, Ballantine Books, New York, 1996, p. 58.
2. Ibid. p. 59. See also my article, "Problems Warned about in 'Fahrenheit 451' Threaten Today's Word" published in Katie de Koster, editor, *Readings on Fahrenheit 451*, Greenhaven Press, Inc. San Diego, Cal., 2000. Available on-line as, "Fahrenheit 451 Trends Threaten Intellectual Freedom" at http://codoh.com/library/document/995
3. Online: http://en.wikipedia.org/wiki/Book_burning
4. On several occasions, this author has provided the ALA with details of the censorship and burning of revisionist books. To this day, they have never responded nor have they made mention of such events on their Website. See "Banned Books and Unmentionable Books: The Hypocrisy of the American Library Association" online: http://codoh.com/library/document/96

5. This author met the late John Sack, who was himself Jewish, at David Irving's first Real History Conference.
6. "Book Detailing Jewish Crimes against Germans Banned," *Journal of Historical Review* Vol. 15 No. 1, Jan/Feb 1995, p. 28. See also: "German Publisher Drops Book on Postwar Camps for Nazis," *The New York Times*, February 16, 1995. The book, *An Eye for an Eye: The Untold Story of Jewish Revenge against Germans in 1945*, was published in the United States in 1993 by Basic Books of New York, a division of the publishing firm of HarperCollins.
7. "St. Martin's Cancels Book on Goebbels," *The New York Times*, April 5, 1996, p. D4.
8. James J. Martin, *An American Adventure in Bookburning in the Style of 1918*, Ralph Myles Publisher, Colorado Springs, Colo., 1988, p.7.
9. Ibid, p.129.

Resistance Is Obligatory

Germar Rudolf

He who argues that peaceful dissidents on historical issues should be deprived of their civil rights for their diverging views, that is: incarcerated, is – if given the power to implement his intentions – nothing else but a tyrant (if enacting laws to support his oppressive deeds) or a terrorist (if acting outside the law).

I. A Peaceful Dissident's Ordeal

Imagine that you are a scientist who has summarized the results of fifteen years of research in a book – and that shortly after publishing this book you are arrested and thrown into prison exactly for this. Imagine further that you are aware with incontrovertible certainty that in the scheduled trial you and your defense attorneys will be forbidden, under threat of prosecution, to prove any factual claims made in that book; that all other motions to introduce supporting evidence will be rejected as well; that all the courts up to the highest appellate will support such conduct; that only a very few of your research colleagues will dare to confirm the legitimacy and quality of your book because they fear similar persecution; but that the efforts of these few colleagues will be in vain as well; and finally that the news media, the so-called "guardians of freedom of speech," will join the prosecution in demanding your merciless punishment. In such a situation as this, how would you "defend" yourself in court?

This is precisely the Kafkaesque situation in which I found myself at the end of 2005 after having been abruptly and violently separated from my wife and child by U.S. Immigration authorities in Chicago,[1] deported to Germany and immediately thrown into jail to await trial, on account of my book *Lectures on the Holocaust*, which I had published in the summer of 2005, and for Web pages promoting this and other similar books. This was no plot against me personally, though, because this is the same situation everyone faces who clashes with Germany's law penalizing the "denial of the Holocaust." The situation is similar in many other nations, most of them in Europe.

Various defense attorneys unanimously assured me that all defense was doomed in principle and that I would have to reckon with a prison sentence close to the maximum term (five years). Other attorneys advised me to recant my political views and feign remorse and contrition, which might gain me the clemency of the Court.

Renouncing my scientific convictions was not an acceptable option for me, though. A defense based on the facts of the case was impossible, and if attempted regardless, it merely would have exacerbated my situation, because in trying to prove that my views are correct I would have repeated once more the very crime of violating state dogma for which I was on trial in the first place.

But even if such an approach had been possible, I still would have rejected it, because I am firmly convinced that no court has the right to pass binding judgment on matters of scientific controversy. It is therefore an impermissible concession to allow a court of law to pass judgment on the correctness of scientific theses – here about history – in the first place. Every such motion to introduce evidence is already a crime against science, because it undermines its independence from the judiciary.

Thus I decided quite early to treat the upcoming trial as an opportunity to document the Kafkaesque legal conditions now prevailing in the Federal Republic of Germany in order to write a book about it after the trial was over. For this reason I wanted to make a thorough statement about the governing legal situation at the beginning of the main proceedings. After a biographical introduction, I explained the actual nature of science as such and its significance for human society. This was followed by a depiction of the Kafkaesque situation prevailing in German court trials today, whose mission is to suppress opinions that are a thorn in the side of the power elite. After analyzing today's practice, which violates all our human and constitutional rights, I posed the explosive question of the extent to which I as a citizen of this State have the right and even the duty to resist such injustice.

Subsequently my seven-day presentation in court turned itself into a *lecture*, this time on the principles of science and on the destruction of freedom of opinion in Germany.

At the end I did receive a prison sentence of 30 months, which is only half of what had been augured by the lawyers, and that in spite of publicly re-affirming my right to express my revisionist views and in spite of calling for resistance against the German authorities.

Here I would like to give a condensed excerpt of my courtroom lectures, a complete version of which with ample documentation is forthcoming.[2] In section VIII, I will add a few observations on my experiences in prison, which are not included in said upcoming book.

II. Defense Strategy

I began my courtroom lectures with a few general remarks about my defense strategy, which, in a way, were a declaration of war to the German authorities. I stated:

1. During my defense, statements about historical subjects will be made by me only in order:

    a. to explain and illustrate my personal development;

    b. to illustrate by examples the criteria of the nature of science;

    c. to place the District Attorney's charges regarding my statements in a larger context.

2. These statements are not made in order to buttress my historical opinions with facts.

3. I will not file motions asking the Court to consider my historical theses – for the following reasons:

    a. Political: German courts are forbidden by orders from higher up to accept such motions to introduce evidence, as is stated in Article 97 of the German Basic Law:[3] "Judges are independent and subject only to the Law." Please pardon my sarcasm.

    b. Opportunistic: Item a) above does not prohibit me from submitting motions to introduce evidence. However, since they would all be rejected, it would all be an effort in futility. We should all spare ourselves this waste of time and energy.

c. Reciprocal: Since present law denies me the right to defend myself historically and factually, I in turn am denying my accusers the right to charge me historically and factually on the basis of the maxim of equality and reciprocity. Thus I consider the prosecution's historical allegations to be non-existent.

d. Juridical: In 1543, Nicolaus Copernicus wrote [4]

> *"If perchance there should be foolish speakers who, together with those ignorant of all mathematics, will take it upon themselves to decide concerning these things, and because of some place in the Scriptures wickedly distorted to their purpose, should dare to assail this my work, they are of no importance to me, to such an extent do I despise their judgment as rash."*

Nicolaus Copernicus (19 February 1473 – 24 May 1543) was a Renaissance astronomer and the first person to formulate a comprehensive heliocentric cosmology which displaced the Earth from the center of the universe. Public domain, via Wikimedia Commons

No court in the world has the right or the competence to authoritatively decide scientific questions. No parliament in the world has the right to use penal law to dogmatically prescribe answers to scientific questions. Thus it would be absurd for me as a science publisher to ask a court of law to determine the validity of the works I have published. Only the scientific community is competent and entitled to do this.

III. Dignity

One hideous feature of German legal standards is that, when it comes to "the Holocaust," it pits human dignity against the right to search for the truth. According to this "logic," the human dignity of all Jews – those who suffered back then and those who live today – depends on everyone accepting the orthodox Holocaust narrative. And since the protection of human dignity is the first and most important article in the German constitution, this has priority over everything else.

What I pointed out first in court was the fact that denying us the search for the truth is an even more serious violation of human dignity than denying the Jews a certain narrative of a detail of their history. After all: what sets us humans apart from bacteria and insects? Isn't it the capacity to doubt our senses and to systematically search for the reality behind the mere semblance? To bolster my case, I quoted several famous personalities of western culture, such as Socrates, who observed:[5]

> "The unexamined life is not worth living."

Aristotle was expressing the same thought when he observed:[6]

> "All men by nature desire to know."
> "[...] for men, therefore, the life according to reason is best and pleasantest, since reason more than anything else is men."[7]

Konrad Lorenz described human curiosity, that is, the will to learn the truth, with these words:[8]

> "There exist inborn behavioral systems that are equivalent to human rights whose suppression can lead to serious mental disturbances."

The philosopher Karl R. Popper described the difference between us humans and the animals as follows:[9]

> "the main difference between Einstein and an amoeba [...] is that Einstein <u>consciously seeks for error elimination</u>. He tries to kill his theories: he is <u>consciously critical</u> of his theories which, for this reason, he tries to <u>formulate</u> sharply rather than vaguely. But the amoeba cannot be critical because it cannot <u>face</u> its hypotheses: they are part of it. (Only objective knowledge is criticizable. Subjective knowledge becomes criticizable when we <u>say</u> what we think; and even more so when we <u>write</u> it down, or <u>print</u> it.)"

Skepticism and curiosity, doubting one's senses and theories and looking deeper in search for the truth, is therefore what brought us down from the trees and out of the caves. They are what made us what we are and what sets us apart from animals. Hence the rights to doubt and to search for the truth are not negotiable. It is therefore perfidious when the State pits freedom of science against human dignity, when in fact they are inseparable. We all are entitled by nature to seek the truth and announce what we think we have found. We do not need any official permission for this.

IV. Enlightenment

When it comes to the Holocaust, the most important values of western civilization are turned upside down. To prove this, I quoted philosopher Immanuel Kant's classic definition of enlightenment:[10]

> "Enlightenment is man's leaving his self-caused immaturity. Immaturity is the incapacity to use one's intelligence without the guidance of another. Such immaturity is self-caused, if it is not caused by lack of intelligence, but by lack of determination and courage to use one's intelligence without being guided by another. Sapere Aude! [dare to know] Have the courage to use your own intelligence! is therefore the motto of the enlightenment."

Yet when it comes to the "Holocaust," most governments discourage us from using our own intelligence. Some of them even threaten us with prosecution, and they insist that we follow the guidance of others. Karl Popper characterized a society where the authorities enforce a "state belief" and impose taboos as a closed, dogmatic, archaic society.[11] The modern, open society, in contrast, encourages criticism of traditional dogmas. In fact, this is its foremost hallmark.[12]

Hence, dogma and criticism stand opposed to each other as antipodes. In our case, this is the State opposed to revisionism; or in other words the Enemies of Science on one hand versus Science on the other:

Dogma vs. Critique

State vs. Revisionism

Enemies of Science vs. Science

For the scientist, however, dogmas and taboos are strictly unacceptable.

V. Science

The two non-negotiable main pillars of any scientific endeavor are:

1. Freedom of Hypothesis: At the beginning of the quest for creating knowledge any question may be asked. Doubt as the intellectual basis of all humans can be expressed as a simple question: "Is this really true?" Thus curiosity is nothing other than reason posing questions in search of answers.

2. Undetermined Outcome: The answers to research questions can be determined exclusively by verifiable evidence. They cannot be determined by taboos or official guidelines laid down by scientific, societal, religious, political, judicial or other authorities.

If answers to scientific questions are prescribed, then posing questions is degraded to a mere rhetorical farce, and science becomes impossible. This is therefore not just an undermining of the essential nature of science, but its complete abolition.

I therefore told the German court:

> *"As a scientist and science publisher, it is my duty to actively combat the gutting of the pillars of science by promoting such doubt, skepticism, and critiques, and by providing them a venue."*

Next I presented a thorough discussion about the nature of science and how to determine whether a paper or book is scholarly/scientific in nature, reyling mainly on the works by my favorite philosopher and epistemologist Karl. R. Popper.[13] I will spare the reader the details of this discussion and will merely reproduce the summary here:

What Is Science?

* There are no (final) judgments, but rather always only more or less reliable (preliminary) pre-judgments.

* The reasons, that is to say the evidence, for our pre-judgments must be testable/verifiable as well as possible.

* We must both actively and passively test and criticize:

> • Test and criticize pre-judgments and reasons of others.
>
> • Invite others to test and criticize our pre-judgments and welcome this activity. This includes the *duty* to publish one's findings in order to enable others to critique them.
>
> • We must address the tests and critiques of others and test and criticize them in turn. This also means that one should not back down too fast in the face of criticism.

* We have to avoid immunizing our pre-judgments:

> • Avoid creating auxiliary theories designed to prop up an untenable or awkward main hypothesis.
>
> • Select data only according to objective criteria, using the technique of source criticism.
>
> • Use exact, consistent and constant definitions of terms.
>
> • Avoid attacks on persons as substitute for factual arguments.

The motivation of my lengthy elaborations to define the nature of science is that the mainstream disparages revisionist works as merely "pseudo-scientific," *i.e.*, false science. After having defined the formal characteristics of scientific works, I then juxtaposed several cases of orthodox scholarship clearly bearing the hallmarks of "pseudo-science" with revisionist works which meet the definition of scientific works much better.

I restrict myself here to summarizing only one case presented to the court, which deals with the arbitrary selection and elimination of data. It concerns a Polish attempt[14] at refuting revisionist claims based on the results of chemical analyses of wall samples taken at Auschwitz by Fred Leuchter[15] and by myself.[16] The problem the Poles had to overcome was that the analytical results as such were undeniably true and reproducible. What they subsequently did amounted to a scientific fraud: They chose a different analytical method which simply eliminated all the unwanted data – with the "reason" given that they didn't understand the issues at hand. If that was really the case, however, then they should not have gotten involved in the first place and should have left the field to those who do understand what they are doing.[17]

VI. The Law

It was Frederick the Great, King of Prussia, who once stated – and I quoted him in court as well for good reason:[18]

> "A legal council which exercises injustices is more dangerous and worse than a gang of thieves; one can protect oneself against those, but nobody can protect himself against rogues who use the robes of justice to carry out their vicious passions; they are worse than the biggest scoundrels in the world and deserve double punishment."

I will not strain the Anglo-Saxon reader's patience by reiterating my elaborations on the German justice system's perversions to persecute peaceful dissidents. I will merely restrict myself to a summary of a comparison with which I introduced my legal observations in court. It is a juxtaposition of the conditions of the current German judicial system in general and when dealing with revisionists in particular with that of another country, whose identity I revealed only at the very end of this comparison: The Soviet Union under Joseph Stalin. This comparison is based on the one hand on Alexandr Solzhenitsyn's trilogy *The Gulag Archipelago,* in which he describes his own experiences and those of others as political prisoners in Stalin's Soviet Union.[19] It is based on the other hand on my experiences with, and insights into, the German judicial system.

The first parallel concerns the existence of special government units serving the prosecution of politically motivated "crimes," which mostly refer to undesirable expressions of opinion. Stalin had his NKVD. In today's Germany this role is fulfilled by the Police Department for State Protection (*Dezernat Staatsschutz*), whose main focus is, statistically seen, on the prosecution of usually peaceful "thought crimes" committed by persons harboring right-wing views.

Another astonishing parallel between Stalin's judiciary and the current German system was described by Solzhenitsyn as follows:

> *"Another very important thing about the courts today: there is no tape recorder, no stenographer, just a thick-fingered secretary with the leisurely penmanship of an eighteenth-century schoolgirl, laboriously recording some part of the proceedings in the transcript. This record is not read out during the session, and no one is allowed to see it until the judge has looked it over and approved it. Only what the judge confirms will remain on record, will have happened in court. While things that we have heard with our own ears vanish like smoke – they never happened at all!"* (vol. 3, p. 521)

In today's Germany the situation is even worse, since in proceedings before District Courts, which handle "serious" offenses, *no* protocol is kept at all about who says what and when. Needless to say this opens the floodgates to error and arbitrariness. And here is the perverted reason given by the German authorities why protocols are allegedly obsolete: Since one cannot appeal the decisions handed down by a District Court on matters of fact anyway, a protocol laying out the facts of the case is unnecessary. So here you have the core of the German judiciary: no appeal possible, hence no protocol. It has its internal logic and consistency, but doesn't that sound more like a totalitarian banana republic?

Another parallel is that defending yourself in front of such a court by trying to argue that you are right will merely exacerbate your situation, as Solzhenitsyn wrote:

> *"Even if you were to speak in your own defense with the eloquence of Demosthenes [[20] ...] it would not help you in the slightest. All you could do would be to increase your sentence [...]."* (vol. 1, p. 294)

That's what happened to Ernst Zündel in Germany, whose lawyers ferociously defended his right to speak his mind, as a result of which Zündel got the maximum sentence for being recalcitrant. Plus his lawyers got indicted too, which is another parallel to Uncle Joe's Soviet paradise, as Solzhenitsyn reported:

> "*The tribunal roared out a threat <u>to arrest</u> [...] the principal defense lawyer [...]*" (vol. 1, p. 350)

As if prosecuting defense lawyers for their perfectly legitimate defense activities weren't bad enough, here is how to top it off: threaten witnesses with prosecution, too, who dare to speak out for defendants on trial for "thought crimes," or as Solzhenitsyn put it (*ibid.*):

> "*And right then and there the tribunal actually ordered the imprisonment of a witness, Professor Yegorov, [...]*"

That happened to me in 1994, when I was summoned by a defense lawyer in order to testify as an expert witness. When the Presiding Judge heard to what effect the defense wanted me to testified, he warned me succinctly that I would be liable to prosecution if testifying along the lines of the lawyer's motion. Of course it never came to this, because, as Solzhenitsyn correctly observed:

> "*Defense witnesses were not permitted to testify.*" (vol. 1, p. 351)

In Germany they are never allowed to testify, when it comes to revisionists on trial. And worse still: not only witnesses supporting the views of a revisionist defendant are rejected, but all kinds of evidence: witnesses, documents, experts. Germany's judiciary claims that everything about the Holocaust is "self-evident," thus requiring no proof at all. In fact, they go so far as to indict anyone who merely dares to file a motion to introduce such evidence, be he a defendant or a defense lawyer. Yes, Germany has made it *illegal* to move for the introduction of exonerating evidence! Not even Stalin had such an ingenious tool in his repertoire of repression! This way the German judiciary manages to eliminate all unwanted data from the record – not that there is much of a record to begin with...

Although there are more parallels I quoted during my courtroom lectures, I will leave it at that here, as the message I want to convey is probably clear.

It goes without saying that there are also important differences between the Soviet and the current German systems of justice: torture does not exist in German prisons, and I am very grateful for that – although it is quite ironic to read in Solzhenitsyn's work that a Soviet prosecutor once stated:

> *"For us [Soviets…] the concept of <u>torture</u> inheres in the very fact of holding political prisoners in prison…"* (vol. 1, p. 331)

With that he referred to the methods of the Tzarist regime, not to his own system's abuses, just as Germany criticizes the offenses against justice of others (like Iran or China), yet ignores the trampling of justice in its own courts.

When I revealed at the end of this comparison with which system I had compared the German system, the judges were visibly shaken. Maybe they realized that something about the system they are a part of is indeed fishy?

I continued my presentation with a definition of a political prisoner and the subsequent proof that we revisionists are a perfect match. Here are the ten criteria I listed, and I explained and proffered evidence that all these points are seen in the cases of prominent revisionists:

- We are dealing with peaceful dissent, peacefully presented; with "peaceful" I mean that no justification or advocation of violations of the civil rights of others occurs.
- The prosecuted offense is not punishable in the vast majority of nations.
- The dissident is supported by civil rights organizations.
- The dissident receives statements of solidarity from strangers (correspondence, visits, interventions at authorities, demonstrations).
- The government attempts to suppress such statements of solidarity.
- Prominent individuals make statements of solidarity.
- Statements of solidarity or criticism against prosecution are published by media & politicians, especially abroad.

- The dissident's rights to a defense are restricted.
- The persecuting nation refuses to recognize political prisoners as such despite the above features.
- Dissidents receive worse treatment than regular inmates.

The last point results from the fact that the prison authorities expect that we revisionists recant and cease all contacts with like-minded persons. Since most of us refuse to do this, the consequences are harsh: no early release on parole, no reliefs in our prison regimen. Needless to say, the same authorities do not expect a drug dealer, for example, to recant his views on drugs nor to cease any contact with his pals and clients. Views, opinions and social contacts are simply not of any interest when it comes to "normal" criminals. Hence dissidents in Germany are subjected to a special treatment. This is not only meant to mentally "heal" the thought criminal, but also to deter others from dissenting. In legalese, deterring the general populace from committing a crime is called "general -prevention." According to Solzhenitsyn, imprisoning dissidents in the late Soviet Union was a measure of "social prophylaxis" (vol. 1, p. 42), which probably amounts to the same thing.

Ironically I had committed the "thought crimes" for which I was imprisoned in Germany in countries where these acts had been and still are perfectly legal: the U.S. and the UK. Germany simply claims the right to prosecute dissent anywhere in the world, if their dissenting voices violate German law and could he heard or read in Germany. In the Internet era, this basically amounts to prosecuting anybody, anywhere, at any time, if only the German authorities can get their hands on the dissident.

For anyone not residing in Germany or any other persecuting nation, the question is: what law should one abide by to stay out of trouble? I don't think there is a satisfactory answer to this question. I've therefore decided to abide by a higher, uncodified law, which was summarized succinctly by Immanuel Kant in his Categorical Imperative:[21]

> "Act only according to that maxim whereby you can at the same time will that it should become a universal law."

If we apply this to the present case, we will see immediately that the legal concepts of "stirring up the people" and "endangering the public peace," as listed in the German law used to prosecute revisionists, are untenable, as they do not describe acts of a perpetrator but rather the effects it has on others.

If an act justifies or advocates the violation of the civil rights of others, then this itself is the act that one might consider prosecutable. Whether this act has any other consequences, like disturbance of the public peace, should be an aggravating circumstance at worst. In fact, many scenarios can be imagined where a perfectly peaceful opinion could wreak havoc in a society which considers such an opinion to be heretical or blasphemous. The history of mankind is full of innocent, peaceful individuals who were persecuted because they upset certain, usually powerful, parts of the populace: Socrates, Jesus Christ, Martin Luther, Galileo Galilei, Mahatma Gandhi. Or take the founding fathers of the U.S. constitution: Did they not disturb the public peace, stir up the populace, and commit sedition?

In all these cases it was *not* the dissident causing havoc, but it was the mindset of the people in their environment and the way they reacted to the dissent. Luther neither advocated the Church to be split in two nor did he ask for the Peasants' War or the Thirty Years War, yet they all ensued as a repercussion. Was Luther responsible for all this? No he was not. The social, political and economic injustices of the time were the cause. So where and how do we draw the line when it comes to punishing disturbers of the "public peace"?

Let me give one more example to make even the most hardcore anti-fascist agree that concepts like "disturbing the public peace" belong in the dustbin of history: During the Third Reich the German Catholic priest Rubert Mayer was publicly indicted because with his sermons he had "repeatedly made public, inciting statements" and because he had discussed matters of the state "in a way capable of endangering public peace."[22] He was subsequently imprisoned at Sachsenhausen concentration camp for seven months. Compare this with the multi-year prison terms revisionists get nowadays in "democratic" Germany!

Although I argued during my defense lecture that the German law I was prosecuted under was unconstitutional, this is of little relevance for people acting within other legal frameworks. What is more important is a universal, holistic approach to the issue of how to react to authorities persecuting peaceful dissidents, no matter what legal trappings they wrap around it.

VII. Resistance

Karl R. Popper wrote in his classic work *The Open Society and Its Enemies*:[23]

> *"those who are not prepared to fight for their freedom will lose it."*

The tragedy is that the enemy threatening our freedom is the very entity – the State – whose "fundamental purpose [is…] the protection of that freedom which does not harm other citizens."[24]

So what are we to do as generally law-abiding citizens, when the law itself has become fundamentally unjust? The answer was given some 160 years ago by Henry David Thoreau in his classic essay "Civil Disobedience":[25]

> *"Unjust laws exist: shall we be content to obey them, or shall we endeavor to amend them, and obey them until we have succeeded, or shall we transgress them at once? Men generally, under such a [democratic] government as this, think that they ought to wait until they have persuaded the majority to alter them. They think that, if they should resist, the remedy would be worse than the evil. But it is the fault of the government itself that the remedy is worse than the evil. It makes it worse. Why is it not more apt to anticipate and provide for reform? [...] Why does it always crucify Christ, and excommunicate Copernicus and Luther, and pronounce Washington and Franklin rebels? [...]*
>
> *A minority is powerless while it conforms to the majority; [...] but it is irresistible when it clogs by its whole weight. If the alternative is to keep all just men in prison, or give up war and slavery, the State will not hesitate which to choose. [...]*
>
> *Under a government which imprisons any unjustly, the true place for a just man is also in prison."*

So if you are a true fighter for freedom of speech and haven't been in prison yet, you've done something wrong! Or you were just plain lucky.

This essay by Thoreau inspired Mahatma Gandhi, from whose writings I quote some pivotal sentences which, in turn, were an inspiration for me during my time in prison:[26]

> "So long as the superstition that men should obey unjust laws exists, so long will their slavery exist."
> "Democracy is not a state in which people act like sheep. Under democracy individual liberty of opinion and action is jealously guarded."[27]
> "In other words, the true democrat is he who with purely non-violent means defends his liberty and therefore his country's and ultimately that of the whole of mankind."[28]
> "I wish I could persuade everybody that civil disobedience is the inherent right of a citizen. He dare not give it up without ceasing to be a man. [...] But to put down civil disobedience is to attempt to imprison conscience. [...] Civil disobedience, therefore, becomes a sacred duty when the State has become lawless, or which is the same thing, corrupt. [...] It is a birthright that cannot be surrendered without surrender of one's self-respect."[29]

But when exactly and how is a minority in a constitutional democracy under the (claimed) rule of law allowed to resist its government? In my defense speech I elaborated on this by quoting numerous experts, most German, on the topic. In summary, most experts agree that civil disobedience against a government, that is to say peaceful disregard of the law, is permissible only if the government's violation against which the protest is directed affects valid constitutional principles or general principles of human rights. This also means that the protesters may ignore or violate only those laws against which the protest is directed. In other words, the protesters may not set their private views as absolute, and they are not allowed to violate other laws, which are generally accepted even by them. Hence violent protests are unacceptable.

This is what we revisionists should insist upon: The right to doubt and to peacefully dissent on any topic is an integral, inalienable part of our human condition, and thus of our human rights, whether it is enshrined in our country's constitution or not. Any government enacting laws or regulations infringing on that right must be resisted with peaceful means by consciously and deliberately violating the law which violates our human dignity.

And that is exactly what I told the German court in 2007.

Curiously enough, the German constitution even grants all German citizens the right to resist their government. In article 20, paragraph 4, of the German Basic Law it says:

> *"All Germans have the right to resist against everyone who endeavors to remove this [constitutional democratic] order, if no other remedy is possible."*

The question is, of course, at what point it is permitted to invoke this right? Do we have to wait until the government has turned into an outright tyranny, or should we be allowed to put our foot down at the outset of government excesses? Since it is always easier to resist the onset of governmental abuse rather than to wait until resistance has become mortally dangerous for the resister, the wise answer to that question ought to be obvious.

Let me quote Germany's highest authority on this question: Prof. Dr. Roman Herzog, former President of the German Federal Constitutional High Court and later President of the Federal Republic of Germany. He stated repeatedly that "from time immemorial there has been a right to resist by those violated and a right to emergency relief for all citizens" in case of encroachments on human dignity and on the human rights.[30] According to Herzog, each article in Germany's constitution – the statutory civil rights also among them – is,

> *"viewed by daylight,... nothing else but the specific elaboration on a fundamental principle of the constitutional nature of the state, so that assaults on almost any individual article at once touch upon the principles of Art. 20 of the Basic Law [the right to resist]."* [31]

Since it is the primary obligation of the State to protect the dignity of its subjects, it is in turn also the primary right of all human beings to resist encroachments of the State on human dignity.[32]

This closes the circle of my argumentation, at the beginning of which I demonstrated that the right to doubt, to search for the truth, and to communicate the results of this activity is simply constitutional for being human, hence for human dignity as such.

Hence, resistance is obligatory!

VIII. Prison

Between the years 1993 and 2011 I had, in a certain way, a Jewish experience: I was persecuted by my own government, saw my career chances destroyed, fled from one country to another in an attempt to avoid incarceration, but eventually I was caught and deported. I subsequently spent many years in a number of detention facilities: Rottenburg, Stuttgart, Heidelberg, Mannheim, and again Rottenburg. In those prisons I had to do work in order to pay for the costs I was causing the German prison system (forced labor, anyone?). After being released, I eventually, after an agonizingly long legal struggle, managed to emigrate for good from the country of my birth.

However, I am also very fortunate that in many ways my experience was much more benign than what many Jews had to experience during World War II: the detention conditions were rather favorable, my family was left unharmed, my health uncompromised, my spirit unbroken, and my property untouched (except maybe for a quarter million dollars in lawyer bills that accumulated over these 18 years).

"So, what is it like in prison?" people ask me once in a while. On the one hand I recommend that you better not find out. But then again, maybe you should. Although not a nice one, it still is a part of the human condition.

Being arrested and thrown into jail is traumatic. The first weeks and months are the worst. But humans are creatures of habit, and so you adjust to your life's circumstances even in such a dismal environment. You find a way to organize your day, to focus on some activities which you enjoy and which make time pass: you write letters, draw pictures, sing songs (Karaoke-style, for the most part…), and you join many of the recreational activities offered: volleyball, working out, Bible studies, discussion groups, church choir, prison band (yes, we had jailhouse rock, and it rocked!). And, needless to say, you play games with fellow inmates and also work out in your cell: push-ups, sit-ups, pull-ups at the toilet curtain rail, and other exercises with self-made "weights" (I had ten one-liter milk cartons placed in an undershirt knotted shut at the bottom; worked nicely).

You even make friends, sort of. Not ones you keep once you are out, but every prison is a tiny world with all the social dynamics you have outside as well. So, even though you initially thought you could never adjust to it, eventually you settle in. You have your time well organized and even feel kind of comfy in your little nook that you've carved out for yourself.

It comes to the point where, after having been out of your cell for a number of hours partaking in some activities, you mumble to yourself: "I'm tired, I want to go home" – by which you mean your cell... Makes you worry, doesn't it? Yet making yourself feel at home even in such a gloomy place is the art of living, is the way to limit emotional damage.

And then, for whatever reason, you are transferred to another jail. That's bad news. You can read it frequently in survivor testimonies: You get ripped out of your routine. You lose all the informal privileges you've won, all the friends you've made. You get to a place where you know nobody. You need to start from scratch organizing yourself and your daily routine: how to get the food you prefer, how to join the recreational groups you like, and so on. Hence every transfer is a new traumatic experience.

I therefore understand today why prisoners who had been at Auschwitz for a while and had managed to carve out a little niche for themselves feared being transferred to anther camp – provided of course there was no extermination going on at Auschwitz.

But all the adjusting notwithstanding, make no mistake: I stood for many hours behind those iron bars in my various prison cells longing to be able to finally go home, and during our courtyard time my eyes followed many an airplane in the sky flying west craving that Scotty might beam me up there…

Which brings up another astounding fact of life: In Germany every prisoner has the right to spend one hour a day in the courtyard, and I assume that the law is similar in most countries. Since that's the only time the inmates can get out of their cells (apart from going to work and recreational activities), most of them make the most of it. The result is that during summer time most inmates get quite a tan, which led my mother to ask me one day whether we have a tanning studio in prison. Well, no, but count the hours which you, as a free person, spend outside each day, and you will realize that a free person on average spends considerably less than an hour outside. So, statistically speaking, prison inmates are more often "out and about" than free people. Amazing, isn't it? Well, I admit, maybe they are out, but not about...

Nothing is worse than the feeling of losing a sizeable part of your lifetime being locked up. So you look for something which helps you feel that you've used your time for something constructive and of use in your later life. Hence I obtained a Cambridge Certificate in Advanced English, learned Spanish, and extended my English vocabulary by learning the words in *Roget's Thesaurus* (one hour of word learning every day, religiously). I read as I've never read in my entire life. I subscribed to the weekly *Science* magazine and read it for three years from cover to cover, thus broadening my scientific knowledge in numerous fields considerably. I also read the works of classic and philosophical literature which I had never managed to look into while free: the ones I like (Aristotle, Kant, Popper, Tolstoy, Dickens, Schopenhauer, to name the most impressive) and the ones I learned to dislike (Dostoyevsky, Hegel, Hemingway).

Now my wife calls me a walking thesaurus. Speaking of whom… she is a psychologist specializing in helping people who have been traumatized by their life's experiences. So she announced toward the end of my incarceration that she would take good care of me and help me to efface my emotional scars. But after my release she quickly realized that these 45 months of incarceration had passed by me without leaving any apparent trace. I was still the same man she had lost back then, and so she fell in love with me all over again…

Even though the authorities treated me worse than other inmates because I did not recant my views and showed no signs of remorse – they rebuked me repeatedly for spreading my views among the inmates – my lot was far better than that of the other inmates from a psychological point of view: being incarcerated did not tarnish my reputation, quite to the contrary. I wear it like a badge of honor, or as the German historian Prof. Dr. Ernst Nolte wrote to me in a letter after my release, I can now count myself among the men of honor who have gone to prison for reasons of conscience. Whereas most inmates lose most of their friends and often even the support of their families, my friends and family have stood firmly by me. Whereas most prisoners struggle financially and get in deep debt during their incarceration, as they lose their jobs and subsequently often also their homes and property, I was very fortunate to find so many generous supporters that not only my legal expenses were covered, but also the support for my children. There were even some funds left over which I could use after my release to restart my life.

Most important and in contrast to most inmates, political prisoners don't lose their feeling of meaning; they feel neither guilty nor ashamed of what they have done. Or as David Cole expressed it once: We are loud, we are proud, and the best of all: we are right!

This attitude, more than anything else, makes you wing even the toughest of times, and it keeps you going afterwards as well, as the *New York Times* correctly observed in an article entitled "Why Freed Dissidents Pick Path of Most Resistance." This article, which was fittingly published five weeks prior to my release from prison, describes how Arab dissidents who were incarcerated for their peaceful political views went right back to their acts of civil disobedience once released from prison.[33] As one of them expressed it:

> *"It is a matter not only of dignity, it is the sense of your life. It's your choice of life, and if you give up, you will lose your sense of your life."*

He said he had no choice but to go right back to where he had left off.

Just like us revisionists!

Resistance Is Obligatory may be purchased in the USA through The Barnes Review.

Notes:

1. I will not dwell on my trials and tribulations with U.S. immigration authorities. My case is thoroughly documented online at www.germarrudolf.com.
2. G. Rudolf, *Resistance Is Obligatory* published privately, forthcoming.
3. Germany's Basic Law, which was negotiated between German politicians and primarily the U.S. occupational forces right after WWII, is considered to be its constitution, although it has never been approved by a referendum of the German people, hence lacks formal legitimacy.
4. Nikolaus Kopernikus, *Über die Kreisbewegungen der Weltkörper*, Thorn 1879, p. 7; English.: Nicolaus Copernicus, *On the Revolution of*

Heavenly Spheres, Prometheus Books, Amherst, NY, 1995; here quoted from Dorothy Stimson, *The Gradual Acceptance of the Copernican Theory of the Universe*, Hanover, N.H., 1917, p. 115; original: *De revolutionibus orbium coelestium*, 1543; from 1616 to 1822 this book was "suspended" by the Catholic Church, which means that, when quoting the book, it had to be emphasized that the heliocentric system is merely a mathematical model.
5. Socrates, *Apologia*, Sec. 38.
6. Aristotle, *Metaphysics*, book 1, chapter 1, first sentence; Richard Keon (ed.), *The Basic Works of Aristotle*, Random House, New York, 1941, p. 689.
7. Aristotle, *Nicomachean Ethics* book X, chapter 7; *ibid.*, p. 1105.
8. Konrad Lorenz, *Der Abbau des Menschlichen*, Piper, Munich 1983, p. 1; *The Waning of Humaneness*, Little, Brown & Co., Boston 1987, p. 186.
9. Karl Popper, *Objective Knowledge*, 4th ed., Clarendon Press, Oxford 1979, pp. 24f.
10. Immanuel Kant, "Beantwortung der Frage: Was ist Aufklärung?," *Berlinische Monatsschrift*, December 1784, pp. 481-494; see "What Is Enlightenment?" at http://en.wikiquote.org/wiki/Immanuel_Kant.
11. Karl R. Popper, *The Open Society and Its Enemies*, Routledge & Paul, London 1962, vol. 1, p. 202.
12. Karl Popper, *Objective Knowledge*, *op. cit.* (Note 9), pp. 347f.
13. Based mainly on his works *The Logic of Scientific Discovery*, Hutchinson & Co., London 1968, and *Objective Knowledge*, *op. cit.* (Note 9).
14. J. Markiewicz, W. Gubala, J. Labedz, "A Study of the Cyanide Compounds Content in the Walls of the Gas Chambers in the Former Auschwitz and Birkenau Concentration Camps," *Z Zagadnien Nauk Sadowych*, Vol. XXX (1994) pp. 17-27.
15. F. Leuchter, R. Faurisson, G. Rudolf, *The Leuchter Reports*, 3rd ed., The Barnes Review, Washington, D.C., 2012, pp. 44-46, 59.
16. Originally presented in: Ernst Gauss (=Germar Rudolf), *Vorlesungen über Zeitgeschichte*, Grabert, Tübingen 1993; English see G. Rudolf, *The Rudolf Report*, 2nd ed., The Barnes Review, Washington, D.C., 2011, pp. 230-278.
17. For details see Germar Rudolf, Carlo Mattogno, *Auschwitz Lies*, 2nd ed., The Barnes Review, Washington, D.C., 2011, pp. 45-67.
18. Bruno Frank, *Friedrich der Große als Mensch im Spiegel seiner Briefe*, Deutsche Buch-Gemeinschaft, Berlin 1926, p. 99.
19. Aleksandr Solzhenitsyn, *The GULag Archipelago*, Collins & Harvill, London 1974-1978.
20. Leading Greek orator and statesman of Athens (384-322 B.C.).
21. Immanuel Kant, *Kritik der praktischen Vernunft*, Riga 1788, p. 54 (§ 7 "Grundgesetz der reinen praktischen Vernunft"; new: Meiner, Hamburg 2003, p. 41); English: *Grounding for the Metaphysics of Morals*, 3rd ed., Hackett, Indianapolis 1981, p. 30.
22. Otto Gritschneder (ed.), *Ich predige weiter. Pater Rupert Mayer und das Dritte Reich*, Rosenheimer Verlag, Rosenheim 1987, p. 89.

23. Karl Popper, *The Open...*, *op. cit.* (Note 11), vol. 2, p. 287.
24. *Ibid.*, vol. 1, p. 110.
25. Henry David Thoreau, *Walden and Other Writings*, Bantam, Toronto 1981, pp. 92, 94.
26. Shriman Narayan (ed.), *The Selected Works of Mahatma Gandhi*, vol. 4, Navajivan Publishing House, Ahmedabad 1969, p. 174.
27. *Young India*, 2 March 1922; Ministry of Information and Broadcasting, Government of India (ed.), *The Collected Works of Mahatma Gandhi (Electronic Book)*, Publications Division Government of India, New Delhi 1999, 98 volumes (www.gandhiserve.org/e/cwmg/cwmg.html), subsequently *CWMG*, here vol. 26, p. 246.
28. *Harijan*, 15 April 1939, *CWMG*, vol. 75, p. 249.
29. *Young India*, 5 Jan. 1922; *CWMG*, vol. 25, pp. 391f.
30. Roman Herzog, "Das positive Widerstandsrecht" in: *Festschrift für A. Merkel*, Munich 1970, p. 102; quoted acc. to Klaus Peters, *Widerstandsrecht und humanitäre Intervention*, Osnabrücker Rechtswissenschaftliche Abhandlungen, vol. 61, Carl Heymanns Verlag, Cologne 2005, p. 184 (Dissertation at Univ. Osnabrück 2004/2005).
31. R. Herzog, *ibid.*, p. 100; K. Peters, *ibid.*, p. 188.
32. R. Herzog, in: Theodor Maunz, Günter Dürig, *Grundgesetz Kommentar*, 41st Supplement (Ergänzungslieferung), Munich 2002, Art. 20, para. 4, Rn. 17-19: acc. to K. Peters, *ibid.*
33. Published online at www.nytimes.com/2009/05/2 7/world/middleeast/27egypt.html on 26 May 2009. A version of this article appeared in print on 27 May 2009, on page A6 of the New York edition under the headline "Once Freed from Prison, Dissidents Often Continue to Resist."

Ritual Defamation: A Contemporary Academic Example

Daniel McGowan

The term *ritual defamation* was coined by Laird Wilcox to describe the destruction of the reputation of a person by unfair, wrongful, or malicious speech or publication. The defamation is in retaliation for opinions expressed by the victim, with the intention of silencing that person's influence, and making an example of him so as to discourage similar "insensitivity" to subjects currently ruled as taboo. It is aggressive, organized and skillfully applied, often by a representative of a special interest group, such as the ironically named Anti-Defamation League.

Ritual defamation is not called "ritual" because it follows any prescribed religious or mystical doctrine, nor is it embraced in any particular document or scripture. Rather, it is ritualistic because it follows a predictable, stereotyped pattern which embraces a number of elements, as in a ritual.

Laird Wilcox enumerated eight basic elements of a *ritual defamation:*

First, the victim must have violated a particular taboo, usually by expressing or identifying with a forbidden attitude, opinion or belief.

Second, the defamers condemn the character of the victim, never offering more than a perfunctory challenge to the particular attitudes, opinions or beliefs the victim expressed or implied. Character assassination is its primary tool.

Third, the defamers avoid engaging in any kind of debate over the truthfulness or reasonableness of what has been expressed. Their goal is not discussion but rather condemnation, censorship and repression.

Fourth, the victim is usually someone who is vulnerable to public opinion, although perhaps in a very modest way. It could be a schoolteacher, writer, businessman, minor official, or merely an outspoken citizen; visibility enhances vulnerability to *ritual defamation*.

Fifth, an attempt is made to involve others in the defamation. In the case of a public official, other public officials will be urged to denounce the offender. In the case of a student, other students will be called upon; in the case of a professor, other professors will be asked to join the condemnation.

Sixth, in order for a *ritual defamation* to be most effective, the victim must be dehumanized to the extent that he becomes identical with the offending attitude, opinion or belief, and in a manner which distorts his views to the point where they appear at their most extreme. For example, a victim who is defamed as a "subversive" will be identified with the worst images of subversion, such as espionage, terrorism or treason.

Seventh, the defamation tries to bring pressure and humiliation on the victim from every quarter, including family and friends. If the victim has school children, they may be taunted and ridiculed as a consequence of adverse publicity. If the victim is employed, he may be fired from his job. If the victim belongs to clubs or associations, other members may be urged to expel him.

Eighth, any explanation the victim may offer is dismissed as irrelevant. To claim truth as a defense for a tabooed opinion or belief is treated as defiance and only compounds the offense. *Ritual defamation* is often not necessarily an issue of being wrong or incorrect but rather of "insensitivity" and failing to observe social taboos.[1]

Ritual defamation is not used to persuade, but rather to punish. It is used to hurt, to intimidate, to destroy, and to persecute, and to avoid the dialogue, debate and discussion that free speech implies. Its obvious maliciousness is often hidden behind the dictates of political correctness and required sensitivity to established myths.

Ritual Defamation at Hobart and William Smith Colleges: A Textbook Example

In the September 2009 I wrote an op-ed for the local newspaper, *The Finger Lakes Times*, defining "Holocaust Denial." I submitted it in response to the media frenzy and demonization of Iranian President Ahmadinejad, who was scheduled to address the UN General Assembly. After several delays, it was published on September 27th under a quarter-page picture of Ahmadinejad and under the headline "What do deniers really mean? (See Appendix 1)

Although the definition I presented has been widely accepted, both by those who affirm and by those who contest or "revise" the current narrative of the Holocaust, and although the facts I presented were not challenged, the op-ed sparked a classic case of *ritual defamation*. Questioning the Holocaust narrative, or even defining what it means to question it, is arguably the most serious taboo in the United States today. It is considered "beyond the pale" and even touching the subject is like touching the third rail on the subway – instant death to your career.

First Blood

On October 3rd a "colleague" from the Education Department, James MaKinster, "facilitated" a smear letter, signed by six additional colleagues, and circulated it by email to over 300 other professors and people in the Hobart and William Smith Colleges community. Their letter was addressed to the colleges' President Mark Gearan; it denounced me with lies and insidious innuendos and demanded the revocation of my status as a faculty emeritus.

I heard about the MaKinster letter quite by happenstance soon after it was circulated, but neither the President nor any of the original seven who signed it was willing to provide me with a copy. It was not until May 2011 some 20 months later that I finally got a copy of the email version, not of the final letter with all the signatures. (See Appendix 2)

My Response

In a vain attempt to clear my name and set the record straight I sent a message to the entire community rebutting the charges made in the MaKinster smear letter. I stated that:

1. Contrary to the feigned outrage of my ritual defamers as to the date of publishing the op-ed, I had nothing to do with the timing of the article and make no apology for when it appeared vis-à-vis a Jewish holiday.

2. My ritual defamers' egregious claim to know my "personal beliefs" and their claim that I used my title to win them credence was untrue. Nowhere were my personal beliefs stated. Moreover my article included an exceptionally long disclaimer showing that The Colleges neither condone nor condemn what I had written.

3. My ritual defamers' claim that "Holocaust denial carries absolutely no weight among academic scholars in any field whatsoever" was also untrue. There are a number of scholars who dare to criticize the typical Holocaust narrative and are willing to fight the slime hurled at them by ardent Zionists who feel it their duty to protect the current version that serves as the sword and shield of apartheid Israel. (As a footnote, our former provost and former dean of women (both Jewish) demanded that I not use the word "apartheid" in connection with Israel. Although the term was used in the Israeli press and later by ex-President Jimmy Carter, they did not consider it to be "suitable discourse" on our campus where, ironically, we routinely claim to support free speech and diversity of opinion.)

4. My ritual defamers said that "denying undisputed facts of the holocaust (sic) is not a way to show support for the Palestinians." First, the three tenets of Holocaust revisionism are clearly not "undisputed." To the contrary, these taboos are hotly and passionately disputed; people's lives are ruined when they dispute these "facts" or even mention them. In fourteen countries you can get jail time for disputing "facts" surrounding the Holocaust.

Second, disputing purported facts is what science and historical analysis are all about. We academics have no problem discussing and disputing whether or not Jesus Christ is truly the son of God, or if President Obama's birth certificate is real, or if Jewish slaves built the Egyptian pyramids, or if Roosevelt knew a Japanese attack on Hawaii was imminent, but we are not allowed to discuss or dispute the six-million figure, which was bantered about before World War I. (Yes, before World War I; see for example, "Dr. Paul Nathan's View of Russian Massacre", *The New York Times*, March 25, 1906.) To question the six million figure on most American campuses is simply taboo.

Finally, what gives these ritual defamers the credentials to pontificate on what supports or hurts Palestinians? None of them are experts on Palestine and none are activists for Palestinian human rights. To the contrary, some of them have been responsible for feting at Hobart and

William Smith Colleges anti-Palestinian demagogues including Elie Wiesel and even Benyamin Netanyahu. They have also endorsed giving Madeleine Albright our highest *humanitarian* award, which was not only ironic, but disgraceful in light of her statement that the deaths of over 500,000 Iraqi children were "worth it".

5. Labeling Holocaust revisionism "Holocaust denial" is unwarrantedly pejorative. It might be fine for Fox News, but it is not conducive to, and often precludes, intelligent discourse. To call Holocaust revisionism "thinly veiled anti-Semitism" is simply untrue and it defames scholars and others, including Jews, who question the Holocaust doctrine as we are fed it in hundreds of films, books, articles, and commentaries. Terms like Holocaust Industry, Holocaust Fatigue, Holocaust professional, Holocaust wannabes, and Holocaust High Priest were not coined by "deniers" or anti-Semites; they were coined by Jews. (The High Priest quip is an obvious reference to Elie Wiesel; it was made by Tova Reich in her book *My Holocaust*. Tova's husband, Walter Reich, was the former director of the US Holocaust Museum in Washington.)

In 1946 the US government told us that 20 million people were murdered by Hitler. Now that figure is said to be 11 million; it has been "revised" downward and literally carved in stone at the US Holocaust Memorial. For years we were told that over 4 million were killed at Auschwitz alone, but by the early 1990s that figure was "revised" downward to 1.5 million. Wiesel tells us that people were thrown alive onto pyres; he claims to have seen it with his own eyes; today even Israeli-trained guides at Auschwitz say that is not true. They have already "revised" his narrative. These are but a few examples of historical revisionism, examples that are not inherently anti-Semitic and no longer considered taboo.

6. It is most interesting to see academic colleagues say, "(a)s we all know ... the term 'ethnic cleansing' was introduced to make genocide sound more palatable." That means they either deny that Palestinians have been (and continue to be) ethnically cleansed or they agree that Israel is performing genocide on the Palestinian people.

7. While the ritual defamers found my piece to be "abhorrent," they seemed unable to find fault with a single fact I presented. So they resorted to name-calling and labeled the piece "hate speech" and "unsupported vitriol" and smeared my name to hundreds of people. I

am surprised that the Anti-Defamation League or the Mossad did not come knocking on my door.

8. The ritual defamers genuinely were concerned about the op-ed's impact on our Jewish students, staff, and faculty. But maybe it is time for all members of the community to see the Holocaust for what it really was and not the unquestionable, unimpeachable, doctrine that makes Jewish suffering superior to that of other people. Maybe it is time to recognize that Zionism as a political movement to create a Jewish state in Palestine began long before the Holocaust and that Zionist discrimination, dehumanization, and dispossession of the Palestinian people should not be excused by it. Maybe it is time to see that since over half the population (within the borders controlled by Israel) is not Jewish, the dream of creating a Jewish state has failed. Walling in the non-Jews or putting them in Bantustans or driving them into Jordan will not make Israel a Jewish state. Nationalistic allegiance to "blood and soil" has been a failure in Germany and in Israel. That should be the real lesson of the Holocaust.

9. To say that my op-ed "does not meet our expectation of minimally rational and minimally humane discourse" is pure nonsense. The piece is well written, well substantiated, and quite humane.

10. The ritual defamers are quite right about one thing; they were deeply disturbed and saddened to see a Hobart and William Smith Colleges title attached to it, even with a lengthy disclaimer. Diversity and perspectives outside the mainstream are to be encouraged, but not if they question Jewish power, Israel, or Holocaust doctrine. Apparently those topics are totally taboo.

11. The demand to President Gearan to remove my title of Professor Emeritus is both classic and stupid. Would it save Hobart and William Smith Colleges from being associated with my writings? Of course not; I would simply become "Former Professor Emeritus at Hobart and William Smith Colleges" with no disclaimer.

But what it would really do is to cast me into the briar patch with Norman Finkelstein, Marc Ellis, Paul Eisen, Henry Herskovitz, Gilad Atzmon, Rich Siegel, and Hedy Epstein (a Holocaust survivor), all friends of mine and all anti-Zionists.

Lest I seem irreverent or unscathed by this widely-circulated smear letter from my ritual defamers, allow me to admit that I have been hurt by it. Many faculty and other HWS folks now shun me as a *persona non grata* largely because they only read the slime and never my rebuttal. My former student and long-time friend, David Deming, who is now the Chair of the HWS Board does not answer my letters. President Gearan does not answer them either. Board member Roy Dexheimer, disparages me and wonders if I "fell off my meds." Another Board member, Stuart Pilch, took it a step further and made a threatening phone call to my home and a promise "to hunt me down."

Recourse? Most Doors Are Closed

For twenty months I did not know the contents of the MaKinster email. When I discovered it as an email draft, my first inclination was to sue him and the other six faculty members who circulated it. I wanted to sue for libel and defamation of character. I knew it would be expensive, but I was determined to correct the lies they had spread about me. The problem was that in New York State the statute of limitations for libel is one year from the date it was committed, not one year from the date it was discovered.

I went to the Provost, who is the head of our faculty, and asked her to get me a copy of the final letter as it was sent to President Gearan. (I had seen only the email draft of it shown in Appendix 2) I wanted a copy of the final letter including the names of all those ritual defamers who had signed it -- MaKinster and the six other "facilitators" and any others of the 300 they sent it to who might have also signed). She refused on the grounds of "confidentiality".

I went to the President and asked for a copy; he refused. I asked MaKinster; he refused to give me a copy of the letter and refused to meet with me to discuss it. I asked the other six "facilitators". Three agreed to meet with me, but were unable to give me a copy of the final letter. They all told me that they thought additional people had signed, but they could not or would not name a single one for sure. Like MaKinster, the remaining three "colleagues" refused to meet with me or give me a copy of what they had collectively written in their smear letter.

I went to The Grievance Committee, but I was told that I could not bring the issue before it, since that committee does not hear such matters. I asked to address the faculty at large, but I was told that only faculty can attend an HWS Faculty Meeting and not those who are retired, with or without emeritus status.

I tried a market approach and publicly offered a $1,000 contribution to Hobart and William Smith Colleges in return for a final copy of the MaKinster ritual defamation letter with the names of all signatories. I made the offer by email to all current faculty members. No response. I raised the offer to $1,500. Some faculty called on me to stop; some even charged me with smearing MaKinster. Others counseled me to "turn the other cheek" and "get over it."

But others thought that withholding the letter and the names of those who signed it was "cowardly," "inappropriate," and "unethical." They asked rhetorically if my critics should not "openly stand by their words and acts?" They supported my right to peacefully and non-violently discover the smears and slime thrown at me by "colleagues" who now piously claim their right to anonymity.

Via college email to all members of the faculty I raised the public offer to $2,000, then $2,500, then $3,000, and so forth. At $5,000 the current acting Provost and long-time friend, Pat McGuire, came to my home (11/22/11) to discuss the "situation" and to advise that my email offers were annoying some people and that Hobart and William Smith Colleges was considering restricting or terminating my email privileges. I raised the offer to $10,000, not by campus-wide email, but in specific offers to several alumni.

Resolution?

Not yet. But I am optimistic. I have been a part of the Hobart and William Smith Colleges community for almost 40 years. I am proud of my record of teaching and activism on behalf of Palestinian human rights. And I am proud of having fought against academic hypocrisy and cowardice, especially when it comes to Israel.

I am also proud that Hobart and William Smith Colleges did not completely roll over in the face of the *ritual defamation* initiated (or facilitated) by otherwise well-meaning "colleagues," especially by those who are too cowardly to reveal or defend their participation in this injustice. And I am eternally thankful that the institution has allowed me to keep my emeritus status and my walking pass at the gym.

Appendix 1

Finger Lakes Times, September 27, 2009, Section D, p.1+ (not available online)

What Does Holocaust Denial Really Mean?

In April 2007 the European Union agreed to set jail sentences up to three years for those who deny or trivialize the Holocaust.[2] More recently, in response to the remarks of Bishop Richard Williamson, the Pope has proclaimed that Holocaust denial is "intolerable and altogether unacceptable."

But what does Holocaust denial really mean? Begin with the word Holocaust. The Holocaust[3] (spelled with a capital H) refers to the killing of six million Jews by the Nazis during World War II. It is supposed to be the German's "Final Solution" to the Jewish problem. Much of the systematic extermination was to have taken place in concentration camps by shooting, gassing, and burning alive innocent Jewish victims of the Third Reich.

People like Germar Rudolf, Ernst Zündel, and Bishop Williamson who do not believe this account and who dare to say so in public are reviled as bigots, anti-Semites, racists, and worse. Their alternate historical scenarios are not termed simply *revisionist*, but are demeaned as *Holocaust denial*. Rudolf and Zündel were shipped to Germany where they were tried, convicted, and sentenced to three and five years, respectively.

Politicians deride Holocaust revisionist papers and conferences as "beyond the pale of international discourse and acceptable behavior."[4] Non-Zionist Jews who participate in such revisionism, like Rabbi Dovid Weiss of the Neturei Karta, are denounced as "self-haters" and are shunned and spat upon. Even Professor Norman Finkelstein, whose parents were both Holocaust survivors and who wrote the book, *The Holocaust Industry*, has been branded a Holocaust denier.

But putting aside the virile hate directed against those who question the veracity of the typical Holocaust narrative, what is it that these people believe and say at the risk of imprisonment and bodily harm? For most Holocaust revisionists or deniers if you prefer, their arguments boil down to three simple contentions:

1. Hitler's "Final Solution" was intended to be ethnic cleansing, not extermination. 2. There were no homicidal gas chambers used by the Third Reich. 3. There were fewer than 6 million Jews killed of the 55 million who died in WWII.

Are these revisionist contentions so odious as to cause those who believe them to be reviled, beaten, and imprisoned? More importantly, is it possible that revisionist contentions are true, or even partially true, and that they are despised because they contradict the story of the Holocaust, a story which has been elevated to the level of a religion in hundreds of films, memorials, museums, and docudramas?

Is it sacrilegious to ask, "If Hitler was intent on extermination, how did Elie Wiesel, his father, and two of his sisters survive the worst period of incarceration at Auschwitz?" Wiesel claims that people were thrown alive into burning pits, yet even the Israeli-trained guides at Auschwitz refute this claim.

Is it really "beyond international discourse" to question the efficacy and the forensic evidence of homicidal gas chambers? If other myths, like making soap from human fat, have been dismissed as Allied war propaganda, why is it "unacceptable behavior" to ask if the gas chamber at Dachau was not reconstructed by the Americans because no other homicidal gas chamber could be found and used as evidence at the Nuremburg trials?

For more than fifty years Jewish scholars have spent hundreds of millions of dollars to document each Jewish victim of the Nazi Holocaust. The Nazis were German, obsessed with paperwork and recordkeeping. Yet only 3 million names have been collected and many of them died of natural causes. So why is it heresy to doubt that fewer than 6 million Jews were murdered in the Second World War?

"Holocaust Denial" might be no more eccentric or no more criminal than claiming the earth is flat, except that the Holocaust itself has been used as the sword and shield in the quest to build a Jewish state between the Mediterranean Sea and the Jordan River, where even today over half the population is not Jewish.

The Holocaust narrative allows Yad Vashem, the finest Holocaust museum in the world, to repeat the mantra of "Never Forget" while it sits on Arab lands stolen from Ein Karem and overlooking the unmarked graves of Palestinians massacred by Jewish terrorists at Deir Yassin. It allows Elie Wiesel to boast of having worked for these same terrorists (as a journalist, not a fighter) while refusing to acknowledge, let alone apologize for, the war crimes his employer committed. It makes Jews the ultimate victim no matter how they dispossess or dehumanize or ethnically cleanse indigenous Palestinian people.

The Holocaust story eliminates any comparison of Ketziot or Gaza to the concentration camps they indeed are. It memorializes the resistance of Jews in the ghettos of Europe while steadfastly denying any comparison with the resistance of Palestinians in Hebron and throughout the West Bank. It allows claims that this year's Hanukah Massacre in Gaza, with a kill ratio of 100 to one, was a "proportionate response" to Palestinian resistance to unending occupation.

The Holocaust is used to silence critics of Israel in what the Jewish scholar, Marc Ellis, has called the ecumenical deal: you Christians look the other way while we bludgeon the Palestinians and build our Jewish state and we won't remind you that Hitler was a good Catholic, a confirmed "soldier of Christ," long before he was a bad Nazi.

The Holocaust narrative of systematic, industrialized extermination was an important neo-conservative tool to drive the United States into Iraq. The same neo-con ideologues, like Norman Podhoretz, routinely compare Ahmadinejad to Hitler and Nazism with Islamofascism with the intent of driving us into Iran. The title of the Israeli conference at Yad Vashem made this crystal clear: "Holocaust Denial: Paving the Way to Genocide."

"Remember the Holocaust" will be the battle cry of the next great clash of good (Judeo/Christian values) and evil (radical Islamic aggression) and those who question it must be demonized if not burned at the stake.

Daniel McGowan Professor Emeritus Hobart and William Smith Colleges Geneva, NY 14456

September 24, 2009

Because of admonishment by the administration, it is hereby stated that the above remarks are solely those of the author. Hobart and William Smith Colleges neither condone nor condemn these opinions. Furthermore, the author has been instructed to use his personal email address of mcgowandaniel@yahoo.com and not his college email at mcgowan@hws.edu for those wishing to contact him with comments or criticisms.

Appendix 2

This is a draft of the letter "facilitated" by James MaKinster, signed by six other "colleagues," and circulated to over 300 others in the Hobart and William Smith Colleges' community.

October 3, 2009

President Gearan,

This letter is a response to Daniel McGowan's defense of Holocaust deniers published in the *Finger Lakes Times* on September 27. The content of the essay and its publication on the eve of Yom Kippur was appalling. We are writing to you because of the disgrace to Hobart and William Smith caused by McGowan's continued use of the institutional imprimatur and his honorary title of "Emeritus Professor" to lend credence in disseminating his personal beliefs. He has every right as a private citizen to hold and spew forth whatever beliefs he may happen to have, but we ask you to prevent the use of his title and the name of Hobart and William Smith from contributing to its effects in the future.

It should be clear that while McGowan is claiming to raise legitimate historical and free speech issues, Holocaust denial has a history of being no more that thinly veiled anti-Semitism. When historians talk about the Holocaust what they mean is that approximately six million Jews and several millions of others were killed in an intentional and systematic fashion by the Nazis using a number of different means, including death by shooting and in gas chambers. This is the position held universally by scholars. The Holocaust deniers reject the historicity of the Holocaust based on three types of assertions. They reject the number of 6 million, the existence of killing camps, and the element of intentionality.

Professor McGowan's article is an example of denying the reality of the most studied and documented event in history. Holocaust denial carries absolutely no weight among academic scholars in any field whatsoever. Additionally, denying the undisputed facts of the holocaust is not a way to show support for the Palestinians. For example, his argument denying the intentionality of the Nazi's execution of Jews is that there is not sufficient proof that it was designed to exterminate the Jewish population. Rather, he asserts, it may have been merely a program of "ethnic cleansing." The suggestion that this somehow makes it less morally reprehensible speaks for itself, as we all know that the term "ethnic cleansing" was introduced to make genocide sound more palatable.

Professor McGowan's position is a classic case of blaming the victims for their own victimization. Promo Levi wrote in *The Drowned and the Saved* that what he most feared was echoed in a remark by one of his SS guards: That if he somehow managed to live through this hell no one would believe his descriptions of Auschwitz. Sadly, for some, that day has arrived.

Freedom of speech is a right for citizens in a democracy that should be vigorously protected, especially when we find the content of that speech to be abhorrent. Colleges and universities have an educational obligation to encourage scholarship that reflects perspectives outside the mainstream of public political discourse, and we encourage that. Hate speech, on the other hand, is a trickier issue for campuses to wrestle with because while free speech has a special value, we have a duty to protect members of our diverse community from unsupported vitriol being espoused under the name of our colleges and its professors. We faculty of all persuasions, Buddhists, Christians, Muslims, Hindus, Jews, and atheists, are deeply offended and also share a special concern about the impact of such hateful messages (and its association with us) upon our Jewish students, staff, and faculty.

Professor McGowan's actions do not meet our expectation of minimally rational and minimally humane discourse. As human beings who see the transparent motivation and effects of such writing, we are deeply disturbed and saddened to see a Hobart and William Smith title attached to it. We therefore request the removal of Professor McGowan's honorary title of "Emeritus Professor."

Sincerely,

Scott Brophy, Professor of Philosophy

Michael Dobkowski, Professor of Religious Studies

Khuram Hussain, Assistant Professor of Education

Steven Lee, Professor of Philosophy

James MaKinster, Associate Professor of Education

Lilian Sherman, Assistant Professor of Education

Charles Temple, Professor of Education

Notes:

1. http://www.lairdwilcox.com/news/defame.html
2. http://www.haaretz.com/hasen/spages/850644.html
3. Holocaust. Dictionary.com. *The American Heritage® New Dictionary of Cultural Literacy, Third Edition.* Houghton Mifflin Company, 2005. Online: http://dictionary.reference.com/browse/Holocaust (accessed: February 09, 2007).
4. Senator Hillary Clinton, statement on Senatorial Web site since disestablished.

Stephen F. Pinter: An Early Revisionist

Klaus Schwensen

In June 1959 the Catholic American Sunday paper *Our Sunday Visitor* printed a letter to the editor that has gained a certain celebrity within the revisionist community. The reason was not only its content, but also the authority of the writer concerning his subject. The letter dealt with a sensitive item, the existence of homicidal gas chambers in the German concentration camps. The author of the letter was a certain Stephen F. Pinter, Attorney at Law in St. Louis, Missouri. After the end of the war Pinter had served as an Attorney for the U.S. War Department within the U.S. War Crimes Program. Through his letter a competent witness of the Allied side had appeared—someone who must have known details about the existence of gas chambers. Therefore, the most important statement of Pinter´s letter, that there were no gas chambers in the camps he had visited, is of considerable value.

The letter to the editor, presumably via German correspondence partners, soon found its way to national circles in the Federal Republic. Nothing was known there about the person of Stephen F. Pinter except for the few things he had mentioned about himself. Thus, some people tried to fill the gap by speculation, which led to erroneous statements, e.g. that Pinter was a German-Jewish emigrant, that he held the title of Doctor or that he had been head of an Allied Investigation Commission in Mauthausen. The following research on Stephen F. Pinter aims to encompass all of his writings and to complete his biography.

1. The Pinter Texts

In addition to the above-mentioned letter from 1959, in the following years Pinter wrote some more texts, and some older texts surfaced which might also originate from him. Today we know of nine texts which (presumably or positively) come from Pinter, and which are designated here in chronological order as follows: Text A[1], Text B[2], Text C[3], Text D[4], Text E[5], Text F[6], Text G[7], Text H[8] and Text I[9]. In *Anthologie révisionniste*[10], a collection of revisionist texts published in 2002 in France, five of the texts (C, D, E, F, and H) are printed in French translation.

The three "presumable" Pinter texts

The two earliest texts (A, B) are anonymous and the third one (C) appeared under a pseudonym. As it emerges from the texts or from some remarks of the respective editors, all three texts originate from an *American*, and from the fact that (in the cases of B and C) he addressed them to a journal in Argentina which was published in *German* we may conclude that he was a *German*-American. In one case (A), the editor mentions that the writer was an American *jurist*. There is no doubt about the author's competence in the field of war-crimes prosecution. All indications are such that one might ask: If Stephen F. Pinter is *not* the author of these texts - who else?

Although the texts A, B and C fit well into the image we have of Pinter, this is of course no proof of his authorship. What actually was the reason that he preferred to remain anonymous? In the case that *Pinter* really was the author, the explanation is obvious:

When the analysis of the Baldwin Report was written in October 1949 (Text A), Pinter had quit the U.S. War Department only one year before. As a freelance lawyer, he depended on a licence to practice before U.S. Military Courts. Thus, he hardly was in a position to contradict the report of a Senate Subcommittee headed by the mighty Senator Raymond E. Baldwin. Finally the Report dealt with malfeasances by members of the U.S. War Crime Commission, which was part of the War Department, i.e. Pinter had to accuse his own former colleagues.

Text B (1954) dealt with the release of "war criminals", who had been still incarcerated in Landsberg prison. The release was "on parole", which meant that the men were strictly forbidden to speak about their cases. Thus, they were practically silenced as witnesses of the events which had brought them before the War Crimes Court. Text B (a letter to the editor of the little journal *Der Weg* in Buenos Aires) describes and denounces the "on parole" practice. The anonymous writer attaches copies of the secret U.S. forms (which he had gained access to through a friend's indiscretion) in order to let them be published in Argentina. This was reason enough to stay anonymous, not least to protect his source.

The third text (Text C) is a letter to the editor (or rather an article) by a certain "Dr. Warwick Hester" to the above-mentioned journal *Der*

Weg in Buenos Aires. The author's name is a pseudonym. The article is especially interesting due to the revisionist position at such an early date (1954). Warwick Hester's observations and arguments are more than 50 years later astonishingly timely. And the forces that deter free discussion are, if anything, stronger. Thus, the reason why the author dared describe his experiences only under a pseudonym needs no explanation.

The known-authentic texts

The six texts D through I (three letters to the editor, one short article, one affidavit and one private letter) are authentic. They contain statements on the following items:

a) Gas chambers in the *Altreich* - yes or no? This question is even today not answered categorically. "*Altreich*" here means Germany within the borders of 1937, and "gas chambers" means only those for killing people (the fact that in German concentration camps gas chambers were used for the delousing of textiles is denied by no one). According to Pinter's letter to the editor (Text E) "there was no gas chamber at Dachau. ... Nor was there a gas chamber in any of the concentration camps in Germany." Pinter had himself not personally investigated every concentration camp in the *Altreich*. On this important item we sought more precision. Years later, apparently on an inquiry of Robert Miller, Pinter answered more precisely (Text I): "I had nothing to do with Mauthausen. However, since I took some months investigating Flossenbürg and all the outcamps connected therewith, while stationed at Dachau, I can talk about those."

b) Flossenbürg Concentration Camp In the 1960s (and perhaps still today) visitors were told that in the former camp existed a gas chamber and a site for mass shootings where thousands of inmates had been murdered. To this Pinter replied: There was in the camp "neither a gas chamber nor a mass shooting site" (Text H). During the existence of the camp "fewer than 300 persons died, by executions or due to other reasons" (Text D).

c) Illegal methods of interrogation In course of preparation for the war crimes and concentration-camp trials (e.g., the Malmedy Case) the American interrogators used methods that were a mockery to the American tradition of justice. The accused, mostly young soldiers of the *Waffen-SS*, confessed to crimes they never had committed and thus, as Pinter put it, "many were unfortunately sentenced and some of them executed" (Text F).

d) The 6-million number "As far as I could find out in six post-war years in Germany and Austria, a number of Jews were killed, but the number of one million was certainly never reached" (Text E). And: "In general, I wrote many years ago to our local daily newspaper, that the allegation of the extermination of the Jewish race was grossly exaggerated, that I had many Jewish clients who had lived in Germany, Poland and other countries at Hitler's time and for whom I collected hundreds of thousands of dollars, thus getting their stories firsthand and could state that the SIX MILLION story was a myth" (Text I). Probably, for such a statement Pinter in Germany of 2005 would face criminal charges of "Holocaust denial."

Some of the texts deserve a comment, but this would exceed the scope of this study. A comment on the interesting text C will follow later. Pinter's statements are of value, since he as an Attorney of the U.S. War Department and due to his activity in the War Crimes Program belonged to those who must have known the truth.

2. Who Was Stephen F. Pinter?

Since the publication of the letter (Text E) in *Our Sunday Visitor* (1959) historians in Austria, Canada, France and Germany have been interested in the person of Stephen F. Pinter. Significantly, private "independent scholars" did all this research. For established historians and commissioned researchers a witness like Pinter has been always a "nonperson." In the above-mentioned *Anthologie révisionniste* Pinter is rightly categorized as an "early revisionist". The editor Jean Plantin succeeded in finding out some personal data, e.g. his Social Security Number (SSN). Thus, at least it was proven that Stephen F. Pinter was no phantom but a man who had walked upon this earth. Nevertheless, it was difficult to find out more about this man. The reason was obviously that he had lived quite a normal life as an American citizen, and had not attracted attention by political or public activities - with the exception of his few texts, most published in remote venues. The life of a respectable lawyer in the American Mid-West is not the stuff of which headlines are made.

In the course of this research, based on the sparse personal data in Pinter's texts, many letters of inquiry were addressed to institutions and organizations in the United States - mostly without result. Benton College, where he had studied, does not exist any more. As a sole practitioner, he was not a member of a lawyers' society or a firm. In the Missouri Bar he had been only a nominal member. A family Pinter living in St. Louis is unrelated to him.[11] Finally, Pinter and his wife had moved in their old age from St. Louis to California - with unknown destination. There were no children. With remote relatives they seemed to have no contact. It seemed hopeless.

Furthermore, it appeared also hopeless to gain information about Pinter's post-war activities. As he mentions in one of his letters in German, he had held the rank of "Oberst" (Colonel) (Text D). An inquiry for "Colonel Stephen F. Pinter" at the National Personnel Records Center was in vain until it turned out that Pinter was registered there not as a military officer but as a civilian employee of the U.S. War Department. Only then a query with the proper authority[12] brought a number of documents from his Personnel File.

All in all, only little, apparently unimportant indications helped to proceed. Thus, from an application for a passport, his birthplace could be found, where a niece of Pinter's still lived, who could contribute some memories of her uncle. Through an Internet search[13] Pinter's date of death was found, but not his last residence. But in the Directory of St. Louis City and County the Christian name of his second wife was registered - Lucia. And in *her* case the Internet led to the couple´s last residence: Hemet, Riverside County, California.

Some information was confirmed by Pinter himself, who wrote - at 85 years of age - a letter (Text I) to the Canadian "Pinter researcher" Robert J. Miller, who presumably had asked him some questions concerning his biography. Summarizing all available data, we can reconstruct now Pinter´s *curriculum vitae* as follows:

Stephen F. Pinter was born on November 23, 1888, in the village of Deutsch-Schützen[14] in Burgenland, Austria. Therefore, Pinter was no German from the Reich, but he was born as a subject of Emperor Franz Joseph. His second (middle) name was not recorded. In his application for a passport[15] the "F." has been completed to "Frank", but in one of his Personnel Questionnaires[16] we read "FRANCIS". Since in old Austria no one was called Stephen or Francis, Pinter's Christian names were most probably Franz Stephan[17], which he had Anglicized in America.

In 1906 Franz Stephan Pinter, 17 years old, emigrated to the United States. His parents could pay not much more than the ship passage for him. He went to St. Louis where there was in that time a "German Quarter" and where he apparently knew someone who was ready to sponsor him. In 1909, at 21 years, he married his first wife Anna Maria, who also came from Austria-Hungary. Due to his ambition, his talents and no doubt the help of his wife, Pinter was able to undertake the study of Law (1912-1918). He attended Benton College of Law in St. Louis and graduated with a "Bachelor of Law."[18] In 1917 he was admitted to the Missouri Bar.[19] In 1920, at 32 years of age, he settled as a lawyer in St. Louis and in 1924 gained United States citizenship.

Until the end of World War II Pinter worked as an independent attorney at law. He employed one stenographer and one investigator. His field of activities he describes as follows: "Trial of all kinds of lawsuits. Preparation of cases and appeals. Some corporation law work and was counsel for a bank."

3. Application for Federal Employment

In September 1945, at almost 57 years, Pinter applied at the U.S. Civil Service Commission for employment as "Lawyer for war criminal trials". One reason for this step was surely the wish to see his home country after forty years again where misery and need now prevailed. Furthermore, the U.S. War Department was seeking jurists with knowledge of the German language for their War Crimes Program. Among the German-speaking jurists who were sent to Germany, German-Jewish emigrants dominated, many of them motivated by sentiments of revenge. In contrast, Pinter was a "genuine" German-American. He got the job, as he was told in Washington, because he "had no axe to grind" (Text I) . On January 13th, 1946, Pinter was sworn in in St. Louis. His employer was the Office of the Secretary of War, Civilian Personnel Division. His position was that of an Attorney and the appointment as civilian employee is of indefinite tenure, but at least for two years. As a civilian employee in a zone of occupation, he was subject to military law and whenever required, had to wear a US military uniform.

The latter requirement may explain a contradiction consisting in that Pinter, as he mentions in one of his texts (Text D) , held the "rank of a Colonel", but was classified as a civilian employee. Obviously in many cases a military rank was given to civilian employees of the War Department, since they had to wear a uniform and a uniform is always associated with a rank. According to Pinter's job and his age the rank of a Colonel is most probable. A comparable case is that of Hollywood director Billy Wilder, who was called to Bad Homburg in 1945 as Head of the Film Department, Office of Psychological Warfare. Wilder, too, mentions that he had then been a Colonel.[20] It appears that the ranks for civilians were merely formalities, and that the U.S. Army clearly differentiated between the "real" and the "formal" ranks.[21]

Immediately after his swearing-in (January 13th, 1946) Pinter travelled by train from St. Louis to Washington, in order to introduce himself and receive final instructions. On January 15th, 1946 he started in New York on his flight to Germany.

4. Activities in the War Crimes Program: Part 1 - Dachau

The Americans had made the former concentration camp Dachau into an internment camp where they had imprisoned accused German war criminals. The camp was also the site of a War Crimes Commission[22] and the site of the Dachau Trials. About January 16th, 1946, Pinter arrived in Dachau. The first of the concentration camp trials, the Dachau main trial, had been finished just four weeks before (November 15 - December 13,1945). Following these were the Mauthausen Main Trial (March 29 - May 13,1946) and the Malmedy Trial (May 16 - July 16, 1946). Pinter had nothing to do with either of them.

In an English letter (Text E) he describes his position as an "U.S. War Department Attorney". According to his Personnel File he had one assistant and one secretary at his disposal. His job was the collection of evidence against the accused (mostly SS personnel from the former concentration camps), the interrogation of former camp inmates as witnesses and preparation of the trial. In Pinter's words, he had "to investigate the former officers and employees of the camp and - as far as this was possible - to release them" (Text D). This formulation is remarkable, since most of his colleagues had quite another conception - namely to bring as many as possible of the accused to the gallows. A typical representative of this mentality was the Chief Prosecutor in the three Dachau Main Trials (Dachau, Mauthausen and Buchenwald Trials), Lt. Colonel William D. Denson.

During the trial the attorney changed his role into that of a prosecutor. In four of his German texts Pinter described his position once as "*Heeresrichter im Rang eines Obersten*" (Text D), once he writes, that he was a "U.S. *Armeeanwalt*" in the function of a prosecutor (*Ankläger*) (Text F), once he spoke of himself as a "*Gerichtsoffizier*" (Court Officer) (Text G) and once as a "U.S. *Armeeanwalt*" (Army Lawyer) (Text H). These contradictory roles - judge (Richter), lawyer (*Anwalt*), prosecutor (*Ankläger, Staatsanwalt*) - can be explained easily, since an American attorney (as advocate for his client) has no counterpart in the continental European system of justice. His activities included the functions of an "inquisitor" (*Untersuchungsrichter*) and those of a prosecutor (*Ankläger*) as well.

When he came to Dachau, he writes, "I was in my department the highest ranking officer and therefore had a free hand". Thus, he was able to choose his first subject of investigation and decided upon the former Flossenbürg camp, "which had not been investigated at all before." Pinter drove to Flossenbürg and ordered the captured SS files of the camp to be brought to Dachau. Then he visited all the DP camps[23] where former Flossenbürg inmates were living. He writes that he had interrogated "Hundreds, if not thousands" and had "spoken with thousands of these people" (Texts D, H). This sounds like an exaggeration, but presumably the former Flossenbürg inmates were called together and asked whether somebody had something to testify. In this way the relevant witnesses could be quickly filtered out and their statements be documented. After visiting the DP camps for several months, Pinter returned to Dachau.

The Flossenbürg trial started on June 12th, 1946. Pinter was one of the prosecutors. Although Flossenbürg camp had only been one of the smaller concentration camps, the trial dragged on until January 22th, 1947 – more than seven months. Thus, it became the longest-lasting trial of all concentration-camp trials before American Military Courts. The long duration is not necessarily due to the number of 52 accused, for e.g. the Mauthausen trial with 61 accused had lasted only six weeks. Possibly the long duration of the Flossenbürg trial was caused by other reasons.[24]

Father Lelere, a former prisoner, testifies at the trial of former camp personnel and prisoners from Flossenbürg. On the right is Fred Stecker, a court interpreter. Could one of these men be Stephen Pinter? Photo 21 June 1946. Source: USHMM - [Photograph #43018] Public domain, via Wikimedia Commons

According to all we know about Pinter, he represented a counter position to the thesis of "conspiracy" and "common design", a more "old-fashioned", more pragmatic - and more humane - interpretation of law. This was certainly in accord with his Christian beliefs, but not with the spirit of the post-war time. As a genuine German-American (his Austrian origin is irrelevant in this connection) Pinter was an exception among his colleagues in Dachau, for most of the German-speaking Americans engaged in the War Crimes Program were German-Jewish emigrants. Pinter, who apparently felt some sympathy for the defeated Germans and tried to do his duty objectively and justly, must have seen with abhorrence what methods were used by some of his colleagues to obtain "confessions." The treatment of the prisoners was a mockery of the American tradition of justice, and led to investigations by the Secretary of War and the U.S. Senate. Pinter in his sober manner writes:

> "While I did my best to represent the real and decent justice and to prevent a justice of hate, there were a number of persons who repeatedly brought in false or unfounded accusations against the German prisoners, and who, by means of obviously perjured witnesses gained successes before the military courts, which did not accord with the real facts. As a result of such miscarriages of justice, many were unfortunately sentenced although not guilty, and some of them were executed. Of the great trials in Dachau it was especially the Malmedy Trial and the Mauthausen and Buchenwald Concentration Camp Trials which became - during my stay in Dachau but without any involvement on my part in the trials - infamous due to their malfeasances."

After the end of the Flossenbürg main trial there was a series of subsequent trials. Pinter describes his activities at that time in a questionnaire[25] as follows:

> "Was Assistant Trial Judge Advocate in principal case. Participated as trial attorney and had charge of administration and filing system. Am now in charge of subsequent proceedings of same case. Engaged in staging and questioning suspected perpetrators so as to determine whether they should be tried or released."

It seems that in summer 1947 Pinter applied for a relocation to Salzburg, or that he had been offered one, which certainly was welcome to him since Salzburg was nearer to his old Burgenland home. At this time in Dachau the Mühldorf Trial (April 1 - May 13, 1947) and the Buchenwald Trial (April 11 - August 14, 1947) took place. Pinter was not involved in these trials. Probably in July 1947 he moved to Salzburg (Text F).

5. Activities in the War Crimes Program: Part 2 - Salzburg

The relocation to Salzburg meant a change from the 7708 War Crimes Group to the Judge Advocate Section. Pinter was promoted to Chief Defense Counsel in Austria (Text I, for the defense in Military Courts was performed by American jurists. His residence became the 5-Star Hotel "Bristol," which had apparently been commandeered by the American Occupation Power.[26],[27]

About his activities in Salzburg nothing is known. After one year in Salzburg (about August 1948) Pinter made a surprising decision: he applied for resignation from the service of the U.S. War Department in order to settle in Austria as an independent lawyer. This step is unusual. His application is not contained in his Personnel File (or has not been released), and so we know nothing about his motives. Financial motives can be ruled out, since as a freelance lawyer in Salzburg he could hardly earn more than with the War Department.[28] Therefore, we must seek the motives in the professional field. We do not know which trials Pinter had to take part in during his service in Salzburg. Maybe he did not agree with the war crimes prosecution policy as it was practiced by the U.S. War Department. Maybe he wanted to do something more expedient in helping accused Germans and Austrians with his experience in Anglo-Saxon Law and knowledge of the English language. But all this is mere speculation.

The last document available from Pinter's Personnel File[29] is a Notification of Personnel Action: "Resignation upon completion of minimum period of employment for the purpose of engaging in the private practice of Law in Austria." Pinter is subject to the restriction to practice only before Military and Military Government Courts, not before Austrian courts. He retains some minor privileges, but has to waive others, e.g. his shopping privileges at the PX (post exchange, a store for American occupation personnel exclusively) and government transportation to the United States.

About November 1948 Pinter applies for a US passport in Vienna, which is issued on December 17th, 1948. Meantime, he had to leave the "Bristol," and move to the modest Gasthof "Ziegelstadl" in Salzburg-Aigen. At this time Pinter is visited by his sister and her daughter from Burgenland. His niece, then 25 and today over 80, still lives in Deutsch-Schützen and recalls well that visit with "Uncle Stephan."[30]

Pinter in Mauthausen?

Pinter's name is in a strange way connected to the former concentration camp Mauthausen. This camp had been taken on May 5th, 1945 by American troops, who immediately started an investigation of atrocities by the SS. The results were set forth in a report[31] dated June 17th, 1945, where the existence of a gas chamber is mentioned. Pinter was not connected with the Mauthausen Trial at Dachau (March 29 - May 13, 1946).

Mauthausen is situated on north side of the Danube River some kilometres downstream of Linz, at a straight-line distance of only 120 km from Salzburg. But since the Americans had pulled back, the camp lay in the Soviet Zone of Austria. It emerges from the so-called Lachout document, which surfaced 1987 under mysterious circumstances in Vienna, that in 1948 there was an Allied Investigation Commission consisting of representatives of the four Allied powers which investigated the camp in order to ascertain whether there had been a gas chamber or not. Robert Faurisson, who had flown to Vienna to inform himself about this document, remained skeptical. Apparently he was the first who recognized that, "if this document is genuine and if Emil Lachout is telling the truth", it would constitute a verification of Pinter's letter (Text E), but he he had formulated this as a mere possibility and as a question yet to clarify.[32] It was not long thereafter that Emil Lachout stated that "U.S. Colonel Dr. Stephen Pinter" had been head of the Allied Commission in Mauthausen and author of a (second) Mauthausen report.[33]

However, the (leftist) "Documentation Centre of Austrian Resistance" (DÖW) had from the beginning declared the Lachout Document to be a forgery[34],[35], and a recent study has confirmed this accusation.[36] There was never an Allied Commission in Mauthausen, and therefore Pinter could not have been the head of it. This result has been confirmed by a letter (Text I) of Pinter that surfaced recently. Apparently answering a question of Robert J. Miller, the 85-year-old Pinter wrote in his curt manner: "I had nothing to do with Mauthausen."

6. The Biographic Lacuna

The notification of Pinter's resignation is the last available document from his Personnel File. From there all traces of him are lost until about 1954. Neither in the list of the Lawyers Bar nor in the City Directory of Salzburg is he registered. Thus, we do not know how long he stayed in Salzburg, what he did in his job as a lawyer, which cases he was engaged in, whether he took part in any war-crimes trials, nor when he left Austria.

At the beginning of 1949 Pinter might have started his activities as a lawyer in Salzburg. About this time presumably his wife died in St. Louis. And at some time he must have become acquainted with his second wife Lucia (Lucy), who came from Bavaria. Pinter was about 60 at the time and the woman about 40.

In 1949 emerged the first anonymous text (Text A) that may originate with Pinter. The text appears not so much as an article for a broader public but rather as a working paper for specialists. The background was the malfeasances of American war-crimes investigators in Germany. The methods of some interrogators against the accused were criminal violations of the American tradition of justice (Malmedy case). There were protests by German bishops and lawyers, and in the U.S. a campaign started under the motto: "Stop the hanging machine". Two Commissions were established to investigate the behavior of the war-crimes investigators: first the van Rhoden/Simpson Commission (established by U.S. Secretary of the Army Kenneth C. Royall) and later the so-called Baldwin Committee (established by the U.S. Senate). There were objections to the composition of the Baldwin Committee from the beginning, since Baldwin and other members of his commission were professionally related with some of the officers whom they were investigating. In October 1949 the "Conclusions" of the Baldwin Report were read out before the Senate, and the critics found their worst apprehensions confirmed. Text A is a critical analysis of the "Conclusions of the Baldwin Report". It was obviously a professional work that could only be performed by a specialist - Pinter?

In his letter to *Our Sunday Visitor* (Text E) Pinter mentions "six post-war years in Germany and Austria." Since he came to Dachau in mid-January 1946, this would correspond to the time up to January 1952. Accordingly Pinter must have returned with his wife to the United States at the beginning of 1952.

The "Warwick Hester" Problem

The identity of the author of Text C is one of the most fascinating problems connected with Pinter. The mysterious "Dr. Warwick Hester" is a "Great Unknown", since the name is doubtless a pseudonym and we do not know his real identity. Was it Pinter? Warwick Hester mentions some unusual journeys for that time: Barcelona, Cairo, Rio de Janeiro. The purpose was to question some former SS members who lived there in exile, and who all had witnessed and confirmed grave war crimes and atrocities committed by Germans (Text C). Doesn't that fit very well with a lawyer who is engaged in the defence of such clients? Considering the years 1949-1951, where nothing is known about Pinter, he had time enough to undertake those journeys.

Also Mauthausen camp is mentioned by Warwick Hester:

"The fifth of this strange category of men was a former SS soldier, who pretended he had belonged for a time to the guard unit of Mauthausen. He told me there had been gas chambers where not only Jews, but also other inmates had been killed. He himself had not seen that, but it was no secret in the camp. I [Warwick] visited this camp in the same year. Even the Jews did not pretend that humans had been gassed there. There was no installation which in any way could be used [for that purpose] ..."

It would be interesting to know *when* Warwick had been in Mauthausen. When he spoke with the above-mentioned SS man, he had not yet seen the camp. Many years later the 85-year-old Pinter wrote that he had nothing to do with Mauthausen (Text I). But this formulation does not exclude that he sometime had visited the camp, and probably Pinter's statement related only to a question of Robert Miller, whether he had been head of the mysterious Allied Mauthausen Commission. In summary, owing to the lack of hard data, an identity between "Warwick Hester" and Stephen Pinter cannot be proven but can also not be excluded.

As his niece recalls, Pinter (accompanied by his wife) in 1954 or 1955 visited his old home Deutsch-Schützen - almost 50 years after his emigration. Maybe it was in 1955, when Austria regained her sovereignty (May 15th, 1955), and when American citizens could visit the former Soviet Occupation Zone without risk.

7. From Missouri to California

Although Pinter on his return to the United States (about 1952) was at an age when some people think of retirement, he started again to work as a lawyer. Apparently he was appreciated as a specialist for the compensation of the "politically and racially persecuted" (which was the correct expression in those days), and where he could make use of his law experiences in post-war Germany and Austria and his knowledge of the German language. Years later he wrote:

> *"In general, I wrote many years ago to our local daily newspaper, that the allegation of the extermination of the Jewish race was grossly exaggerated, that I had many Jewish clients, who had lived in Germany, Poland and other countries at Hitler's*

> *time and for whom I collected hundreds of thousands of dollars, thus getting their stories first-hand and can state that the SIX MILLION story was a myth."*

Considering these activities for Jewish people who had been persecuted under the National Socialist regime, and the confidence which he obviously enjoyed, one could hardly have blamed Pinter had he become a Nazi sympathizer or an anti-Semite.

In the St. Louis Directory [37] he appears for the first time in the edition of 1955, which of course does not preclude an earlier return. In Text B the anonymous writer mentions that he attended a meeting in Detroit, which took place at the beginning of 1954. And "Warwick Hester" sent his article (Text C) in the middle of 1954 from the U.S.A. to Buenos Aires. Both are compatible with Pinter´s (apparent) whereabouts.

As late as 1966, Pinter was still registered in the Martindale-Hubbell Law Directory. Between 1958 and 1966 he wrote the texts that make him so interesting as a witness. Not until 1968, at 80 years of age, did he retire. In 1976, at the age of 88 years, he is mentioned in the St. Louis City and County Directory for the last time - as "retired". Apparently in the same year he moved with his wife to Southern California, to Hemet, Riverside County (near San Diego), where he had purchased a house.

Pinter was obviously interested in politics and observed the events of the day - also in Germany. We know, that he had a correspondence with the journalist Helmut Sündermann, who had been the deputy of *Reichspressechef* Dr. Dietrich from 1942 to 1945.[38] Possibly he corresponded with other partners in Germany or Austria. This is the only explanation for the fact that his letter to *Sunday Visitor* (Text E) in the faraway State of Indiana became known so soon in Germany. Thus, Pinter would have heard of Sündermann´s trial in Munich (1960), which caused him to help the accused with an affidavit (Text F). Also the article for *Nation & Europa* (Text G) may have been caused by Sündermann´s request. And finally it was supposedly Sündermann who sent an article from the *Coburger Tageblatt* to Pinter concerning the former Flossenbürg camp, with which Pinter was "connected" in a special way. This article moved Pinter, then 78, once more to a response.

From occasional remarks in his texts it emerges that Pinter was a conservative man, and this tendency is also recognizable in the earliest texts (A, B, C), where we can only presume that they originate from Pinter. Thus, the author of Text A tends to the line of Senator Joseph McCarthy who committed himself to a thoroughgoing review of the malfeasances committed by members of the War Crimes Commissions in Germany. Most revealing is Pinter's remark (Text I) that he corresponded with Austin J. App, since App was (at least among German-Americans) a well-known personality.

Dr. Austin Joseph App, born the son of German immigrants in 1902 in Milwaukee, Wis., was a professor for English language and literature at the (Jesuit) University of Scranton, Pa. and at the (Catholic) La Salle College, Philadelphia, Pa. Thus, App as well as Pinter were Catholic, conservative German-Americans. Both of them were among the earliest American revisionists of the Second World War, although App sought publicity whereas Pinter went public only on a few occasions. It is probably a mere accident but symptomatic, that in the *Anthologie révisionniste* Pinter's famous letter to the editor (Text E) is directly followed by a letter of Austin App.

Since 1942 App had criticized Roosevelt's politics in articles and letters to editors and politicians.[39] After the war App became founder and president of the "Federation of American Citizens of German Descent". As a "lone wolf" he published numerous articles and brochures, in which he pleaded for the defeated Germans.[40] In 1952 he organized an "American-German Friendship Rally", where Senator McCarthy was expected to speak (threats of counter-demonstrations led him to withdraw). App found little support by the American mass media, and thus, his articles were printed mostly by obscure German-American or Catholic publishers. In the 1960s Austin J. App visited the Federal Republic of Germany several times and worked up to his old age for American-German understanding. He died in 1984.

We may assume that Pinter agreed in principle with App's point of view. Like App (and McCarthy, too) he had his roots in the Roman Catholic faith. He read his *Sunday Visitor* regularly. He was at odds with one of his sisters who also lived in the United States since she had converted to a Protestant church.[41] In his last years he went almost daily to Mass. Stephen F. (Franz Stephan) Pinter died on March 30th, 1985, 96 years old, in Hemet, Riverside County, California.

Mrs. Lucia Pinter, born May 17th, 1907, survived her husband by 14 years. She died on Nov. 18th, 1999, at age 92, in Hemet. The estate went to relatives of hers in Germany, including the house in Hemet. A lady who had been a neighbor to the Pinters was kind enough to forward a letter to the heirs who live in Germany (address not disclosed). Finally - what a chance to discover some unknown "Pinter papers"! But the heirs refused any contact. Alas - maybe they had at least a photo of Stephen F. Pinter.

An earlier version of this article appeared in German in *Vierteljahreshefte für freie Geschichtsforschung* Volume 9, Number 3. April 2006.

Notes:

1. Anon., "Analyse der Schlußfolgerungen des Baldwin-Berichts—Untersuchung des Malmedy-Massakers"; in: Ralf Tiemann, *Der Malmedyprozess—Ein Ringen um Gerechtigkeit*, Munin-Verlag, Osnabrück 1990, S. 282-311.
2. Anon. [Eberhard Fritsch?], "Freiheit in Ketten," in: *Der Weg* (Buenos Aires), Heft 4 (April 1954), S. 268-272.
3. Dr. Warwick Hester, "Auf den Straßen der Wahrheit," in: *Der Weg,* Heft 8 (Aug. 1954), S. 572-578, Dürer Verlag, Buenos Aires 1954. This text, slightly shortened, was reproduced by Udo Walendy, *Historische Tatsachen* Nr. 43, Vlotho 1990, S. 20-23.
4. S. F. Pinter, letter to *Deutsche Wochenschrift*, St. Louis, Missouri, dated 20.11.1958; reproduced in „Suchlicht", a supplement to *Nation Europa,* Heft 10 (Okt. 1959) Whether the date 20.11.58 given in „Suchlicht" relates to Pinter's letter or to the respective edition of *Deutsche Wochenschrift*, is unclear.
5. Stephen F. Pinter, Letter to the Editor, in: *Our Sunday Visitor* (Huntington, Indiana), June 14, 1959, p. 15.
6. Stephen F. Pinter, Beeidigte Erklärung (Affidavit), St. Louis, Mo., dated 9. Februar 1960; in: *Nation Europa*, X. Jahrgang, H. 4 (April 1960), S. 68.
7. S. F. Pinter, „Die Kollektivschuld," *Nation Europa* , Jahrg. X. H. 9 (Sept. 1960), 9-11.
8. Stephen F. Pinter, letter to *Deutsche National-Zeitung*, no date; partly printed in: *National-Zeitung* Nr. 26, dated 1 July 1966, pp. 1 and 11.
9. Stephen Pinter, private letter, dated March 22nd, 1974, to Robert J. Miller.
10. Jean Plantin [editor], "Anthologie chronologique des textes révisionistes des années quarante et cinquante," in: Jean Plantin [publisher], *Etudes Révisionistes*, Vol. 2, privately published by "Le cercle antitotalitaire", France 2002. The collection contains five of the texts in French, namely Text C ("Sur les chemins de la vérité," p. 199), D (lettre du 20 novembre

1958, p. 234), E (lettre du 14 juin 1959, p. 235), F (Affidavit, p. 197, endnote 1) und H (letter to *Deutsche National-Zeitung*, p. 198, endnote 1).
11. Questions to 10 addresses with the name Pinter in St. Louis, which were found in the St. Louis Directory, resulted in only one answer (2.7.2001). According to this the respective Pinter family is the only one in St. Louis, but not related to Stephen F. Pinter (Information by Jean Plantin, Sept. 10, 2001).
12. National Personnel Records Center, Civilian Personnel Records, 111 Winnebago Street, St. Louis, Missouri 63118-4199 (Personnel Records of Pinter, Stephen F., DoB 11-23-1888).
13. Family Search U.S. Social Security Death Index (https://familysearch.org/pal:/MM9.1.1/J54H-CZQ).
14. Burgenland then belonged to the Hungarian half of the Double Monarchy. Deutsch-Schützen is situated on the "Pinka Valley Wine Road" (*Pinkataler Weinstraße*), which leads along the Austrian-Hungarian border. The next town is the Hungarian Szombathely (*Steinamanger*), at a distance of 15 km Northeast.
15. Stephen F. Pinter, Application for Passport, Salzburg, 1948 (front page only). According to stamp of Vice Consul in Vienna the passport was issued on Dec. 17th, 1948.
16. Request of Headquarters US Forces in Austria to FBI (Standard Form "Request for Report on Loyalty Data"), dated 17 Nov. 1947.
17. The name Franz Stephan was very popular in Austria then, after Franz Stephan Duke of Lorraine (1708-1765), spouse of Empress Maria Theresia, who as Holy Roman-German Emperor called himself Franz I.
18. *Martindale-Hubbell Law Directory*: "Pinter, Stephen..... '88, '17 C & L.. 16 Ll.B. 4 N. 8th". Explanation: '88 = born in 1888, College & Law School Benton College of Law, St. Louis, Ll.B. in 1917. (Ll.B. = Legum Baccalaureus = Bachelor of Law). These data we received in a letter of the Saint Louis Public Library dated April 8th, 1982, to Robert J. Miller.
19. Missouri Bar, Letter to the author dated 8.10.2002.
20. Interview with Billy Wilder, in: Neyl Sinyard und Adrian Turner, *Billy Wilders Filme*, Berlin 1980.
21. In an order announcing the composition of the Flossenbürg Military Court, from 15 members of the court four are declared as civilian employees (US CIV, WCB USFET), including "MR. STEPHEN PINTER" - without any military rank (Headquarters Third U.S. Army, APO 403, Special Orders No. 123, dated 17. May 1946).
22. The War Crimes Commissions in Dachau, Augsburg and Schwäbisch Hall were subordinate to the 7708 War Crimes Group under Lt. Colonel Burton Ellis. Each of the War Crimes Commissions had several War Crimes Investigating Teams.
23. DP = Displaced Persons, i.e. mostly people from Eastern Europe, who had lived during the war in Germany and who could not or would not return to their home country since it belonged now to the Soviet sphere of control.
24. The files of the Flossenbürg trial consist of 16,000 pages and have not yet been evaluated. It is strange that the first Chief Prosecutor, whose name

is not known, was replaced during the trial by Lt. Colonel William D. Denson, Chief Prosecutor in the Dachau and the Mauthausen trial, a proponent of the "common design" thesis.

25. Application for Federal Employment, dated Dachau, May 12th, 1947.
26. Headquarters United States Forces in Austria to Pinter, Stephen F. dated 28 Sept. 1948.
27. Headquarters United States Forces in Austria to Pinter, Stephen F. dated 18 Oct. 1948.
28. Pinter's last service grade (Aug. 1947) was P-5, according to a salary of $715 monthly (incl. "differential").
29. Notification of Personnel Action dated 21 Dec. 1948.
30. Personal information by Mrs. Elisabeth S. to the author (June 2003).
31. Mauthausen Report, 3rd U.S. Army Chemical Corps, dated 17.06.1945. The author of this report was Investigation Examiner Major Eugene S. Cohen, 514th Quartermaster Group, QMC, JA Section, Third US Army. The report (Document PS-2176) was introduced as evidence not only into the Mauthausen Trial, but also into the Nuremberg Main Trial.
32. Robert Faurisson, "The Müller Document", *Journal of Historical Review* Vol. 8, No. 1 (Spring 1988), 117-126. Online: http://vho.org/GB/Journals/JHR/8/1/Faurisson117-126.html
33. Anon., Exclusive Interview with Mr. Emil Lachout, *SIEG* Nr. 6 (1989), 16-19.
34. Brigitte Bailer-Galanda, Wilhelm Lasek, Wolfgang Neugebauer, Gustav Spann [DÖW], *„Das Lachout-Dokument - Anatomie einer Fälschung"*, Vienna 1989.
35. DÖW and Federal Ministry for Education and Arts [Editors], *Amoklauf gegen die Wirklichkeit - NS-Verbrechen und 'revisionistische' Geschichtsschreibung*, DAÖW, Vienna 1992.
36. Klaus Schwensen, „Zur Echtheit des Lachout-Dokuments", *Vierteljahreshefte für freie Geschichtsforschung (VffG)* Jahrg. 8 H. 2 (2004), S. 166-178.
37. St. Louis City and County Directories (1940-1979), Type County, Section People.
38 Personal information by Dr. Gerd Sudholt to the author (Febr. 2002).
39. In *Lexikon des Rechtsextremismus* of the *Informationsdienst gegen Rechtsextremismus (IDGR)* http://lexicon.idgr.de/index we find this, under "App, Austin J." is noted: *"In the years 1942 to 1945 besides his teaching activities, he inundated newspapers and politicians with attacks against the U.S. intervention in World War II and justified therein the war of aggression and politics of the N.S. regime. For all problems of post-war Germany he blamed Roosevelt's Secretary of the Treasury Henry Morgenthau (see Morgenthau Plan). His letters to the editor were blatantly anti-semitic. Although they were hardly published App did not relent in this undertaking".*
40. Articles, brochures, and books by Austin J. App: "Ravishing the Women of Conquered Europe" (1946), "Slave-laboring of German Prisoners of War", "Our Lend-Lease Pals in East Prussia", "The German Food Problem This Winter Is an American Problem" (Nov. 1946, several periodicals),

"History's Most Terrifying Peace" (1946), *Morgenthau Era Letters* (1966) and many others.
41. Personal information by Mrs. Elisabeth S. to the author (June 2003).

A Postcard from Treblinka

Thomas Dalton

The following is a true account of my personal visit to the camp. Certain names and dates have been changed to protect privacy. All photos are my own.

Mid-summer, Warsaw. Partly sunny, mild—a nice day to visit a death camp. I had just finished with an academic conference in the suburbs of Warsaw, and had one free day (a Tuesday) before moving on to my next European engagement. This was very fortunate, as I knew that the Treblinka concentration camp was only some 100 km away, and I was very much hoping for a chance to see it in person. My local Polish contacts were supportive, if slightly puzzled why an American professor of humanities would bother visiting a place "with nothing there to see." But I insisted, and so they complied. A Polish colleague, Lech, agreed to travel with me. He had no car, so we booked a taxi—reasonably priced, considering the distance—and by 9:30 am we were on our way to Treblinka.

We would not be arriving as mere tourists. Another colleague previously contacted the camp and spoke with museum director Edward Kopowka. He agreed to meet with us, show us the small museum, and then walk the camp grounds with us for two full hours. Good luck for us, though perhaps not for him.

We made good time, arriving in Malkinia before 10:30 am, and only some 10 km from the camp. But then a problem: the bridge over the Bug River was out of service. We would have to go down to the next crossing at Leg Nurski, about 20 km away, and then work our way back to the camp. This little detour threw our Warsaw-based cabbie for a loop, and with signage virtually nonexistent, I knew we were in a bit of a fix. So we crossed the river, worked our way down to Kosow Lacki, stopped two or three times for directions, drove up past Wolka Okraglik, and on to the entrance of the camp—after 45 extra minutes. But we were there. We drove right in—no gate, no guard, no entrance fee—and parked. Only two other cars in the lot, a relief; no Auschwitz-style Disneyland here.

Lech and I walked over to the small museum (Photo 1). Edward was in his office, ready to see us. He was a clean-cut fellow, probably in his late 40s, and seemed happy to have us. Lech introduced us (in

Polish), and I immediately learned that Edward "spoke no English." Lech would have to translate back and forth—a bit of an inconvenience, I thought, and strange for someone whose job it is to interact with many visitors. But here I was the foreigner, so I couldn't much complain.

Photo 1: Treblinka museum.

Inside the museum we viewed a large wall map, showing both the labor portion of the camp (Treblinka I), and the "extermination" zone, Treblinka II—see Photo 2. We were presently located at the far right, near the parking "P", with the museum marked "M".

Edward then introduced to us—with Lech patiently translating—a large scale model of the extermination camp (Photo 3). Edward explained the standard extermination process: the arriving train cars, the separation by sexes, the "tube" pathway to the gas chambers, and then the gassing itself—with diesel engine exhaust. Not being your typical ignorant tourist, I asked if diesel exhaust had enough carbon monoxide to efficiently kill masses of people. Edward's answer: the Germans used "dirty fuel"! This was a new one for me; I am unaware of any witness or perpetrator describing the deliberate use of contaminated diesel fuel in order to increase CO content, nor do I know if it would even work. But it was an interesting response.

Evidently he knew that ordinary diesel exhaust cannot kill masses of people, so the story had to be modified. But who am I to challenge the director of the Treblinka museum himself?

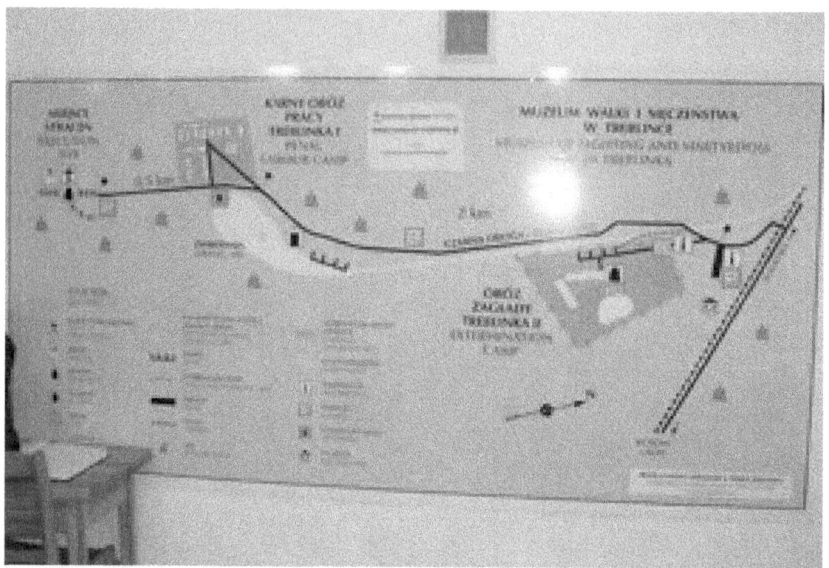

Photo 2: Camp layout.

Edward then explained that a total of 912,000 people were killed over the brief, 11-month lifetime of the camp. In fact this is precisely the figure offered by Manfred Burba in his 1995 German book, *Treblinka*. Why Edward preferred this number over the other "expert" estimates—including van Pelt's 750,000, Hilberg's 800,000, Arad's 870,000, or Benz's 974,000—he did not say.

Of the 912,000, the first 700,000 were initially buried in mass graves, he said, and then later exhumed for cremation on open-air pyres—the usual story, but rife with problems. He pointedly did not discuss the timeframe, so I asked (knowing already) if *all* 700,000 were buried first, prior to exhumation. He hesitated, but finally answered 'yes.' So I asked: where *exactly* were these 700,000 bodies buried? He pointed to a few areas marked "mass grave" on the model. And how much space did they require? A lot, he said. How deep were the graves?, I asked. Eight meters—some 26 feet, a very impressive hole. Isn't there a ground water problem here, I asked, being a flat landscape so close to the Bug river? Not a concern, Edward replied; the water table is some 10 meters deep. No problems here!

Photo 3: Scale model of extermination camp.

Photo 4: Symbolic camp entrance.

We then proceeded to walk to the extermination camp. One quickly notices that many things about the camp are "symbolic": symbolic camp entrance (Photo 4), symbolic fence (Photo 5), symbolic railroad tracks (Photo 6). Necessary, Edward says, because the Nazis obliterated every trace of the original camp. How convenient, I thought to myself.

Photo 5: Symbolic camp fence.

Photo 6: Symbolic railroad tracks.

Along the way we passed a large map of the camp area (Photo 7). Unfortunately it bore little resemblance to the present memorial layout, and it was nearly impossible to locate the various "symbolic" markers that we had seen. But perhaps it was just as well—fewer difficult questions to answer this way.

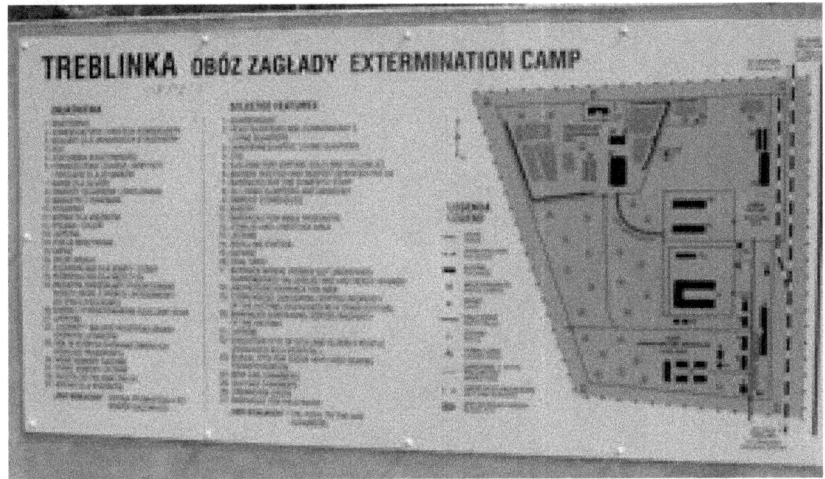

Photo 7: Camp layout.

Soon enough we arrived at the pathway (the symbolic "tube") that led to the famous central monument: a toadstool-like monolith located at the very spot of the alleged gas chambers (Photo 8). Here we were, at the heart of Treblinka, the site of the most horrendous kill rate of the entire Holocaust: of the 912,000 victims, 837,000 were killed in just six months of 1942, according to the camp's (and Burba's) "official" tally. (The remaining 75,000 died in 1943.) This works out to nearly 140,000 per month, 35,000 per week, or *5,000 per day*, every day, rain or shine, for six months. Not even Auschwitz during the alleged Hungarian massacre could match this rate.

Surprisingly, gassing that many people per day was no problem, on the traditional view. Treblinka had, for most of its existence, 10 chambers with a combined capacity of nearly 40,000 gassings per day; 5,000 would have been a walk in the park. Corpse disposal, on the other hand, would have been a nightmare. Burying the first 700,000 victims would have required astoundingly huge graves. If we accept Arad's claim of four such graves, each would have had to be something like 15 x 120 meters in area, and 8 meters deep (as Edward claimed), to hold all those bodies. Combined, this is an area equivalent to 1.4 times as large as a professional American football field, and 26 feet deep. (And where did they put all that dirt, by the way?) Upon dumping the bodies for nine months, the Germans then, allegedly, covered the whole mess up—just in time to *change their minds* and decide to burn them all.

Photo 8: Central monument, marking the gas chambers.

So they uncovered the graves, dredged up 700,000 rotting, decaying corpses, and dragged them over to…a fire pit. To burn them all. Down to *pure ash*, down to *nothing*. In the open air. Using wood logs. I asked Edward where this miracle happened. He walked us over to the "symbolic" pit where the Germans had constructed grills of elevated railway rails, on which they could stack the corpses—see Photos 9 and 10. Wood was placed underneath, ignited, and the bodies all but vaporized. And not only did they have the 700,000 exhumed corpses, but they also had to contend with the ongoing supply of 212,000 "fresh" bodies that were still being gassed—at a rate of 5,000 per day. All 912,000 bodies, reduced to ash, in the very spot we were standing. And they did this in *just 16 weeks*, according to the experts—more than 8,000 per day, every day. Those Germans were brilliant indeed, and *efficient*.

Photo 9: Symbolic cremation pit.

Where is the ash?, I asked. It's still in the ground, said Edward. He reached down, scraped around in the dirt with his hand, and said, "Here is some." He handed me 5 or 6 bits of something that certainly looked like ash: two were black (wood ash?), one was grey, and two white—bone fragments, perhaps? I was quite impressed: here in my hand were the likely remains of actual Treblinka victims. I stuffed the bits of ash in my pocket. I have them still.

During our discussion the question of excavations arose. On the traditional view, the ash was reburied in the graves that held the bodies; even today, there would be literally tons of it remaining. But as we know, there have been no attempts to unearth evidence of mass graves, or to measure or quantify ashes or human remains—not one single attempt, in nearly 70 years. It is almost as if the powers that be did not want to confirm the truth. Perhaps they suspected, in the back of their minds, that the conventional storyline would not hold up. So, I was quite surprised to hear that a team from Birmingham University (UK) was preparing to conduct a non-invasive study of the mass graves, using a ground-penetrating radar. I made a note to myself to follow the progress of this very interesting development.

Photo 10: Edward Kopowka, at the ash pit.

Our time about up, we walked on back to the museum. Along the way we stopped at a little gift-shop kiosk and purchased two small books: a photo album titled *Treblinka: The Stones Are Silent* (2007) and a historical overview, *Treblinka II – The Death Camp* (2007). The latter reiterated that "around 900,000" Jews were killed there, but it included a surprising statistic: "one third of the deportees were dead or on the verge of death when they reached [the camp]" (p. 9). This was a shock: something like 200,000 or 250,000 of the Treblinka victims were *dead on arrival?* I am unaware of this estimate in any conventional academic work; it would significantly alter the whole story.

The book also mentions the 10 gas chambers, each of 16 square meters in area, which could collectively gas "up to 5000 victims at a time" (p. 13). So: 500 victims per room, which works out to *31 persons per square meter of area*. Evidently the authors count on the reader being incapable of basic math—otherwise they wouldn't put forth this obvious nonsense.

Such was my day in Treblinka. Back in the parking lot, our cabbie was waiting—arising from a little nap. His time might have been better spent. Heading back to Warsaw we took "the direct route," meaning, we got lost three more times. Finally, two hungry hours later, we arrived back at our hotel. Quite a day. I wouldn't have missed it for the world.

Postscript

For a long time after my visit, I heard nothing at all about any Birmingham study of the camp using ground-penetrating radar. I was disappointed, but not surprised. Then to my astonishment, just one week ago, came a blazing headline in the British paper *The Daily Mail*: "British archaeologist destroys Holocaust deniers' argument with mass grave find at Treblinka" (18 January 2012). The short article reads, in part:

A British forensic archaeologist has unearthed fresh evidence to prove the existence of mass graves at the Nazi death camp Treblinka— scuttling the claims of Holocaust deniers who say it was merely a transit camp. ... Forensic archaeologist Caroline Sturdy Colls has now undertaken the first coordinated scientific attempt to locate the graves.

Ms. Colls is quoted as follows: "I've identified a number of buried pits using geophysical techniques. These are considerable in size, and very deep, one in particular is 26 by 17 meters." This is the full extent of the details that we are offered—a very strong sign that Ms. Colls did not, in fact, "destroy" the revisionists' arguments. The presumably largest grave is 26 by 17 meters, or 442 square meters in area. Recall above where I noted that the orthodox story requires a total grave area of roughly 7200 square meters. So Ms. Colls's one large grave is about 6% of the necessary area. She claims to have found "a number" of graves, but unless this was something like 30 or 40, she is far short of the mark. More likely, of course, the "number" was quite small, or we would surely have been given specifics.

I would further add that, on the revisionist thesis, many thousands of people did indeed die in the camp, of various causes. A high-volume transit camp would have received thousands of incoming dead (recall the "one third" statistic above), and many more would have died of disease and, yes, execution (likely by bullet) at the camp. So it is fully expected that mass graves exist in the camp. But the anticipated number of victims is much smaller—perhaps 10% of those claimed. Thus we might expect to see a total grave volume of around 10,000 to 12,000 cubic meters, rather than the 120,000 required by the conventional account.

So what grave volume did Ms. Colls find? BBC Radio 4 ran a 30-minute exclusive story on this event, on January 23. She spoke several times, but offered very few additional details. She confirmed that a "number" of graves were found, with the largest as mentioned above. But of course, we also need to know how deep they are. The newspaper article quoted her as saying they were "very deep." But it turns out that her high-tech ground-scanning system cannot record the depth! All she knows is that the graves are "at least 4 meters deep"—evidently the scanning limit of her system. Unbelievable. This is a case of either blinding incompetence, or willful neglect. Any serious attempt to understand the graves would have obviously recorded their depth, at least to the full 8 meters claimed by Edward Kopowka. As it is, and for all she knows, the graves may indeed be *no more than* 4 meters deep—in which case, her large "26 x 17" grave is a mere 3% of the needed size.

Colls added one further fact on the radio program: the "main area" for graves, right behind the presumed gas chambers, showed evidence of "five graves in a row." And all five, presumably, are significantly smaller than her largest. This again suggests that she has found only a small fraction of the necessary grave area. The conventional story, and the 700,000 buried corpses, may well have been fatally undermined by this latest discovery. But we won't know until we see the details of her report—if they ever reach the light of day.

Lacking the details, it's hard to draw firm conclusions. But all signs point in one direction. They imply that, as at Belzec, ground surveys provide far more support for the revisionist thesis than the traditional one. Things are looking up; the truth is at hand.

REVIEW

The Wandering Who: A Study of Jewish Identity Politics

by Gilad Atzmon. Zero Books, Washington, D.C, 2011, 202 pp. US $14.95/UK £8.99

Ezra MacVie

Cover reproduced with permission of Gilad Atzmon

In a way, this latest book by Israeli-British saxophonist-commentator Gilad Atzmon is a case study. It is a study of the situation of mastery by a Zionist cabal over the foreign policies of the United States and the United Kingdom and of the critical centers of public opinion that guide these policies. What makes this subject a case is the broader conception of Jewish-led enterprises as a sort of evolved parasite first infesting, then controlling institutions and structures of human organization generally, going back to hosts as ancient as the Roman Empire. Whenever and wherever systems of human order and power have developed to a scale that justifies the effort, strategic networks organized and staffed largely by Jews have sprung up to move matters in the directions that favor them (the major exceptions to date seemingly confined to East Asia). This applies not only to empires and republics, but to dictatorships, kingdoms, professions, labor unions, media, banks, and supra-national organizations—wherever power of any sort intersects organization of any kind.

The case Atzmon delineates in 202 trenchant, eminently readable pages is a beast in whose belly—Israel—he was born and raised, up to and including a stint in the vaunted Israeli Defense Forces, in which the future saxophonist's billet was in a military band that he reports played as badly as possible in order to keep its future workload to a minimum. But Atzmon's experiences were not limited to blowing the horns such as those with which his ancient forebears reduced the walls of Jericho. He also witnesses numerous cases, described in this book, of cruelty and murder visited by his comrades-in-arms on their hapless opponents, the natives of the Palestine that Israel is relentlessly swallowing up in the finest traditions of the ancient Roman and all succeeding empires.

It was primarily these experiences that opened the young jazzman's eyes to the inhumanity of the Zionist project in the Middle East, one to which his own parents and grandparents had been fervently—fanatically—devoted throughout his life. His account is, however, not excessively personal beyond the undeniable fact that his publishing it places him squarely in his subjects' murderous crosshairs. While there is a grippingly human "personal journey" to be discerned in the thread of its argument, this is not an autobiography. At a time now well over a decade past, Atzmon left the fold of his native country and its noxious ambitions and took up residence in a place at least relatively distanced from it: Britain. But even in the heart of a distant empire whose own death throes gave rise to Israel, he finds himself monitored and hectored by agents—sayanim, as they are called in Hebrew—of the perfidy he fled. So, perhaps for that reason, he has turned to make his stand, to fight a fight he would have no chance of being able to fight on his native soil.

He conducts this fight informed by a distinctly "left" (perhaps collectivist) vision, no doubt a vestige of his origins in the "tiny, faraway, socialist theocracy," as Joseph Sobran once memorably styled it. His second chapter is titled "Credit Crunch or Zio Punch," in which he details a correct view of recent economic developments as arising from the policies of the Jewish Chairman of the Board of Governors of the US Federal Reserve Alan Greenspan. He styles Greenspan as formulating his policies in league with "capitalists" whose own satanic profit motive expels them irretrievably from the pale of the righteous, or even the respectable, in doing which Atzmon conflates the inherent adaptability of entrepreneurs to pernicious government policies with complicity in those policies. This jaundiced view of private enterprise is effectively confined to the one chapter in which it appears, and does not spoil even that chapter. It only leaves this reader with the disturbing suspicion that Atzmon might actually envision some statist (or law-based) solution to the problems he laments—a solution that, as history has amply demonstrated, invites back in the very Problem (see first paragraph above) that he seeks to abate.

In his penultimate chapter "Truth, History and Integrity," Atzmon devastatingly exposes the myriad ways in which the Israeli juggernaut defends, expands, exploits the myths of the Holocaust to serve its own evil agenda. He even confesses an innocent reaction as a teenager upon first confronting the noise generated by this program: "I wondered why they bragged so much about being resented"—an unassailably logical reaction that invites comparison with the wonderment of another innocent child as he beheld crowds ogling the magnificent raiment of an utterly naked emperor. His analysis of the exploitation of this mendacious narrative is conclusive: yesterday's "victims" are today's perpetrators, shielded by the tragic legacy borne for the most part by the parents or grandparents of some of them. And those perpetrators do all they can to make the most of that legacy, even to flying their young to the Polish sites of concentration camps in order to imbue in their minds the sights and sounds of a place where terrible things must have been done to ... people those young might suppose they might somehow be descended from.

The final chapter, "Being in Time," is by far the most philosophical of a book thoroughly laced with deep understandings of both personal and group emotions and dynamics, including perspectives in full depth over the course of time measured in centuries and, in fact, millennia. In a few short pages, "Being in Time" delivers a fundamental definition of historical understanding that will delight the soul of any committed revisionist, whether of the specific histories concerned with Atzmon's story or the history of any other times and places whatsoever. And through the lens of this concisely delineated metahistory, he is able to describe the distortions characteristic of Jewish/Zionist thought that offers an appreciation of profound import.

From Britain, Atzmon has been at a disadvantage to witness and chronicle the takeover of the mind, if not the heart, of the American Behemoth for purposes of world domination. America, however, is large and important and open enough (still) to be observed in considerable detail from a distance, particularly for a speaker of English. Atzmon in fact has toured the United States in person with his jazz ensemble, along with many other countries besides. But ultimately it is his heritage in the dragon's very bosom that enables him to deliver a penetrating perspective of its nature, its aims, and its methods.

In the end, the work is an object demonstration of what George Orwell meant when he wrote, in *1984*, "He who controls the past, controls the future."

The Wandering Who? is available from

Amazon.com and Amazon.co.uk

www.gilad.co.uk

www.myspace.com/giladatzmon

www.jazzaproductions.squarespace.com

COMMENT

The Palestinians as an "Invented People"

Rich Siegel

The name "Palestine" has been around for a long time. "Peleset", transliterated from Egyptian hieroglyphics as "P-l-s-t", is found in numerous Egyptian documents referring to a neighboring people or land starting from around 1150 BC. The "Philistine" States existed concurrently with the ancient Kingdoms of Israel and Judah, making up the coastal plain below Jaffa and south to Gaza. In the 5th Century BC Herodutus wrote of a "district of Syria, called Palestine". About a century later, Aristotle described the Dead Sea in *Meteorology* and located it in Palestine:

> "Again if, as is fabled, there is a lake in Palestine, such that if you bind a man or beast and throw it in it floats and does not sink, this would bear out what we have said. They say that this lake is so bitter and salty that no fish live in it and that if you soak clothes in it and shake them it cleans them."

This writer has had the misfortune of frequently engaging in debates with Zionists (a bad habit I need to kick!) who often tend to seize on small ideas. "When did the Palestinians ever have their own country?" In order to win such an argument one would have to reduce oneself to their terms, and produce a map that shows a country and borders: "Palestinian Kingdom, 1587- 1702", and then let them present their map of ancient Israel and Judea, and then get into a wrestling match the winner of which would claim the territory for their own. Or perhaps the issue would be better settled the way the New York colony won Staten Island from New Jersey: with a boat race. If the goal is exclusivity, as it always has been with Zionism, then the only criterion in achieving it is winning, whether a war or a race.

There was no 17th-Century Palestinian Kingdom, or 18th- or 19th-. There were, prior to Allied victory in World War One and the League of Nations "mandates" which granted European powers control of the region, various provinces in a larger Ottoman empire, ruled from Istanbul (previously known as Constantinople, and before that,

Byzantium), much as there are today various American states governed from Washington. Objectors will cry "Foul!", as Americans are governed by Americans in Washington, whereas Arabs were governed by Turks, a different ethnic group with a different language. Fine. So I modify my comparison to the Spanish speaking Puerto Ricans governed from Washington, or the French speaking Quebecois governed from Ottawa. Neither the Puerto Ricans nor the French Canadians are being ethnically cleansed.

11059—A Coffee-house in Palestine.

"A Coffee-house in Palestine." Scanned from a period stereoscope card. Printed by Keystone View Company, Manufacturers and Publishers, Meadville Pennsylvania & St. Louis Missouri. Copyright 1900 by B. L. Singley. Photo is in the Public Domain, via Wikimedia Commons

Prior to Zionism, there was no need for the Arabs of Palestine to focus on Palestinian identity. They were citizens of the Ottoman Empire. When, during the mandate years the British made contradictory promises to the Zionists and the Arabs, and the Arabs expected, and had the right to expect, eventual self-rule, it was certainly not a foregone conclusion that there was going to be an independent Palestine. Palestinians might well have been a part of a larger South Syria, or of a Greater Syria, and happily so. They certainly would not have been ethnically cleansed under those circumstances. The Arabs of Palestine have always had their own distinct Arabic dialect, and various other cultural attributes that set them apart from other regional Arab cultures, but that was never particularly relevant. Many various subcultures existed within the Ottoman Empire, and continued to exist within British and French mandates.

Interestingly, during the years of the *Yishuv*, the pre-Israeli-statehood Zionist community in Palestine, Jewish-Zionist settlers called themselves "Palestinians". In this way, the Zionists ironically affirmed the thing that many of them wish now to deny: Palestinian identity. In 1948, amid the massacres and military forced mass expulsions of the "nakba" (Arabic for catastrophe, the name commonly given to the events of 1948), when the state of "Israel" was declared, all of the Jews who had been calling themselves Palestinians became "Israelis", and when the dust cleared, the Arabs who remained within the green line became "Arab Israelis", like it or not. (It was not known until the state of "Israel" was declared, what it was to be named. "Zion" was considered as a possibility, but rejected, as the result would have necessitated referring to "Arab Israelis", the Arab citizens of Israel, as "Arab Zionists".)

The designation "Palestinian" was more actively embraced beginning in 1964, with the forming of the PLO (Palestine Liberation Organization), this *out of necessity*, because a people who had been ethnically cleansed, who were in a state of shock and humiliation, and who were desperate to recover and regain what was rightfully theirs, found it useful to rally around symbols representing themselves: A name and a flag are two of the basics.

Golda Meir famously said in 1969, during her tenure as Israeli prime minister;

> *"There were no such thing as Palestinians. When was there an independent Palestinian people with a Palestinian state? It was either southern Syria before the First World War, and then it was a Palestine including Jordan. It was not as though there was*

> *a Palestinian people in Palestine considering itself as a Palestinian people and we came and threw them out and took their country away from them. They did not exist."*

Golda is actually right on this point and that point. I would not have been able to show her a map that says "Kingdom of Palestine" or "Grand Duchy of Palestine" or any of dozens of designations that might have satisfied her. But this I can say for sure: There were human beings on that land, and they had been there all their lives, and their families for many generations before them down through the centuries. And many of them were actually descended from ancient Jews who later converted to Christianity and Islam, while our ancestors, Golda's and mine- the Ashkenazi Jews, were converting to Judaism in the Khazar Kingdom on the shores of the Caspian Sea.

Golda actually knew when making this statement, the information which has become available to the general public in the decades since: We Jews *did* come and throw them out and take their country away from them. It's been thoroughly documented. It wasn't, when she made this statement in 1969. She was able to get away with it then. But since then an entire generation of Jewish-Israeli scholars, (and many others, but we Jews need to hear it from Jews first!) has carefully documented the ethnic cleansing of Palestine and presented the history that she personally knew, but actively hid and denied. She and her colleagues concealed the truth from Jewish supporters of Israel all over the world including my family, who taught me lies quite innocently, because they didn't know any better.

In 1984 a book written by Joan Peters, entitled *From Time Immemorial: The Origins of the Arab-Jewish Conflict over Palestine*, was released to the world. The book claimed that the Palestinians were not resident in Palestine long-term, but were recent arrivals, having come to take advantage of economic opportunities in Palestine which were largely the result of Zionist Jewish settlement. What a perfect way for us Zionist Jews to massage ourselves (I was one at the time!) and drive a wedge between ourselves and the growing awareness about Palestine in the world around us! So it really *was* a "land without people for a people without a land"! Those Arabs were all immigrants! And how ungrateful that they hate us after all the opportunity we gave them! A wave of related claims surfaced among the Zionist community. An essay by Mark Twain describing his touring of a sparsely populated 19th-Century Palestine, was offered up into the mix of "Palestinian-denier" evidence. Twain, whose writing was full of humorous and ironic opposition to human bullshit, was no doubt rolling in his grave over this. And claims were often heard that prominent Palestinians, from Edward Said to Yassir Arafat, were "not really Palestinian".

Enter another book, in 2003, *The Case for Israel* by Alan Dershowitz. In case 19 intervening years had given anyone a memory lapse since the publication of Peters's book, Dershowitz borrowed heavily from same, giving the same statistics and making the same conclusions.

Enter yet another book, but this one very different: In *Beyond Chutzpah: On the Misuse of Anti-Semitism and the Abuse of History*, published in 2005, Norman G. Finkelstein exposed Peters's statistics as fraudulent, and with that revelation both her argument and that of Dershowitz, collapsed. However, the damage is done among those who wish to ignore Finkelstein, and there are many! "Isn't he a holocaust denier?", I've been asked. I respond: "No. His parents were holocaust survivors." Zionists have long used a familiar tactic against those who challenge their propaganda: Defamation. And so the lies persist. This writer *still* has people putting *From Time Immemorial* in his face to prove their argument. They refuse to be embarrassed.

At the time of this writing (January 2012), the American public is being treated to an entertainment we get every four years: the run up to our presidential election. As the Democratic candidate will obviously be the incumbent, we are witnessing the Republican candidates claw at each other in their striving to win support for the Republican nomination. Enter a billionaire Jewish American Zionist named Sheldon Adelson, casino magnate and the 8th wealthiest American alive, who along with his wife has donated $10 million to candidate Newt Gingrich. Adelson, whose holdings include the Israeli newspaper *Israel HaYom* (*Israel Today*) made some interesting statements while in Israel at an Israel Media Watch event in 2010:

> "I am not Israeli. The uniform that I wore in the military, unfortunately, was not an Israeli uniform. It was an American uniform, although my wife was in the IDF and one of my daughters was in the IDF ... our two little boys, one of whom will be bar mitzvahed tomorrow, hopefully he'll come back– his hobby is shooting – and he'll come back and be a sniper for the IDF."

And:

> *"All we (the Adelson family) care about is being good Zionists, being good citizens of Israel, because even though I am not Israeli born, Israel is in my heart."*

Does it sound like this guy has "divided loyalties?" Maybe like the Jewish neocons in the Bush administration who got us to fight a proxy war for Israel in Iraq? No- you can't say that! It would be "anti-Semitic"!

So is it any wonder that Newt Gingrich has made the utterly incorrect and profoundly idiotic statement that he has made about the Palestinians being an "invented" people? It has nothing to do with any education on the subject of the history, or any awareness of the current situation. It's simply a question of wanting to win, and of reiterating nonsense he has heard in conversations with a very rich and generous supporter, nonsense which jives with the general impressions that Americans get from our Zionist-controlled media, and that no doubt circulate in Gingrich's Republican circles. Does anyone think Gingrich has read Finkelstein? I doubt it! And if he did, would he turn down $10 million in favor of truth and justice?

The people native to the land of Palestine were not "invented". It is indeed unfortunate that someone who is supposedly educated, and who has achieved position in life where he is poised to potentially become the next president of the United States, is putting forth such foolishness.

COMMENT

Relegation—A Formula for Blowback

Jett Rucker

Pre-emptive censorship is a nefarious but effective form of suppression that is as close as this issue's editorial, in which Richard Widmann reports the peremptory expungement of *Inconvenient History*'s two bound annual books of our Website's articles from the offerings of their erstwhile publisher, Lulu Publishing. Not only are our laboriously compiled books no longer listed in Lulu's catalog, they aren't even supplied to our own private order. It's not only not our book, it has in fact become a nonbook, in the manner of nonpersons as depicted in George Orwell's *1984*.

But for cases where the impermissible thoughts have already been expressed (published, spoken, or uploaded), there is yet another evil device in the censor's torture chamber, known technically as censorship after the fact. One case of this form of censorship is described in detail in Prof. Dan McGowan's article, also in this issue, in which a gang of his former colleagues at Hobart and William Smith Colleges punished him by circulating an e-mail that called for withdrawal of Dr. McGowan's emeritus professorship at their institution. He further cites (or recites, actually, verbatim), Laird Wilcox's eight Elements of Ritual Defamation, which represents the archetype of a form of punishment by which censorship after the fact is commonly practiced. Ritual defamation, as Wilcox originally explained in his 1990 essay, "… is the destruction or attempted destruction of the reputation, status, character or standing in the community of a person or group of persons by unfair, wrongful, or malicious speech or publication." My own term for the crime is "reputational terrorism."

The primary purposes of reputational terrorism are twofold: (a) to incent the original offender to desist from any repetitions of his offense—to silence him; and (b) to discourage others who might come out publicly in agreement with the original offender or with other material in effect committing a similar offense—to make an example of the victim. Item (b) can work, if the defamation reaches a wide enough audience, makes clear what the offense was, and properly intimidates members of the audience without inflaming them with disgust or hatred for the defamer. Accusations of "Holocaust denial" remain effective for the present thanks to a long tradition in the West of training students to reflexively revile people to whom such a label is affixed, but overuse of the label together with overtraining in the requisite reaction may be eroding the effectiveness of this particular ritual. Where the process is effective in deterring other would-be publicizers of a proscribed viewpoint, the censorship-after-the-fact becomes pre-emptive censorship, always the preferred form of suppression for undesirable opinions.

But Item (a), causing the offender to desist from attacks on whomever or whatever the defamer wishes to protect, can backfire badly through various mechanisms, including arousing in the victim a desire to avenge the defamation by manifesting exactly the reaction he knows unmistakably the defamer wishes to discourage. Where once the offender—say, someone who expresses a disbelief in the full authenticity of most claims for Holocaust reparations payments—might have doubted, disagreed with, or disapproved of one or two sensitive, but minor points in the ideology or myth the defamer wishes to defend, the defamation attracts from its victim a greatly increased level of attention and zeal to the entire program that the defamer is seen to be protecting. Seeking more points on which to get back at his (typically remote, usually anonymous) detractor, the defamed party might, in the case just cited, expand his animus from mere fraudulent reparations claims to the underlying historical claims for the event itself (the Holocaust, in this case), discovering and promoting the growing forensics-based debunking of major aspects (e.g., gas chambers) of the Holocaust legend that has been so carefully and successfully nurtured and propagated these 65 years, now.

Continuing in his quest, the aggrieved victim of reputational terrorism might even proceed from broad-spectrum Holocaust revisionism to a review of the uses various Jewish organizations, the state of Israel foremost among these, make of the mythology, and discover an entire new world of atrocities being justified and obscured by the traditions of the long-cultivated Holocaust legend, and take up public opposition to these programs as well. In extreme cases, it is readily imaginable that the desire for revenge could even lead, in a case like that hypothesized, to anti-Semitism, in which the victim is likely still to be committing no moral offense any worse than the one that was originally committed against him.

The foregoing outlines a series of developments culminating possibly in full-blown fanaticism, understandably and perversely arising from the motive of revenge against those who commit ritual defamation in a treacherous defense of some ideology or program of propaganda. But compounding the dynamic and motivation of revenge just described is a further dimension of reaction that, while possibly less calculated or willful, is fully as potent in leading the defamed party to a course of action precisely opposite to the desired reaction of "standing down," or even recanting, as some Holocaust revisionists have done under various forms of duress or enticement. This amplifying consequence of ritual defamation, which is entirely consistent with the defamer's frequent desire to actually harm his victim, I call "relegation." It consists of the denial of the defamed party's *alternatives* to (continuing with the illustrative case) public behaviors which got him defamed in the first place, including, particularly, whatever profession (likely one involving some level of public visibility) the target may have been a member of, or preparing to be a member of.

One rather spectacular case displaying indications of this scenario is that of perhaps a leading Holocaust revisionist, Germar Rudolf, formerly of Germany. While a candidate for the Ph.D. in chemistry at the University of Stuttgart, Rudolf was hired to provide expert testimony in the trial of a person accused of the crime (in Germany) of Holocaust denial. Rudolf's testimony was confined to the subjects of chemistry in which Rudolf was already in his late twenties an eminent authority. After the trial, Rudolf's testimony, together with other non-contrite commentary by the defendant in the trial, was published as a book in Germany. For his contributions to the contents of this book, Rudolf found himself facing criminal charges of Holocaust denial. The process of Rudolf's relegation began with the university's threatening to withhold the Ph.D. degree for which Rudolf had in fact completed his dissertation.

Denied the premier credential in his chosen field for which he had trained for many laborious years, and further feeling a powerful compulsion to resist the pressures being brought to bear on him, Rudolf defiantly extended his scientific inquiries into the forensic bases of the Holocaust legendry, and branched out into publishing activities through which he disseminated his consistently earth-shaking discoveries. The one-man avalanche called Germar Rudolf (no "Dr." for Herr Rudolf) continued gathering momentum and force until 2005, when he was finally arrested in the United States, taken away from his American wife and child, deported to Germany, and there made to stand trial for his "crimes," at the conclusion of which he was sentenced to 30 months in jail. Rudolf shares with his thousands of supporters all over the world an eminently justified outrage at what he has suffered for voicing his soundly based opinions, and what measures this treatment may move him to take now that he has regained his freedom fuels the hopes of Holocaust revisionists everywhere. And these hopes run squarely and powerfully against the results that obviously were hoped for by those who launched their vicious campaign against him so long ago.

Perversions of this kind are by no means unknown in other areas, and in processes other than ritual defamation. In fact, it is *punishment for belief,* or the expression of belief, that leads to the "recidivism" of which the Rudolf case is but one of many going back through history at least to Martin Luther. The perpetual stigmatization by employers, often in compliance with governmental regulations, of ordinary criminals who have served their terms in prison relegates those who, as the phrase goes, "have paid their debt to society" to ways of making a living that are open to ex-convicts—that is, crime. So also with "thought crimes" such as Holocaust revisionism, with the exception of the fact that expounding analyses of the evidence for the Holocaust is for most of us less profitable than, say, robbing a bank. But if you are denied your intended career in, say, chemistry as in Rudolf's case, or journalism as in the case of the late commentator Joseph Sobran, you are as good as confined to the very sphere of activity from which your malefactors obviously intended to dissuade you in the first place, especially if you regard its continuation as an ennobling duty rather than a degrading necessity.

It is, perhaps, only just that the perpetrators of reputational terrorism receive such fierce blowback as reward for their skullduggery. In the case of many such perpetrators, such as the Anti-Defamation League, this blowback only serves their purposes by aggravating the very problem they gain their donations for combating, rather like a glazier who discourages vandals from breaking windows by throwing rocks at the vandals—often missing and instead breaking the windows. Like arms dealers, they thrive on discord, and this how they go about fomenting it, assuming the poses of saints even as they do it.

Every now and then, a well-meaning friend notes how much of my time I devote to revisionism and asks, "Don't you have anything *else* to do?"

Of course, I *don't* have much else to do.

Not anymore, anyway.

Volume IV

Number 2, Summer 2012

EDITORIAL

The Clash of the Nobelists

Jett Rucker

Nobel-Prize-winning German writer Günter Grass sent shock waves through the international community when, on April 4, he published a poem in the *Süddeutsche Zeitung* titled "What Must Be Said." In that poem, for his first time, he voiced his deep concerns about the fact that his country was supplying to Israel, a nuclear power, submarines from which missiles with nuclear warheads could be launched. In fact, Germany has supplied—*given*, actually—three of these so-called Dolphin-class submarines to Israel, and is building three more for the same "customer."

Grass's spectacular statement soon drew fire from another Nobel laureate, one who though of neither nationality, had publicly urged the hatred of Germans, and who holds a converse devotion to Israel, Elie Wiesel. This winner of the Nobel Prize in Peace, not for the first time, assumed the position of supporting Israel's bellicose threats against Iran on the charge of seeking to develop a nuclear capability to offset that possessed secretly at least these 45 years now by Israel. In articles in Israeli and American newspapers, the rampant self-styled "survivor" of World War II slave-labor camps saw fit to impugn not only Grass's reprehensible nationality, but his 1945 service in a military unit mounting a doomed defense against the Soviet conquest of his hometown, Danzig (now Gdansk, Poland).

The entire matter is redolent in the history of the Third Reich and that regime's dealings with Jews in the territories it controlled, among whom, according to his stories, Elie Wiesel himself numbered. In fact, Wiesel's 1958 novel *La nuit* (*Night*) not only launched its writer on a spectacular career culminating in the Nobel Prize, but has, along presumably with its translations into numerous other languages, recently been promoted from its initial classification as fiction to a status much more like actual fact, a memoir. Meantime, a growing but scrupulously ignored contingent of investigators [see especially the work of Carlo Mattogno and Carolyn Yeager— Ed.] advances the report that *La nuit* itself was plagiarized from a preceding (and much longer) book in Yiddish, *Un di velt hot geshvigen* (*And the World Remained Silent*), to which Wiesel claims authorship under the most dubious of circumstances. They assert that Wiesel relied upon that book, rather than actual presence in a labor camp, for the vivid portrayals he published of life as a slave of the Third Reich.

Günter Grass, 20 March 2010. By Blaues Sofa from Berlin, Deutschland (Günter Grass beim Blauen Sofa) [CC-BY-2.0 (http://creativecommons.org/licenses/by/2.0)], via Wikimedia Commons

Günter Grass, as a conscript into the Waffen-SS, actually shares with his critic the fate of being enslaved in the service of the Third Reich, except that Grass, serving in combat, had to undergo enemy fire, and was in fact wounded. And after the war, unlike Wiesel's hometown in Romania, Grass's city of birth was taken over by a hostile power and if he had returned to it somehow, he would undoubtedly have been thrown into a POW camp, ending up like as not in Siberia, as millions of his comrades in arms did. As to history, Grass is known as a founding member of a literary genre known by the German term *Vergangenheitsbewältigung,* or coming to terms with the past, and Grass's career was launched in 1959 with his novel (*still* a mere novel) *The Tin Drum,* gaining him the Nobel Prize forty years later. Grass's past, which is considerably better documented than that of the enigmatic Wiesel, is extensively reflected in the Danzig Trilogy, of which *The Tin Drum* is the first book. It would appear that Grass's claim to a mastery of history and its implications for the present day is at least the equal of, if not considerably superior to, that of his detractor.

The matter of which Grass wrote in his notorious poem is, of course, like all such matters, very much the outgrowth of the history involving World War II Germany and that of the country whose population acquired critical mass by 1948 from the large numbers of Jews it succeeded in collecting from among the millions who, quite like millions of non-Jews in the same continent, found post-war Europe a hostile place riven by poverty, ruin, cold, hunger and hatred. Wiesel, though he remained in Europe and later sojourned in South America and finally the United States, appears to have taken up the service of Israel in which he remains to this day, at around that time. Germany began in 1952, very early in its long recovery from the war's devastation, paying direct reparations to Israel, as it still does today, continuing to increase a sum running to many billions of dollars.

Grass, who visited Israel in 1967 and 1971, has never complained about nor even mentioned this transfusion of German economic lifeblood to its sanctified beneficiary, but the day after "What Must Be Said" was published, Eli Yishai, interior minister of Israel, took the trouble to declare that Grass would be refused if at any point in the future he attempted a third visit. For his part, Grass merely noted that he had been similarly banned from entering the former German Democratic Republic (East Germany).

The strategic implications of Grass's fears actually range far beyond those mentioned in his verses, in which he points with exaggeration reminiscent of Wiesel's descriptions of the Holocaust, to the extermination of the Iranian people by nuclear missiles launched from Israel's submarines. Yet, in some ways, even that horrific eventuality is an understatement of the scope in which Israel is able to menace humanity with its seaborne nuclear capabilities (capabilities that, in fairness, belong also at least to the United States, Russia, Great Britain, France, China, and soon India).

Israel's missiles as yet have nothing like the range of missiles deployed by the United States and Russia, not to mention the other powers mentioned. And it is this fact that makes submarine launching of their missiles so crucial (virtually all of Iran lies within range of Israeli missiles launched from the Persian Gulf).

Israel's submarines, unlike those of the other powers, are not nuclear powered. They incorporate elaborate but potent technology that enables them to cruise underwater using their Diesel engines for as long as a week without surfacing or using a snorkel device. It would be possible, for example, for such a nuclear-armed submarine to travel from Haifa to New York without refueling or even surfacing. With refueling, of course, such a submarine, of which Israel will soon have six, well over 90 percent of the population of the globe will live within range of Israel's nuclear missiles.

Israel's defense rationale for seaborne nuclear launch capabilities actually makes sense at first blush in the framework of a doctrine of mutually assured destruction, in which an attacked power retains the ability to launch a nuclear retaliation even after sustaining widespread, devastating destruction from an attacker's first strike. Having an area little greater than New Jersey's, Israel, unlike the United States or Russia, could conceivably lose its entire land-based retaliatory capacity in an extensive first strike. In such an event, the only retaliatory capability at Israel's disposal would be its nuclear-armed submarines.

At present, however, the only powers capable of such a first strike on Israel are its devoted ally, the United States, and Russia, whose exposure to attack from the sea is severely limited to begin with. So Israel's development of a seaborne retaliatory capability must be seen as preparation to deal with a threat that can only lie in the future.

Israel has, as recorded in Grass's apocalyptical lines, made a great deal of noise over the past few years about the possibility of Iran's developing an atomic weapon, though even if Iran developed such a weapon, it would lack a delivery system for it capable of deploying it against Israel. And for Iran to develop sufficient capability to deliver a pre-emptive first strike capable of neutralizing all of Israel's numerous land-based retaliatory capabilities would take many years beyond such time as they first succeeded in producing even the first weapon and delivery system.

Israel's air force, in any case, can maintain an air-based retaliatory capability by the expedient of keeping nuclear-armed aircraft aloft at critical times, as the United States and no doubt other countries have done. Israel's crucial gain from establishing seaborne nuclear strike capabilities vis-à-vis the airborne alternative just described is, in fact, the attainment of global reach.

With this global reach, provided at bargain-basement prices by its contrite benefactor of the past half-century, Israel acquires the ability to threaten every country, and every city and hamlet, within 200 miles of the sea.

How it is possible not to share Grass's abiding concern at this development from his own country's policies can be explained only by an attachment to Israel's devastative capacities that transcends concern for the safety of the other 99.9 percent of the world's population.

Historical Revisionism and 'Relativising the Holocaust'

K.R. Bolton

Whether the received wisdom on an historical event can be subjected to scholarly scrutiny depends upon the method by which the subject is utilized by entrenched interests. Hence, let the scholar or student who embarks on the questioning of certain sacred cows beware lest he be damned for heresy. This essay examines a polemical technique branded 'relativising the Holocaust', toward the end of extending the limits of scholarly enquiry. The essay examines several examples of acceptable and unacceptable forms of revisionism from the relativist perspective.

Winston Churchill & Gassing Primitives

The Churchill Centre was formed in 1994, emerging from the International Churchill Society of the United States.[1] The Centre is dedicated to promoting the memory of Winston S. Churchill. This includes debunking allegations against Churchill that put the democratic idol in less than a Godlike light. Much of its work is, then, like that of the Institute for Historical Review, *Inconvenient History*, or David Irving's Real History, revisionist. However, unlike these three mavericks, The Churchill Centre's revisionism is not only of an acceptable nature, but is regarded as laudable, and attracts notable patronage.[2]

An entire section of the centre website is devoted to Churchillian historical revision, under the title 'Leading Churchill Myths'.[3] One item that might be of particular interest to revisionists is the repudiating of the allegation that Churchill ordered the gassing of Iraqi rebels during the 1920s. This is of particular interest because it is, on several significant points, analogous to the 'historical revisionist' contentions in regard to the gassing of Jews by the Hitler regime during World War II. My comparison, as will be shown below, is a form of 'relativism'. The Churchill Centre, in recognising that the gassing of Iraqis is a matter that is generally accepted by historians, quotes from *Science Daily*,[4] that:

It has passed as fact among historians, journalists and politicians, and has been recounted everywhere from tourist guidebooks to the floor of the U.S. Congress: British forces used chemical weapons on Iraqis just after World War I.[5]

The *Science Daily* article reproduced by The Churchill Centre goes on to state that R. M. Douglas, Associate Professor of History at Colgate University, has repudiated the allegation. The article continues:

Allegations of chemical bombings by the British erupted into the public sphere during the run up to the U.S. invasion of Iraq in 2003. Iraq's history of chemical weapons did not start with Saddam Hussein's gas attack on the Kurds, scholars and critics asserted. It was Great Britain when it controlled the region under League of Nations mandate in the 1920s that first used chemical weapons in the region to quell Arab uprisings. Many scholars went so far as to root Arab distrust of the West in Britain's brutal chemical attacks.[6]

Douglas, however, finds that these claims - oft repeated in books, newspapers and political speeches - rest on very shaky foundations. The first blunt assertion of British chemical weapons use in Iraq comes from a 1986 essay by historian Charles Townshend.[7]

According to Douglas, the allegation of gassing derives from a letter written in 1921 by J. A. Webster, an official at the British Air Ministry. Townshend cited the Webster letter to the British Colonial Office that tear gas shells had been used against Arab rebels with 'excellent moral effect'. According to Douglas however, Townshend had been wrong: The Army had asked permission to use the shells and the Webster comment on the 'excellent moral effect' was only an estimation of what might occur. Shortly after the Webster letter the British Colonial Office had sought clarification from Army General Headquarters in Baghdad and was informed that gas shells had not been used in any manner. From this letter, however, the allegation took on a life of its own, with varying accounts blaming either aerial bombardment or artillery shelling. 'Though the specifics differed, each allegation treated the incident as a matter of unassailable fact. Douglas's research suggests it is anything but'.[8]

Winston Churchill voiced support of the use of poison gas against Arabs, "I am strongly in favour of using poisoned gas against uncivilised tribes." Canadian Prime Minister Robert Borden (1854-1937) is shown with Churchill (then First Lord of the Admiralty) in 1912. By Agence photographique Rol (Bibliothèque nationale de France) [Public domain], via Wikimedia Commons

The article relates that giving credence to the story was the desire by British Ministers of the Crown to use gas shells or bombs against the Iraqi rebels, 'But wanting to use them does not mean they did'. Douglas states that during 1920-21 there had been two instances where British policy had been to use gas against insurgents but, 'In both cases practical difficulties rather than moral qualms ...prevented their use'. Indeed, it remains undisputed even apparently by the Churchill Centre that, to quote from the report, when in 1920 an Arab rebellion occurred, Churchill as Secretary of War, was 'a vocal advocate of nonlethal gas use' and gave field officers permission to use existing stocks of tear gas shells. However, the nearest stock was in Egypt and by the time the shells arrived, the rebellion was over. Anticipating renewed hostilities, in 1922 a Royal Air Force Commander sought permission to convert the shells into aerial bombs, and Churchill signed off on the request, which was rescinded two days later only because the Washington Disarmament Conference passed a resolution banning the use of tear gas. The article states:

> *There is little doubt had the timing of these events been slightly different - had the 1920 rebellion lasted longer or if there had been time to convert the shells to aerial bombs - that British forces would have used their chemical ordnance. And that, says Douglas, may have vastly changed the course of history. Churchill had given authorization to use chemical agents without consulting his colleagues in the Cabinet, most of whom would have vigorously objected.*[9]

Douglas opines that had such weapons been used, an outcry, with memories of the use of mustard gas during World War I, might have resulted in 'an abrupt end' to Churchill's career'.

Despite 'faulty evidence', appeals to this alleged use of gas against Iraqis in the 1920s resurfaced in regard to allegations of Saddam Hussein's gas attacks against Kurds during their 1988 rebellion.

"The symmetrical appeal of history faithfully repeating itself no doubt accounts for much of the public and scholarly credence accorded to claims that the British used chemical weapons in Mandatory Iraq, their inconsistency and implausibility notwithstanding," Douglas writes.[10]

Gassing – Hitler & Churchill

While one might think that the new (2009) revelations as to Churchill's 'innocence' in regard to gassing Iraqis does not do much to enhance his moral character, my primary interest is not the veracity of the allegations against Churchill. Rather, it is the analogous character of the allegations against Churchill and those against Hitler, in regard to claims of gassing Arabs and Jews respectively, and how re-examinations of these allegations are treated differently. Here are some parallels between the two:

1. Both allegations involve ethnic groups: Arabs and Jews, and both involve attitudes towards those ethnic groups based on race theories. Winston Churchill stated of the issue: 'I am strongly in favour of using poisoned gas against uncivilised tribes'.[11]
2. Both allegations involve the use of gas: (a) tear gas on Arabs, (b) Cyanide gas on Jews.
3. Both rely on documents the implications of which are open to interpretation.
4. Both have become oft-repeated allegations, the repetitions of which have been sufficient of themselves to sustain the allegations. The gassing of Iraqis and the gassing of Jews have therefore both taken on the characters of myth and legend. This is what Douglas calls, in regard to a Churchill order for Iraqi rebels, 'The symmetrical appeal of history faithfully repeating itself [accounting] for much of the public and scholarly credence accorded to claims... their inconsistency and implausibility notwithstanding'.
5. Because an alleged event 'has passed as fact among historians, journalists and politicians' should not render it an 'unassailable fact'.
6. Wanting to do something or discussing the option does not make it an accomplished fact. Hence, in regard to the support by Churchill and other Government Ministers, 'wanting to use [tear gas shells] does not mean they did', any more than discussions on the possibility of exterminating Jews at some levels of the Third Reich administration does not prove that any such policy was put into effect.

It is not my purpose here to argue the merits or otherwise of 'Holocaust Revisionism' as some call it, or the (much) less-than-scholarly 'Holocaust Denial' as it is called by others, but rather to question what has been termed 'relativism' which Lipstadt et al. apply to aspects of historical revisionism not to their liking, while applying 'relativism' as a technique of their own.

The primary questions raised by Prof. Douglas in repudiating the widely accepted belief that the British military used gas against Arab rebels in the 1920s, have also been raised in regard to the widely held view that 6,000,000 Jews were exterminated – mainly by gassing - by the Hitlerite regime as part of an official policy. Suffice it to mention, when this allegation was subjected to rare challenges in Canadian courts in 1985 and 1988 in the prosecution of Ernst Zündel, many of the primary elements of the 'Holocaust', regarded as a matter of unassailable fact by academia, took a hammering under the cross-examination of Zündel's defence lawyer, Douglas Christie. Dr Robert Faurisson, in summarising the cross-examination of the Prosecution's expert witness, Raul Hilberg, who declined to return to Toronto for the 1988 trial, stated that Hilberg was 'forced to admit that for what he called the policy of extermination of the Jews there was neither a plan, nor a central organisation, nor a budget, nor supervision'. The Allies had never carried out a forensic examination of the primary 'weapons', the gas chambers, nor had there ever been an autopsy of a corpse that had allegedly been gassed with Zyklon B. No written orders from Hitler or Himmler for the extermination of Jews had ever been found.[12]

The case for the British gassing of Iraqis in the 1920s seems neither more nor less convincing than the case for the Germans having gassed Jews during the 1940s. Whether one, neither, or both events actually took place is not the concern here. The question is: why are those who raise the same questions in regard to the 'Holocaust' as those raised by Prof. Douglas and promoted by the prestigious Churchill Centre, published by *Science Daily*, and as a scholarly paper in *The Journal of Modern History*,[13] not accorded the same hearing as those involved with any other form of historical revisionism? Why has 'holocaust revisionism' been excluded, on pain of banishment, imprisonment, pillorying, and even death[14], as just another aspect of historical revisionism? The questions raised by the so-called 'Holocaust deniers' are in substance no different from those raised in regard to numerous applications of revisionism, such as those of Prof. Douglas.

Dr Robert Faurisson, whose scholarly qualifications and record have been impressive by any criteria, was recognised as an 'expert witness' in both the 1985 and 1988 trials of Ernst Zündel in Toronto. He was a tenured professor at the University of Lyon where he taught Modern Literature and Text and Document Criticism. He applied his scholarly discipline to an examination of the documents at the Centre de Documentation Juive Contemporaine in Paris, the National Archives of the USA, the State Museum at Auschwitz, and the Bundesarchiv in Koblenz, West Germany. He also conducted on-site examinations of Auschwitz and other concentration camps.[15] Dr Faurisson has posed the same types of questions in regard to the gassing of Jews as those posed by Prof. Douglas in regard to the gassing of Iraqis. Among those questions are the different interpretations that can be applied to key texts in regard to the 'Holocaust', in a manner that seems analogous to Prof. Douglas's contention that statements of opinion do not necessarily prove the realisation of those opinions as policy; in this instance, Churchill's opinion of 'primitives' is analogous to the anti-Semitic opinions of some National Socialist leaders, which are marshalled to 'prove' that these opinions were translated into a policy of genocide.

When Dr Faurisson published his first major article on the 'Holocaust' in *Le Monde* in 1978 he was teaching at the University of Lyon. As a result he was subjected to many demonstrations and 'punched many times'. He had 'many, many lawsuits' against him, and 'many trials'.[16] His teaching career was 'permanently ended' in 1979.[17] It would be superfluous to further relate Dr. Faurisson's predicament since applying his expertise to the subject of the Holocaust. The record is easy enough to find.

My interest in this regard is not the veracity of Dr. Faurisson's contentions. They might be totally erroneous. I frankly do not know, as the 'Holocaust' has only ever been of marginal interest to me. My concern is that such questions are as legitimate as any other form of historical revisionism, and that Dr. Faurisson and countless other scholars, should no more be subjected to outright persecution for their research than Prof. Douglas or any other researcher pursuing a revisionist study on any subject.

What is of particular relevance in regard to the question of 'relativism' in scholarship is that Prof. Douglas is pursuing an important aspect of World War II revisionism. His latest book *Orderly and Humane: The Expulsion of the Germans after the Second World War*,[18] is intended to show that the mass expulsions of ethnic German populations from central and southern Europe after World War II was anything but 'orderly and humane'. This historical revisionism, so far from being suppressed or driven to the fringes of underground publishing, is being published by Yale University Press. The advertising blurb from Yale University Press states of the book:

> *Immediately after the Second World War, the victorious Allies authorized and helped to carry out the forced relocation of German speakers from their homes across central and southern Europe to Germany. The numbers were almost unimaginable—*

> between 12,000,000 and 14,000,000 civilians, most of them
> women and children—and the losses horrifying—at least 500,000
> people, and perhaps many more, died while detained in former
> concentration camps, while locked in trains en route, or after
> arriving in Germany exhausted, malnourished, and homeless.
> This book is the first in any language to tell the full story of this
> immense man-made catastrophe.
>
> Based mainly on archival records of the countries that carried out the
> forced migrations and of the international humanitarian organizations
> that tried but failed to prevent the disastrous results, *Orderly and
> Humane: The Expulsion of the Germans after the Second World War*
> is an authoritative and objective account. It examines an aspect of
> European history that few have wished to confront, exploring how the
> expulsions were conceived, planned, and executed and how their
> legacy reverberates throughout central Europe today. The book is an
> important study of the largest recorded episode of what we now call
> 'ethnic cleansing,' and it may also be the most significant untold story
> of the Second World War.[19]

Douglas's book *Orderly and Humane* is not due for release until May 2012, and it is therefore too early to see what type of reception it will receive. What stands out from the Yale University Press blurb for the book is that Douglas appears to be undertaking one of the cardinal sins of 'Holocaust revisions' and their fellow-travellers: 'relativising the Holocaust'. The question might be one of Douglas being too secure in his position for the Holocaust lobbyists and professional Jewish organizations to wish to confront. While Douglas does not seem to be Jewish, certainly being Jewish has not saved others from opprobrium when dealing with subjects that are regarded as related to 'Holocaust revisionism', namely John Sack for *An Eye for an Eye*, dealing with Jewish-run concentration camps in Poland after World War II and the treatment there of German prisoners by Jewish personnel; and *The Holocaust Industry: Reflections on the Exploitation of Jewish Suffering*, by Prof. Norman Finkelstein.[20]

Will Douglas escape condemnation, when even Jewish Leftists such as Sack and Finkelstein have not, for his having, no doubt inadvertently, 'relativised the Holocaust'?[21] *Orderly and Humane* is unlikely to *directly* challenge Zionism and Israel, unlike the late (d. 2004) Sack's *An Eye for an Eye*[22] which directs attention to the role played by Jews in the NKVD and concentration camps, thereby casting doubt on the Jewish status as history's most martyred; while

Finkelstein's *Holocaust Industry* focuses directly on how Jews individually and collectively have profited from the 'Holocaust'. Another problem for Sack, acknowledged as a 'founder of literary journalism',[23] is that his book exposes the role of Israel in protecting these Jewish murderers under the 'Law of Return' and refusing to extradite them to face trial, while, as is well known, Organized Jewry and Israel have been relentless in pursuing alleged 'war criminals'. Sack's exposé of Jewish culpability in post-war atrocities brought allegations against him from Deborah Lipstadt that he was a 'worse than a Holocaust denier', Lipstadt's claim to academic fame being that she seems to have coined the widely used but – from a scholarly viewpoint – useless, terms 'Holocaust denial' and 'Holocaust denier',[24] the present-day equivalents to 'Witch' or 'Heretic'.[25] Hence, Sack had the following exchange with Lipstadt, where it is apparent that she was referring to what she calls 'relativising the Holocaust':

> *On the Charlie Rose Show I was called an 'anti-Semite' and a 'neo-Nazi' by Deborah Lipstadt. I called her up after that and reminded her that I'd read her book, and I sent her a nice note about it and told her what I was trying to do in my book, and I said 'How could you have said that about me?' She said 'You are worse than a "Holocaust denier,"' and I said 'Deborah, I'm worse than a 'Holocaust denier?' and she said 'You are worse than a "Holocaust denier"'. I said 'Could you explain why?,' and she said 'No. I have a faculty meeting,' and that's the last I talked to her. It doesn't scare me. It doesn't hurt me. It amuses me.*[26]

It is heartening that John Sack was by then in a situation where he could afford to be 'amused'. Others have sustained considerable injury in challenging some aspect of history that has affronted the Holocaust Lobby and/or Zionism.

'Relativising the Holocaust'

It remains to be seen whether the Holocaust Lobbyists will harass Prof. Douglas for 'relativism' in regard to *Orderly and Humane*. It is more likely that such a reaction would be seen as counter-productive and the book best ignored. However, the fact remains that *Orderly and Humane*, albeit of necessity at the moment judged only by the Yale University Press description, is an example of 'Holocaust relativism'. As mentioned, Lipstadt gives much attention to this 'relativism' in *Denying the Holocaust*, and opines that it is the logical strategic direction for 'Holocaust deniers', with Chapter 11 being devoted to the subject. Lipstadt castigates socialist historian Dr Harry Elmer Barnes, for example, for 'relativising the Holocaust', and the issue of German atrocities in general, by claiming that they were no worse than Allied atrocities; indeed, less so.[27] Concerned that this 'relativism' undermines Germany's guilt complex and its 'moral obligation to welcome all those who seek refuge', she condemns German historian Ernst Nolte as coming 'dangerously close to validating the deniers' in his work *The European Civil War 1917-1945*, because he states that 'more "Aryans" than Jews were killed at Auschwitz'.[28] Lipstadt explains:

> *These historians are not crypto-deniers, but the results of their work are the same: the blurring of boundaries between fact and fiction and between persecuted and persecutor. Ultimately the relativists contribute to the fostering of what I call the 'yes, but' syndrome. ... Yes, there was a Holocaust, but it was essentially no different than an array of other conflagrations in which innocents were massacred.*
>
> *Relativism, however convoluted, sounds far more legitimate than outright denial... In the future, deniers may adopt and adapt a form of relativism as they attempt to move from well outside the parameters of rational discourse to the fringes of historical legitimacy.*[29]

Hence, Lipstadt finds it essential to deny even the existence of certain well-documented Allied atrocities, and to repudiate any suggestion that America's role in Vietnam or the activities of Pol Pot are the moral equivalents to the killing of Jews. All other atrocities are relatively insignificant because it was only Jews who were killed as Jews. One might then ask whether the real bone of contention is that more value is put on the life of a Jew than a Gentile, a question that often occurs in regard to Israel's actions against Palestinians, and one that was broached by another Jewish heretic, Dr Israel Shahak.[30] Therefore Lipstadt considers it unacceptable that historians such as Nolte have 'relativised' the 'Holocaust' by comparing it to 'a variety of twentieth–century outages, including the Armenian massacres that began in 1915, Stalin's gulags, US policies in Vietnam, the Soviet occupation of Afghanistan, and the Pol Pot atrocities in the former Kampuchea. According to them the Holocaust was simply one among many evils'.[31] Lipstadt objects that these relativists are 'obscuring crucial contrasts between Stalinism and Nazism', because the terror allegedly perpetrated by Stalin, and others, was 'arbitrary, whereas that of the Nazis 'targeted a particular group'.[32]

Lipstadt's denial in regard to group persecution other than that involving Jews is of course nonsense: Stalin targeted the *kulaks* as a class, and many other groups for centuries have been targeted for class, religious and ethnic reasons, such as the 40,000 Cossacks who were repatriated from Austria back to the USSR and to death, with the connivance of the (western) Allies after the war. Since the deportees included women and children, and therefore non-combatants, the Cossacks were presumably being deported as an ethnic group. [33] Hence, in making the 'Holocaust' a unique experience in history, Lipstadt's methodology seems to include simply denying the existence of any non-Jewish genocidal experience—itself a denial of surpassing scope and depth. For example, the genocidal character of the *Morgenthau Plan* for the starvation of the German population, she claims, 'was never put into effect'.[34] 'Furthermore', she states, 'there was no starvation program in Germany, and the rations Germans received far surpassed anything concentration camp inmates were ever given by the Nazis'.[35] James Bacque, who would certainly be regarded as a 'Holocaust relativist, documents a different view.[36]

Which returns us to the problem of Prof. Douglas's forthcoming book on the mass deportation of ethnic Germans in the aftermath of World War II. There are, as described by Yale University Press, salient features of Douglas's book that make it a seminal work on 'Holocaust relativity':

- The numbers involved are higher than those of dislocated Jews in Europe during World War II: 12,000,000 to 14,000,000.
- Most were women and children, deported after the conclusion of hostilities, and cannot therefore be regarded as 'enemy aliens', such as the Jews in Reich Territory during World War II or German, Italian and Japanese civilians in Allied states during that war.
- At least 500,000 died en route.
- The deportation of the ethnic Germans is described as: 'the largest recorded episode of what we now call "ethnic cleansing"'.
- The book is said to describe perhaps 'the most significant untold story of the Second World War'.

These factors tick all the boxes in regard to the scholarly heresy termed 'Holocaust relativism'. Will Prof. Douglas be subjected to the same persecution that has been meted out to others, for being, like

John Sack, 'worse than a holocaust denier'? Prof. Douglas remains oblivious to the possibility. I put to him the following:

> ...*I assume then, you would not regard your forthcoming book on the expulsion of ethnic Germans from central Europe as 'relativising the Holocaust', which is the contention of Dr. Lipstadt on such subjects? I note that the Yale University Press description of your book states that the expulsions were the worst examples of 'ethnic cleansing', which would certainly qualify for Dr. Lipstadt's term.*[37]

Prof. Douglas, already probably put on guard from my prior questions as to whether his repudiation of the allegations against Churchill also apply in principle to allegations relative to the 'Holocaust',[38] commented simply: 'Indeed I would not, for reasons that are set forth in the book itself'.[39] Yet, whatever the rationalisations Prof. Douglas has used to try and dodge the question of 'relativising the Holocaust', any suggestion that there was a large-scale 'ethnic cleansing' of any people other than Jews, let alone being described by Yale University Press as the 'largest recorded' in history, is going to mark Prof. Douglas down as a 'Holocaust relativist' and like John Sack, 'worse than a Holocaust denier'. A frank opinion was not forthcoming from Dr. Lipstadt when I asked her opinion of the forthcoming Douglas book:

> *Dear Dr Lipstadt*
> *Could I direct your attention to an advertising blurb from Yale Uni. Press for a forthcoming book by Dr. R. M. Douglas:* Orderly and Humane: The Expulsion of the Germans after the Second World War? *Yale Uni. Press describes the book as dealing with, 'the largest recorded episode of what we now call "ethnic cleansing", and it may also be the most significant untold story of the Second World War'.*
> *The Yale link is at: http://yalepress.yale.edu/yupbooks/book.asp?isbn=9780300166606. While we do not yet have the advantage of the book being published, wouldn't the description by Yale Uni. Press suggest an example of 'relativizing the Holocaust'?*[40]

In the meantime, the thorny question of the alleged Turkish genocide against Armenians has again been raised. Raffi K. Hovannisian, first Armenian Minister of Foreign Affairs, has raised the matter in an article published by *Foreign Policy Journal*. He writes that, 'On

February 28, the Constitutional Council of the French Republic struck down a bill, previously enacted by its legislature, that would have made it a crime to deny the Armenian Genocide'.[41] While supporters of freedom of historical enquiry will, frankly, be supportive of the decision by the Constitutional Council for having refrained from a further curtailing of freedom of opinion, the double-standards cannot go unnoticed in regard to France's draconian laws prohibiting any questioning of Holocaust dogma. It seems clear that the Armenian attempt to get such a law passed would have been inspired by France's criminalization of 'Holocaust revisionism'. Certainly, what Hovannisian writes can only be described as the worst form of Lipstadtian 'Holocaust relativisation':

> *What befell the Armenian nation in 1915 was* more than genocide, more than holocaust. *It was not only the premeditated taking of human lives. It was the collective murder of a nation, a culture, a civilization, and a time-honored way of life.... The Armenian Genocide was the Young Turk regime's comprehensive and violent dispossession,* unprecedented in its evil and effect, *of the Armenian nation.*[42] [Emphases added].

As referred to above, Lipstadt vehemently condemns those who have the *chutzpah* or the naiveté to suggest that any event in history is even comparable to 'The Holocaust'. She refers specifically to the alleged Armenian genocide as one such example. She states that 'it was not part of a process of total annihilation of an entire people',[43] while Hovannisian asserts, to the contrary, that it was 'more than genocide, more than holocaust'. If Mr. Hovannisian is not in hot water for such heretical views then the Anti-Defamation League, The Wiesenthal Center, and the rest of the multitudinous Judaeocentric gaggle throughout the world, are off their game.

Notes:

1. 'About the Centre', The Churchill Centre, http://www.winstonchurchill.org/support/the-churchill-centre/about-the-centre (Accessed on: 27 February 2012).
2. Ibid.
3. 'Leading Churchill Myths', The Churchill Centre, http://www.winstonchurchill.org/learn/myths/myths (Accessed on: 27 February 2012).

4. 'Despite Claims, UK Did Not Gas Iraqis in the 1920s, New Research Finds,' *Science Daily*, 22 October 2009, http://www.sciencedaily.com/releases/2009/10/091022064745.htm
5. 'New Research: UK Did Not Gas Iraqis in the 1920s', 25 October 2009, The Churchill Centre, http://www.winstonchurchill.org/learn/in-the-media/churchill-in-the-news/771-new-research-uk-did-not-gas-iraqis-in-the-1920s (Accessed on: 27 February 2012).
6. 'Many scholars' might have sought the explanation for Arab distrust here, since it would be professionally unwise to point out that the roots of distrust are to be found in the betrayal of T. E. Lawrence's Arab rebels who fought Turkish occupation during World War I, the Balfour Declaration supporting a Jewish state in the midst of the Arab world, and other promises to the Arabs on which the French and British reneged. See: K. R. Bolton, 'Anders Breivik and the "Clash of Civilizations"', *Counter Currents*, http://www.counter-currents.com/2011/08/anders-breivik-and-the-clash-of-civilizations-part-1/
7. 'New Research: UK Did Not Gas Iraqis in the 1920s', 25 October 2009, The Churchill Centre, op. cit.
8. Ibid.
9. Ibid.
10. Ibid.
11. 'Winston Churchill's Secret Poison Gas Memo, Winston S. Churchill, Departmental Memo' (Churchill Papers 16/16), War Office, 12 May 1919; cited by: Global Research, http://globalresearch.ca/articles/CHU407A.html (Accessed on: 27 February 2012).
12. Robert Lenski, *The Holocaust on Trial: The Case of Ernst Zündel* (Decatur, Alabama: Reporter Press, 1990), p. 23.
13. R. M. Douglas, 'Did Britain Use Chemical Weapons in Mandatory Iraq?', *The Journal of Modern History*, No. 81, December 2009, pp. 859-887, University of Chicago Press.
14. Such as the killing of French academic Francois Duprat in 1978 by the 'Remembrance Commando'. 'Jewish Militants: Fifteen Years, and More, of Terrorism in France', *Journal of Historical Review*, March-April 1996 (Vol. 16, No. 2), pages 2-13, http://www.ihr.org/jhr/v16/v16n2p-2_Faurisson.html (accessed: 29 February 2012).
15. Barbara Kuluszka (ed.) *Did Six Million Really Die? Report of the Evidence in the Canadian "False News" Trial of Ernst Zündel – 1988* (Toronto: Samisdat Publishers, 1992), pp. 286-287.
16. Ibid., p. 289.
17. Robert Lenski, op. cit., p. 280.
18. R. M. Douglas, *Orderly and Humane: The Expulsion of the Germans after the Second World War* (Yale University Press, 2012).
19. Yale University Press, http://yalepress.yale.edu/yupbooks/book.asp?isbn=9780300166606 (Accessed on: 29 February 2012).

20. Norman G Finkelstein, *The Holocaust Industry: Reflections on the Exploitation of Jewish Suffering* (New York: Verso, 2001).
21. Deborah E Lipstadt, *Denying the Holocaust: The Growing Assault on Truth and Memory* (London: Penguin Books, 1994). See especially Chapter 11: 'Watching on the Rhine: The Future Course of Holocaust Denial', pp. 209-222.
22. John Sack, *An Eye for an Eye: The Untold Story of Jewish Revenge against Germans in 1945* (Arizona: Basic Books, 1993).
Sack's description of 'Holocaust deniers' at a 2001 conference of the Institute for Historical Review, to which he was invited to speak, was that,

> *They were affable, open-minded, intelligent, intellectual. Their eyes weren't fires of unapproachable certitude and their lips weren't lemon twists of astringent hate. Nazis and neo-Nazis they were certainly not. Nor were they antisemites....*

John Sack, "Daniel in the Deniers Den," *Esquire*, February 2001, http://www.johnsack.com/daniel_in_the_deniers_den_1.htm (Accessed on: 29 February 2012).
23. The John Sack Site, 'About John Sack', http://www.johnsack.com/about_john_sack.htm (Accessed on: 29 February 2012).
24. Deborah E. Lipstadt, op. cit., inter alia.
25. For a Medieval account analogous to the scholarly tomes denouncing 'Holocaust deniers', see: Heinrich Kramer and James Sprenger (1486) *Malleus Maleficarum* (London: Arrow Books, 1986).
26. John Sack, 'Behind "An Eye for an Eye": Revenge, Hate and History', http://www.ihr.org/jhr/v20/v20n1p-9_Sack.html (Accessed on: 29 February 2012).
27. Deborah E Lipstadt, op. cit., pp. 74-75.
28. Ibid., p. 214.
29. Ibid., p. 215.
30. Israel Shahak and Norton Mezvinsky, *Jewish Fundamentalism in Israel* (London: Pluto Press, 1999).
31. Deborah E Lipstadt, op. cit., p. 211.
32. Ibid., p. 212.
33. Nikolai Tolstoy, *The Minister and the Massacres* (London: Century Hutchinson, 1986).
34. Deborah E. Lipstadt, op. cit., p. 44.
35. Ibid., p. 45.
36. James Bacque, *Crimes and Mercies: The Fate of German Civilians under Allied Occupation 1944-1950* (London: Little Brown & Co., 1997).
37. Bolton to Douglas, e-mail: 2 March 2012.
38. Bolton to Douglas, e-mail: 28 February 2012.
39. Douglas to Bolton, e-mail: 3 March 2012.
40. Bolton to Lipstadt, 3 March 2012.

41. Raffi K. Hovannisian, 'France, Turkey, and the Armenian Genocide', *Foreign Policy Journal*, 2 March 2012, http://www.foreignpolicyjournal.com/2012/03/02/france-turkey-and-the-armenian-genocide (accessed on: 2 March 2012).
42. Ibid.
43. Deborah E. Lipstadt, op. cit., p. 211.

Christian Gerlach and the "Extermination Camp" at Mogilev

Carlo Mattogno

Christian Gerlach's article, "Failure of Plans for an SS Extermination Camp in Mogilev, Byelorussia"[1] is a typical example of the historically baseless conclusions reached by Holocaust historians due to their technical ignorance, particularly in the field of crematory ovens and cremation.

The article attempts to deduce an intention, on the part of the SS, to create an extermination camp for Western European Jews at Mogilev (Byelorussia), in late 1941, according to a nonsensical technical conjecture, upon which – in order to justify his hypothesis – the author then constructs a series of inconsistent historical conjectures spiced with misleading interpretations.

The article notes that Hitler ordered the deportation of German Jews to the East by mid-September 1941 and comments (the source citations refer to Gerlach's original article):

> "It is not clear if the German leadership actually intended to resettle the Jews as it had before or whether the phrase 'sending the Jews to the East' had now become a code for murdering them. In fact, some Jews deported in the Soviet Union (all who came to Kaunas, one entire transport to Riga) were murdered in 1941, whereas the others – brought to Riga, Minsk, Lodz and to the Lublin district – survived for several months, a few until 1943 and 1944." (pp. 60-61)

In fact, this explanation is utterly incompatible with any plan for the total extermination of the Jews launched as early as September 1941.

Gerlach continues:

> "At the Wannsee Conference on January 20, 1942, Heydrich indicated that forced labor was only a temporary placement for some European Jews; all were to be murdered in the end." (p. 61)

To demonstrate the presumed homicidal intention, Gerlach, in the related footnote, cites the well-known passage from the Wannsee Protocol.

> *"Unter entsprechender Leitung sollen nun im Zuge der Endlösung die Juden in geeigneter Weise im Osten zum Arbeitseinsatz kommen...* [OMITTED: in großen Arbeitskolonnen, unter Trennung der Geschlechter, werden die arbeitsfähigen Juden straßenbauend in diese Gebiete geführt] *wobei zweifellos ein Großteil durch natürliche Verminderung ausfallen wird. Der allfällig verbleibende Restbestand wird, da es sich zweifellos um den widerstandfähigsten Teil handelt, entsprechend behandelt werden müssen...* [OMITTED: da dieser, eine natürliche Auslese darstellend, bei Freilassung als Keimzelle eines neuen jüdischen Aufbaues anzusprechen ist. (Siehe die Erfahrung der Geschichte)]*"* (note 6 on p. 70).

The complete passage, translated into English, is as follows. Gerlach simply omits the sentences in italics set off by square brackets.

> *"Under appropriate supervision, in the course of the final solution the Jews are to be allocated for appropriate labor in the East.* [OMITTED: Able-bodied Jews, separated according to sex, will be taken in large work columns to these areas for work on roads], *in the course of which action doubtless a large portion will be eliminated by natural causes. The possible final remnant will, since it will undoubtedly consist of the most resistant portion, have to be treated accordingly* [OMITTED: because as a product of natural selection these would, if released, act as the kernel of a new Jewish resurgence (per the experience of history.)].

It is obvious that these passages were not omitted by accident; rather, the omissions are intended to lead readers to believe that the expression 'treated accordingly' (*entsprechend behandelt*) means killing. In reality, as I have documented elsewhere[2], the actual meaning of the passage is quite different: it means that those Jews remaining after the natural reduction (*natürliche Verminderung*) would, upon their release (*bei Freilassung*) then constitute the kernel of a new Jewish resurgence (*Keimzelle eines neuen jüdischen Aufbaues*) and should, therefore, not be released. In fact, however, the opposite of "release" is not [necessarily] "murder" but (possibly, or even likely), "continued detention."

The omissions concealed by Gerlach therefore prove that he was well aware that this is the correct interpretation.

Registration of the population of Mogilev, July 1941. Bundesarchiv, Bild 101I-138-1084-24 / Kessler, Rudolf / CC-BY-SA [CC-BY-SA-3.0-de (http://creativecommons.org/licenses/by-sa/3.0/de/deed.en)], via Wikimedia Commons

He then sets forth the central argument of his article:

> *"During recent years surprising new revelations have emerged about activities of the SS in the Byelorussian city of Mogilev.*[3] *Jean-Claude Pressac has shown that, in mid-November 1941, the Topf Company of Erfurt received a commission to construct a huge crematorium at Mogilev; the order came from Amt II of the SS Main Office for Budget and Building (Hauptamt Haushalt und Bauten). On December 30, 1941, an oven with four cremation chambers was delivered and assembled. Three more ovens were available by August 1942 for delivery to Mogilev and were then "diverted" to Auschwitz. The SS Building Administration of "Russia Center" already had paid most of the money for all these ovens."* (p. 61)

Gerlach, therefore, raises the following objection to Pressac's hypothesis that the crematorium at Mogilev "was to dispose of the bodies of those German soldiers and Soviet POWs who had died of typhoid fever":

> *"Out of 300-400,000 soldiers in December 1941, 252 soldiers and officers fell sick with typhoid fever, 150 more in January, 161 in February, and 27 in the first half of March 1942, most of them guards of POW camps. During the same period there were 4,907, 4,270, 3,776 and 648 cases among Soviet POWs, and roughly as many among Soviet civilians from that area. [...]. The death rate among Soviets in POW Camp Dulag 185 in Mogilev in December 1941 was noticeably lower than in other camps: 50 per day."* (p. 61)

At this point, Gerlach introduces the nonsensical technical conjecture constituting the linchpin of his entire article:

> *"But the estimated capacity of the crematorium the SS had ordered was more than 3,000 corpses a day."* (p. 61)

Hence the "logical" conclusion:

> *"An epidemic of typhoid fever was not the reason for constructing a crematorium in Mogilev. Rather, the crematorium was connected with the relatively unknown SS labor and extermination camp in that city."* (p. 62)

The presumed crematory capacity of 3,000 bodies a day, therefore, is alleged to prove that the SS intended to create an extermination camp at Minsk.

This conclusion is technically nonsensical and historically false.

Let us begin with Pressac's "surprising new revelations."

On 4 December 1941, the *Hauptamt Haushalt und Bauten* at Berlin ordered from Topf four double 4-muffle crematory ovens (*4 Stück Doppel-Topf-4-Muffeleinäscherungsöfen*), that is, 4 double 4-muffle ovens" (4 eight-muffle crematory ovens, for a total of 32 muffles), for Mogilev.[4] Topf confirmed receipt of the order on 9 December, but only sent half of one such oven (since the complete oven had 2 x 4 = 8 muffles), i.e., 4 muffles, on 30 December.

In receipt of the proposal filed on 19 August 1942 by Topf engineer Kurt Prüfer during his visit to Auschwitz, the *SS-Wirtschafts-Verwaltungshaupt*, on 26 August, ordered the shipment to Auschwitz of two ovens based on the Mogilev order.

Of the 4 ovens ordered, one half of one oven (i.e., 4 muffles) – as stated above – were delivered to Mogilev, 2 ovens with a total of 16 muffles, to Auschwitz and the remaining one and one half ovens were stored for disposition by the *Reichsführer-SS* in the Topf warehouses.[5]

In consequence of the letter from Topf dated 7 July 1943, the remaining one and a half ovens (8 + 4 muffles) were drawn down by the *SS-Wirtschafts-Verwaltungshauptamt*. On 16 August, the SS-Wirtschafter (the SS official responsible for commercial enterprises) at the *Höherer SS- und Polizeiführer* of the General Gouvernement sent the *Zentralbauleitungen der Waffen SS und Polizei* of Heidelager, Cracow, Lemberg, Lublin and Warsaw, and the Neubauleitung of Radom a note informing them that: "Office CIII has at this time one and a half crematory ovens available = 12 muffles (= 8 + 4)" (*Dem Amt CIII stehen z.Z. 1 ½ Einäscherungsofen = 12 Muffeln zur Verfügung*), asking the above mentioned offices to let him know by 1 September whether they needed them.[6]

As for the payment for the ovens, Rudolf Jährling, the civilian employee forming part of the Auschwitz *Zentralbauleitung*, unequivocally clarified something -- apparently garbled in an earlier rendition-- which had misled even Pressac himself. Jährling made two hand-written annotations, one dated 31 January, the other dated 21 February 1944, on the copy of the letter from the *Bauinspektion Russland-Mitte* dated 2 June 1943 received by the *Zentralbauleitung*, in which he explained that the SS had ordered 4 ovens with 8 muffles (each), costing a total of 55,200 RM; the *Bauinspektion Russland-Mitte* had already paid Topf 42,600 RM on account, followed by the addition – on 7 February 1944 – by the *SS-Standortverwaltung* of Auschwitz, of another part payment of 10,000 RM,[7] as a result of which Topf was still entitled to 2,600 RM.[8] The oven-and-a-half stored in the Topf warehouses were therefore, for all intents and purposes, the contractual property of the *Reichsführer-SS*.

Now let us consider the question of the crematory ovens at Mogilev.

As noted above, Gerlach attributes "an estimated capacity" of 3,000 bodes per day to the 4 ovens, [each] with 8 muffles (for a total of 32 muffles), intended for Mogilev. What is the source of this estimate? Gerlach, in support of this claim, refers to pages 34 and 40 of Pressac's book, *The Crematory Ovens of Auschwitz* (note 14 on p. 71). But Pressac says nothing here about the crematory capacity of the Mogilev ovens. Rather, he adduces the presumed crematory capacity of the 2 ovens. [Each] with 8 muffles (for a total 16 muffles), installed in crematoria IV and V at Birkenau, making a distinction between theoretical capacity, 768 bodies per day each, and the "effective" capacity of 500 bodies.[9] Gerlach therefore uses the theoretical figure instead of the "effective" one: 768 x 4 = 3,072 or approximately 3,000.

But the crematory capacity estimated by Pressac is technically baseless.

The 8-muffle ovens were designed for Mogilev, where coke was difficult to procure, and were therefore equipped with wood-burning fire boxes (*Holzfeuerungen*) without doors, which Topf, for the ovens sent to Auschwitz, had adapted to coke-burning grates using sloping and horizontal short-beam bars. In view of the very short useful life of the sloping short-beams, Topf advised the *Zentralbauleitung* to order grate bars intended for reserve coke and refractory-clad furnace doors. Due to transport problems, moreover, the ovens for Mogilev were not insulated; Topf was prepared to supply the insulation material at the specific request of the *Zentralbauleitung*.[10]

In conformity with the proposal by Topf dated 2 September 1942, concerning the change in the fueling of the ovens and resulting changes, on 15 September the *Zentralbauleitung* ordered 4 cast iron doors (*gusseiserne Türen*) for the fire boxes, and, to insulate the 2 ovens, 2,500 insulating bricks (*Isoliersteine*), 600 kg of rock wool (*Schlackenwolle*) for each oven, in addition to the spare short-beams for the gas-generator furnaces, at a price of 3,258 RM.[11] Naturally, since the 2 ovens had 8 gas generators, there were also 8 fire box doors, and not 4, as hastily rectified by Topf.[12]

Pressac was well aware of this problem, which he summarized as follows:

> "This oven was a field design, which was greatly simplified. As desired by the Bauleitung *of Mogilev, it was wood-fired, since coke was rare in the region. The generators had no doors, and the oven was not thermally insulated on the interior, since these parts would have been very heavy to transport.*" [13]

In reality, the 8-muffle ovens at Birkenau were capable of cremating no more than 160 bodies per day (per day total), i.e., a cremation rate of one body per muffle per hour, for a twenty-hour working day,[14] (8 muffles x 1 corpse per hour x 20 hours = 160.)

With regard to the Mogilev ovens, it was quite a different story, since the use of wood for fuel (coke has a calorific value at least double that of seasoned wood) and the absence of thermal insulation and fire box furnace doors (with the consequent enormous increase in heat loss by irradiation and conduction) would have seriously affected cremation economy, including cremation times, drastically increasing the duration of cremation.

What is more, only one half oven, i.e., 4 muffles, was ever sent to Mogilev, which means that, even under the most favorable circumstances, the crematory capacity of the installation would have been 80 bodies per day (20 hours), in reality, less than one third as many. This is fully compatible with Pressac's hypothesis that the ovens were (only) used for the victims of typhoid fever.

In practice, Gerlach assumes asserts a crematory cremation capacity for the Mogilev ovens 50 times greater than that which was actually available, destroying the basis for his conjectures on the presumed extermination camp in that locality.

In this regard, he writes:

> "*One hint of this project emerged on October 10 [1941] at a conference in Prague on "Jewish questions" in the Protectorate of Bohemia and Moravia. During the meeting Heydrich stated that the heads of* Einsatzgruppen *B and C, SS-*Brigadeführer *Nebe und Rasch [,], could take Jews into the camps for communist prisoners in the operational area. According to [a] statement from SS-*Sturmbannführer *Eichmann this is already being done (*eingeleitet*).*" (p. 62)

In reality, this document only speaks of deportations to the East and of the arrival of the deportees to the appropriate camps, without even the vaguest mention of any extermination:

> *"Difficulties arose due to the evacuation. It was therefore expected to begin on about 15 October, in order to get the transports rolling gradually by 15 November, reaching a maximum of about 5,000 Jews (no precise information as to time period) – just from Prague. For the time being, much consideration must be given to the officials at Litzmannstadt. Minsk und Riga are to receive 50,000 [...]."*
>
> *(Wegen der Evakuierung entstanden Schwierigkeiten. Es war vorgesehen, damit am 15. oktober etwa zu beginnen, um die Transporte nach und nach bis zum 15. november abrollen zu lassen bis zur Höhe von etwa 5000 Juden – nur aus Prag. Vorläufig muss noch viel Rücksicht auf die Litzmannstädter Behörden genommen werden. Minsk und Riga sollen 50000 bekommen. [...].)*

> *"5,000 Jews will now be evacuated from Prague in the next few weeks. SS Brigade Leaders Nebe and Rasch could include Jews in the camps for Communist inmates in the operational area. This is already being done, according to* Sturmbannführer Eichmann.*"*[15]
>
> *(In den nächsten Wochen sollen 5000 Juden aus Prag nun evakuiert werden. SS-Brif. [Brigadeführer] Nebe und Rasch könnten in die Lager für kommunistische Häftlinge im Operationsgebiet Juden mit hineinnehmen. Dies ist bereits nach Angabe von SS-Stubaf. [Sturmbannführer] Eichmann eingeleitet.)*[16]

It should be noted in passing that this program is fully compatible with the content of the Wannsee Protocol:

> *"The evacuated Jews will first be sent, group by group, to so-called transit ghettos, from which they will be transported to the East."*[17]

This is also confirmed by the telegram from Georg Leibrandt, leader of the Political Division in Rosenberg's Ministry, as *Reichskommissar für das Ostland*, Heinrich Lohse, dated 9 November 1941, "on Jewish transports to the East."

> "Full details in the post. Jews are being shipped further and further East. Camps in Riga and Minsk only temporary measures, therefore no objections here."
>
> *(Genaues Schreiben unterwegs. Juden kommen weiter nach Osten. Lager in Riga und Minsk nur vorläufige Massnahme, daher hier keine Bedenken.)*[18]

On the same day, Lohse sent Rosenberg the following secret telegram:

> "Security Police report transport of 50,000 Jews to the East. Arrival of first transport in Minsk 10.11., in Riga 19.11. Urgent: please defer transports, since the Jewish camps are to be transferred considerably further east."[19] [20]
>
> "It is a good thing for fear that we are exterminating the Jews to travel on ahead of us." (p. 64)

Thus, mention of a mere "fear" amounts, "in fact", to a confession!

Gerlach then produces the following as additional proof:

> "Mogilev is linked to another aspect of German extermination policy. In September 1941 a notorious killing experiment with exhaust gasses took place there under the command of the head of Einsatzgruppe B, Arthur Nebe."(p. 64)

He adds that, at the time, there were "two gassing experiments, one at Mogilev and one at Minsk." (p. 65) These presumed experiments are said to have been performed in compliance with the order to find more humane methods of execution than shooting, issued by Himmler to Nebe during his visit to Minsk in August 1941. But this anecdote is based solely on post-war testimonies, beginning with that of Erich von dem Bach-Zelewski, who had been *Höherer SS-und Polizeiführer* in Russia. Similarly, even the presumed gassing experiments – using pipes connected to motor vehicles – are attested to solely by more or less unreliable witnesses, as demonstrated in my studies *Il campo di Chelmno tra storia and propaganda* (Effepi, Genoa, 2009), the American English translation edition of which is now in preparation under the title *Chelmno: A German Camp in History and*

Propaganda, and *Schiffbruch. Vom Untergang der Holocaust-Orthodoxie* (Castle Hill Publishers).

In the end, after two pages of conjecture, Gerlach is compelled to admit that "the SS apparently did not give up the idea of an extensive extermination in camp in Mogilew until 1942, when the crematoria intended for Mogilev were delivered to Auschwitz" and that "it seems that a gas chamber in Mogilev never existed," (p. 68) Mogilev was not, therefore, even a Jewish extermination camp! He then informs us that "instead, three gas vans were at that time located in the city, as in February 1942. This is proven by a newly found report of the Einsatzgruppe B." (p. 68) In the related note, Gerlach claims that, according to the "*Tätigkeits- und Lagebericht der Einsatzgruppe B für die Zeit vom 16. bis 28 Februar*, of 1 March 1942," on 23 February 1942 this *Einsatzgruppe* received two large "*Gaswagen.*" (note 83 on p. 77) It only remains to be established whether these vehicles were the presumed homicidal gassing vehicles, or mere gas-generator vehicles (*Generatorgaswagen*) or producer-gas vehicles (*Holzgaswagen*), referred to, for purposes of brevity, as *Gaswagen*, vehicles operating on gas produced by gas generators.[21] Incidentally, the term "*Gaswagen,*" as a homicidal gassing vehicle, gas van, only entered the language after the war; the documents mentioned in support of the reality of the presumed homicidal gassing vehicles were in fact referred to as *Sonder-Wagen, Sonderfahrzeugen, Spezialwagen* or *SWagen*. As documented by myself in the book *Schiffbruch. Vom Untergang der Holocaust-Orthodoxie,* one of the above-mentioned vehicles was sent to Auschwitz in September 1944 and was, in reality, a gas-generator vehicle. The document cited by Gerlach has also been discussed by Santiago Alvarez.[22]

Gerlach then mentions the victims at Mogilev: "at once up to 4,000 people were said to be killed;" (p. 68) that is, for a total of 25,000-30,000 civilians between 1941 and 1942 (p. 69), but the sources are merely witness testimonies made several years after the war before the Soviet War Crimes Commission investigating German crimes at Mogilev (notes 89, 91 and 92, p. 78)! Here as well, there is not the slightest trace of any real documents.

Gerlach concludes as follows:

> *"Although there can be doubts about some details, it is at least probable that the SS intended in autumn 1941 to send part of European Jewry to Mogilev to kill them there. Mogilev was one*

option; others were Lodz, Riga, and Minsk, precisely as mentioned during the conference in Prague on 10 October." (p. 69)

To return to reality, Gerlach's inane conjectures are based on an audacious egregious distortion of the facts: the SS plan to deport Western European Jews to the transitory ghettos (*Durchgangsghettos*) of Riga and Minsk as a temporary measure (*vorläufige Massnahme*) prior to transporting them further east (*weiter nach dem Osten*) and the delivery of 4 muffles to Mogilev with a crematory capacity well below 80 bodies a day!

This is how the Holocaust historians write "history."

Translated by Carlos W. Porter

Notes:

1. *Holocaust and Genocide Studies*, Spring 1997, pp. 60-78.
2. "'Leugnung der Geschichte?' - Leugnung der Beweise! Teil 2. " Keine "Beweiskonvergenz" in Holocaust. Antwort an M. Shermer und A. Grobman, in: *Vierteljahreshefte für freie Geschichtsforschung*, vol. 8, no. 3, November 2004, pp. 299-301 ("Das Wannsee-Protokoll")
3. Gerlach writes "Mogilëv".
4. Letter from the HHB to Topf dated 4 December 1941. RGVA (Russian National War Archives, Moscow) 502-1-327, pp. 47-48.
5. Letter from Topf to the *Zentralbauleitung* dated 7 July 1943. RGVA, 502-1-327, pp. 43-45.
6. WAPL (Lublin National Provincial Archives), Zentralbauleitung, 268, p. 132. Document 166.
7. WAPL, Zentralbauleitung, 268, p. 132. Document 166.
8. *Zentralbauleitung, Abschlagszahlung Nr. 1* dated 1 February 1944. RGVA, 502-1-310, pp. 16-16a.
9. Letter from the *Leiter der Gruppe C Baugruppe* of the *Höherer SS-und Polizeiführer Russland-Mitte* to the *Bauinspektion der Waffen-SS und Polizei Reich-Ost* of 2 June 1943 and handwritten notes by the civilian employee Jährling dated 31 January and 21 February 1944. RGVA, 502-1-314, pp. 36-36a.
10. J.-C. Pressac, *Die Krematorien von Auschwitz. Die Technik des Massenmordes.* Piper, Munich-Zürich, 1994, p. 164.
11. Letter from Topf to the *Zentralbauleitung* dated 31 August 1942. RGVA, 502-1-313, p. 150.
12. Letter from the *Zentralbauleitung* to Topf dated 15 September 1942. RGVA, 502-1-312, p. 22; letter from Topf to the *Zentralbauleitung* dated 22 September 1942. RGVA, 502-1-313, pp. 127-127a.

13. Letter from Topf to the *Zentralbauleitung* of 30 September 1942. RGVA, 502-1-313, p. 118.
14. J.-C. Pressac, *Die Krematorien von Auschwitz. Die Technik des Massenmordes*, op. cit., pp. 40-41.
15. Notes on the conference of 10.10.41 on the solution to the Jewish question. T 37/299. Transcribed in: Miroslav Kryl, *Deportacja więźniów terezinskiego getta do obozu koncentracyjnego na Majdanku w 1942 roku*, in: "Zeszyty Majdanka", XI, 1983, pp. 38-41.
16. See my study *Auschwitz: The Case for Sanity*. Published by The Barnes Review, Washington, 2010, pp. 282-289.
17. NG-2586-G. Photocopy of the original in R.M. Kempner, *Eichmann und Komplizen*, Europa Verlag, Zurich-Stuttgart-Vienna, 1961, pp. 133-147, p. 8 of the original.
18. GARF (National Archives of the Russian Federation, Moscow), 7445-2-145, p. 54.
19. G.ARF, 7445-2-145, p. 52.
20. Adolf Hitler, *Monologe im Führerhauptquartier 1941-1944*. Albrecht Knaus, Hamburg, 1980, p. 106.
21. F. P. Berg, Diesel Gas Chambers: Ideal for Torture - Absurd for Murder, in: G. Rudolf (Ed.), *Dissecting the Holocaust. The Growing Critique of "Truth" and "Memory"*. Theses & Dissertations Press, Chicago, 2003, pp. 460-461.
22. Santiago Alvarez, Pierre Marais, *The Gas Vans. A Critical Investigation*. Published by The Barnes Review, Washington, 2011, pp. 92-94. The document is reproduced on pp. 343-344.

John Demjanjuk: The Man More Sinned Against

Nigel Jackson

I am a man more sinned against than sinning!

—King Lear in Shakespeare's King Lear

John Demjanjuk is dead. *The Age*, Melbourne's more intellectual daily newspaper, reported this on 19th March under the prejudicial and ambiguous heading 'Nazi camp guard dead.' Quoting the *Washington Post*, the newspaper referred to Demjanjuk as 'the target of a decades-long international effort to prove that he participated in genocide as a guard at Nazi prison camps'. The report summarised the legal history of cases against him and noted that he was finally charged in Germany 'with 27,900 counts of being an accessory to murder as a prison guard at Sobibor', one of the alleged Nazi 'death camps'. In May 2011 Demjanjuk was found guilty and sentenced to five years in prison. There is no suggestion in this report by *The Age* that anything was amiss in the treatment of this man by the USA, Israel or Germany, although it is noted that he maintained 'that war-crime accusations against him were a matter of mistaken identity.'

The purpose of this essay in memorial to Demjanjuk is to suggest that there was indeed much amiss in the treatment meted out to him - as indeed there has been in the reporting of his cases and life history by Melbourne newspapers - and to indicate the significance of the whole story to world politics and to the Australian political order.

II

Immediately on 19th March I emailed the following letter to the letters editor of *The Age*:

> The death of John Demjanjuk ('Nazi camp guard dead', 19 Mar) brings to a close one of the most repulsive and inhumane persecutions of a human being in European history. Yoram Sheftel, Demjanjuk's Jewish lawyer, provided in his 1995 book *Show Trial* a thorough exposure of the massive corruption involved in the staging of the first Israeli trial of Demjanjuk,

> whose verdict had to be overturned in the appeal trial because of irrefutable evidence found after the collapse of the Berlin Wall.
> There is plenty of evidence, too, that corruption was involved in the further campaign against Demjanjuk, which resulted in his cruel deportation to Germany in his late eighties. As for the charges on which he was then found guilty, they are thoroughly preposterous. Moreover, revisionist historians have mounted a strong case that Sobibor was not, in fact, a death camp at all, but a transit camp. The continuing persecution of these historians in more than a dozen countries merely adds to the conviction that there is something very rotten indeed in contemporary Western European political orders.

This letter was not published and so I appealed to the letters editor next day, giving these reasons:

> *There is a strong body of opinion that John Demjanjuk was treated most unjustly in America, in Israel and in Germany. It includes eminent and thoughtful persons such as Patrick Buchanan, a former candidate for the American presidency. Even* The Daily Telegraph *in the UK in its obituary has written: 'In 2011, doubt was cast on the very identity card that had seemed so damning, with FBI analysis appearing to show it might have been tampered with.'*
> *It is notable that, in contrast to their coverage during the Israeli trials, coverage of the Demjanjuk story throughout the second campaign against him including the German trial that this led to by major Australian media,* The Age *included, has been deplorably one-sided. I do not think that The Age published one pro-Demjanjuk letter throughout that whole period. Now that the man is dead, please at least let his defenders have some say!*

The letters editors remained unmoved by this appeal and next day there was nothing published sympathetic to Demjanjuk.

Even more depressing than this has been the response of our national newspaper, *The Australian*. Neither on the 19th nor the 20th of March did it publish any news about Demjanjuk's death. Thus, on the 20th I emailed to its letters editor a letter very similar to that sent to *The Age*. It included the information about the statement by *The Daily Telegraph* and identified the identity card as having been issued by the Trawniki training camp.

This letter did not appear on the 21st and so I emailed an appeal to the letters editor, giving my reasons as follows:

> *After the first Israeli trial of John Demjanjuk,* The Australian *expressed triumphant joy in a spread that ran to several full pages. Even then it was possible to see that justice had not been done and* The Australian *published a letter of mine pointing this out. We now know, thanks to Sheftel and others, that there was massive corruption in both the USA and Israel that led to that verdict.*
>
> *It seems extraordinary that, now that Demjanjuk has just died,* The Australian *has made no reference at all to that death or the man's life.*
>
> *It is also odd that major print media in Australia, including* The Australian, *have treated the second campaign against Demjanjuk, which resulted in his deportation to Germany and the trial there, as a relatively minor news story and have virtually silenced debate on the rightness or otherwise of the treatment of him. Quite a number of influential and informed persons, including former USA presidential candidate Pat Buchanan, have expressed grave reservations about the integrity of proceedings against Demjanjuk. I think I am correct in saying that, since the second campaign against him was first publicised in Australia,* The Australian *has not published a single pro- Demjanjuk letter.*
>
> *Isn't it therefore time to allow this side of the controversy some coverage, especially as it bears on the case of Australian citizen Charles Zentai, whose case is still in progress?*

(Certain Jewish bodies have been agitating for years to have Australia deport Zentai, now in his late eighties, to face 'justice' (really a show trial) in Hungary over his alleged killing of a Jewish youth during World War Two.) The letters editor of *The Australian* remained unmoved by my appeal; and the newspaper continued to remain silent about Demjanjuk's death.

III

Yoram Sheftel's book *Show Trial*, first published in Israel in Hebrew in 1993, establishes clearly that there was serious corruption in the USA to get Demjanjuk deported to Israel to stand trial, that Israeli authorities flouted true justice by deliberately turning the first trial into the theatre of a show trial, and that there was unacceptable bias against Demjanjuk in the way in which that trial, leading to a death sentence, was conducted.

John Demjanjuk hearing his death sentence. Demjanjuk Trial Jerusalem, 25 April 1988. USHMM Photograph #65266, courtesy of Israel Government Press Office [Public domain], via Wikimedia Commons

That it was possible to know wrongdoing was occurring before Sheftel's book was published is proved by the full text of the first letter I sent *The Australian* on 2nd May 1988 and which was not accepted for publication (the one that finally appeared was much, much shorter). Here is that text.

>*In your* Weekend Australian *for April 30-May 1 you employ nearly 5,000 words apparently in order to convince your readers that Ukrainian Christian John Demjanjuk has received justice in Israel and that the current drive to pursue up to 600 suspected "Nazi war criminals" in Australia is a splendid jihad. [Several trials were eventually held, but resulted in no successful prosecutions; hence the intense eagerness in some quarters to at last get Australia 'on the hook' by having Zentai sent to Hungary.]*
>
>*'With luck, it seems, we may even find some bigger fish than the one Israel has just hooked; and there may be a gladiatorial "trial" of even more superb dimensions in the Land of the Yellow*

and Green [Australia] (or is it the Red, the Yellow and the Black?)! [The colours of the "Aboriginal flag"]

May I employ somewhat fewer words to suggest to you and your readers that John Demjanjuk may well have suffered immense injustice in Israel (making comparisons with the Dreyfus affair thoroughly apt) and that Australia's "leadership" in pursuing the New Inquisition is something of which we should all feel deeply ashamed?

Your page 18 news report ("Cocky Ivan's world collapses") uses a pejorative word to encourage hostility in the reader towards Demjanjuk; and this is particularly mean-spirited in view of the fact that, whether justly or not, this man is facing a sentence of death and is thus entitled to the traditional courtesies.

We soon find from the first five paragraphs that Demjanjuk is alleged to be in much poorer psychological shape after being sentenced than when he arrived in Israel in February 1986 – the implication being, presumably, that the scoundrel's bravado has received an excellent punch in the guts after his just denunciation. But this report depends only on unnamed "prison guards" and an unnamed "eyewitness" and may well be a propaganda fabrication.

A fatal anonymity continues. We are told that "according to legal experts" Demjanjuk "has little to hope for" from his appeal; but the only such expert actually named is a "specialist in criminal law at Harvard, Professor Alan Dershowitz, who has followed the case closely." Frankly, I suspect that this academic is a Jew and not a disinterested and impartial observer. [He is.] It is noteworthy that The Australian has not told its readers that the author of its 3,800-word "summary" of the trial, Gitta Sereny, is Jewish.

The "legal experts" (we are informed by "Douglas Davis in Jerusalem") claim that Demjanjuk's defence is based on "a series of implausible contentions." I shall list three of these and comment on them.

(1) "That a succession of Treblinka survivors and a former SS guard inaccurately identified him as Ivan the Terrible." But there were just such a series of proven inaccurate "identifications" in the trial of Frank Walus!

(2) "That the Soviet authorities conspired to forge an identity document which placed him in the Trawniki camp, where Red Army deserters were trained to be guards at SS death camps." But, as Chapman Pincher showed in The Secret Offensive (UK,

1985), the Soviet Union are past masters at such forgeries and have a whole political arm devoted to disinformation.

It must be noted that Count Nikolai Tolstoy, who testified on Demjanjuk's behalf for three days in Israel, told a Melbourne audience on March 4 that not only he but all the other experts consulted were confident that the card is a forgery, and he made it utterly clear that he had no confidence in the Israeli court's turning aside of such evidence and that he could not imagine such a position being taken in a British or Australian court.

Count Tolstoy was emphatic and unqualified in his view that Demjanjuk was not receiving justice in Israel.

Gitta Sereny does admit in her article that the defence have a good case that the card is a forgery: "there is (very curious for an ID) no date either of issue or validity. Strange too, that Demjanjuk's two postings are written by hand so that the bearer could have written in and transferred himself anywhere he wished.

"The most important witness brought, Dr Julius Grant, one of Britain's most distinguished forensic scientists, considered Demjanjuk's signature, in Cyrillic writing, 'unlikely' to be genuine."

And she admits that "The prosecution case hangs on a less-than-satisfactory card plus photo-identifications that many people feel were carried out with less than impeccable proceedings."

Yet she does not question the judge's statement: "The court accepted the contention of two prosecution witnesses – a German police expert and an Israeli academic – who testified that the document was authentic, rather than the defence witnesses, whose expertise in the field had been undermined during cross-examination."

A first-class and disinterested journalist would surely have felt obliged in a 3,800-word article to either show the tenable grounds for the judge's decision or to oppose it.

(3) "That he was at the Chelm prisoner-of-war camp when he was alleged to have been at Treblinka – a claim that was proved to be historically impossible." But was it proved to be historically impossible? There are many relevant aspects of World War II history which remain extremely controversial and which will continue to do so until the research of the "revisionist historians" is clearly rebutted in an academic manner (if it can be). The enormous efforts made to defame these historians and to suppress their writings only makes one more suspicious that some of them

must have exposed at least something that is true and iconoclastic.

Furthermore, the references in Gitta Sereny's article to the Chelm issue do not in fact add up to a harmonious and fully articulate story. Her report of Judge Dorner's interrogation of Demjanjuk concerning his "forgetting" of his time at Chelm "when the Americans had been interrogating him about his early life" may well be correct; but it is impossible to fit this American interrogation into her earlier account of how Demjanjuk changed his testimony.

As one reads Ms Sereny's article, all sorts of questions and problems arise.

Firstly, there is the positive evidence in Demjanjuk's favour. "Three other survivors of the upper camp (at Treblinka) – two in Israel and one in Australia – did not see a resemblance." Ms Sereny has already admitted that "The documentary record is scanty; our knowledge of it depends, in the final analysis, on human memory." Is it justice to execute Demjanjuk 43 years after the war on the basis of "human memory"?

Bishop Scharba (from Demjanjuk's church, St Vladimir's) has stated: "I cannot bring together the man I know and the man he is accused of being." Ms Sereny was very ready to proffer the opinion of an Israeli psychologist (Dan Bar-On): "If he is really innocent, though, then however often he has heard these accusations, he would have to show anger."

Why? Psychologists, like historians, often have differing opinions. Reports of Demjanjuk's trial have at times indicated that he showed anger. And Ms Sereny produces no psychologist to explain the discrepancy noted by Bishop Scharba.

Instead, she rather deftly uses innuendo to suggest that Bishop Scharba is uneasy at defending Demjanjuk ("Bishop Scharba very soon veers away from Demjanjuk to talk about 'the Ukrainians' general sense of group victimisation.'")

Similar innuendo is used to seek to discredit Demjanjuk's supporter Jerome Brentar, who is made to sound like a dedicated helper of fleeing Nazi monsters (Eichmann's name is tenuously linked to him on a "guilt by association" ploy). Yet we are told that Brentar succeeded in "getting statements from three Polish villagers near Treblinka that Demjanjuk's photograph in no way resembled the Ivan they had known: a giant approaching his 40's with greying hair" and that "He then visited Kurt Franz, Treblinka's deputy commandant... and acquired an affidavit with an identical description."

Ms Sereny never uses innuendo to discredit any Jews or Israelis.

Moreover, she gives no reason why the evidence of Franz was not accepted by the judges, while they did fulsomely accept the testimony hostile to Demjanjuk, of Otto Horn. The way Ms Sereny writes about Horn should also be noted: "a 77 year-old (in 1981) German SS sergeant who had been in charge of burning the bodies at Treblinka. He had been acquitted at the 1965 Treblinka trial in Dusseldorf, had turned State's evidence and was described by the survivors as 'inoffensive'. His identification of Demjanjuk as Ivan was important: he had no axe to grind."

But did he have no axe to grind? From one point of view, Horn may be seen as a turncoat. What were his motives for turning State's evidence? Is it possible that he was subject to blackmail or bribery? Is it possible that he has a position to maintain? We cannot lightly accept the Israeli judges' assertion about Horn: "(He) had already served a prison sentence for his wartime activities... and had no personal motive for implicating Demjanjuk."

Another most unsatisfactory element in Ms Sereny's account concerns her handling of the evidence of Pinhas Epstein (that on arrival at Israel Demjanjuk clearly walked like "Ivan the Terrible"): "It was one of those moments when one's doubts dissolve: this was no horror story, no prepared scenario by a professional witness. He could not have known this question would be asked... the memory of how a man walked, a characteristic that does not change with age."

My doubts did not dissolve at all. The question asked by the defence was an obvious one, which any eyewitness could have easily anticipated being asked ("When you saw John Demjanjuk get off the plane, did that man fit the memory you couldn't forget?"). And is it true that a man's walk does not change after 40 or so years? My podiatrist has just been explaining to me how damage to the feet can throw out knees, hips and spine, as one ages.

Ms Sereny also tells us: 'Historians called by the prosecution said it was impossible (that Demjanjuk was at Chelm as long as he claimed): no prisoner stayed there for 18 months." But the fatal anonymity intrudes again. Who were these historians? Count Nikolai Tolstoy, in his Melbourne address on March 4, specifically stated that the prosecution had been able to present no world class historian to support their case and had had to "bring in a few nonentities." He said that he did not believe that the world class historians would have lent themselves to the sort of proceedings being carried out against Demjanjuk. Count Tolstoy is a successful professional historian with a world reputation.

It is not surprising to read, then, that "The last week of the trial has produced the angriest confrontation between judges and defence. Defence lawyer Paul Chumak... warned the judges to be 'careful' – Israeli justice 'is on trial'." Indeed, it is. The truth is, however, that Israel has never had the slightest right to try this Ukrainian Christian on the basis of retrospective and ex post facto legislation.

The judges asserted: "We are satisfied that we have remained objective. This has not been a show trial or another Dreyfus case, as the defence has suggested." But they cannot claim to pass judgement on themselves. Impartial and competent students of their proceedings will in due course do that.

And this brings us to the extraordinary front page article which The Australian has gleefully headed: "How we lead hunt for the next Ivan."

The Simon Wiesenthal Centre, the group that vociferously maintained that Frank Walus was someone he was not, is described, in good sporting terminology, as "the world's top Nazi-hunting group."

We learn that the centre is "promoting Australia as a leader in the 'revolution' that in two years has swept the West from apathy to action in the pursuit of untried war criminals from the Holocaust." Rather, the whole international charade has been organised behind the scenes, no doubt with enormous financial and psychological pressure on governments, politicians and the media, and has imposed one community's war psychosis on nations.

Your report includes the choice advice: "The apparent success of direct approaches by Australia to Eastern bloc countries, including the Soviet Union, for access to information and witnesses has enhanced other countries' prospects of doing the same." What a poisonously clever way of using the word "enhanced" (which smacks of virtue and beauty)! Translated (for I write in the tradition of Orwell) this sentence means that we have been bootlicking tyrants so successfully that others will not sustain as much damage to their tongues as might have been expected.

> *So much for the coverage by The Australian of these events which are so threatening to our traditional freedoms and to the cause of Truth. But I have more to add.*
>
> *I accuse.*
>
> *I accuse the State of Israel of engaging in monstrous injustice, as already indicated, and call upon it to surrender my fellow-Christian to his family.*
>
> *I accuse the Christian leaders and peoples of the West, including those in Australia, of disgraceful apathy and craven turpitude in allowing this wickedness to occur without the most energetic and articulate resistance.*
>
> *I accuse the Jewish people, in Australia and overseas, of complicity in the actions of their misguided leaders; for there has been almost no Jewish criticism of their deeds.*
>
> *I accuse the United States of America for yielding one of its citizens to a kangaroo court on the basis of deportation proceedings without due process.*
>
> *I accuse The Australian of encouraging a New Inquisition and Witch Hunt when it is the responsibility of all decent intellectuals to plead in this context for an attitude of mercy and forgiveness.*
>
> *The Australian Senate will later this month have an opportunity to put an end to Australian participation in this demonic crusade.*

Unfortunately the Senate voted to support the passage of the War Crimes Amendment Bill, which had already been passed in the House of Representatives with bipartisan support. The Liberal-National Coalition voted against the proposed Bill in the Senate, but did not have the numbers to win the day. As a result, a small number of 'Nazi war crimes trials' were held in Australia, some aspects of the proceedings being quite farcical, but leading to no convictions.

IV

A letter from Count Tolstoy was published in the London *Daily Telegraph* on 12th April 1988. Here is the complete text:

> *Political considerations have been blatantly permitted to override the rule of law in the recently concluded case of John Demjanjuk (report, 19th April).*
>
> *Last autumn I spent three days in the courtroom, testifying as an expert witness for the defence. There was scarcely an aspect of*

the court's procedure which did not strike at the most vital principles of natural justice.

The lack of a jury and the specious pretext employed to deny the defence any financial resource are apparently staple Israeli practice about which no more need be said. The case was regarded as a show trial in every sense of the word, as was evident by its being conducted in a theatre with continuous live television coverage.

Judge Levin's conduct of proceedings represented an appalling travesty of every principle of equity. He regularly intervened with bitter sarcasm or crude personal attacks, always at the expense of the accused, his counse,l or witnesses called for the defence. He repeatedly took especial care to forbid without explanation the hearing of much of the evidence most damning to the prosecution case.

The intervention of Shamir [the then Israeli leader] and other political figures in the proceedings would have been unthinkable in any civilised country, though it may be conceded that the Prime Minister possesses a closer acquaintance than some with the theory and practice of terrorism. Specially bussed-in audiences were repeatedly permitted to boo and hiss at appropriate moments, Judge Levin smilingly calling for order after an appropriate time-lapse.

Neither defence nor prosecution laboured under any delusions with regard to the outcome. In conclusion, the overwhelming impression one received was that no judge or prosecution (in this case virtually indistinguishable) could possibly have found it necessary to act in the way they did, were they genuinely convinced of the defendant's guilt. It can only be hoped, for Israel's sake almost as much as Demjanjuk's, that the Appeal Court does not display the blind intransigence which (alas) most concerned observers anticipate.

One distinguished Australian who was alive to the improprieties of the first Israeli trial of Demjanjuk was B. A. Santamaria, the president of the National Civic Council, an anti-communist pressure group with a distinctly Catholic atmosphere. In his Point of View column in the NCC journal *News Weekly* for 11th May 1988 entitled 'War crimes trials... a matter of justice', he pointed out that, as the Senate was due to debate the proposed War Crimes Amendment Bill on 17th May, what mattered were 'the danger signs which the procedures in the Demjanjuk case signal as to the forthcoming trials of alleged war criminals in Australia.'

Santamaria noted that Demjanjuk's conviction 'was secured in large part by the Court's acceptance of the genuineness of an identity card supplied by the Soviet KGB' and that it was well known that this organisation had often framed people.

He then quoted a letter by Lord Denning, Master of the Rolls, whom he described as 'the most prominent legal member of the House of Lords over the last quarter century', in the 28th April issue of the *Daily Telegraph*. This deserves to be reproduced here in full, as it shows the kind of treatment, well outside the realm of the lawful, to which Demjanjuk had been subjected by *force majeure*.

John Demjanjuk,' wrote Lord Denning, 'has been tried by the judges of Israel and sentenced to death.'

> *I would ask these questions.*
> *First, against what law has he offended?*
> *Not against the law of Israel. The offences were committed in the years 1942-1943 before the State of Israel existed or had any laws of its own. It was not founded until 1948.*
> *Nor were the offences committed against the laws of Germany or Poland. They were committed in the concentration camp at Treblinka and were done by the orders of those in authority in those states.*
> *The only law against which he had offended was the international law in respect of crimes against humanity. It was defined in the Charter of Nuremberg: "Murder, extermination, and enslavement, deportation and other inhuman acts, committed against any civilian population before or during the war."*
> *Second, what state had jurisdiction to try such crimes against humanity?*
> *According to international law, a single state after the war might have jurisdiction to set up its special court to try such crimes committed by persons in its custody.*
> *The four powers who signed the Charter for Nuremberg acted on this principle by agreeing to set up the Nuremberg Court to try war criminals then in custody in Germany.*
> *But I know of no principle by which the State of Israel could set up such a court to try crimes said to be committed over 40 years earlier in a far off country by a man not in its custody.*
> *In my opinion it was contrary to international law for the State of Israel to arrange with the United States for the*

deportation of Demjanjuk to Israel to stand trial there; and for the Court of Israel to try him there for a crime against humanity.

If he was to be tried at all, it should have been by an international court of justice like the one set up in Nuremberg for he was a war criminal just like Goering and the rest.

I am afraid too that the trial shows signs of racial and political vengeance. Whereas at the trial at Nuremberg the prosecution's case against those convicted was clear on the documents and undisputed, here there was room for doubt.

The prosecution's case was rested on identification by witnesses over 40 years later. But we all know how mistakes are made by the witnesses at identification parades here. The accused protested his innocence throughout.

The atmosphere at the trial can be seen by the report that there was "clapping, cheering and dancing" by the packed "audience" when he was sentenced to death.

When I have sentenced to death, there was a hushed calm and solemn silence.

(Lord Denning should have referred to Demjanjuk as 'a person accused of being a war criminal' and not as 'a war criminal' *tout court*. His complete confidence in the integrity of the proceedings at Nuremberg also appears most questionable.)

Santamaria felt that Lord Denning's arguments made it wrong for Australia to hold 'Nazi war crimes trials' of its own. If, despite this, the ALP government led by Robert Hawke, set such trials up, 'certain prerequisites were indispensable'.

One of these was that 'under no circumstances should there be any deportations.' Santamaria, had he lived long enough to see it, would have opposed the current campaign to deport Zentai to Hungary. Unfortunately his successors at the NCC think differently.

Another prerequisite listed by Santamaria was that 'Soviet, Yugoslav or other similar evidence should be totally disregarded unless corroborated by independent evidence clearly beyond Soviet (or similar) control.' That, too, would stymie the attempt to deport Zentai, as the case against him rests essentially on proceedings carried out in Hungary under a communist government in 1948.

Five years later, after Demjanjuk's acquittal by the Israeli Court of Appeal, Melbourne Jewish columnist Robert Manne published an important opinion piece in *The Age* on 29th September 1993 entitled 'Justice and John Demjanjuk". A number of his comments are worth recalling. For instance, reflecting on the first trial, he noted how difficult it had been for any Israeli court to provide a fair trial and explained: 'For many Jews in Israel and abroad, anyone who assisted with the defence of Demjanjuk was a Nazi collaborator or a traitor. In the course of the trial a Holocaust survivor actually threw acid in the face of Demjanjuk's tenacious defence counsel, Yoram Sheftel.'

Manne also commented on a failure of the court visible 'in the rougher than usual handling visited upon certain expert witnesses called for the defence'. One of these 'was so distressed by her experience in the witness box that, on the evening following it, she attempted suicide by slitting her wrists.'

Manne rebuked the judges for never admitting 'what common sense should always have made clear: that the memories of a face shown in an old photograph of those who had passed through a hell 40 years earlier, was no basis for sending a man to the gallows.' He even accused them of deliberate fabrication in that they 'concocted a story which had Ivan travelling to Sobibor in early 1943 and back to Treblinka in time for the uprising there in August.'

Manne especially condemned the role of the Office of Special Investigations (an arm of the US Department of Justice): 'If the reputation of the Israeli court has been tarnished by the Demjanjuk affair, the reputation of the OSI has been shattered. Since Sheftel uncovered the crucial Soviet depositions that revealed Ivan the Terrible's identity, it has been discovered by Demjanjuk's friends in the US that a considerable amount of this very evidence had been in the possession of the OSI since the late 1970s! It now seems clear that the OSI deliberately withheld this evidence from the Israelis... To have concealed evidence which might have saved Demjanjuk from the gallows and the Israelis from a major act of injustice is no small matter.'

Manne concluded, alas without prescience, that, while there was a strong possibility that Demjanjuk had served as an SS guard at Sobibor, 'since the death of Danilchenko [a man who had allegedly testified to the KGB that Demjanjuk was at both Trawniki and

Sobibor] and in the absence of other evidence, it is highly unlikely that any civilised court would find him guilty of such a charge.'

Manne ended his piece with two telling rhetorical questions to which his implied answers were obviously no and yes: 'Can these or other failings be avoided in future Nazi war crimes trials? Is it not time to bring this process to a close?'

That Demjanjuk should never be sent for trial to Israel was well known in some quarters months before the trial began. For example, Patrick Buchanan, then a speech-writer for President Reagan, published an article substantiating that position which was republished in *News Weekly* on 12th November 1986.

Buchanan attacked the claims of various alleged eyewitnesses, after pointing out that no less than eleven survivors, as well as Simon Wiesenthal himself, had been wrong in identifying Chicago's Frank Walus as the 'Butcher of Kielce'. 'For six years,' Buchanan commented, 'Walus's life was living hell because of the testimony of such eyewitnesses. Finally, overwhelming proof turned up that all were wrong, that Walus had spent the entire war in Germany as a farm labourer, that he was too short, too young and of the wrong nationality (Polish) even to belong to the Gestapo.'

Buchanan summed up his findings in a single devastating sentence: 'In brief, as many Treblinka survivors claim "Ivan" was killed in 1943 as say he survived the war, and the number who do not identify Demjanjuk as "Ivan" far exceeds the number who do.'

As for the identification card placing Ivan Demjanjuk at Trawniki, which the Soviets conveniently produced in 1980, Buchanan provided the following critique.

> *An expert who examined the card found that an "umlaut" was missing on a word on the ID card and that the card used, instead of a separate letter, a combination of letters not common in German until about 1960.*
>
> *The former paymaster at Trawniki claims he never saw a card similar to this one at the camp: "Missing is the date of issue, missing is the place of issue, missing is the officer's signature."*

> *The photograph of Demjanjuk on the card has been tampered with – parts are blocked out. Demjanjuk – from a blow-up – is wearing a Russian tunic.*
>
> *The photograph was obviously stapled to some other document before being placed on the card.*
>
> *The seals on the card are misaligned – as though separate documents were placed together.*
>
> *The card gives Demjanjuk's height as roughly 5ft 9in – he is actually 6ft 1in.*
>
> *We have no card; the Soviets have only provided a photostat copy.*

We are entitled to ask how the Office of Special Investigations could consider itself in a position to recommend the deportation of Demjanjuk to Israel. A strong presumption exists that it was fatally biased in its handling of the whole matter.

V

It is to the great credit of *News Weekly* that between 1986 and 1994 it reported regularly on the Demjanjuk case, often providing information that did not appear in the major newspapers.

It had much to say about the alleged Trawniki training camp ID card with Demjanjuk's name on it. On 18th May 1988 it reported Edward Nishnic, son-in-law of Demjanjuk, as documenting faked Soviet evidence against his father-in-law. 'He has a copy of an article from a Soviet magazine which showed an ID card, made out in John Demjanjuk's name, but with the photograph of another person on it.'

On 25th May 1988 *News Weekly* provided an edited transcript of a talk given by Nishnic in Melbourne the previous week. Nishnic said: 'Without this document [the ID card], there is not another document in the world, any record, any form, anything with the name John Demjanjuk, anywhere. I have here a report from Warsaw from the Ministry of Justice Main Commission investigating Nazi Crimes in Poland. The top line reads, "with reference to your letter, the [Commission] wishes to inform you that we do not have any data concerning Demjanjuk." They literally had never heard of him. The same report came back from the Berlin Documents Centre.'

Nishnic pointed out another suspicious matter: 'Appearing on this identity card which is the back of this card, it has the wrong man's picture on it. This picture just so happened to be the picture next to the alleged picture of Mr Demjanjuk on the Soviet photo spread.' He implied that the card had been supplied to a Soviet journalist by the KGB.

Nishnic further pointed out: 'On the card, which was actually on the original, it said that this card was translated in the year 1948 after the Red Army had swept these camps… One thing we couldn't figure out and brought to the attention of the court – if in fact this card was translated in 1948, why would they pay his mother a Hero's Pension until almost 1960? The card disappeared and later reappeared with a section which as you can see clearly a blank was put over it before it was copied. We took this to the Soviet embassy in Washington DC and said this was altered; explain why you took that date off. Vice-Consul Valery Nkubinov in Washington said, "That's in the interests of the Soviet Union, and it's none of your business."

On 26th October 1991 *News Weekly* published a review by Michael Fitzgerald of a book entitled *Ivan the Terrible* and sub-titled *The Trial of John Demjanjuk* by Tom Teicholz, published by the prestigious firm of Penguin. The book was a Jewish writer's attempt to whitewash the findings of the first Israeli trial. Fitzgerald reported and commented on Teicholz's tale: 'The most telling piece of documentary evidence was the so-called Trawniki card. This was "uncovered" by the relevant KGB department following a request for information on an "Ivan Demjanjuk at Trawniki". It was made available to the prosecution through the good offices of Armand Hammer, a confidant to the Soviet leadership since the time of Stalin.' [On 14th August 1993 *News Weekly* described Hammer as 'the disgraced industrialist'.] Fitzgerald noted that the defence had 'disputed the card's details relating to Demjanjuk's hair colour, complexion and facial shape' and that the judges in their judgement had stated that it was 'not the technical details [of the documentary evidence] which will seal the fate of the accused.'

On 11th April 1992 *News Weekly* published an article titled 'Germany's *Stern* uncovers Demjanjuk fraud.' Here are excerpts from this important item:

> 'The so-called Trawniki Card was provided to the Israelis by Soviet authorities. It was given to the Federal Criminal Police in

> Wiesbaden in January 1987 so that forensic experts could determine if it were genuine. The Germans concluded at first sight that the document contained a series of distinctive features that placed some doubt over its authenticity. The head of the unit, Dr Louis-Ferdinand Werner, recorded in a memo that: (1) The card did not have – as was customary – a date of issue; (2) The rank of the issuing officer, SS *Hauptsturmfuhrer* (Captain) Streibel was printed on the card and not entered by hand or by typewriter, as was customary because ranks would change rapidly; (3) The photograph of Demjanjuk's head had been mounted to the neck with two different types of glue; (4) A quite unusual typeface (for that period) was used; and (5) The SS-runes shown on the card had been drawn by hand before being copied by the printer.
>
> The forensic experts informed the Israeli embassy in Bonn of these initial observations and said that a fortnight would be needed to allow a meticulous examination. The Israelis responded that 'further examinations are no longer required.' Dr Werner concluded in his memo: "In this case the experts' doubts are to be subordinated to political considerations" and that "finding out the true facts of the case does not really matter here."'

Stern reported: 'Undeterred by these events, Police Major Bezaleli [from the Document Laboratory in Jerusalem] subsequently proceeded...to the Federal Archives in Koblenz and other places to look for any material substantiating the authenticity of the document – this was likewise unsuccessful. He searched for a comparable SS identification card – in vain – for there is not one single specimen in Germany.'

Stern added: 'Also, the signatures on this [card] have obviously been forged: The former *SS Hauptsturmfuhrer* Karl Streibel, who allegedly signed the ID-card, as well as Rudolf Reiss, the former pay-sergeant of the SS training camp at Trawniki, where, according to the ID-card, Demjanjuk served in 1942, emphatically denied in sworn statements in the presence of German detectives, ever having signed, handed out or even having seen such a document.

Contemptuously and sarcastically, *Stern* noted that the Israeli court had 'accepted the judgement of Professor Scheffler, a historian, who, without training in forensic science, believed the card to be authentic, adding that "anyone who would like to falsify such a [card] would have to be an absolute expert."'

On 28th August 1993 *News Weekly* published a report that the German weekly news magazine *Der Spiegel* had reached a similar conclusion about the ID card. 'Bavarian writing analyst Dieter Lehner examined the Trawniki ID closely. He pointed out a false service seal had been used on the card, the improper usage of German words, and a letter 'k' in the wrong style, which led to the manipulation of the signature. Other indications: grammatical markings were missing or were hand-marked rather than printed; the service number 1393 had been assigned even before Demjanjuk was captured by the Germans and the photograph was probably removed from Demjanjuk's 1947 Regensburg driver's licence, added to the Trawniki card and then retouched.'

It should now be apparent to the reader how totally unreliable the card is and that it is the product of deliberate Soviet efforts to frame Demjanjuk to secure his conviction for American and Israeli interests.

VI

News Weekly's coverage also had much to tell about the Office of Special Investigations. On 4th May 1988 an article referred to 'a three-year Freedom of Information battle' to obtain Soviet documents from the OSI for Demjanjuk's defence. On 18th May 1988 it commented, again relying on Nishnic, that this evidence 'was withheld from Demjanjuk's lawyers, apparently because the Office deeply resented its failure to secure convictions in the Walus and Fedorenko cases.'

On 25th May 1988 in the Melbourne statement by Nishnic *News Weekly* published significant information of how the world campaign against 'Nazi war criminals' began: 'The Demjanjuk case started in the Soviet Union – I can back it up to before Elizabeth Holtzman – the originator of the Holtzman Amendment which initiated the Nazi hunt – had gone to the Soviet Union to discuss two basic issues. First and foremost was for freer immigration of Soviet Jews into the USA and secondly was to collaborate with the KGB on bringing back to justice their accused war criminals. Several years later a man by the name of Michael Hanusiak – the head of the Communist Party in the US – went over to the Soviet Union and had evidently open access to their archival centres. He came back to the United States with a list of suspects. One of the names on that list was Ivan Demjanjuk.'

So the whole campaign against Demjanjuk and others was initiated by a collaboration between totalitarian communists and elements within the world Jewish community. The role of the latter deserves comprehensive investigation by impartial researchers in the future.

Nishnic also referred to the testimony of Danilchenko (or H. Daniel Shenko) who claimed to have been with Demjanjuk in Sobibor, Regensburg and Flossenbürg from March 1943 to the end of the war; and Nishnic described him as 'an official Soviet eye-witness.'

On 16th January 1993 *News Weekly* published some more damaging information about the OSI: 'One former prosecutor, George Parker, stated under oath that he had sent a memo to his superiors warning that to proceed with the Treblinka allegations would violate professional ethics. Parker produced a copy of the memo – the existence of which has been repeatedly denied by government lawyers. It carefully details that the evidence presented two factually irreconcilable scenarios regarding Demjanjuk's alleged whereabouts during World War II.' The first placed him in Treblinka, the second at Sobibor at the same period. 'We have little admissible evidence that the defendant was at Sobibor,' the memo stated. *News Weekly*'s report continued: 'Parker and former colleague Martin Mendelsohn have testified about the degree of pressure brought on the OSI by a former member of Congress, Joshua Eilberg of Pennsylvania. Eilberg wrote to the then Attorney-General Griffin Bell to say that the Justice Department "could not afford to lose" the Demjanjuk case. Parker told the court that he left the OSI because he could not ethically continue to prosecute Demjanjuk on the Treblinka charges. He said that his misgivings were dismissed by his superiors.'

It is not surprising that US authorities eventually turned the spotlight on to the OSI. In its edition of 3rd July 1993 *News Weekly* noted that 'The United States Supreme Court has approved the current investigation into the US Government's extradition and denaturalisation case against John Demjanjuk. Two former OSI attorneys had sought a Supreme Court order to halt the investigation by the Circuit Court of Appeals on the grounds that the Circuit Court had no jurisdiction once Demjanjuk was extradited to Israel in 1986.'

The same news report quoted London *Daily Telegraph* writer Herb Greer as likening the past treatment of Demjanjuk to a 'positive lynching' in which 'officials charged with enforcement take it upon themselves to bend or ignore the due processes of law.' Greer remarked of the Demjanjuk case: 'During the deportation proceedings the American Government perverted its own due process by rigging a photo-identity routine, refusing close examination by the defence of a disputed identity card, and by throwing away evidence that would have helped Demjanjuk's defence. Later the American authorities suppressed a cable from the Russian Government that clearly established Demjanjuk's plea of mistaken identity.'

On 14th August 1993 *News Weekly* noted the infamous manner in which the US could obtain denaturalisations and extraditions: 'Unlike Australia, the United States did not enact legislation to try Nazi war crimes cases. Instead, civil hearings – which require far less rigorous evidence than criminal trials – are used against suspected Nazis to strip them of the protection of US citizenship. Thus exposed, they are deported to their former countries or – in Demjanjuk's case – to whoever wants them.'

On 28th August 1988 *News Weekly* reported a second legal victory for Demjanjuk on 3rd August 'when a US federal court in Cincinnati ruled that [he] must be permitted to return to the United States.' After the Israeli appeal trial, the judges had taken over nine months to give their verdict (only two months had been needed for a verdict in the first trial). There had been calls to have Demjanjuk re-tried as a Nazi war criminal in the Sobibor camp.

News Weekly noted that the US Court of Appeals had 'criticised the US Justice Department's prosecution of Demjanjuk, calling it "careless at the least." The court also questioned how Attorney-General Janet Reno could have supported the legal position that Demjanjuk should continue to be barred from the US while federal courts reconsider their earlier decision to revoke his American citizenship.'

Nishnic, *News Weekly* added, had said that 'in the Cincinnati courtroom the US Government had argued that Judge Thomas Wiseman's report to the Court of Appeal had cleared the Justice Department of fraud. "At that point", Nishnic said, "Chief Judge Gilbert Merritt advised Douglas Wilson (the attorney for the US Government) that the issue had not been resolved and would be the subject of arguments to be presented on 3rd September in Cincinnati."'

The OSI was finally nailed, as *News Weekly* reported in its edition of 4th December 1993: 'A United States court of appeals has ruled that the prosecution case against alleged war criminal John Demjanjuk "constituted a fraud on the court." In a unanimous verdict, the Sixth Circuit Court of Appeals struck down its own previous decision approving Demjanjuk's extradition and said that federal prosecutors [had] "acted with reckless disregard for the truth." It found that the OSI had withheld documents which supported Demjanjuk's contention that he was a victim of mistaken identity.'

VII

The picture of the mistreatment of Demjanjuk can be fleshed out still further by looking at other information provided by *News Weekly*. On 18th May 1988 its report of statements by Nishnic included the following: 'Contrary to press reports in Australia, Demjanjuk made no 'confession' either to the American marshals who escorted him to Israel, or to an Israeli policeman who spoke Ukrainian, he said… the reports were false, and no such evidence was introduced at the trial.' A comprehensive study on the reporting by the major Australian print media of the Demjanjuk affair between 1986 and 1993 would almost certainly show a continued bias in favor of his accusers. We are entitled to ask why.

A number of items in *News Weekly* raise the strong suspicion that the Israeli trial of Demjanjuk was being used for reasons other than the authentic conduct of justice. For example, in his review of Tom Teicholz's book on 26th October 1991, Michael Fitzgerald commented: 'It also serves to show the motivation of the "war crimes lobby" which has succeeded in convincing countries such as Canada and Australia to spend millions of dollars bringing alleged war criminals (but only those associated with Nazi Germany) to justice. One gets the impression that this is basically an educational exercise aimed at a number of targets: (1) the younger generation of Jews which is apparently showing a lack of interest in the Holocaust; (2) non-Jews, to remind them of their role in anti-Semitism; and (3) to overshadow and discredit the activities of "revisionist" historians whose claims that the Holocaust has been exaggerated or substantially invented have gained ground in France, Germany and North America.

Alan Dershowitz... fully endorses Teicholz's book, saying that it is... "for a world which must never be allowed to forget."'

On 3rd July 1993 in the previously mentioned article by Herb Greer quoted by *News Weekly* from the UK *Daily Telegraph*, we read: 'One witness was seen to contradict his own written statement made decades before when memories were fresh and more dependable, yet the contradiction was ignored and the testimony taken as true, because the witness was a Holocaust survivor. His transparently vengeful malice and the consequent possibility of reasonable doubt was also ignored. Even after the lucky discovery of post-*glasnost* documents from KGB files made it clear that Demjanjuk's plea of mistaken identity was valid, the self-contradicting Israeli witness still stuck to his story... This raised the question of whether some survivors of the Holocaust have been corrupted by their own suffering and their longing for justice perverted into a desire for vengeance at any cost.'

Returning to the review of Teicholz's book, we may note that Michael Fitzgerald wrote very scornfully about the Israeli attempt to discredit Demjanjuk: 'The historical experts called by the prosecution to demolish Demjanjuk's alibi must have spent their lives hiding their lamps under a bushel. They were... unknown in their field, with one, a Dr Meisel, even arguing that Poland was Germany's ally in World War II.'

In its report of 14th August 1993 *News Weekly* reminded its readers that for sixteen years Demjanjuk had been facing one trial or another. 'He has been imprisoned in Israel since 1986 in a 7 foot x 12 foot cell in which a light burns constantly, with his every word and movement recorded on audio-visual equipment.'

VIII

News Weekly on 10th November 1990 published shocking information about an earlier 'Nazi war crimes case' under the heading 'False evidence claim in US extradition case'. The report began: 'There is a growing body of evidence that an alleged war criminal, Andrija Artukovic, was extradited from the US to Yugoslavia in 1986 on charges of massacres that never occurred. The uncorroborated evidence used by the American Office of Special Investigations has been challenged by four experts, and the OSI is now being investigated by the Justice Department's Office of Professional Responsibility over its handling of the case.'

This story is of especial personal interest to me. Artukovic was in his late eighties when he was extradited on 11th November 1986; and a two paragraph story about this appeared in Melbourne on the front page of either *The Age* or *The Australian*, probably on 12th November. I read this story and was profoundly horrified. I thought: 'You simply do not treat men of that age in such a way, no matter what they have been accused of! How can someone of such an age defend himself effectively? And why on earth is a 'free nation' sending him to a totalitarian communist country behind the "Iron Curtain"? This is positively evil behaviour!'

It was from that moment that I became a committed opponent of the campaigns to 'obtain justice' by placing on trial alleged 'Nazi war criminals'. That was why I could oppose from the start the procedures by which Australia was drawn into the ungodly action by means of the unethical and, I believe, unlawful altering of our War Crimes Bill to enable retrospective legislation under which the alleged criminals could be charged. If ever a fully impartial study is written of how the War Crimes Amendment Bill became Australian law, I believe it will establish that corrupt practices were involved.

That was also why I have been able to follow the Demjanjuk case from before his extradition to Israel.

Artukovic died in prison awaiting a firing squad following his conviction in what was almost certainly an unjust trial.

Here is an extended quotation from *News Weekly*'s analysis of the Artukovic case. It casts further light on the machinations of the OSI.

> *His extradition derived from a Yugoslav petition based on two affidavits. One claimed the murder of a single individual, and was unsubstantiated by other information. The second was an affidavit by Bajro Avdic, a Croat who had been imprisoned by the Yugoslav Government after the war. He claimed that Artukovic was personally involved in a number of massacres, some involving as many as 5,000 victims.....*
>
> *Ironically, Dennis Reinhartz, a University of Texas at Arlington historian, was one of the OSI's consultants on the*

Artukovic case. He recently told the Washington Times *that while Artukovic was an important member of a Nazi puppet government, he does not believe the evidence of Avdic. "He was quite clearly cutting himself a deal with the government that had him imprisoned. On those events there is no corroboration," Reinhartz said.*

OSI officials said that Reinhartz had never challenged the accuracy of the charges contained in the Avdic affidavit during the Artukovic trial.

However, under America's rules of extradition used against Artukovic, his supporters could not testify to anything that contradicted the evidence put forward by the Yugoslavian Government. According to an OSI brief in the case, Artukovic and his supporters also could not attack the credibility of any of the affidavits in the case, nor could they attack the communist Yugoslavian system of justice.....

When the case came to trial, witnesses for Artukovic were not allowed to describe what they considered proof that the Yugoslav evidence was fraudulent.

Another historian, Charles McAdams of the University of San Francisco, said of the specific evidence against Artukovic: "It was absurd, a joke. The crimes never happened." McAdams was also prevented from testifying at Artukovic's extradition proceedings.

McAdams told the Washington Post: *"...There was no credible evidence against Artukovic on these crimes. The OSI wanted him badly and they got him. None of the standards of justice used in the US were applied."*

A fourth piece of evidence comes from Dr Milan Bulajic, a former Yugoslav diplomat who..... has published a book in Yugoslavia claiming that the massacres for which Artukovic was convicted were inventions. Bulajic told a Belgrade newspaper, "There was no legal reason for the extradition. Andrija Artukovic was sentenced for crimes that never took place."

This was known in 1990. The corruption of the OSI in its campaign to have Demjanjuk tried in Israel was established by 1994. Yet the USA allowed the OSI, after that, to organise another campaign that resulted in Demjanjuk being deported to Germany at the age of eighty-nine. How could this be? And how can anything that the OSI and its associates then alleged against Demjanjuk possibly be believed? Perhaps the Demjanjuk family has grounds for a massive damages claim against the US Government.

IX

There is no doubt whatsoever that, in his deportation to Israel (including the processes in the USA that led to it) and in his experiences in the two trials there between 1986 and 1993, John Demjanjuk was subject to monstrous injustice, including the reception of a sentence of death for crimes he had never committed. A thorough investigation is called for by the historians of the future into all the circumstances that led to this colossal miscarriage of justice.

One would have thought that any person known to have been so mistreated would not be further pursued in campaigns for 'justice' in the relevant context of wartime activities allegedly carried out fifty or more years earlier. One would have thought that ordinary human-kindness and compassion would have moved the hearts of any accusers to leave this man alone and to the judgement of God after this life. One would have thought that a care for their own dignity and public image would have kept such accusers silent.

This was not the case. It is time to examine the second campaign against Demjanjuk, which began as soon as he arrived back in America after release from Israeli custody.

X

Despite Demjanjuk's complete exoneration from the charges brought against him in Israel (whether or not he was formally acquitted or merely, as some of his opponents claimed, released from custody), certain persons and groups were unable to, or unwilling to, concede that he should now be allowed to live out his life in peace. There were some indications during the Israeli trials that he might have served as a guard not at Treblinka, indeed, but at another alleged extermination camp, Sobibor. Accordingly a new campaign against him began at once, spearheaded by the OSI. No apologies or regrets were extended to Demjanjuk by the OSI or the US Department of Justice over his wrongful extradition to Israel and wrongful subjection to imprisonment there. Nor was any compensation offered to him or his family.

He regained his citizenship in 1998, but a new campaign against him led to a second denaturalisation in 2002. In 2005 US judicial authorities found that he could be extradited to the Ukraine (his land of birth), Poland (the land in which his alleged crimes at Sobibor took place) or Germany (the land whose nationals operated the Sobibor camp). After a series of legal battles, Demjanjuk was finally extradited from the US to Germany in 2009, when he was eighty-nine years old. He was found guilty by a German court in Munich in 2011 of having been an accessory to the murder of 28,060 Dutch Jews in 1943 and sentenced to five years' imprisonment. His lawyers appealed the decision and he then died in a German nursing home, technically a free man. During the trial, which lasted over a year, he attended the court in a wheelchair or on a stretcher. Apart from denying the charge at the trial's beginning, he remained silent throughout the proceedings.

His opponents and enemies, those who had initiated or supported this second campaign to bring him to 'justice', were happy with the verdict; but was he really treated justly during this second courtroom ordeal, after he had been removed from the care and comfort of his family in the USA?

XI

One answer in the negative has been provided by Thomas Kues in an article entitled 'Demjanjuk Sentenced to Five Years in Prison', published online in the blog of the revisionist journal *Inconvenient History* and republished by Bradley Smith in *Smith's Report*, No. 182 for 11th June 2011.

Kues noted that 'the only existing testimonial evidence consists of a few vague statements of dubious value from former Ukrainian auxiliaries made behind the Iron Curtain. Not one of the surviving Sobibor inmates has placed Demjanjuk at Sobibor.' Furthermore, the only piece of documentary evidence supporting the presence of Demjanjuk at Sobibor was the suspect ID card from the SS training camp at Trawniki, whose counterfeit nature had been exposed in the Israeli trials. A month before the sentence was passed on Demjanjuk a formerly classified FBI report had surfaced which stated that the card was 'quite likely fabricated' by the Soviet Union. There exists a very strong presumption that the OSI held this information before the denaturalisation hearing that enabled Demjanjuk to be deported to Israel!

Experts, or those thought to be so, have disagreed throughout the whole Demjanjuk process, including the three trials, as to whether or not the card is genuine; but it seems safe to sum up that the burden of doubt about it is such that it should not have been relied on, as it was, by the German judge.

Kues pointed to a serious anomaly about the German prosecution: 'The mere presence as a guard at Sobibor, or any of the other "pure extermination camps", has until now not been considered punishable. In fact, at the Sobibor trial in Hagen in 1966, five out of the eleven accused former German camp personnel were acquitted, despite their admitted presence in the camp..... All these men were of higher rank than Demjanjuk.'

Then Kues brought out his heavy artillery.

> 'There exists no documentary or material evidence whatever supporting the official claim that Sobibor served as a "pure extermination camp" where hundreds of thousands of Jews were gassed, buried and later dug up and burned on open-air pyres. The only documentary evidence mustered by prosecutors and Holocaust historians consists of reports and transports lists confirming that large numbers of Jews were sent to the camp..... On the other hand, a directive issued by Himmler on 5th July 1943, as well as a reply from Oswald Pohl on 15th July 1943 (Nuremberg document No. 482) speaks of "the Sobibor transit camp located in the Lublin district."'

Kues continued with a second devastating assertion: 'In 2001 and 2008 two teams of archaeologists, the first headed by the Polish professor Andrzej Kola, the second by the Israelis Isaac Gilead and Yoram Haimi and the Pole Wojciech Mazurek, went over the whole of Lager III, the "death camp" proper of Sobibor – corresponding to an area of less than four hectares – using probe drillings as well as numerous excavations without finding any trace whatever of the camp's alleged homicidal gas chambers. As it is radically impossible, given the limited area and the time available, that these well-equipped teams of specialists would fail to locate any remain or trace, however slight, of the large concrete or brick building described by the self-styled eyewitnesses, only one conclusion is possible: the alleged homicidal gas chambers never existed.'

Kues also argued that, contrary to the official story of 'orthodox historians' that not a single Dutch Jew was ever deported further east than Poland, there exists abundant evidence otherwise (of which he provided several examples), so that 'There is ample reason to believe that the 28,060 alleged victims were in fact sent on to the German-occupied territories of the Soviet Union and the Baltic states.'

This set of arguments challenging the official or received version of the history of the Sobibor camp could not be used to assist Demjanjuk. Commented Kues: 'The defence, undoubtedly aware that any mention of said facts would run afoul of Germany's laws against "Holocaust denial", settled on the usual strategy: accepting the officially sanctioned version of events while insisting on the personal innocence of the defendant.'

What this means is that, because of pre-existing unjust laws in Germany which are an affront to intellectual freedom and judicial integrity and should never have been enacted in the first place, Demjanjuk could never enjoy a fair trial on the charges against him. The OSI and other American officials who combined to have Demjanjuk deported to Germany knew of this situation. There is thus an overwhelming presumption that both the second campaign to extradite Demjanjuk from the USA and the German trial that followed were every bit as corrupt as the first Israeli trial.

XII

A little earlier, in 2009, Paul Grubach had published, also online at *Inconvenient History*, a detailed essay contesting the received account of the Sobibor camp. Entitled 'The "Nazi Extermination Camp" of Sobibor in the Context of the Demjanjuk Case', it drew attention in detail to the host of contradictions in 'survivor testimony' about the happenings at Sobibor, a phenomenon which leads to very serious doubt indeed that Sobibor was a 'death camp'.

For example, some alleged that carbon monoxide was the gas used for the murders, but others asserted that it was chlorine, others a different gas, others that electricity and not gas was used. Then again, some witnesses claimed that the engines supplying the gas were diesel, but others asserted that they were benzene. 'Even mainstream Sobibor expert Christopher Browning admits that the type of engine used to generate the death gas cannot be determined.'

There were also discrepancies on the number, dimensions and capacities of the 'gas chambers', so that 'even the official mainstream historian of Sobibor, Jules Shelvis, finally admitted that the capacities of the chambers cannot be determined.'

Various witnesses also disagreed with each other about the structures of the gas chambers, some saying that they were made of wood, others saying they were made of brick, still others claiming that they were made of stone.

Conflicting accounts were also given of the length of time it took to asphyxiate victims, varying from ten to thirty minutes. Disagreements are on record, too, about how the corpses were removed from the 'gas chambers' and how they were disposed of.

Another suspicious detail is that while the official US government position, in the hearing that denaturalised Demjanjuk in 2002, was that Sobibor was a top secret camp, yet other witness stories assert that 'virtually everyone in the surrounding area soon realised what was going on' there, because the flames, glow and smoke of 'mass burnings' could be seen for miles around.

Further disagreement exists as to the number of persons murdered at Sobibor, from 'half a million' to around 150,000 or 167,000.

Grubach took particular aim at the ruling of US District Court Judge Paul. R. Matia at the end of the 2002 hearing. The judge stated that 'In serving at Sobibor, Defendant [John Demjanjuk] contributed to the process by which thousands of Jews were murdered by asphyxiation with carbon monoxide.' He also claimed that 'This [case against John Demjanjuk] is a case of documentary evidence, not eyewitness testimony.' Grubach pointed out that that second statement is misleading. 'The current case about Demjanjuk allegedly serving at Sobibor is based upon purportedly authentic documents. But what Matia asserts about Sobibor being an "extermination camp" is based exclusively upon eyewitness testimony.'

As a result of his detailed analyses of the inconsistencies and contradictions in the testimonies of alleged eyewitnesses, Grubach posed a question for Judge Matia: 'Since [he] effectively sealed John Demjanjuk's fate, I would like to ask him this pointed question. Since we cannot determine how many 'gas chambers' there were, nor their dimensions and capacities; what the exact death gas really was; what type of engine was used to generate the death gas; what the chambers were made of; where these structures were located; how long it took for the victims to be asphyxiated; how the corpses were removed from the chambers; how the bodies were buried in a lake-like area; what substance was used to burn the bodies; how the millions of unburned bones and teeth were disposed of; and how many were killed: how then can Judge Matia rule with any confidence that John Demjanjuk "contributed to the process by which thousands of Jews were murdered?"'

Grubach pointed to serious credibility problems with the testimony, hostile to Demjanjuk, of Thomas Blatt: 'The mere fact that Blatt was allegedly at Sobibor for six months and was not murdered is consistent with the Revisionist hypothesis that Sobibor was not an extermination centre for Jews, but rather a transit camp where Jews were deported further east.' Blatt's testimony is suspect for several reasons. For example, he stated that the special barrack where the women's hair was cut off before entering the gas chambers was "just steps away" from them, whereas Sobibor historian Yitzhak Arad claims that the path (the 'tube') that led from the reception area for Jews (Lager II) to the extermination area (Lager III) was 150 metres long.'

Grubach also dealt with the claim that the Nazis destroyed Sobibor Camp to destroy evidence of exterminations and suggested instead that they were aware of false atrocity stories circulated by the Allies and wanted to prevent the camp being used to create new propaganda that could ultimately be used against them after the war.

Grubach proceeded to argue that the official extermination story of Sobibor is utilised as 'a non-scientific axiom, because it cannot be falsified. It is just assumed to be true – just like a religious dogma. He explained, also, that the reason that German soldiers 'confessed' to 'Nazi gas chamber' crimes after the war was to save their skins or mitigate punishment for themselves and their families. 'The "Nazi extermination camp" mythology was declared "historical truth" at the Nuremberg trials, and it was then used as an ideological cornerstone for the Allied-installed governments in post-war Germany.....From a legal standpoint they [the accused German soldiers] had no choice but to give credence to this legend..... It was out of the question for them to contest this in court, so they simply built their defence strategies accordingly.' Grubach quotes the revisionist German judge, Dr

Wilhelm Stäglich, and mainstream historians Browning and Ian Kershaw, who all testified to this need of the soldiers to lie.

In a document prepared for the Penguin Books/Deborah Lipstadt team in the famous UK High Court action brought and lost by David Irving, Browning argued in effect that a convergence of evidence proved the Sobibor extermination story despite the many contradictions and inconsistencies in eyewitness testimonies. However, Grubach argued in contrast that 'A series of false testimonies can converge on a falsehood.'

Grubach summed up his rebuttal of Judge Matia's 2002 ruling: 'The traditional extermination story at Sobibor has no authentic war-time documentation to support it, nor does it have any forensic or physical evidence to prove it. It is based exclusively upon the testimony of former Sobibor inmates and the post-war testimony of former German and Ukrainian soldiers who served at Sobibor….. Even if it is proved that Demjanjuk served as a guard at Sobibor, there is no evidence he ever contributed to the process by which Jews were murdered in "gas chambers" – because there is no credible evidence the "gas chambers" of Sobibor ever existed….. there is no credible evidence that he ever harmed a single person. Recently a Canadian court ruled in a similar case… that Ukrainian-born Wasyl Odynsky's citizenship should not be revoked, even though he served at the German forced labour camp of Trawniki. Odynsky served as a perimeter guard, and the Federal Court of Canada ruled there is no evidence he harmed a single person. The same could be true for John Demjanjuk….. What Matia and the official history assert about Sobibor being an extermination camp is based upon the grossly unreliable testimony of former Sobibor inmates and the equally unreliable testimonies of German soldiers that were given years after the events in question and in grossly unfair courts.'

XIII

In this section of this essay I will provide additional information suggesting that Demjanjuk has been cruelly and wrongfully treated. Sometimes I will append a comment, sometimes not. These items are in random order and will be separated by centered asterisks.

*

Upon his return home from Israel, Demjanjuk and his family were subjected to harassment and menace by Jewish vigilantes. *News Weekly* on 12th March 1994 published an account by Myron Kuropas, a columnist with the US newspaper the *Ukrainian Weekly*, which reported that 'one of the more visible and active leaders of the Jewish nomenklatura in the United States', Rabbi Avi Weiss, had 'led Jewish demonstrators in front of the home of John Demjanjuk in Seven Hills, Ohio, terrorising his family and demanding that the US Government deport [him] for "Nazi war crimes." And the UK newspaper *The Economist* recalled on 24th March 2012 that, after the appeal trial in Israel, 'He was not declared innocent, and his old life could never be resumed as before. He kept the house blinds drawn so as not to see the Jewish protesters circling silently outside.'

*

In 2005 and afterwards the US Supreme Court chose not to consider Demjanjuk's appeal against Judge Matia's deportation order. Why?

*

In Munich the court hearings during the 2009-2010 trial were restricted to two 90-minute sessions per day, because of the state of Demjanjuk's health. Does that really convince us that the 'Establishment' doctors who claimed he was fit enough to undergo the trial were right?

*

There is controversy over Demjanjuk's health. His defence team claimed that he was suffering from myelodysplastic syndrome, psychological torment, spinal pain and deterioration, hip and leg pain including gout, kidney disease and stones, anaemia and arthritis. Even if his condition was exaggerated for tactical reasons, is it likely that such a man was fit to endure such a complicated trial? Is it not more likely that the German doctors who claimed he was well enough to take part were exaggerating in the other direction to accommodate political requirements placed upon them?

*

The defence pointed out that the alleged statements by Danilchenko are all suspect and may have been obtained under torture or fabricated by the KGB. On 14th May 2011 Patrick Buchanan noted: 'Danilchenko has been dead for a quarter of a century; no one in the West ever interviewed him and Moscow stonewalled requests for access to the full Danilchenko file. His very existence raises a question. How could a Red Army soldier who turned collaborator and Nazi camp guard survive Operation Keelhaul, which sent all Soviet POWs back to Joseph Stalin, where they were murdered or sent to the Gulag?' And on 8th February 2011 Andrea Jarach of Associated Press wrote that a 1985 statement by Danilchenko refers to several other guards but never Demjanjuk. Danilchenko said in that statement that none of the Ukrainian guards were able to go into the areas where Jews were...gassed.'

*

Eight Sobibor survivors chosen by a Holocaust museum in the USA could not testify they had seen Demjanjuk at Sobibor. Patrick Buchanan on 14th April 2009 noted: 'One witness in Israel who was at Sobibor and says he knew all the camp guards, says he never saw Demjanjuk there.'

*

It can be argued that Demjanjuk was subjected to double jeopardy in being sent to Germany. It is not certain that Germany's claim to have had jurisdiction over him is valid. The claim by the prosecution that, when he agreed to serve as a camp guard, he became a German civilian, seems very tenuous.

*

Erik Kirschbaum, reporting for Reuters on 25th February 2009, reported that Germany's chief Nazi war crimes investigator in Ludwigsburg, Kurt Schrimm, had claimed that his office had evidence that Demjanjuk had been a Sobibor guard and personally led Jews to the gas chambers there in 1943.' Schrimm is also reported as having claimed: "It's now possible to give the precise names and birth dates of the victims.' Fran Yeoman in Berlin for the *London Times* reported on 15th April 2009 that Demjanjuk's oldest victim was 99 and the youngest were babies in what had been described as being 'as close an approximation of Hell as has ever been created on this planet.'

One suspects that all Schrimm really had was a list of persons transported to Sobibor and that the rest is eyewitness allegations and/or propaganda fabrications – possibly designed to assure ordinary newspaper readers around the world that everything was reasonable and in order in the Munich courtroom.

*

Two extraordinary reports surfaced during the trial. Were they propaganda to blacken Demjanjuk's name and stop ordinary people from protesting against the injustice of the trial?

One report (possibly from the London *Daily Mirror* of 15th May 2009) stated that Demjanjuk might be proven guilty of rape by DNA tests on the grandchildren of a woman he allegedly raped, a person who lived near the camp and bore a son.

The other reports were in the *Jerusalem Post* on 14th and 18th December 2009. Here it was alleged that Demjanjuk might have deliberately run over and killed a Jew named Moshe Lisogorski on 20th August 1947 in Ulm while driving a truck.' The allegation was being investigated by German authorities.

*

On 31st May 2009 the *Plain Dealer* reported that a 92 year-old man named Alexander Nagorny could state that he worked with Demjanjuk at the Flossenbürg camp. He did not, however, have anything to say about Sobibor. Flossenbürg was not a death camp.

*

John Rosenthal, writing in *Pajamas Media* online on 21st May 2009 stated that 'captured Red Army soldiers were notoriously permitted to starve to death. It is estimated that over half of the Soviet soldiers captured by the Germans died in captivity.' This suggests that, if Demjanjuk did serve anywhere as a guard for the Nazis, he had chosen to do so out of self-preservation. There seems to be agreement on both sides of this controversy that Demjanjuk lied about his past in order to emigrate to America; but whether he did this purely to avoid being repatriated to death or the gulag, or whether he really did have infamous behaviour to hide, is a question to which no certain answer is now likely to be found. In that case, he should have been given the benefit of the doubt.

*

A Dutch historian, Professor Johannes Houwink ten Cate, was allowed to give expert testimony despite defence objections that he could be suspected of bias and should not be allowed such status. (He had stated both before and during the trial that he was certain Demjanjuk was guilty.)

Former US Secret Service forensics expert Larry Stewart may have committed perjury in giving evidence about the ID card for the prosecution, according to Andrea Jarach of Associated Press in 2010.

Was the actual conduct of the trial biased against the defense, as it was in Israel? Only detailed analysis in the future will answer that.

*

There were only twenty German SS troops stationed at Sobibor. Is it likely that such a small number would have been assigned there if it was a death camp?

*

On 5th December 2009 the prestigious UK newspaper, *The Guardian*, apologised for publishing a letter by John Mortl on 3rd December, saying, inter alia, 'The underlying meaning, we now realise, implied Holocaust denial.'

John Mortl had, in fact, made the key objection to the trial that we have seen Thomas Kues and Paul Grubach explain. He wrote: 'What kind of justice is it that proscribes the normally accepted right of an accused to challenge the assumption that a crime had, in fact, occurred?'

Normally the prosecution is obliged to prove beyond a reasonable doubt that the crime of murder had taken place.

> *This is not the case in the German trial of John Demjanjuk. The prosecution will not have to present such evidence. The court will, without proof, arbitrarily accept that the alleged crime took place. His legal counsel will be prohibited on pain of prosecution from presenting evidence contradicting this assumption. Being stripped of his most powerful defence, the accused is reduced to pleading mistaken identity or that he had nothing to do with an unproved murder.*

It is disgraceful that the newspaper disowned this letter, grovelling to complainants, rather than investigating afresh the truth or otherwise of its claims – or at least asserting Mortl's right to express that opinion and the paper's right to publish it.

*

In the Winter 1994 issue of *Human Rights*, the journal of the Section of Individual Rights and Responsibilities (Vol 21, Issue 1, pages 28-29) Alfred de Zayas commented on aspects of the Demjanjuk case. The author was at the time a visiting professor of international law at DePaul University School of Law in Chicago. A graduate of Harvard Law School and a member of the New York bar, he also held a doctorate in history.

De Zayas argued that the Department of Justice and US judges 'ought to take international law into consideration, including the obligations undertaken by the United States pursuant to the Covenant on Civil and Political Rights' of 1966, when considering 'suits at law pursuant to the 1979 Holtzman Amendment in denaturalisation and deportation cases.'

De Zayas referred to Demjanjuk's ordeal up to 1994, including the 'further proceedings in the US following his return' from Israel. Rights which he felt Demjanjuk had been partly or wholly denied included: (1) the right to a fair hearing. 'Subjecting Demjanjuk to a criminal proceeding more than 40 years after the offences in question raises issues under this provision, because it is extremely difficult for him – or anyone in his positions – to properly represent himself, in view of old age and the near impossibility of obtaining exculpatory documents and witnesses, or even of remembering the events under investigation.' (2) the right to liberty and security of the person. 'It is questionable whether the length of detention was appropriate in the circumstances of this case.' (3) the right to family life and privacy. 'The [further] deportation of Demjanjuk would violate this right, because he would be separated from his entire family. (4) the right to equality of treatment. 'Currently one particular category of immigrants is being singled out for de-nationalisation and deportation: persons who served the Nazi regime, whether voluntarily or through conscription.' (5) the prohibition of inhuman or degrading treatment. 'The nature of the proceedings against Demjanjuk, the hostile atmosphere that accompanied the [first] extradition, the surrender for trial in Israel, the initial trial in Israel, the demonstrations of jubilation following his being sentenced to death in April 1988, the ensuing years of uncertainty, the continued detention for eight weeks following acquittal by the Israeli Supreme Court – all these elements, taken cumulatively, may be deemed to amount to cruel and degrading treatment. (6) the right to compensation. 'The question arises whether he is entitled to compensation for miscarriage of justice.'

*

A version of an article that appeared in *The American Almanac* and which was made available by *The New Federalist* newspaper online on 6th July 1998 had this to say about the context of the first Israeli trial: 'No one could foresee in 1986 that, three and a half years, four years onwards, the Soviet Union would collapse, and the entire communist regimes in Eastern Europe would collapse, as happened, and make it possible, to get this material [the new evidence from the Soviet Union archives]'.

How easily Demjanjuk could have been unjustly executed in Israel!

*

Also from that excerpt from an edition of *The American Almanac* comes this account of a significant US official's response to the collapse of the Israeli case:

> *Five minutes after Demjanjuk was acquitted, Janet Reno, the Attorney General of the United States, was asked to comment. We are talking about a man who spent seven years, six months, and 21 days in prison in Israel for being what he's not, because of the Justice Department that Janet Reno heads. Now, she didn't have*

one word of criticism about the organisation she's in charge of. The only thing she said is that the Justice Department would do everything in its power to prevent the return of Demjanjuk to the United States.....

When that same Sixth Circuit [judge] said that the Justice Department, through the OSI, had committed a fraud upon the court, which almost led to the execution of an innocent man, she again was asked to comment. The only thing she had to say was that she would try to appeal the 6th Circuit decision to the Supreme Court, which she did. The Supreme Court refused to even certify the case. No investigation, nothing has been done since then by anybody in this country; no government body, not the US Congress or any other body within the government of the United States, has moved to investigate, let alone to actually prosecute. Why not? The activity of those responsible for this terrible travesty, didn't end with the case of Demjanjuk.

*

An important article published in the *Toronto Sun* newspaper in Canada on 21st May 2011 was 'No satisfaction in Demjanjuk case' by Peter Worthington. He reminded readers of the passions aroused by the Demjanjuk case in Israel, when a defence lawyer, Dov Eitan, a very distinguished Israeli jurist, was found dead after a fall from a fifteen-storey building. Passed off as suicide, it may well have been a murder, like the similar death of James Forrestal, opponent of the creation of the state of Israel, in the crucial weeks before the UN established the new state. Worthington reminded readers of the acid thrown by a Holocaust survivor in the eyes of Yoram Sheftel at Eitan's funeral.

Worthington also recalled Sheftel's comment in his book blaming two former OSI directors, Allan Ryan and Neal Sher, for 'the worst cover-up in concealing evidence in a major case taken by an American public prosecutor in modern history..... Sher was disbarred in 2002.'

The writer's scepticism about the German verdict is evident: 'There was no evidence he [Demjanjuk] had committed a specific crime, but the state argued just being there was evidence of guilt – the first time such a legal argument has been used in a German court.' In Australia we call that 'moving the goalposts'.

*

Demjanjuk authorised a statement on his behalf which was read to the German court on 13th April 2010. Included in this were the following points: 'I have already defended myself against the accusation of the Munich prosecutor while in Israel. In Israel I was accused of being connected to Nazi crimes in Sobibor. The Israeli Supreme Court specifically recognised that this accusation of the Israeli Prosecutor could not be proven..... I feel it is not compatible with fairness and humanity that for over 35 years I have had to defend myself as a constantly chased legal victim of the Office of Special Investigation of the USA and the circles behind it, especially the World Jewish Congress and the Simon Wiesenthal Centre, which live off the Holocaust.'

*

An important statement was published on 29th June 2009 in *The National Law Journal* in the USA by Michael E. Tigar, Professor of the Practice of Law at Duke Law School and professor emeritus at American University Washington College of Law, John H. Broadley, the lawyer who represented Demjanjuk in the deportation case brought against him by the US Government, and Demjanjuk's son John. They declared that after the result of the Israeli appeal trial, 'Israel's attorney general said that the acquittal barred prosecution for other offences, including the ones now being pressed in Germany. Ironically, at that time, the OSI allowed Jacob Tannenbaum, a 77-year-old admitted brutal Jewish kapo, to live out his life at home in the US due to age and health reasons.'

The signatories confirmed that 'the OSI has never apologised to anyone, let alone Demjanjuk and his family, nor offered compensation. Nor were the perpetrators of the fraud punished or even reprimanded.'

Another important point they made was that 'the allegations now being made against Demjanjuk have been reviewed in Poland, the site of the death camps, and that government has pronounced the evidence insufficient and closed the investigation.'

*

Paul Grubach, in a short essay entitled 'Hunting Demjanjuk: Injustice, Double Standards and Ulterior Agendas', made another significant point:

> '*Noted journalist John Sack has documented how Jewish officials in Poland persecuted and murdered large numbers of German prisoners in the aftermath of World War Two in his book* An Eye for an Eye. *After committing such dastardly deeds, many of these Jews came to America. If it is right and just that alleged non-Jewish war criminals like Demjanjuk be legally hounded and deported, then Jewish war criminals should be met with the same fate. If the US Government devotes resources to the rooting out of non-Jewish war criminals, then they should devote resources to the rooting out of Jewish war criminals. To concentrate only upon non-Jewish war criminals is selective justice. And selective justice is in fact injustice. Why the hypocritical double standard? What really lies behind this campaign?*'

What indeed? It is time now to consider that question and to reflect on the overall political significance of the Demjanjuk case.

XIV

On 21st May 2010 Andriy J. Semotiuk published an important essay on the case in the newspaper *Kyiv Post*. Semotiuk at the time was an attorney with a practice in international law dealing with immigration. He was a member of the bars of California and New York in the US and Ontario, Alberta and British Columbia in Canada.

Semotiuk asserted that the use of an immigration procedure [in order to secure Demjanjuk's deportation to Germany] 'should have set off alarm bells about what this may mean for the rule of law and a fair and balanced judicial system in the US.' He rehearsed several unsatisfactory aspects of the ways in which Demjanjuk had been treated and then said: 'What troubles me the most about this case is the silence of individuals and organisations ostensibly dedicated to human rights and their failure to speak up in support of Demjanjuk. For example, I was a member of the American Civil Liberties Union, an organisation dedicated to the protection of the civil liberties of Americans, including protecting the due process rights of individuals. I asked them specifically to speak up in the Demjanjuk case and was met with silence.'

Semotiuk concluded that 'the Demjanjuk case is little more than a Western show trial to reinvigorate the memory of the Holocaust..... It is a show trial along the lines of what we saw in the former Soviet Union and Nazi Germany previously.'

Semotiuk noted that Patrick Buchanan had been 'the only prominent political commentator who has spoken out about this witch hunt' and asked: 'Where are all the others? It appears they are not concerned that the Demjanjuk case demonstrates that American courts can be politicised and made to bow to the pressures of expediency. It appears they are prepared to accept that America cannot always be relied on to be balanced, fair and to protect the rights of its citizens and the rule of law.'

Paul Grubach, in his aforementioned essay 'The "Nazi Extermination Camp" of Sobibor in the Context of the Demjanjuk Case', eventually asked 'What really lies behind this campaign [to "bring to justice" alleged "Nazi war criminals"]?' Here is his answer: 'Holocaust revisionism, the theory that the traditional view of the Jewish Holocaust contains lies, exaggerations and other falsehoods, is a serious threat to Zionist power and the German Government that is subservient to Israeli/Zionist interests. Various governments have resorted to "war crimes trials" to combat its phenomenal growth. Indeed, Israel's former Attorney General, Yitzhak Zamir, publicly admitted that this was one of the major purposes of the Israeli Demjanjuk trial: "At a time when there are those who even deny that the Holocaust ever took place, it is important to remind the world of what a fascist regime is capable of... and in this respect the Demjanjuk trial will fulfil an important function." In 1993, as the case against Demjanjuk was falling apart, an Israeli prosecutor close to the case [quoted on page 402 of the US Regnery edition of Sheftel's book] acknowledged a political motive for continuing the campaign. "So the important thing now is at least to prove that Demjanjuk was part of the Nazi extermination machine... otherwise... we will be making a great contribution to the new world-wide movement of those who deny the Holocaust took place."... The promoters and the beneficiaries of the Holocaust ideology – International Zionism, Israel and the current German Government – want to use a Demjanjuk show trial to fight the phenomenal growth of Holocaust revisionism, a movement that poses a dire threat to the Zionist government in Israel and the government subservient to Zionism in Germany.'

Australian journalist Michael Barnard, who steadfastly spoke out against the 'Nazi war crimes' campaign until he was removed from his position as a columnist for *The Age* newspaper in Melbourne, wrote in the issue of that paper on 10th December 1991 an article headed 'Will Israel play fair over this disturbing "war crimes" case?' Contemplating the second Israeli case, whose result had not yet been announced, he wrote: 'If guilt is upheld, the court will be seen by many as pursuing a cause – publicising the Holocaust, for this in part is what such trials are about – to the exclusion of significant doubt that would fail to sustain a conviction in such countries as Australia.'

Barnard was not optimistic: 'But whatever the nature of the evidence, the pressures to maintain the conviction must be immense. Many reputations, of both individuals and organisations such as the Simon Wiesenthal Centre, are at stake. Additionally, the key educational purpose of the protracted trial – which took place, appropriately, in a theatre adapted as a television studio – will have been squandered if innocence is accepted.'

As for those arguing that there is no such thing as a statute of limitation on murder, Barnard responded by stating that 'A far more telling regulatory statute is the unwritten one so relentlessly applied by Nature, namely the Statute of Fallibility, which decrees that with advancing age even the finest mind can become subject to tricks of memory. A war crimes judge in Ontario Supreme Court acknowledged the problem of failing memory this year. Canada's war crimes process – which, as in Australia, was preceded by a lot of peculiar lobbying and impassioned pleas for "justice" that took no account of the practical difficulties involved or the threat to the stature of the law itself – seems to be dying on its feet. The "flagship" trial of Imre Finta resulted in acquittal.'

Finally, Barnard observed that 'a certain symbolism has been attached to Demjanjuk'. Here he touched one of the most crucial aspects of the whole Demjanjuk story. By 1993 Demjanjuk had become widely known throughout the world as one whose vindication in Israel had cast an extremely strong spotlight on the whole campaign against 'Nazi war criminals' and, by extension, on the received view of World War Two history including the Holocaust.

It seems clear that elements in the Jewish world community, who, as it is also clear, have great power over Western governments, including those of the US and Germany, decided that Demjanjuk must be given his comeuppance and the success gained for opponents of the 'Nazi war crimes' process cancelled out by the finding of another guilty verdict somewhere else. And the evidence suggests that, once again, truth and the cause of true justice and rightly conducted law processes were not to be allowed to stand in the way.

Of course, the pursuers of Demjanjuk were now going out on a limb. To many people Demjanjuk's age and the fact that he had experienced unjustly such a terrible ordeal in Israel would have seemed overwhelming arguments against further litigation. Perhaps some of the pursuers felt a little like Shakespeare's Macbeth. They may have been beginning to wish that the whole 'Nazi war crimes' operation had never been started in the first place. However, they may have thought, in Macbeth's words,

> *For mine own good*
> *All causes shall give way. I am in blood*
> *Stepped in so far, that, should I wade no more,*
> *Returning were as tedious as go o'er.*

Their awkward position surely explains the very different presentation in the major media of the German trial compared to the Israeli trials. Judging by the behaviour of the Australian newspapers *The Australian* and *The Age*, there exists a strong presumption that a plea went out behind the scenes for a very muted coverage of the German trial, with a strong censorship to prevent widespread public discussion such as might raise concerns in many heads that once again justice was being violated.

'He who pays the piper calls the tune.' There is ever-increasing evidence, of which the Demjanjuk affair is part, that Western nations are already in the grip of a covert tyranny which, in order to preserve and extend its power, wealth and cultural influence, is steadily trampling on intellectual freedom and the honourable administration of laws firmly based in principles of true justice. The books of UK writer Nicholas Hagger, especially his 2004 study of 'the coming world government', *The Syndicate*, provide strong support for this view.

An ominous aspect of the second phase of the Demjanjuk affair is the widespread silence by intellectuals who, one feels, should have spoken out strongly in defence of him. Are Western communities losing the nerve and the will to fight to maintain the integrity of their cultures? And why has the Christian Church, at the highest levels, done so little to expose and check the incipient tyranny?

In the meantime, after Demjanjuk's death, it was pitiful in the extreme to read that his opponents were bewailing the fact that he died technically a free man and that, if his body was returned to his family for burial in his home town, his grave might become 'a shrine for neo-Nazis'. How low can meanness of spirit and pusillanimity descend?

Today I was listening to the exquisite music of Adolphe Adam's ballet suite for *Giselle*. This enabled me to contemplate again the ballet's wonderful presentation of the power of love. Prince Albrecht had betrayed the peasant girl; she had died of a broken heart; but when the Wilis, the spirits of maidens who had been jilted like her and died, came out at night to try to dance him to death, so great was the love of Giselle's spirit that she danced with him until six o'clock sounded and the power of the Wilis was no more. The strength and magnanimity of love had triumphed over the hatred of those who felt themselves wronged.

The spirit of Giselle had to return to the grave. The soul of John Demjanjuk has passed from Earth into God's care and moved beyond our sight. His long travail, and the nobility of his endurance of it, remain in our memory. Like Giselle, we who still live must go on in the spirit of love, that spirit which is ultimately stronger than any hatred. Saint Paul wrote well about love in *1 Corinthians 13*. He could have added that love is not cowed by the threats and machinations of tyrants, and that it is not afraid to speak out at risk to itself in the defence of those who are treated unjustly. In that spirit, let us work around the world, wherever we are, to gradually defang the present malign presence within our nations, of which the 35 years of mistreatment of John Demjanjuk is a permanent witness.

Melbourne, 30th March 2012

A Postcard from Auschwitz

Thomas Dalton

The following is a true account of my personal visit to the camp. All photos are my own.

Krakow is a beautiful city in early summer, the stand-out among southern Polish cities. Miraculously, the old city center survived both world wars unscathed. The huge central square is a sight to behold, and with no less than three major universities, Krakow bristles with youthful energy. Coming down by train from Warsaw, I was able to arrange a two-night stay before continuing on my way to Vienna. As with most major European cities, one quickly learns of the "must-see" sites: St. Mary's Basilica, Wawel Castle, the salt mines, and of course, Auschwitz.

This being my first visit to Auschwitz, I decided to see it as a tourist would. This was not only easier (I was travelling alone), but allowed me to better understand the "official" portrayal of the camp and of events there. Auschwitz is the number one tourist destination in all of Poland; about 1.3 million visit the camp every year—coincidentally, about the same number as is alleged to have been killed there. The official guided tours dictate a particular image of the camp, and I was as interested in this image as the camp itself. I wanted to see what the public sees.

So I went to one of the many tourist information offices around town and purchased a standard "day trip" to Auschwitz. The package, which included free pickup and return delivery to my hotel, cost 90 złoty, about $30—quite a deal. My pick-up time was set (8:30 am), and the van would be at my hotel the next morning, for the "6-hour tour." Plenty of time to see the place, I thought, given that Oswieçim—the Polish name of Auschwitz—was only some 70 kilometers (about 40 miles) from Krakow.

The van dutifully arrived the next morning. But I soon realized that, as at Auschwitz itself, the tour was not quite as expected. The vehicle—a bit larger than I anticipated, more like a small bus—had a capacity of about 25 people. I was one of the first in, and the driver proceeded to cover much of the city in order to pick up our remaining guests. But between rush hour traffic, construction delays, and people slow getting out to the bus, a good hour went by before we were even ready to depart Krakow. So my "6-hour tour" was now down to five. And of course it would require another hour or so to return everyone; in other words, I was really getting a "4-hour tour." Not sure that that counts as a "day trip," but such is the life of a tourist in Poland. (I'm no tour planner, but it seemed to me that, if everyone simply walked to the central tourist office and met the bus there, that we could have saved a couple hours...)

It turned out that this little time crunch would impact our tour itself, and, in my suspicious mind, served an ulterior purpose. But I will come to that matter in due course.

There are three distinct and roughly parallel paths from Krakow to Oswieçim: the (longer) expressway route, and two cross-country routes via two-lane roads. In good traffic, as I learned, all three take about one hour—a rather long time for a mere 40 miles. But Poland has only two kinds of roads: expressways and two-lane roads, and the latter are painfully slow. Our driver opted for one of the scenic country rides.

As soon as we were clear of Krakow city, the driver pulled out a DVD and popped it into a dashboard player. A small screen above us lit up: this was our complimentary 20-minute documentary about the camp (in English). No surprises here. We were treated to the usual recounting of the "extermination camp" history, the appalling conditions, the emaciated inmates, the gas chambers, and the "over one million" Jewish deaths. Horror awaits, it seemed to say.

The remainder of the trip was uneventful. The forecasts called for rain that day, but supposedly not until later in the day; with luck it would hold out for our visit. Around 10:30 am—a good two hours after my pickup—we rolled into the town of Oswieçim. It was a typical smallish European town, nicely maintained, with the usual amenities. We drove only a few minutes through the town when, suddenly, we arrived at the main camp, Auschwitz I. For those not familiar, "Auschwitz" is comprised of three primary facilities, and dozens of smaller sub-camps. The original and main camp is Auschwitz I, also called the *Stammlager*. It opened as a Nazi camp in 1940, but was originally built by the Polish army as a military barracks complex, apparently during World War I. This camp allegedly had a single gas chamber, which we were about to see. But the vast majority of the gassings are said to have occurred at Auschwitz II, known as Birkenau. This would come later in the day. The third facility,

Auschwitz III (Monowitz), was located some three kilometers from the town, and served as an industrial facility; no mass murder is alleged to have happened there, and consequently it receives few tourists.

Knowing all this, I was still surprised at how integrated the main camp was into the town. This, I think, is not the usual image we have: the dreaded "Auschwitz death camp" located in the heart of a civilian village. But we have a good explanation for this, of course. Its original function, as a Polish military camp, had nothing to hide. And even as a German camp, when constructed in 1939 and 1940, it was not originally intended, even on the traditional view, as an extermination camp. The Germans were simply making good use of a captured military barracks.

Pulling into the parking lot, we were immediately confronted with a mass of vehicles: passenger cars, taxis, tour buses like our own, and full size long-haul buses packed with people. The place was a frenzy of activity—see Photos 1 and 2. Our bus disembarked, we merged with another small group, and then were assigned a tour guide: a cheerful young woman with a good knowledge of English, and of the standard story she was scripted to present.

Photo 1: Auschwitz parking lot. By Thomas Dalton

Photo 2: Auschwitz museum entrance   By Thomas Dalton

We pushed through the mob into the entrance building, past the gift shop, and on into a small alcove. There we were given our headsets and radio receivers. It is a rather high-tech affair: with all the commotion and simultaneous tours in multiple languages, the Poles gave the tour guide a radio voice transmitter; each of us could then hear her speaking through our headsets. Thus each group heard only their personal guide. On the one hand, this was a clever and useful solution. No confusing cross-talk, and even if you drifted away from the group, you could still hear your guide speaking loud and clear. On the other hand, it had a noticeable (and to me, suspicious) side effect: questions from individuals to the guide *could not be heard by the group*. They were necessarily individual questions between you and the guide. When I did this on a couple of occasions, she answered me personally, but *shut off the transmitter*. No one else in the group heard either my questions, or the answers. Very clever, I thought to myself.

Moving into the camp grounds, we immediately came upon the famous "Arbeit Macht Frei" sign—"Work Makes (You) Free" (Photos 3 and 4).

Photo 3: "Arbeit Macht Frei" By Thomas Dalton

Photo 4: "Arbeit Macht Frei" By Thomas Dalton

In the background of Photo 4 is Block 24, the building that housed the brothel and library for (non-Jewish) inmates; the main entrance is shown in Photo 5. Photo 6 shows a typical view in the camp, of barrack buildings and a guard tower.

Photo 5: Block 24 (brothel and library). By Thomas Dalton

Photo 6: Walking through the Stammlager. By Thomas Dalton

Our group wandered through the camp, following the guide as she made stops in various barracks to tell us stories of the appalling conditions faced by the inmates. The buildings were mostly empty. Some contained walls of inmate photos; others, simulated sleeping bunks. One final barrack was set up rather as a standard museum. It had exhibits displaying inmate suitcases, personal items, and hair (cut from inmates as a precaution against lice). One large glassed-in exhibit showed an apparent mound of "thousands" of shoes—though, as Germar Rudolf has noted, the mound is displayed on an unseen elevated board, which is empty beneath. This is the same trick that grocers use to display fruit, to give the illusion of a vast quantity. The mound was not so vast after all.

At one point the guide mentioned the total Auschwitz death count as roughly 1 million Jews and thousands of others. I caught up to her and asked if the toll wasn't previously claimed to be 4 million. (microphone *off*.) Yes, she said, but better research in the 1980s and 1990s had confirmed the new, lower figure. Any chance it would be lowered still in the future?, I asked. Unlikely, she said.

By this time, people were beginning to talk among themselves about the as-yet-unseen gas chambers. The guide then reminded us that, indeed, we were about to come to the gas chamber itself. "And oh, by the way," she added, "most of the gassings were at Birkenau. But we'll see that later." It was already approaching 12:00 noon.

Finally we arrived at "the" gas chamber in the main camp, also called Krematorium #1 (or Krema 1, for short). It was a partially underground structure with a flat roof and sloping, grassy side walls with large trees—see Photo 7. Few statistics were given on the details of the gassings: no start or finish date (in fact, February to November 1942), no details on the gassing procedure (Zyklon pellets thrown in through roof vents), and only rough numbers of Jews allegedly gassed there (about 20,000—a mere two percent of the claimed Auschwitz toll). We could not enter via the "inmate entrance," as this was blocked off (Photo 8), so we went around to the other side (Photo 9).

Photo 7: Alleged Gas Chamber (Krema 1) By Thomas Dalton

Upon entering the building, we were treated to what must have been the world's shortest tour of a gas chamber. We walked in, took a hard right turn into a small room, then a hard left into the gas chamber itself. It was a windowless, rectangular room, about 25 x 5 meters. The guide said little more than "this is the gas chamber, no photos please," and then she was off into the adjoining room with the cremation ovens. Rebel that I am, and not wanting to miss an opportunity, I lagged behind the group and then snapped a quick photo (Photo 10). But the guide was gone—no chance to ask about the many post-war modifications to the room (chamber size, door location, chimney), nor about its history as a morgue and an air raid shelter. No chance to ask how 800 to 1000 people were jammed into that room, nor how the deadly Zyklon pellets were collected up without killing the guards handling the dead bodies. No chance to ask why the four Zyklon vents appeared to be added later than the original construction. No chance to ask about French traditionalist Eric Conan's claim that "everything there is false."

Photo 8: "Inmate entrance" By Thomas Dalton

Photo 9: Entering Krema 1. By Thomas Dalton

Photo 10: Alleged Gas Chamber Krema 1 By Thomas Dalton

In the oven room (Photo 11), we had about one minute to view the ovens themselves—"no photos please"—and our guide was off. No chance to ask why the reconstructed chimney was not attached to the ovens. No chance to ask why the six cremation muffles, which could handle six bodies per hour, were such a capacity mismatch with a gas chamber that could kill 800 to 1000 at a shot. Note: it would have taken roughly 150 hours—or more than 6 days working round the clock—to dispose of all the bodies from a *single* gassing.

Photo 11: Krema 1 oven. By Thomas Dalton

Outside again, our guide was suddenly much more relaxed. Now we have time for a break, for bathrooms, for a visit to the gift shop, she said. "Be out front at the bus at 12:30, for the ride over to Birkenau." Finally, I thought—the highlight of the trip.

Again, the "ride to Birkenau" was surprising—all of about five minutes. Out of the small village, across a field, and there we were, at the famous entrance building, complete with train tunnel (Photo 12— a poor exposure, as my camera was beginning to fail me). There we were, at the site of the greatest mass killing in human history: 1.1

million people, the vast majority Jews, killed over two years (1943 and 1944), 90 percent of whom were gassed in the four crematoria.

I was very anxious to get inside and look around. Then another surprise. "Because we are running late," said our guide ("late"?), "we will only have time to see the main guard tower and one of the barracks. Unfortunately we won't be able to see the gas chambers." What?! You must be kidding me, lady! No gas chambers?! Like hell!, I said to myself. "How much time do we have until the bus leaves?," I asked our guide. "About 25 minutes." "I'm going to the gas chambers." "Ok," she said as she headed off with the group. I didn't care if I had to *walk* back to Krakow; I was going to see the Birkenau gas chambers.

Photo 12: Birkenau main gate. By Thomas Dalton

Inside the main gate, one sees the train tracks going out into the distance, to a dead end, and flanked by guard towers and a loading area (Photo 13). Being familiar with the camp layout, I knew that the main objectives were Kremas 2 and 3, and that they were straight ahead of me, at the end of the tracks, about 800 meters—almost half a mile—away. Quick calculation: I can walk there in 10 minutes, and 10 minutes back, leaving 5 minutes for the chambers—or I can run. I ran.

Photo 13: Train tracks heading to gas chambers. By Thomas Dalton

So, after an earnest five-minute run, I could at last see the ruins of the infamous Krema 2—site of the single greatest death toll at Auschwitz: some 300,000 people, on the conventional view (Photo 14). Across the way, its twin facility, Krema 3—site of another 275,000 gassings (Photo 15). Both buildings were destroyed by the Germans upon abandoning the camp, though Krema 2 retains some very relevant and important structures.

Photo 14: Krema 2 ruins. By Thomas Dalton

Photo 15: Krema 3 ruins. By Thomas Dalton

Standing there in front of the remains of both buildings, one gets a real sense of the improbability of the conventional story. Each building had an almost completely underground chamber, roughly 30 x 7 meters, at right angles to the main building, which contained the cremation ovens. On the revisionist view, this chamber was a morgue—a large, unventilated, but cool, place to store dead bodies (many infectious) until they could be cremated. On the standard view, this room was the gas chamber—a place in which 2,000 people were collectively gassed in less than 20 minutes. Photo 16 shows the collapsed roof of the Krema 2 chamber as it exists today.

Now, imagine this: You are somehow able to pack 2,000 frightened, sick, angry people, wall to wall, into this underground room—a room with only a single narrow doorway from the main building. You then kill them all by sprinkling pellets of Zyklon-B over their heads, through openings in the roof. Now you have to *quickly* extract the dead bodies, steeped in poisonous gas, without killing yourself or your fellow workers. No problem—if you could peel the roof off and scoop them out with a backhoe. Lacking that option, it would be *nearly impossible* in any reasonable amount of time. And yet the experts, like Francizek Piper, claim that it took only three or four hours. Incredible—that they can make such claims, and no one (except the few revisionists) challenges them.

Photo 16: Alleged Krema 2 gas chamber. By Thomas Dalton

There are other stories in these remains. One is the search for residue of the deadly cyanide gas. If the chambers were used on as many people as claimed, the remaining bricks should have detectable cyanide compounds still in them. And yet none are to be found. Another story is the search for the roof openings into which the Zyklon pellets were poured—supposedly four per chamber. Krema 2's roof is sufficiently intact that we should be able to find evidence of these holes. And yet they are not to be found—not one single indisputable hole.

But my time was running short. A quick dash over to Krema 3 for a last shot or two (Photo 17), and then back to the bus. The other two crematoria, Kremas 4 and 5, were across the camp, a good 600 meters away, in the wrong direction; they would have to wait for my next visit. So too would the two "bunkers," or small converted farm houses, that were allegedly used to pilot the Birkenau gassing project in 1942. Almost nothing remains of them, yet it would be interesting to hunt down their locations—the sites of some 250,000 Jewish gassings, it is said. But now it's time to go. Heading back along the tracks toward that most infamous of buildings, I couldn't resist pausing for one more shot (Photo 18).

Photo 17: Alleged Krema 3 gas chamber. By Thomas Dalton

Photo 18: Birkenau main entrance. By Thomas Dalton

I arrived back at the bus just as the crowd was loading up—perfect timing. After an hour ride we returned to Krakow around 2:00 pm. But rather than sitting it out for another hour circuit of the city as we returned my fellow riders, I opted to hop out at the first stop and walk home. A good move. I was back at my hotel for less than an hour when the skies unleashed a pounding rain. So luck was with me after all, that day—my day in Auschwitz.

On the Roads of Truth: Searching for Warwick Hester

Klaus Schwensen

1. Introduction

Between 1947 and 1957 a little monthly journal was published in Buenos Aires under the title *Der Weg - El Sendero* (The Way). Language and readers were German, and the journal is of some historical interest since it was able to publish things in Argentina that certainly would have caused problems in post-war Germany. In July 1954 *Der Weg* had published an article by a certain Guido Heimann which dealt critically with the 6-million number and the Jewish death toll in what since became known as "the Holocaust."[1] In response to Heimann's article an American by the name of Dr. Warwick Hester wrote a letter to the editor[2] in which he agreed with Heimann. The editor Eberhard Fritsch printed the letter (whose length was more that of an article) under the title "On the Roads of Truth" (*Auf den Straßen der Wahrheit*). The title refers to the letter writer Warwick Hester, who had in past years made many journeys in order to interview former German soldiers and SS men who lived now in exile and had testified on alleged German atrocities. Both Heimann and Warwick Hester appear in today's context as early revisionists, and both articles were recently reproduced in the French language.[3]

2. Who Was Warwick Hester?

The author's name Warwick Hester is rather unusual. Warwick is a town in England, and there is also a Warwick in Rhode Island (U.S.A) and in Queensland (Australia). But Warwick is also a surname. Hester is a female Christian name (like Esther), but it can also be a surname. In the introduction to Warwick Hester's article we read: "*Aus einem Brief des bekannten Nordamerikaners*", which means that the author was a man and Hester cannot be his Christian name. Thus, both Warwick and Hester could be surnames here, Warwick Hester a hyphenated name and we would not know his Christian name. On the other hand, the naming of children in the United States is rather permissive, and thus, the Christian name of "Dr. Hester" may have been "Warwick." In the "Contents" of the issue of *Der Weg* we read that his residence was Washington. All in all, "Dr. Warwick Hester" is obviously a pseudonym, and the location "Washington" may be given to protect his anonymity.

But the story goes on. An Internet search for "Warwick AND Hester" leads us into the world of dog breeders, especially to the friends of Great Danes (Celtic Danes). Here we find in the pedigree of some dogs two bitches that apparently originated from the breeding of a Mr. Warwick, since their names were "Warwick's Eunice" and "Warwick's Hester." Since the pedigree does not contain the life data of the dogs, we are not sure whether the noble creatures lived in 1954, but perhaps they had a grandmother called "Warwick's Hester"? It seems he was not without some humor - our Dr. Warwick Hester!

According to his article, Warwick Hester made "from 1946 until now" (1954) "journeys into the European countries", in order to form an opinion about the question of the German guilt and the genocide. He travelled in the three Western Occupation Zones of Germany, to Barcelona, even to Cairo and Rio de Janeiro. The latter cities he visited to interview former German soldiers who lived there in exile and who had testified on German war crimes. As Warwick Hester found out, their statements were mostly based on hearsay. As he writes further, he had numerous talks with former concentration camp inmates, that he had done research of his own and studied files and documents. Such an interest and competence in the field of war crimes was unusual for an American private person, not to mention the costs of the research and journeys. But it could well correspond to a lawyer, who travels in order to sound out former witnesses of the prosecution and thus help his clients. Finally, Warwick Hester mentions his own "collection of documents" - where might it have ended up?

According to its content and tendency Warwick Hester's article could well fit one Stephen F. Pinter, a lawyer from St. Louis, Missouri, who after the war worked in the U.S. War Crimes Program, quit his post in 1948 and settled as a freelance lawyer in Salzburg (Austria). Warwick Hester started his travels in 1946 - like Pinter, who after his arrival in Dachau in mid-January 1946 began to visit many DP (Displaced Persons) camps. Although Pinter does not mention any travels to Barcelona, Cairo and Rio, he could have made such journeys during his "biographical lacuna" (1949-1953) where we have no information at all about his whereabouts.

An identification of "Warwick Hester" with Stephen Pinter is found first in Udo Walendy´s introduction to his reprint of the letter, which he calls "The Dr. Pinter Report."[4] Walendy had relied on a source of information whose name he did not want to disclose. Obviously his informant was convinced that Warwick and Pinter were identical. Maybe the source knew some of Pinter´s texts *and* Warwick´s text, and had by combination or intuition concluded that both must be by the same author. If so, Walendy´s source should have reported his discovery - what he did not do. But there is another possibility: that there were some former correspondence partners of Pinter's, who really knew who "Warwick Hester" was. Pinter had correspondence partners in Germany and maybe also in Austria. Thus, it was quite plausible that he sent copies of the "Warwick Hester letter" to his partners.

3. Origin of the Text and Aftermath

Shortly after its publication Warwick Hester's article was quoted in a little paper *Die Anklage*, (*The Accusation*) which, beginning in January 1955, brought out a series about the number of victims of National Socialism.[5] *Die Anklage* referred to the International Committee of the Red Cross (ICRC) *and* Warwick Hester. Obviously they knew only Warwick Hester's article, but nothing about the author. The information about the article in *Die Anklage* was published by Wolfgang Benz[6], who apparently also knew nothing about Hester.

In 1990 the Warwick Hester article was reprinted almost completely by Udo Walendy. Only the two introductory passages were omitted and two others changed places. In his introduction Walendy brings out some personalia of Pinter, which probably originate from the authentic Pinter texts[7,8,9,10,11]. The other data are speculative or wrong. For example, Pinter was a Bachelor of Law and no Doctor (Ph. D.), and he was not a Jew. Warwick mentions that when talking with former Jewish prisoners of Majdanek camp, these took him "for one of them" - maybe from there the misunderstanding arose. Upon questioning, Mr. Walendy responded that he had received the text in 1990 together with a letter, and he sent from that letter the following passage[12]:

> *"In a private letter to the editor of* La Voce de la Plata, *Buenos Aires, Wilfried [actually Wilfred] von Oven, Pinter described his experiences, which von Oven printed 1954 in* Der

> Weg *No. 8, pp. 572 ff. Pinter was often criticized for this and wrote newspaper articles like in* Our Sunday Visitor. *Concerning his person and competence he let a local notary of St. Louis testify and put it into the papers. Pinter's reports for the U.S. War Department (*heeresamtliche Berichte*) have never been published... .*
>
> *Pinter had been in office since 1920, and during the war he was drafted as an Attorney. 1945/46 he was prosecutor in Dachau and investigated thereafter all concentration and labor camps west of the Russian Occupation Zone."*

The letter is quoted here only to demonstrate that it contains a lot of errors. Apparently Walendy's source knew not only the Warwick Hester article but also some of the authentic Pinter texts. From this base he would have composed his story, a strange brew of data that was picked out of the authentic texts but mostly misunderstood. Thus, the writer of the letter seems to be the source of most of the misunderstandings, errors and speculations about Pinter. For example:

It is not plausible that Pinter was "often criticized" because of the Warwick Hester article, for the article was published in faraway Argentina - under a pseudonym. Then Walendy's source mentions "Pinter's Army Reports" (*heeresamtliche Berichte*), which were never published - how does *he* know of their existence? And concerning Wilfred von Oven, the editor of *La Voce de la Plata*, the source seems to believe that von Oven had been the editor of *Der Weg,* but the founder and editor was Eberhard Fritsch. Herr von Oven, by then 90 years old, said that he at that time had no connection to Duerer House, although he had wished to work for *Der Weg*.[13]

In recent times the Warwick Hester article has been completely printed in French. The editor Jean Plantin seems like Walendy to accept the equation Warwick Hester = Stephen F. Pinter. But he did not rely on speculations but started his own research and published his preliminary results. This again was the encouragement for further research and the findings presented here.

4. Warwick's Points

Warwick Hester's text remains today, more than 50 years later, highly revelatory and his points and arguments are typical "revisionist":

- *The problem of witnesses*

The author complains that evidence in the trials was almost exclusively based on the statements of witnesses, and that numerous statements were false. In this connection he mentions not only Jewish, but also German false statements, e.g., that of Dr. Wilhelm Höttl who had reported the 6-million-victims number, which he allegedly had heard from Eichmann.

- *The gas vans (Gaswagen),*

...which nobody has ever seen.

- *The documentary film* Die Todesmühlen *(The Death Mills)*

The author writes that this film was introduced as evidence in the Nuremberg main trial and that it later turned out to be extensively faked.

Here the writer is partly wrong: The film which was shown in the first week of the Nuremberg Main Trial was not *The Death Mills* but another, quite similar film entitled *Nazi Concentration Camps*. The footage of these films was mostly authentic (although it was sometimes "enriched" by manipulations, e.g. half-burnt bodies in the crematory ovens were shown which were posed for the film). The propagandistic impact of these films was tremendous. It relied on the horrible pictures combined with a propagandistic, false interpretation. For example, hundreds of dead bodies were shown, all victims of typhus, i.e. victims of a pestilence, while the film comment insinuated that killing was the actual aim of German concentration camps.

- *The issue of gas chambers in certain camps.*

- *The general treatment of inmates in German concentration camps.*

- *The issue of Jewish deaths (number of victims).*

Here Warwick Hester mentions the increase of the Jewish world population by 3 million between 1933 and 1950, which of course is in contradiction to the 6 million murdered by the Nazis. In this connection he tells the following story :

> *"Recently when talking to a North American of Jewish origin whom I esteem very much I referred to that discrepancy* [of Jewish population numbers]. *I asked him whether he himself believed in earnest that the Nazis had killed 6 millions. He said:'Naturally not. For that they had neither the time nor the means. What they obviously had, was the intention. Here begins politics* [i.e. the psychology of propaganda]. *Given the imputed intention, you can make any number. We thought that 6 millions are not too much to appear plausible, but sufficient to make mankind shiver for one century. This chance Hitler has given to us, and we make the most of it, to good effect, as you see.'*
>
> *I said he ought to consider that a political lie like this will, in light of subsequent investigation, disclose itself and turn against those who invented it. But this Jew, a psychologist, denied that. It* [the propaganda] *had penetrated too deep into the subconscious of the masses, so that it could never be dislodged. Humans in general are completely uncritical. What is anchored in the subconscious, even an individual with common sense almost never is able to expunge. As a proof he cited the fact that already now* [1954!], *after a relatively short propagandistic campaign, that item required no further discussion.*
>
> *'We have no problem, since we have created a historical fact which from now on is in the history books of schools, like the date of a battle.'"*

Why speculate at all about the author of an article that was published more than 50 years ago in an obscure journal on the Rio de la Plata? The reason is that this article is an early precursor of revisionism. The author was a man who had good knowledge of the war-crimes issue, who thought independently and was not misled by the Allied war-crimes propaganda. Furthermore, he had a sense of justice, some sympathy with the defeated Germans and he must have enjoyed financial independence. The contemporary witness "Dr. Warwick Hester" has only one drawback: we do not know who he really was. This is a pity since the value of his experiences and observations would increase if it did not originate from a "Mystery Man" but, say, from the U.S. War Department Attorney Colonel Stephen F. Pinter. There are many indications for it, but a real proof is still lacking.

Notes:

1. Guido Heimann, „Die Lüge von den sechs Millionen," in: *Der Weg*, Heft 7 (Juli 1954), p. 479-487, Dürer Verlag, Buenos Aires 1954.

2. Dr. Warwick Hester, „Auf den Straßen der Wahrheit," in: *Der Weg*, Heft 8 (Aug. 1954), p. 572-578, Dürer Verlag, Buenos Aires 1954
3. Jean Plantin, editor "Anthologie chronologique des textes révisionistes des années quarante et cinquante ("Chronological Anthology of Revisionist Texts of the 1940s and 1950s"), in: Jean Plantin (editor), *Etudes révisionistes*; Vol. 2, private printing through "Le Cercle antitotalitaire", France 2002.
4. Udo Walendy, „Der Dr. Pinter-Bericht", *Historische Tatsachen.* Nr. 43, pp. 20-23, Verlag Volkstum u. Zeitgeschichte, Vlotho 1990
5. N.N., „Die gemeinste Geschichtsfälschung", in: *Die Anklage*, Bad Wörishofen, Jan. 1955 ff.
6. Wolfgang Benz, Dimensions of the Holocaust, http://140.149.134.79/Journal/wbenz002.htm
7. S. F. Pinter, letter to the editor of *Deutsche Wochenschrift*, St. Louis, Missouri, dated November 20, 1958; printed in „Suchlicht", a supplement of *Nation Europa*, Heft 10 (Okt. 1959) (Text D)
8. Stephen F. Pinter, Letter to the Editor, in: *Our Sunday Visitor* (Huntington, Indiana), June 14, 1959, p. 15 (Text E)
9. Stephen F. Pinter, „Beeidigte Erklärung, St. Louis, Mo., vom 9. Februar 1960;" in: *Nation Europa*, X. Jahrgang, H. 4 (April 1960), p. 68 (Text F)
10. S. F. Pinter, "Die Kollektivschuld," *Nation Europa* , Jahrg. X. H. 9 (Sept. 1960), p. 9-11 (Text G)
11. Stephen F. Pinter, letter to the editor of *National- Zeitung*, dated ?; partly quoted in: *National-Zeitung* Nr. 26, dated July 1, 1966, p. 1 and p. 11 (Text H)
12. Udo Walendy; letter dated September 6, 2002.The letter of Walendy's source is in German. The passage quoted here is author's translation.
13. Wilfred von Oven, letter dated October 4, 2001

REVIEW

Night

by Elie Wiesel. Bantam Books, New York, 1982, 109 pp.

D.D. Desjardins

Night, written by Elie Wiesel, winner of the 1986 Nobel Peace Prize has, for such a small book, a very large reputation. I hasten to mention, however, the Bantam Books edition I am reviewing boasts the complete text of the original hardcover, of which "NOT ONE WORD HAS BEEN OMITTED." A. Alvarez, reviewing for *Commentary*, wrote "As a human document, *Night* is almost unbearably painful, and certainly beyond criticism." And while I too am not here to criticize, in the course of examining, I do wish to question. For there are many odd and contradictory things in this book. And if you do not come to it with obedient reverence, you will find those things readily.

Mr. Wiesel tells us about his family, his father and mother who ran the family business, and his three sisters Hilda, Béa, and Tzipora. This book, in fact, is dedicated to the latter.[1] Even before mention of his family, however, we are introduced to Moshe the Beadle, a master at the Hasidic synagogue of Sighet, the town in Transylvania where Elie grew up. Elie wants to undertake studies of the Zohar, the cabbalistic books, which contain secrets of Jewish mysticism. In an ensuing conversation, Moshe tells Elie:

> "There are a thousand and one gates leading into the orchard *of mystical truth. Every human being has his own gate. We must never make the mistake of wanting to enter the orchard by any gate but our own. To do this is dangerous for the one who enters and also for those who are already there."*

And this is revelatory in more ways than one. For it perhaps serves not only as an overview regarding studies of the Kabbala, but the journey Elie will be describing regarding his experiences of the Jewish Holocaust; descriptions where "mystical" truth often becomes the touchstone of what he is striving for. The "gate" would be his personal experience, the "orchard," the actual events themselves. If what is now being said about Elie is true, that he assumed the identity of another person, that he is not the person he pretends to be, then woe to him, for he has broken with the advice given by his own master, creating great danger for himself as well as for others.[2]

A ready example of employing the wrong gate to enter the orchard is Elie's use of Moshe's testimony to set the stage. It begins this way: one day in the life of Sighet, "they" (the Hungarian authorities) expell all *foreign* Jews, Moshe the Beadle being one of these. Moshe is crammed into a cattle train by Hungarian police and shipped to Poland. Once across the Polish frontier the Gestapo take charge, immediately loading Moshe and other foreign Jews onto trucks to be taken to a forest. Once there, the condemned are required to dig their own graves, whereafter the Gestapo – "without passion, without haste" – undertake a systematic execution. Each is shot in the neck with a bullet, while the babies are thrown in the air as "target practice" for the machine guns. Moshe, however, is merely shot in the leg... "and taken for dead."[3] Hence, he escapes... one presumes on foot, all the way back to Sighet. When he gets there, his fellow Jews don't believe his story, including Elie. After all, despite Moshe's reputation as a member of the Hasidic synagogue, the claim he was miraculously saved to return on a wounded leg all the way through Slovakia and Hungary to Translvania in order to tell the story of... "his death," must have appeared nothing less than sensational.[4] And it must have appeared at least ironic to Elie, who describes him earlier as "a past master in the art of making himself insignificant." Now Moshe wants to be other than insignificant, that is, more significant, risking his life to warn others while there is still time. But the question is not whether this man has changed his character, but the character of a story about wanton murder against "foreign" Jews when so many "native" Jews were left in peace. Now this "foreign" Jew who returns to what should be arrest and a second expulsion is allowed to walk the streets in plain day without further ado.

In fact, according to Elie, there is no further disturbance for anyone, including Moshe, for a full one and a half years. Not until the Spring of 1944 when Admiral Horthy is forced to ask one of the leaders of the Nyilas Party to form a new government allowing the Fascists come to power. Now the Germans are granted permission to station troops in the country and within a few days they suddenly appear at Sighet. At first all is well, some even billeting in Jewish homes and acting friendly. But then they lower the boom with harsh decrees and designated ghettos. Not to mention deportation. In a spirit of cooperation it is the Hungarian and Jewish police who move the Jews into the Big Ghetto, followed by the Jewish Council which takes the final step of transferring them to the main synagogue and then the train station. Once there, it is now the Hungarian Police, assisted by the Gestapo, who load them onto cattle cars bound for what is at first an unknown destination.

Elie Wiesel at the Time 100 Gala, 3 May 2010. By User:David Shankbone [CC-BY-SA-3.0 (http://creativecommons.org/licenses/by-sa/3.0)], via Wikimedia Commons

The train stops at Kaschau, on the Czech border, and it is only now the Jews realize they will not remain in their native Hungary. Only now, when it is "too late," are their eyes opened. Elie tells us this because as recently as their stay at the Big Ghetto they might have escaped, the ghetto being unguarded, but the Jews stayed nevertheless thinking the Germans would not have time to expel them, the front was too close, et cetera. Now they are to cross into Czechoslovakia where they soon find themselves at Auschwitz. And surprisingly, no one had ever heard this name before. As the train arrives, a certain Madame Schächter, who had become hysterical on four separate occasions crying about flames and fire and furnaces where none were to be seen, now cries out a fifth time that flames are leaping from a tall chimney into the black sky.[5] And this time her visions are apparently real. Adding to the scene is an abominable odor and odd-looking characters dressed in striped shirts and black trousers who enter the wagon beating people with truncheons, yelling for everyone to evacuate the cars quickly. Maybe to insure they do not end up somewhere else. For soon we discover these prisoners are somehow no longer at Auschwitz, but nearby Birkenau. Not that there is any difference. They are still confronted by the sight of flames and the scent of burning flesh.

At Birkenau, along about midnight, with SS men every six feet, "tommy guns" at the ready, Elie and his father are permanently to be separated from Elie's mother and sisters.[6] The men are formed in columns of fives and while they are so doing, an unknown prisoner comes telling what is in store for them... at Auschwitz (sic?). "Haven't you heard about it?" And because they have not, he tells them. "See that chimney over there? See it? Do you see those flames?... You're going to be burned. Frizzled away. Turned into ashes." And here my readers you will be astounded to realize is the modus Elie thought proper and fitting to propound for his Nobel Peace Prize winning novel: flames, not gas, but flames![7]

There is thought of revolt then and there but the older ones beg the younger ones not to do "anything foolish." So they instead march toward a square where they encounter "the notorious Dr. Mengele." And here Elie may be expressing a post-war attitude or maybe it is an indication the notoriety of the doctor was simply greater than the place where he worked. In any event, Elie describes him as having a cruel face, but not devoid of intelligence. To complete the picture he is wearing a monocle and holds a conductor's baton. And he actually addresses Elie, asking his age. To be sure, it is surprising a man of his stature would intercede in such matters, even to the point of becoming chatty. For he also asks if Elie is in good health and what he does for a living. And it is just as surprising Elie has the nerve to answer these questions falsely. For his pains he is directed to the left. As is his father. But lo, they soon learn this means the crematories! Not the indoor crematories Madame Schächter raved about, but a ditch with gigantic flames!

At this juncture we return to an aspect of Moshe's incredible story, only this time it is Elie who is telling us: a lorry delivering babies. A full load of them. He sees it with his own eyes – babies thrown into the flames! But gruesome as this pit is with its large, leaping flames, this is not their pit. There is an even larger one for adults. And it is so terrible Elie wonders if he is awake. He pinches himself to make sure. For his part, the father is sorry Elie couldn't have gone with his mother. We learn that apparently, despite specific orders women had to go one way and men another, several boys Elie's age (he is 15) somehow and nevertheless went with their mothers. Naturally, we wonder how this could happen? Could it be the Germans were lax in their strictures or were they simply not paying attention? Both seem improbable. Elie speaks of wanting to run to the electric wire and electrocute himself rather than "suffer a slow agony in the flames." Apparently, he thinks there is a chance for this. And we can't be sure, for he says nothing about the guards. His father meanwhile, weeping, recites the Kaddish, a prayer for the dead. This makes Elie angry. Why should he bless the name of God, a Lord of the Universe who is silent? Here one might counsel Elie not to make matters worse by blaspheming the All-Powerful and Terrible. Something bad might happen. And we see it almost does. Closer and closer Elie and his father march toward the ditch and its leaping flames. And oddly, nothing is said of being forced there, of guards beating them forward with truncheons or whips. They are not even shouted at. It is instead like a dream. Maybe Elie is dreaming? Closer, and closer they go: twenty paces, then fifteen. The inferno's heat rises up and by now must be stifling. Ten steps, eight steps, seven. It is like a funeral march, not forced, suggestive of trance. Odd too, is the fact Elie's teeth are chattering, not from the cold, obviously, so we suppose this is from nervousness. Four steps, three steps. And now the pit is directly in front of them, right there in front, and they are not even singed nor withered by what must be tremendous, overwhelming heat, but instead Elie retains the presence of mind and the gathering strength to think he might still break from the ranks and make it to the barbed wire. But suddenly it is not necessary. At the last moment he, his father and their remaining comrades are miraculously ordered to make a quick turn to the left and proceed to the barracks. They are saved! But what's this? Like the odd ratcheting of a broken mechanism, it appears Elie and his father were not at the edge of the pit after all. For when the order comes, somehow they are again two steps away and not quite there. Still, it was a close call.

The blows that were not in evidence forcing prisoners into the flaming pit now rain down volubly to encourage those who survived to go to the barber to get their haircut! And the people wielding the truncheons are fellow prisoners. Not only is Elie's hair cut with clippers, but his whole body is shaved. He and his companions are all the while naked, carrying only their original belt and shoes. And apparently they are still naked afterward as they wander into the courtyard meeting old friends and acquaintances. Some are joyful and some are weeping. And Elie admits to something that would become more and more pronounced as his story progresses, viz., that those who were dead and departed "no longer touched even the surface of our memories." They would speak of them, but with little concern for their fate. Elie tells us why: because their senses are blunted. Because "everything was blurred as in a fog." Or a dream? In any event, it was no longer possible to grasp anything. Self-preservation, self-defense, pride – all had deserted them.

At five in the morning they are beaten once more, and made to run naked through icy winds with their shoes and belts to yet another barracks, where disinfection is waiting for them in the form of a barrel of petrol. Everyone is soaked in it. Picturing how they did this requires some imagination. Then everyone takes a hot shower. And what comes out isn't gas, but real water for genuine cleaning. All at high speed, mind you – no wasting water! Now they are made to run to another barracks where they receive their prison clothes, to discover nothing fits! But unlike the usual G.I. lament where a soldier must adapt to the clothes he is issued, these prisoners are allowed to swap clothes and make the necessary adjustments.

In case the reader has gotten the wrong idea, Elie describes an SS officer with fleshy lips and "the odor of the Angel of Death" who tells everyone they are at Auschwitz... a concentration camp. You can nearly imagine some editor who has advised this, e.g., stop the descriptions making Auschwitz appear like a country club and get back to the evil of those murderous Germans. So now we have Elie reading crime not only on the SS man's brow, but also in the pupils of his eyes. And we know Elie is not being technical because any book on the human visual system will tell you that the pupil is the aperture in the iris that controls the amount of light entering the eye, where the larger the diameter the more light rays reach the edges of the lens, thereby reducing the quality of the image. Rather than reading evil there, the best that can be inferred is that the SS man's pupils were dilated because the room was dark. But apart from the dilated pupils, the SS man is certainly focused on his topic of discussion. For he tells them Auschwitz is not a convalescent home. It is a place of work. And if one doesn't work they will "go straight to the furnace." Not to the gas chambers, but directly to the crematory! "Work or the crematory..." This is what Elie quotes the SS man as saying. And it is again apparent the mention of gas chambers is avoided in preference to the word "furnace." Why? Speculation suggests this might be because up until the time of Edith Stein's beatification in 1987, Elie Wiesel had been attempting to introduce the word "Holocaust" into our vocabulary (from the Hebrew *ola*, i.e., burnt offering). The twenty-fifth anniversary edition I am reviewing was printed in 1986. Controversy at the time of Edith Stein's beatification apparently persuaded him to use the word "Shoah" (from Isaiah 47:11, meaning "disaster").[8] I leave it to the reader to determine if more modern editions mention "gas chambers" in addition to crematories.

Returning to our story, we again find force being used for unusual purposes. For we have a scene where ten gypsies join a lone gypsy wielding whips and truncheons to force everyone outside into the spring sunshine. One wonders why prisoners must be forced to do this? Naturally we assume spring sunshine is preferable to the inside of a barracks. But maybe they have an intimation of the short march and coming confusion? For they are formed into ranks of five and marched through the gates between electric wires. And near or on the electric wires there are a series of white placards brandishing a death's head with this caption: "Warning. Danger of death." And the irony is not lost on Elie, who has been telling us all along they are in a death camp! The gypsies are soon replaced by SS who march the prisoners outside the barbed wire of the camp, and now there is some uncertainty whether this is a march of half an hour or only a few moments before they reach the barbed wire of another camp: Auschwitz! Yes, that's right. They were in Auschwitz which they left to enter another camp which is also Auschwitz. Elie is obviously confused and I wonder if his editors are so mesmerized by the sanctity of his descriptions there has been no attempt to correct this anomaly. For the obvious correction is that Elie has left Auschwitz for nearby Birkenau, else re-entered Auschwitz through another gate. For he specifically mentions an iron door with the inscription: "Work is liberty!," claiming this is Auschwitz.[9] But then he confuses his reader again by saying this camp is better than Birkenau! He was at Auschwitz, the SS man with the fleshy lips and the odor of death tells him they are at Auschwitz, they leave Auschwitz and enter... Auschwitz! How did this glaring confusion get past the editors?

We learn Auschwitz was better than Birkenau because of its concrete buildings and gardens. Not to mention hygiene. At the entrance to one of the prison blocks, Elie is made to wait his turn to go into the showers. From what we know about how the Germans used showers, we think this is the end, but no, not at all. It is Elie himself who tells us the showers were a compulsory formality at the entrance "to all these camps." Even when passing from one to the other several times a day, e.g., from Birkenau to Auschwitz, from Auschwitz to Birkenau, you had to go through the baths each time. Yet, pleasant as that seems, all is not wine and roses. It is in fact a pretext for complaint. And this is because after the nice, hot shower, they were forced to shiver in the night air. But the case Elie makes for this doesn't stack up. Just a short while ago, Elie and his comrades were marched over in the spring sunshine, the march took only a few moments or half hour at the most, whereafter they queued at the prison block to get a shower and now it is night. One of two things must be true: they waited a long time for their shower or they spent a long time in the shower, or possibly both. Either way, forget the old adage, for here time passes quickly when you're *not* having fun! Their clothes they had to leave behind in "the other block," and since this is the first block they are supposedly entering once reaching Auschwitz, one must imagine they walked naked all the way from Birkenau! But I think instead there was an undressing process at Auschwitz Elie has failed to mention. What he does mention is that time has passed even more quickly and it is now nearly midnight before he and his comrades are ordered to run, not to get clothes, but to go to bed.

Next morning after a good night's sleep, the prisoners are able to wash, get new clothes and drink black coffee. As a point of reference you can read *The Forgotten Soldier* by Guy Sajer and know this is a time on the Eastern Front when German soldiers were eating grass for lack of supplies. What they wouldn't have given for some coffee! You need only make such comparisons to realize the prisoners' life was somewhat gentle by comparison. The German soldier was constantly exposed to death, lived in the same uniform month after month, and rarely got a bath, hot or otherwise. Except for the dishonor, some soldiers might have been glad to trade places. And think. Instead of some muddy ditch or foxhole, Elie tells us his comrades didn't have to leave the relative comfort of their barrack until ten a.m. – so that it could be cleaned. Outside, they chatted with fellow comrades in the warm sunshine. At noon, they are brought a plate of thick soup. Again by way of contrast, Aleksandr Solzhenitsyn tells us about the food in the Soviet camps: gruel with salted carrots September till June, groats in June and shredded nettles in July. At other times there might be cabbage. There was also fish, but it was mostly bones because the flesh was boiled off leaving only a little meat on the tails and heads.[10] Who had the better system? Both the German and the Russian camps had a bread ration, but it must be remembered that while the Gulag was meant to hold prisoners for political crimes, the German camps allegedly existed for purposes of extermination. Something to ponder.

Elie tells us despite his hunger he doesn't eat it because he was still "the spoiled child," so his father takes his ration instead. Then they take a siesta. Elie now begins to think the SS officer of the other day was lying: Auschwitz is not a concentration camp, not a death camp where if you do not work you die, but in fact a rest home!

We now come to a description which, in light of recent controversy, should be of particular interest. For this is where Elie tells us how he got his prisoner's tattoo. The scene unfolds as follows: one fine afternoon a line is formed in front of a table with some medical instruments. Three veteran prisoners with needles are assigned to engrave numbers on the arms of the new prisoners. With left sleeve rolled up, Elie tells us he gets his number: A-7713. And the number is important. When at dusk the work units return, greeted by a band playing military marches, roll call is taken. And the SS verifies the tens of thousands of prisoners not by their names but by their numbers. So Elie would have been required to have a number at Auschwitz. No number, no Auschwitz. A-7713, left arm. Of course any other legitimate number would have served the purpose, but this is the one he says he received. If no number or a false one, we must toss out the whole idea of his ever being at Auschwitz or the factual basis for what he says in *Night*. Why not believe him?

Apart from the harrowing experience at the flaming pit when first arriving, the next three weeks at Auschwitz are really quite good. In the mornings there is black coffee. At noon there is soup. After roll call at 6 p.m., there is bread and margarine. Then the prisoners are free to roam, looking for friends, neighbors and relatives before going to bed by 9 p.m. Elie and his father have nothing to do but sleep a great deal in the afternoon and at night. Their only worry is to in fact stay at Auschwitz "as long as possible" and avoid being moved. How? Simply by identifying themselves as other than skilled laborers, for "laborers" (i.e., unskilled laborers) "were being kept till the end."

But soon these good days end. A first indication is when the cell block leader is replaced for being too humane, replaced by someone savage, ably assisted by monstrous attendants. This turn of events again causes Elie and his fellow Jews think of their fate, but also of things one doesn't usually expect of a people too proud to believe they are at fault for anything. A fellow Hasidic, Akiba Drumer, one of solemn voice, is given to say God is testing them to find out whether they can dominate their base instincts and "kill the Satan within us," while others speak "of the sins of the Jewish people," but also their future deliverance. This reminds one of the occasional admissions of Jews such as Bernard Lazarre, a French historian who, well before the holocaust, understood national uprisings and the expulsion of Jews in consequence of negative characteristics the Jews themselves possessed. And it also reminds of Edith Stein, the German philosopher and Carmelite, who spoke of the "fulfillment of the curse which my people have called down upon themselves!"[11] But now, during a period of common suffering, these Jewish prisoners come to a similar understanding.

Eventually Elie, his father and some other prisoners are transferred to Buna. And here Elie makes a striking statement. On the one hand he says Buna looks like it was suffering from an epidemic, but on the other hand he says its sparse population of prisoners were well-clad and walking about seemingly healthy. Once there, they go through the ubiquitous showers, joined by the head of the camp – a man with gray-blue eyes who looks kind and even smiles. He takes an interest in the several children who arrive with the convoy and has food brought for them. The newly arrived, meanwhile, are given new clothes. Even the veteran prisoners admit "Buna's a very good camp," yet seem to have misgivings about the building unit. But now we learn what might be behind the niceties of the camp commandant in regard to the children. It seems the head of Elie's tent, a German, also likes children. And despite having an "assassin's face," hands like "wolf's paws," and so much fat he could hardly move, he too, brings the children food: bread, soup, and margarine. Elie explains why by assuming the man is a trafficker in children. He assumes he is an homosexual. Why these assumptions? Because later he would learn "there was a considerable traffic in children among homosexuals here…" It is not proven against the German mind you, nor the camp commandant, but for Elie the rumors are sufficient. And I'm sure for many of his readers, too.

Medical examination seems pretty good – maybe as good or better than what modern-day US military Reservists receive. There are three doctors present and instead of posing questions via some on-line and impersonal form, they ask about the health of a person, in person.

And then there is a dentist - something not even our modern-day Veterans' hospitals provide. The only draw-back according to Elie is that the dentist is not looking for decayed teeth but ones that contain gold. Those who have them, like Elie with his gold crown, have their number added to a list. The secretary of the block soon orders him to return to the camp dentist, despite he has no toothache. It seems those with gold teeth are required to have them extracted (without waiting to remove them from their dead skulls!) But on this occasion the dentist is a Czech Jew, and when Elie explains he is not feeling well, the dentist tells him to return when he is feeling better. When Elie returns a week later, he gives the same excuse and is again given a reprieve. But now there is an end to it, for the Germans discover the dentist is running a private traffic of his own and is "thrown in prison," whence to be hanged. Not gassed, not incinerated, but hanged! And no one replaces him. So Elie gets to keep his gold crown because the Germans don't afterwards assign a new dentist to extract gold teeth and one wonders if the original Jewish dentist was not only working on his own but without authority?

From time to time Elie tells us something unusual about the psychology of concentration camp life and here divulges an instance involving a work detail headed up by Idek, a bully Kapo. Normally, Elie and his father worked in an electronics warehouse at Buna but this incident occurs at a rail depot where they had to load Deisel engines. Idek breaks out into a frenzy over Elie's father's laziness and begins beating him with an iron bar. You can imagine the blows were not light. The father is in fact beaten so badly he is described as "broke in two," like a tree struck by lightning, whereupon he collapses. And here is the strange part. Elie describes his anger as not directed towards Idek but wholly against his father "for not knowing how to avoid Idek's outbreak." If true, this is indeed bizarre. Elie blames the effects on camp life, but seen from a nature versus nurture viewpoint, one wonders at the boy's character and what he is made of. One often learns the worst about oneself under conditions of turmoil and stress. And it is not the last of our friend Idek.

Elie would learn something about his comrades, too. Take Franek, for example. Franek, the former student from Warsaw. Franek, a Pole and fellow Jew, who was also their foreman. It now seems that someone else besides the Jewish dentist wants Elie's gold crown and that person is Franek. Jews, we are told, love gold. And we are reminded of this by Woody Allen of all people, himself Jewish, whose film *Annie Hall* shows actual German newsreel footage of abandoned cars on the outskirts of Paris accompanied by English subtitles telling us these were Jews attempting to flee the Germans with all their… gold! So who can blame Franek? No longer the sympathetic, intelligent youth, Franek attempts to persuade Elie through his father, savagely thrashing the father every time he marches out of step. Elie tries to teach his father how to march correctly, but it is no good. The father remains unregimented, and for that, continues to receive beatings until finally, Elie consents to give up his crown. By now, however, Franek wants a ration of bread for having been kept waiting – this, to go to the famous dentist from Warsaw who's going to do the extraction. It's not much of a fee really and the old adage applies: you get what you pay for. The famous dentist pulls the tooth in a lavatory with a rusty spoon! And this is a Jewish, not a German dentist.

Fresh on the heels of this tale of the lavatory and rusty spoons comes a story that is now salacious, one that is meant to titillate. It again involves Idek. Picture a pleasant Sunday, normally a day of rest, but Idek won't hear of it. Everyone to the warehouse, which is outside the camp. But maybe Idek has relented, for Elie finds there is not much to do there but go for little walks. Elie's little walk takes him to the back of the building where he hears noises from a room next door. Next door is obviously their own barracks inside the camp for next thing we know, Elie is able to spy on Idek and a half-naked Polish girl on a mattress in the building from whence they were forced to leave. It is odd Elie is able to return there, and evidently comical the sight he is witnessing, too. So much so, he laughs out loud and draws Idek's unwanted attention. Soon, he is made to lie on a box during a special roll call to receive twenty-five lashes, during which he passes out. Doused with water and brought before Idek, the latter tells Elie the punishment was for his curiosity and that he will receive five times as many lashes "if you dare tell anyone what you saw!" And he says this during the same roll call in front of some hundred prisoners who presumably are within earshot. Or did Elie forget the scene he had painted? By now we are thinking this happens too often.

And that is not all. For another thing that happens often and by now catches our eye is the fact mass murder in flaming pits or crematories is not the only way the Germans choose to dispatch the undesirable. Those who commit actual infractions are curiously handled individually and in the old-fashioned way: by hanging! The Czech Jew who was hanged for improper dental practices is apparently not an anomaly. And we know this because Elie tells us about gallows erected in the center of the camp for other such executions. And these events are quite formal. He describes one that occurs while all ten thousand prisoners are at roll-call. The gate to the camp is opened and they find themselves surrounded by a "section" of SS, one soldier every three paces.[12] The hanging concerns a youth from Warsaw accused of stealing. He must now die as a warning and example, but also because it's the law. Apparently there is a semblance of law even in a concentration camp. Despite Elie telling us the youth has spent three years in various camps, he is nevertheless described as "strong," and "well-built." And it is odd, if anything any longer can be, that Elie is overwhelmed by the sight of this one impending death by hanging when he says he is otherwise no longer troubled by the thousands who die daily at Auschwitz and Birkenau in the crematory ovens. And his reason is a matter of speculation, but I infer it is because aside from the one incident of the flaming pits, he does not see these thousands of deaths but only imagines them. By contrast, the true sight of someone who is to hang is more poignant and real. And the odd twist is that even after the youth is able to shout an appeal for liberty and a curse upon Germany, following the execution, the assembly is nevertheless commanded to bare and cover their heads as a gesture of respect. Then the prisoners are all made to pass by the dead body and look at the hanged youth full in the face, to see his dimmed eyes and lolling tongue, as if this was to make a special impression when thousands were dying every day by more gruesome means for no particular infraction.

There is yet another hanging into which Elie delves at length concerning a boy who was an assistant to a Dutch *Oberkapo* of the fifty-second cable unit. The boy was known as a *pipel*, a child with a refined and beautiful face, and anyone who has read Oscar Wilde's *Portrait of Mr. W.H.* is struck by certain similarities. After the sabotage of the electric power station at Buna, the Gestapo accuse a certain Dutchman, whereupon they torture and send him to Auschwitz. The *pipel*, however, also tortured, is instead sentenced to death at Buna, along with two others. Consequently, three gallows are erected and it is the same cumbersome process once again: the SS en masse, machine guns at the ready, surrounding ten thousand prisoners at a mandatory assembly. But what's this? Elie tells us the SS seem more disturbed than usual. Why? Because it is no light matter to hang a young boy in front of thousands of spectators! The three are hanged at the same time and in the same primitive manner the Italians used for the Libyans in 1931: by forcing them to mount chairs, placing a noose around their necks, then tipping the chairs over. Again the token of respect, again the forced march past the victims. But during this pass and review the prisoners see the two adults have perished but the *pipel*, "being so light," is still alive, struggling in his noose and experiencing a slow agony on the brink of death. If the SS were reluctant to begin with, what are they feeling now? But Elie doesn't tell us. What he does say is that night the soup tasted of corpses. Corpses? It is a poor analogy. It also poses a strange contrast to the aftermath of the death of the youth from Warsaw where Elie said the soup tasted "excellent." Which is less an artistic twist than a psychological exposé.

It is now the eve of Rosh Hashanah, the end of summer, the last day of the Jewish year. Everyone is given thick soup but no one touches it. You would think Elie and his fellow prisoners are starving, and at other times they are, or he says they are, but this time they are willing to forgo their meal until after prayers. Thousands of Jews gather silently in the place of assembly, the same place as the hangings, to pray. Unlike the Jews of *Exodus* who felt obliged to ask Pharaoh to let them leave Egypt so they could worship their god elsewhere, these Jews ask nothing but to gather and pray uninhibited and unharmed. We are told there are the usual ten thousand, to include the heads of blocks, Kapos, the "functionaries of death." And they are there to "Bless the Eternal…" But Elie questions this blessing. Why should he bless the Eternal who "had had thousands of children burned in <u>His</u> pits" (my underscore), who "kept six crematories working day and night, on Sundays and feast days," and who "created Auschwitz, Birkenau, Buna, and so many factories of death?" Elie tells God He has betrayed these people, allowing them to be tortured, butchered, gassed and burned when previously He took action with Adam and Eve, Noah's generation, and the city of Sodom. And while Elie reviles the fact the assembly is praying to God despite these things, he does not allow himself to ponder why God would indeed act in those biblical instances, yet not here and now. Still, the reader must wonder, as might any person who does not feel God is God for him alone, a personal god for a chosen people. For Elie, however, if God is not doing the Jews' bidding then God is no longer God but something less to where, feeling stronger than the Almighty, Elie is now the accuser and God the accused. And this is curiously reminiscent of that passage in *Exodus* where Moses tells God to turn from His wrath against the people of Israel and repent of evil.[13] More than "chutzpa," it is blasphemy, the unbridled arrogance of a Rashkolnikov who presumes everything and becomes something less.

It is now winter 1944. Elie and his comrades are given winter clothes, thicker striped shirts which the veterans nevertheless deride. Of course there are some people who will appreciate nothing. On Christmas and New Year's there is no work and the prisoners are afforded a slightly thicker soup. And possibly there are some who gripe about this, too. But here Elie must be commended for at least telling us of these things, for we are able to glimpse the Germans as human, respecting the birth of Jesus and sharing with those less fortunate.

Toward the middle of January, Elie's right foot begins to bother him and he goes to have it examined. The examination is performed by an eminent Jewish doctor, also a prisoner. The doctor insists on an operation. If Elie's time-table is correct, we know the Russians are within a week or so of seizing the camp, the Germans are on the verge of evacuation, but the Jewish doctor nevertheless proposes surgery, with no concern for hardship in terms of medical facilities, anesthetics, bandages, etc. Elie in fact tells us he is given a bed with white sheets and "the hospital was not bad at all." In addition, the patients in the hospital are given good bread and thicker soup.[14] Elie is even able to send his father some of this bread. There is a Hungarian Jew who is there for dysentery, mere skin and bones, but rather than let him die, the Germans are treating him to make him well. All the while, Elie has the chutzpa to again mention selections, telling us the hospital has them "more often than outside." On hearing this, however, one gets the impression the true significance is that here in the hospital, with limited beds and large demand, only the more serious cases are able to remain. If death is the purpose, why bother to treat in the first place? And yet despite treatment, the Hungarian Jew exclaims "Germany doesn't need sick Jews"! He therefore tells Elie he should "get out of the hospital before the next selection!" The thought must occur to Elie that if he is being treated, he is needed, and being a thinking person, realizes there may be a personal motive behind the Hungarian Jew's advice. For in fact he decides to stay. And good thing, too. The surgery is performed the very next day. And when it is over, the doctor is able to tell Elie everything is o.k. He will now be allowed to remain in the hospital the next two weeks, will rest comfortably, eat well and relax his body and nerves. Not only that but he will be up and walking like everyone else in a fortnight. Marvelous news, no doubt, to a concentration camp inmate expecting death at any moment from selections lurking round every corner.

But lo, on the same day Elie gets the prognosis about his foot, comes word of evacuation. Not that Elie need worry, for his doctor tells him hospital patients will not be evacuated but can remain in the infirmary. Immediately, the Hungarian Jew predicts all invalids will be summarily killed, sent to the crematory as part of a final liquidation. What Elie doesn't tell us and what the Hungarian obviously doesn't know is that all of Birkenau's crematories have already been shut down, the last being Kremas II, III, and V which, according to official records, ceased operating on 30 October 1944.[15] But truth doesn't stop rumors, nor Elie's speaking of them as if they might be taken seriously. Same for another rumor the camp will be blown up before the Russians arrive. All is belied by the fact Elie tells us death does not worry him. What worries him is being separated from his father. And this is because they had already suffered "so much," borne "so much," that now was not the time. Given what he has written earlier, one wonders. Why is he telling us this? But a few pages earlier, when he was describing the Allied bombing at Buna where his father was working, he was telling us despite the risk to his father he was glad about the bombing because it meant destruction and revenge. Now he is telling us when the Russians are coming he is worried about being separated from his father. What's this leading up to? Elie runs in the snow on his bad foot with no shoe to find his father. What shall we do, he asks him? Elie is confident he can get the Jewish doctor to have his father entered as a patient or a nurse and thereby fall within the rule of allowing those in the infirmary to remain behind. Soft beds, nourishing food, clean sheets, and all they would have to do is wait for the Russians. And it is not a matter of Elie worrying about liquidation or the camp being blown up because he has already and to his credit refused believing what people saying these things have previously said about hospital selections.[16] So rather than the soft beds, clean sheets and nourishing food waiting for liberation, he instead suggests he and his father "be evacuated with the others." That is, he suggests, even with his bad foot, he and his father leave with the retreating Germans to remain prisoners at another camp in Germany! People have made much to do over this and I think they should. It is nothing less than an admission despite all the hubbub about cruelty and mistreatment, despite the descriptions of forced labor and executions, remaining with the Germans was preferable to all other options – including being liberated by the Russians. This is telling. And what it tells is that the Germans may not have been so bad after all.[17]

Elie and his comrades are given double rations of bread and margarine for their journey. They were also allowed to take as many shirts and other clothes from the camp store. Elie in fact tells how next morning everyone is in multiple garments, looking like they are at a masquerade! Those who recognize the name Austin Burke, a Miami clothier of the 1960's, remember how he used to advertise men's suits on television ads this way. Burke or an assistant would come on screen with multiple suits one over the other, stripping them off as Burke would go through purple prose on the virtues of each. In the same way Elie describes these prisoners as "poor mountebanks, wider than they were tall, more dead than alive." That last comment is perhaps necessary. Elie throws this in because it is perhaps beginning to look too good, because we know they are alive and on double rations, willing to go with the Germans. And there is even a German spirit in the block leader who orders only an hour before evacuation that the block be cleaned from top to bottom, washed in every corner, so that the liberating Russians will realize "there were men living here and not pigs."

Departing Buna, the Jews arrive at Gleiwitz, where they are hurriedly installed in their new barracks by the Kapos. In their haste to occupy this refuge, this "gateway to life" as Elie calls it, he also describes how they "walked over pain-racked bodies" and "trod on wounded faces" to get inside. Elie and his father are themselves victim to this, as they are thrown to the ground by a rolling tide of humanity. Elie finds he is now in fact crushing someone he knows, a voice from the past, and in his effort to disengage himself, does some mean and horrible things, e.g., digging his nails into others' faces, and "biting all around." Elie discovers it is Juliek he has been crushing, the boy from Warsaw who played the violin in the orchestra at Buna. Despite the crush, swollen feet and lack of air, it is not his own life Juliek is concerned for, but his violin. He's got it with him and is afraid it will be broken.

But before the conversation can continue, Elie must first extricate himself. We learn he is not face down, but face up, and someone is lying on top of him, suffocating him to where he is now unable to breathe either through his nose or mouth. So again he commences to scratch, to tear with his nails into decayed flesh, yet to no avail. Elie thinks the man on top of him in fact is dead, but isn't sure. Finally, however, he manages to dig a hole – a hole through the wall of dying people, a little hole through which to breathe. Now he calls to his father, who he knows is not far away, and the father, who presumably is also being crushed, answers he is "well!" Elie tries to sleep now, still buried but breathing, when he suddenly hears the sound of a violin. It is Juliek playing a fragment from a Beethoven concerto. And Elie wonders, as the reader must, how when Elie was on top of Juliek and couldn't budge, Juliek got out from under him to play his violin? What miracle allowed this? What flight of fancy? The nice thing of course is that it now allows Elie to trip the light fantastic about Juliek's soul and how it is the bow and how the whole of his life seems to be gliding on the strings, the whole being very beautiful. But despite this beauty Elie again falls asleep and when he awakes this time by the light of day he sees Juliek opposite him, slumped over dead, his violin smashed beside him. And this makes for a sad if wondrous image, something Elie does from time to time for literary effect, even if the image defies reason.

Moving from Gleiwitz, the prisoners continue their journey to Buchenwald, where they are assembled to be counted. And wouldn't you know that right next to where they are standing is the high chimney of a crematory, although by now it hardly makes an impression. They've seen and survived these things before. What really fascinates them, however, is the fact there are hot showers, and beds. The guards in fact have to begin striking the prisoners to maintain order, the prisoners crowding so to get a shower, but to no avail. They obviously believe it is water and not gas that will issue from those showers. Here in the heart of Germany. But now Elie's father is too exhausted to stand in line. He thinks it's the end and drags himself to a snow covered hillock of dead bodies to await the end. Suddenly, interrupting the scene of Elie pleading with his father, of pleading with death itself, there is an air raid siren, the lights go out, and the guards drive everyone into the blocks. The prisoners are only too glad not to have to wait outside in the icy wind, instead letting themselves sink down onto beds arranged in tiers. Even the cauldrons of soup at the entrance to the barracks attracts no one. This reminds us of before. Where formerly they were starving, tearing, biting, even killing for a scrap of bread, suddenly food does not matter to anyone, all they want is sleep.

And here Elie makes another of those less than laudatory revelations. For he tells us he has followed the crowd from where his father was resting at the hillock, where he pleaded with his father to arise and get himself washed before going to the blocks, but left him during the alert to go inside to sleep, not troubling with him further. The father, meanwhile, during the alert and after, was left outside in the snow!

On the brink of death. Abandoned. Only on the following day does Elie go back to look for him. This man, this father whose hand he held just the day before when forming up at Buchenwald's assembly place, not wanting to lose him! But now he has already abandoned him to his fate while he slept inside and confesses as he goes to seek him he in fact doesn't want to find him, instead wishing he could "get rid of this dead weight" so he could use all his strength to struggle for his own survival. What happened over the past 12 hours to bring about this change of attitude? Elie has now rested, has been relatively comfortable and has presumably nourished himself from the cauldrons of soup that were at the entrance to the block, but now instead of being refreshed and invigorated, more generous of spirit, is afflicted by avarice and lack of familial fidelity. He tells us he is ashamed for these thoughts, but still it is puzzling, if not disturbing. Now, searching for his father, he finds him at a block where black coffee is being served. Elie gets his father some coffee, asks a number of questions, then says he cannot stay long because the place is to be cleaned and only the sick are allowed to remain. And in the background we begin to comprehend it was the Germans who did what Elie did not, and that is get his father inside, out of the weather, where he could be sheltered and allowed to survive. And it is another blow, a small one to be sure, adding to an overall picture that the Germans have something else in mind than a systematic plan to kill Jews, even sick ones.

But it is near the end for the father and there is a curious description of him lying in his bunk laid up with dysentery, suddenly raising himself to whisper in Elie's ear where to find the gold and money he buried before leaving their home in Sighet. Elie tries to explain this is not the end, that they would both return together, but the father will not listen. A trickle of saliva mixed with blood comes from his lips, his breath comes in gasps, and when a doctor arrives, Elie pleads he examine his father but the doctor instead insists on an office visit. When Elie brings his father, the doctor announces he can do nothing because it is a case of dysentery and his field is surgery. Returned to the barrack, another doctor comes, but Elie thinks this doctor is just there to "finish off" those who are sick because he hears him shouting that the sick are just lazy and want to stay in bed! And it is just an opinion the doctor wants to finish them off, although Elie tells us he would like to strangle the doctor! And not only the doctor but "the others." In fact, he would like to burn the "whole world," especially his father's murderers. Lest we think he means only the world of the Germans, we learn Elie's father is being beaten by a Frenchman and a

Pole, fellow prisoners who cannot stand the fact the father won't drag himself outside to relieve himself. And they not only beat him, but also steal his bread!

Elie knows his father must not drink water, that water for a person with dysentery is poison, but he gives it to him anyway. A week passes this way, however, and the father still lives. The head of the block advises Elie not to give the father his ration of bread and soup but to instead keep it for himself. He says this because it is clear the father is dying, and there is nothing anyone can do. So Elie holds the bread but gives his father soup, only the father wants water, always water, and Elie obliges. But now comes an SS officer on the scene, passing the beds. And apparently this SS officer is disturbed at the noise Elie's father is making begging for water. He tells him to be quiet, but the father continues to call Elie's name, and when the father ignores the officer, the latter deals him a violent blow to the head with his truncheon. Elie does nothing, afraid to move, afraid he too will be struck. After roll call, he climbs down from his bunk to learn the worst, that his father's skull is shattered. He is still alive, but barely. Elie stares at him for an hour, then climbs back into his bunk. At dawn when Elie awakes, he finds his father has been removed, replaced by somebody else, and naturally assumes "they must have taken him… to the crematory." And if he indeed died, this is likely true, for most cases of dysentery are due to micro-organisms, as is typhus, which is due to a bacillus, so the burning of bodies rather than their burial, is the recommended practice. Elie laments there were no prayers and no candles, but we are shocked when he admits that in the depths of his being, in the recesses of his conscience, was the basic sentiment "free at last!" Such an expression seems wrong and inhuman. Compare, for example, with Henry Fonda who speaks these same words when carrying the limp body of Sylvia Sidney, escaping from a police sharpshooter who is about to pull the trigger.[18]

Let us consider the time-line for a moment. Elie gives the date of his father's death as 29 January 1945. As a satellite camp to Auschwitz, we suppose Buna was evacuated approximately the same time as Auschwitz, that is, 18 January 1945, whereafter there was a two nights' march to Gleiwitz, where the prisoners stayed for three days. Then there was a train ride to Buchenwald, which required "ten days, and ten nights." Then another week while Elie's father was dying of dysentery. We should now be at 9 February, or later, but Elie tells us his father died during the night of 28 – 29 January. Something is wrong here.[19] But there is something else. The father has dysentery while at Buchenwald and the doctors wouldn't or couldn't do anything for him. Fellow prisoners beat him and took his bread. The head of the block, someone sympathetic, advises Elie not to waste rations on the father. And finally, an SS officer finishes him off with a blow from his truncheon. So despite the treatment of fellow prisoners, despite dysentery and even the behavior of Elie himself, the blame comes to rest with the Germans. Elie wants us to see it that way. And technically he is right, but later he would try to establish something evil about the soul of the Germans. There is an interesting comparison in Solzhenitsyn's *Ivan Denisovich* when speaking about "Shukov" (i.e., Denisovich). For he speaks of a Soviet warder who pricked himself on the sewing needle Shukov hid in his prisoner's cap when the former snatched the cap off his head during inspection. And the warder became so angry by this "he'd almost smashed Shukov's head in."[20] And this is not to forgive or excuse what the SS officer did to Elie's father but to understand that temper, violence and brutishness was as much a part of gulags as it was of concentration camps, the type of people these establishments required or bred, and is therefore less particular and more universal than one might otherwise wish to believe.

On 5 April the prisoners are still at Buchenwald where there is an announcement for all Jews to form at the assembly place. All the children of Elie's block are made to do this, motivated by menaces from block leader Gustav and his truncheon. And there is fear this is finally the end. But on the way to the assembly place some prisoners whisper to the children to return to their barracks, so they won't be shot by the Germans. "Shot" mind you, 600 bullets if none of them miss, 600 bullets that might be used to defend against the approaching Americans, but not gas or the flaming pit, theoretically more efficient for mass killings. The whispers come either from members of the camp resistance organization or those who knew about the plans of such an organization, plans that provide the Jews will not be abandoned or allowed to be liquidated. With several thousand prisoners leaving the camp each day beginning 6 April, there are still some twenty thousand who remain on 10 April, including several hundred children. And on this day all are to be evacuated immediately, whereafter the camp is to be destroyed (Elie quotes the camp commandant as saying Buchenwald is to be "liquidated" but it is obvious what the term really means is the camp would be evacuated and destroyed). As everyone is massed in the huge assembly area, there is suddenly an alert and they all must return to their blocks. Now the evacuation is postponed until 11 April. Elie states those present haven't eaten for six days, save for some bits of grass and potato peelings. And so it is with super-herculean willpower, however undernourished or weakened, while the SS are again moving the prisoners to the assembly point, the resistance rises up and after two hours of what must have been a very unequal battle fit for a Hollywood movie, is nevertheless master of the situation. The SS flee and the resistance is now in charge. And by six that evening the first American tank arrives.

Once liberated, the prisoners' first thought is not of revenge, not even of their families, but to seize and consume Buchenwald's remaining provisions. The following day, approximately 14 April, some of the younger men make their way to Weimar to acquire more food and sleep with women. This is not what you'd expect from starved and emaciated men ravaged by years of concentration camp life. The gratuitous photos we've seen of those who were liberated doesn't make this seem possible. But now we learn just three days after liberation, Elie becomes ill with food poisoning. Very ill, and we wonder if it is the American food or the food they stole from the Germans? Either way, this is puzzling, just like the stories relating to the outbreak of typhus at Bergen-Belsen *after* its liberation by the British. Elie's case is so serious he is transferred to a hospital where he spends the next two weeks on the brink of death. During this time he looks into a mirror, and what he sees is a corpse. Not simply a radically changed man like Yuri Zhivago after fifteen months as a doctor with the Red partisans, but "a corpse." And it is just this liberty with modes of expression that defines how he has employed mystical rather than plain truth in describing his ordeal; how if he is pretending to be somebody else he has broken the rules regarding what Moshe the Beadle tried to say about entering the orchard. Yet even now, while viewing "the corpse," never could he dream the fame and honors that awaited when telling his story, the Nobel Peace Prize and the United States Congressional Gold Medal, to name but a few. Proving life can be good if one isn't a corpse, but rather lives to tell the tale.

Notes:

1. It is possible that a Swedish journalist for *Sydsvenska Dagbladet*, researching in 1986, misidentified Elie as one Lazar Wiesel, inmate number A-7713. True, in *Night*, Elie claims his number at Auschwitz was A-7713, but that he was also an only son; there is no mention of a brother named "Abraham." Furthermore, Elie Wiesel would have been age 15 in 1944,

whereas witness Miklos (Nikolaus) Grüner claims Lazar Wiesel was 31 in that same year. Was the genesis of Elie's book in fact something previously written in 1955 by Lazar Wiesel? That is a different matter.

2. Three people have investigated this: Nikolaus (Miklos) Grüner, Carlo Mattogno and Carolyn Yeager. Carolyn Yeager has delved into it and written about it most fully in several articles on her Website, "Elie Wiesel Cons the World." Online: http://www.eliewiesltattoo.com.

3. The distance between the neck and a leg being large, especially at close range, one is not surprised the Germans needed target practice. But killing babies with machine guns seems an absurd matter of overkill!

4. By the Treaty of Trianon, signed 4 June 1920, Hungary lost Transylvania, but it was restored by Rumania on 30 August 1940.

5. In Exodus 19:18 we find: "And Mount Sinai was wrapped in smoke, because the Lord descended upon it in fire; and the smoke of it went up like the smoke of a kiln..." Thus one might infer Madame Schächter is hallucinating about the presence of God.

6. Regarding the SS with "tommy guns," (Thompson submachine guns) one wonders if these are a contingent of the some 50 British volunteers who allegedly served in the Waffen SS during the war?

7. MGM's film *The Search*, released in 1948, starring Montgomery Clift, Ailene MacMahon (and a little Czech boy named Ivan Jandl) has a scene with a young girl who is speaking about her mother being "gassed" at Dachau. And later, there is a scene where Ivan Jandl and other displaced children are being transported in Red Cross trucks who break free and escape the trucks because they smell exhaust gas and believe they are being exterminated. So the idea of gas as a modus operandi was already in the public mind but curiously not in Elie's mind and we naturally wonder why?

8. See Ernst Ludwig Ehrlich, "The Jews Did Not Want to Bring Burnt Offerings," in *Never Forget*, Waltraud Herbstrith, Ed. (Washington: ICS Publications, 1998), p. 129.

9. I myself, when retracing the steps of Fred Leuchter in 1998, passed beneath this "inscription," although by then there was no iron door, nor did there seem ever to have been, just a wrought-iron grill with its Gothic text slogan: *Arbeit Macht Frei*.

10. Aleksandr Solzhenitsyn, *One Day in the Life of Ivan Denisovich* (New York: Bantam Books, 1963), p. 17. Solzhenitsyn's *The Gulag Archipelago* was begun in 1958, the same year Elie Wiesel's *Night* was first published in France. Like Wiesel's book, Solzhenitsyn's claimed eyewitness testimony. However, Solzhenitsyn's massive tome was also supported by the reports, memoirs, and letters of 227 fellow witnesses. Despite its mammoth undertaking as an experiment in literary investigation, covering a 38-year period (1918 – 1956) of torture and murder by the Soviet system, Solzhenitsyn's book did not receive a Nobel Peace Prize, nor was Solzhenitsyn honored with the United States Congressional Gold Medal, the Medal of Liberty, the Presidential Medal of Freedom, the rank of Grand-Croix in the French Legion of Honor, nor an honorary Knighthood from Her Majesty, Queen Elizabeth II of Britain.

11. Cited in *Never Forget: Christian and Jewish Perspectives on Edith Stein*, Waltraud Herbstrith, OCD, Editor, translated by Susanne Batzdorff (Washington, D.C.: ICS Publications, 1998), p. 111. The statement is cited by Friedrich Georg Friedmann (in his article "Not Like That! On the Beatification of Edith Stein"), as taken from the third edition of Sr. Waltraud Herbstrith's book *Das wahre Gesicht Edith Steins*.

12. A "section" in the French scheme of things – Elie's book was translated from the French by Stella Rodway – is equivalent to our American platoon, roughly 50 men. Fifty men would be hard-pressed to surround ten thousand men at three pace intervals, unless, of course, the ten thousand were themselves hard-pressed!

13. The exact quote from *Exodus* 32:12 reads: "Turn from thy fierce wrath, and repent of this evil against thy people." Truly, is there anyone but Jews who presume to tell God to repent of evil?

14. In *One Day in the Life of Ivan Denisovich*, Solzhenitsyn mentions how "Shukhov" (Ivan Denisovich) dreams of getting sick enough to go to the hospital for a few weeks "even if the soup they gave you was a little thin..." (ibid., p. 23). And this was after the war with no special rationing.

15. See *Anatomy of the Auschwitz Death Camp*, edited by Yisrael Gutman and Michael Berenbaum, Indiana University Press, 1994, p. 174.

16. Elie tells us at the bottom of page 78 that he would learn after the war how those who stayed behind were "quite simply" liberated by the Russians two days after the evacuation.

17. Knowing scripture, possibly Elie and his father were also remembering how the Jews had believed themselves traduced during the sojourn in the wilderness of Sin, where the people of Israel murmured against Moses and Aaron saying, "Would that we had died by the hand of the Lord in the land of Egypt, when we sat by the fleshpots and ate bread to the full; for you have brought us out into this wilderness to kill this whole assembly with hunger" (*Exodus*, 16:3). Now, to be fed, they will go into the wilderness with the Germans, not remain according to their own devices and wait for the bread of the Russians.

18. *You Only Live Once*, MGM 1937, directed by Fritz Lang.

19. See especially Carolyn Yeager's "Night # 1 and Night #2 - What Changes were Made and Why, Part One and Part Two." Online: http://www.eliewieseltattoo.com/night-1-and-night-2—what-changes-were-made-and-why-part-one-2/ and http://www.eliewieseltattoo.com/night-1-and-night-2—what-changes-were-made-and-why-part-two/.

20. Aleksandr Solzhenitsyn, *One Day in the Life of Ivan Denisovich* (New York: Bantam Books, 1963) p. 28.

REVIEW

Hitler's Austria 1938-1945: Popular Sentiment in the Nazi Era

by Evan Burr Bukey, University of North Carolina Press, Chapel Hill, N. C., 2000, 320 pp.

Ezra MacVie

In 1938, if you were an Austrian over forty, you, or your brothers, husband, sons, had fought on the losing side of the Great War, and seen the former Austro-Hungarian empire cut up after the war into a dozen or more sovereign pieces, leaving a tiny rump state behind made up of the former Imperial capital Vienna and neighboring Alpine regions encompassing a few nearby towns a fraction of the capital's size. The fate of Hungary was quite similar, while the fate of co-lingual Germany to the north was far less drastic, leaving a Germanic "big brother" that retained a good deal of its previous potentialities among nations. If you were under forty, your parents and grandparents had witnessed these events, and they, along with your teachers, bosses, and mentors, had ineluctably conveyed to you a visceral awareness of these changes they had experienced.

You had undergone the straitening effects of the blockade by the victorious Allies that extended beyond the War well into 1919 and particularly if you lived, as most Austrians did, in Vienna, you noted the great influx of refugees—Jews dominant among them—from areas to the east that had suddenly been stripped of the protections of minorities enforced from the defunct Imperial court in the capital. You may even have seen them as aggravating the privations you were already experiencing before their arrival, that extended after the War even, as you might have supposed, to the present year of 1938. If you paid attention to such matters, you were even aware that the terms imposed by the Allies upon both Germany and Austria for relief from the wartime strictures that the Allies had maintained long past the armistice included the prohibition of a union of Austria with its big Germanic brother to the north.

Adolf Hitler in Vienna with Arthur Seyß-Inquart, 1938. Bundesarchiv, Bild 119-5243 / CC-BY-SA [CC-BY-SA-3.0-de (http://creativecommons.org/licenses/by-sa/3.0/de/deed.en)], via Wikimedia Commons

But then, in 1933, you likely had noticed the ascent to power in the government of Germany of a native son of Austria, one Adolf Hitler, born just this side of the border in Braunau am Inn, to parents quite as Austrian as the others who inhabited the tiny remnant of the former

Hapsburg hegemony. This Hitler was not only Austrian, having spent major portions of his youth in Linz and Vienna, but his National Socialist Workers' Party even set about very openly repressing the Jewish minority in Germany, which was far less obtrusive there than it was in Vienna and thus, in all the national affairs of Austria. Hitler's party, in fact, had its Austrian cousin, and along with union with "the rest" of Germania, this party advocated—occasionally brutally—repression of Those Jews who had attained such prominence in both the affairs, professions, and even the neighborhoods of Vienna. And these Fascists, of course, constituted by far the most-powerful resistance to a scourge that appeared to draw its own potency from among those very Jews, communism.

This, in compressed form, is the setting from which Evan Burr Bukey explores the *Anschluss*, the incorporation of Austria into the Third Reich, that Hitler effected in May 1938 by ordering the German Army to march across its border with Austria to face cheering throngs throwing flowers and kisses in their path. He continues his analysis from the antecedents of this event all the way to the end of the Second War, to the point at which Austria, in common with Germany, was invaded and conquered from both east and west by the onrushing Allies. His study is nuanced, imbued with what seems a profound understanding of the contexts experienced by the many actors in the drama, and on every point, scrupulously detached in a way that exemplifies the very highest ideals of academic inquiry.

Testimony to his rigor might be inferred (or, might be doubted) from the fact that this book proudly bears on its back cover the inscription, "Winner of the 2000 National Jewish Book Award, Holocaust Category, Jewish Book Council." Close reading of its content, however, powerfully yields the conclusion that Bukey has portrayed the vast and complex waves of emotion and reaction that swept across the populace of Austria from 1938 to 1945 in as fair, yet informative, a manner as can be imagined in these times that are still so charged with emotion and outright connivance regarding what was said, thought, and done—and by whom, and to whom—in those times and places.

Bukey's task was made harder—inestimably harder—not only by the detritus of wartime propaganda that still today grossly distorts the public's understanding and feelings regarding the actors in the story, but by the stupendous destruction of both witnesses and records that the events encompassed and by the various forms of repression subsequently visited and maintained on those who had survived the events. Accordingly, the author's sources tend in the main not to be eyewitnesses, neither named nor anonymous, but rather, reports filed and remaining intact to the present from officials both visible and covert whose job it was to monitor public feeling in Austria and convey information about it to government headquarters, chiefly in Berlin. While this approach could be seen as limiting the scope of discovery in certain ineffable ways, it can at the same time be seen as capturing an objectivity at least on the present scholar's part that would seem hard to match via any other possible approach.

The result, while virtually irreproachable from an evidential standpoint, is anything but dry—rather, it is *credible*. The author's insights, while measured and subtle, imbue the result with a momentum and urgency that approach those of a rousing mystery novel, for all that every reader already knows how the story ends. Exactly *how*, by what path, the Austrian people got to the end is the compelling thrust of the account.

That path, of course, was different for every Austrian, and while Bukey does not, as more-popular authors sometimes do, trace the entire arc of experience for any individual real or imagined, he nonetheless provides a "branching" of viewpoints that always exists among populations as variegated as that of 1930s Austria was. He identifies and describes factions, interests, and perspectives as they must have existed among the various communities constituted by the people who inhabited the territory of Austria in the period in question, even to the extent of including prisoners of war, concentration-camp inmates, and German refugees in Austria from the Allied bombing campaigns that affected particularly western Germany so much more than Austria during the course of the war.

He arrives at certain conclusions, which seem to arise not so much from the author's special understandings as from the content itself, and these number two.

First, the modal animosity of Austrians against Jews was greater, even, than that found or aroused among the people of Germany of the time. Reasons for this arise from the material itself; Bukey finds little need to explore the question explicitly.

Second, while the Austrians' devotion to the National Socialist Party waxed and waned during the period in question along with their sanguinity regarding Germany's quest for *Lebensraum* at the time, the faith most Austrians put in their native son in Berlin seems to have held steady in a way conspicuously at variance with their other inclinations. Reasons for this would seem ineluctable—sheer desperation comes to the fore, at least in this reader's mind. Hitler's mystique seems to have had more power in Austria even than it had in the country whose government he gained control of in 1933.

This book may be the definitive study of the Führer's reception in the country where his birthplace happened to be. For anyone interested in that subject, this book is not only indispensable, but it may even be exhaustive.

Volume IV

Number 3, Fall 2012

EDITORIAL

Imprisoned at Ellis Island

Richard A. Widmann

On December 23, 1991, President George H. W. Bush issued proclamation 6398 to recognize National Ellis Island Day. His proclamation began:

> "The ethnic diversity that we so proudly celebrate in the United States mirrors our rich heritage as a Nation of immigrants. 'Here is not merely a Nation,' wrote Walt Whitman, 'but a teeming nation of nations. . . . Here is the hospitality which forever indicates heroes.' One of the greatest symbols of American hospitality stands at Ellis Island in Upper New York Bay."[1]

Bush went on to call America's history, "a story of immigrants."[2] Indeed, according to the Ellis Island Website, "Ellis Island is the symbol of American immigration and the immigrant experience."[3] There can be no doubt that Ellis Island has become a part of the contemporary American mythos. There is an incredible irony however about this symbol of hospitality and liberty — Ellis Island was used as a detention center for Germans and Italians during the Second World War.

In a stark example of inconvenient history, an investigation into the use and function of the facility at Ellis Island undoubtedly results in critical questions about our freedoms, our conduct of war, and even the treatment of ethnic and religious minorities by Americans.

Ellis Island, a small island in New York Harbor, was designated as the site of the first Federal immigration station by President Benjamin Harrison in 1890.[4] It officially opened its doors on January 1, 1892. Ellis Island became the nation's premier federal immigration station. It remained in operation until 1954. During this time, the station processed over 12 million immigrant steamship passengers. The island was made part of the Statue of Liberty National Monument in 1965, and has hosted a museum of immigration since 1990.[5] The main building was restored after 30 years of abandonment and opened as a museum on September 10, 1990.[6]

Immigrants view the Statue of Liberty from Ellis Island. National Archives photo. Public domain.

During the 1940s however, Ellis Island served another purpose—it was the location of an internment camp that held about 8,000 German, Italian, and Japanese U.S. citizens, naturalized citizens, and resident foreigners.[7] Ellis Island also served as a way station for those being transferred to and from other internment camps and for those awaiting deportation, repatriation, or expatriation.[8] At the time, Ellis Island was the perfect prison – easily guarded and reachable only by boat.

While the story of the internment of Japanese-Americans has become more widely known, it remains a largely untold tale that Germans and Italians were interned in at least forty-six locations in the United States during World War Two including Ellis Island.[9]

Internment Camp at Crystal City, Texas. Japanese, Germans, and Italians were rounded up and transferred to dozens of US camps including this one. Public domain.

The majority of aliens arrested in New York and New Jersey were first taken to Ellis Island. According to a 2003 *New York Times* article,

> *"Letters show that the Attorney General's office expected to arrest 600 people from New York and 200 from New Jersey per month and hold them on Ellis Island. On Dec. 8, 1941, the day*

> *after the [Pearl Harbor] attack, the roundup began. Internees were housed in the baggage and dormitory building behind the Great Hall."*[10]

The Ellis Island Reception center held people whose loyalty was in question. Of those interned, there was evidence that some had pro-Axis sympathies. Many others were interned based on weak evidence or unsubstantiated accusations of which they were never told or had little power to refute.[11] During the first two years of the war, Ellis Island was used primarily as a transit and holding camp. By January 1943, the population of German internees had stabilized at about 350 enemy aliens and their dependents. Upon arrival prisoners would have their clothes replaced with a pair of American army shoes, khaki socks, shirt, and underwear.

How did this come to pass?

In 1940, the Alien Registration Act was passed requiring all aliens aged 14 and older to register with the US government. On Dec. 7, 1941, pursuant to the Alien Enemy Act of 1798, Roosevelt issued three Presidential Proclamations 2525–2526 and 2527 branding German, Italian and Japanese nationals as enemy aliens, authorizing internment and travel and property ownership restrictions. A blanket presidential warrant authorized U.S. Attorney General Francis Biddle to have the FBI arrest a large number of *"dangerous enemy aliens"* based on the Custodial Detention Index. Hundreds of German aliens were arrested by the end of the day. The FBI raided many homes and hundreds more were detained *before* war was declared on Germany on December 11.[12]

On January 14, 1942, the Attorney General issued regulations pursuant to Presidential Proclamations 2525-2527 and 2537 requiring application for and issuance of certificates of identification to all *"enemy aliens"* aged 14 and older and outlining restrictions on their movement and property ownership rights. Approximately one million enemy aliens reregistered, including 300,000 German-born aliens, the second largest immigrant group at that time. Applications were forwarded to the Department of Justice's Alien Registration Division and the FBI. Any change of address, employment or name had to be reported to the FBI. Enemy aliens were prohibited from entering federally designated restricted areas. If enemy aliens violated these or other applicable regulations, they were subject to "arrest, detention and internment for the duration of the war."[13]

U.S. President Franklin D. Roosevelt issued the now infamous Executive Order 9066 on February 19, 1942 authorizing the Secretary of War to prescribe certain areas as military zones. Eventually, EO 9066 cleared the way for the incarceration of Japanese Americans, as well as Italian Americans and German Americans in internment camps. In total, 10,905 people of German ancestry were interned, along with 3,278 people of Italian ancestry not counting spouses and children who voluntarily joined internees.[14,15]

While the United States has officially apologized for its treatment of Japanese-Americans for their relocation and imprisonment during the war, we are apparently reluctant to apologize to the German and Italian internees. President Gerald Ford rescinded Executive Order 9066 on February 19, 1976. In 1980, President Jimmy Carter signed legislation to create the Commission on Wartime Relocation and Internment of Civilians (CWRIC). The CWRIC was appointed to conduct an official governmental study of Executive Order 9066, related wartime orders, and their impact on Japanese Americans in the West.

In December 1982, the CWRIC issued its findings in *Personal Justice Denied*, concluding that the wholesale incarceration of Japanese Americans had not been justified by military necessity. The report determined that the decision to incarcerate was based on "race prejudice, war hysteria, and a failure of political leadership." The Commission recommended legislative remedies consisting of an official apology and redress payments of $20,000 to each of the survivors; a public education fund was set up to help ensure that this would not happen again (Public Law 100-383).

On November 21, 1989, President Bush signed an appropriation bill authorizing payments to be paid out between 1990 and 1998. In 1990, surviving internees began to receive individual redress payments and a letter of apology. This bill only applied to the Japanese Americans. German Americans and other European Americans received neither the apology nor the recompense.[16]

While there was no evidence of a military necessity for the incarceration of German, Italian, or Japanese Americans during World War Two, we are faced with a similar situation today, only this time with Arab and Muslim internees. President Obama came into office in 2009 promising to shut down the Guantanamo Bay detention camp and end the extra-judicial system that President George W.

Bush had created to imprison terrorist suspects without trial, often without even filing charges.

On New Year's Eve 2011, President Obama signed his name to the National Defense Authorization Act for Fiscal Year 2012. Buried in this act are provisions that appear to allow indefinite military detention of American terrorism suspects, and to require it of suspected foreign enemies. The Obama administration insists the law merely codifies existing standards, but its strong supporters and vehement opponents are sure it does much more, legally enshrining for the first time in 60 years the authority to hold citizens without trial.[17]

Americans like to think of the Second World War in strict terms of good and evil. It is difficult to consider that our political leadership was making decisions based on "race prejudice" and "war hysteria." And yet that was the determination of the CWRIC. When will the lessons of the past be applied to contemporary political events? When will we realize that the Greatest Generation was not so different from our own—complete with blemishes and warts. It is quite simple to criticize and attack the actions of the vanquished—long-dead enemies and regimes. It is far more difficult to acknowledge that history is always written by the victors.

Notes:

1. Online: http://www.presidency.ucsb.edu/ws/?pid=20385#axzz1snF2DaLC
2. Ibid.
3. Online: http://www.ellisisland.org
4. Online: http://www.ellisisland.org/genealogy/ellis_island_history.asp
5. Online: http://en.wikipedia.org/wiki/Ellis_island
6. Online: http://www.thestatueofliberty.com/ellis_island.html
7. Online: http://ephemeralnewyork.wordpress.com/2011/01/31/the-world-war-ii-internment-camp-on-ellis-island/
8. Online: http://www.foitimes.com/internment/Ellis.htm
9. Arnold Krammer, *Undue Process: The Untold Story of America's German Alien Internees*, Rowman & Littlefield Publishers, Inc., New York, 1997, p.83.
10. Online: http://ephemeralnewyork.wordpress.com/2011/01/31/the-world-war-ii-internment-camp-on-ellis-island/
11. Online: http://www.archives.gov/research/immigration/enemy-aliens-overview.html
12. Online: http://www.issuesandalibis.org/campsa.html

13. Online: http://www.issuesandalibis.org/campsa.html
14. Online: http://en.wikipedia.org/wiki/Executive_Order_9066
15. Krammer, op. cit., p.171.
16. Online: http://en.wikipedia.org/wiki/Executive_Order_9066
17. Online: http://www.huffingtonpost.com/2012/01/11/guantanamo-bay-10th-anniversary-indefinite-detention-american-citizens_n_1197547.html

Count Potocki de Montalk and the Katyn Manifesto

K.R. Bolton

At the time when the USSR was fighting alongside the Allied powers against the Axis, any mention of the atrocities and aggression of the Soviet Union was considered to be seditious and liable to place the exponent of such ideas on the black list of suspected 'collaborators' and 'fifth columnists'. Hence, what eventually became the most infamous of the Soviet atrocities during World War II, the so-called 'Katyn Massacre' of 15,000 Polish Army officers at Katyn Forest by the Soviet invaders in 1940,[1] was prohibited from discussion. Among the first in an Allied state to defy this censorship and risk the consequences was a highly eccentric New Zealand-born poet and claimant to the throne of Poland, Geoffrey Potocki de Montalk, who was residing in England during the war.[2]

Potocki was, in contrast to most of the others of the New Zealand literati, decidedly of the 'Right', and in particular he was a Royalist.[3] His opposition to Communism brought him closer to sympathy for Germany during World War II, and although his loyalty was to the Poland of his noble ancestors, whence his claim to the Throne, he demanded a negotiated peace with Germany with the expectation that a result might be the return of Poland's territorial integrity. Despite this pro-German orientation, Potocki enjoyed the confidence of Poles in exile in England during the war.

Allied Cover-Up

When on April 13, 1943 German radio announced the finding of mass graves of Polish officers in Katyn Forest, near Smolensk, the Allies knew the Soviets were responsible. Prime Minister Churchill had believed from the start that the Russians had been guilty at Katyn, and wrote of his feelings long afterward.[4] The British ambassador to Poland, Owen O'Malley, reported when the discovery was first made, his view of Soviet guilt, writing in a report that 'we have, in fact, perforce used the good name of England to cover up the massacre'.[5] 'But such views could not be admitted to the people in wartime, and O'Malley's messages were kept secret until the official records were opened thirty years later. The governments of Britain and the United States proclaimed at the time of the German discovery that it was all a monstrous lie'.[6] The British ambassador in Moscow also considered Katyn to be Russia's responsibility, and that the Soviet break with the Polish government-in-exile over the matter had been done to cover up their guilt.[7] The only Allied newspaper to carry the story about Katyn from the start and to doubt the Soviet protests of German guilt was the *Chicago Tribune*. The other major press ignored the story as far as possible, before adopting the line that it was German propaganda.[8] On April 20, 1943, the Allied press took up the Soviet line that the Polish Government-in-exile was in collusion with Germany in blaming the USSR for Katyn. *Time* claimed that the Poles had 'promptly remembered' that the Polish officers had been missing for three years, and that the Germans had 'planted' the story.[9] The USSR made this a pretext for breaking off diplomatic relations with the Polish exile government based in England.[10]

French Ambassador Fernand de Brinon visits the place of the mass murder in the forest of Katyn accompanied by German officers. April 1943. Bundesarchiv, Bild 183-J15385 / CC-BY-SA [CC-BY-SA-3.0-de (http://creativecommons.org/licenses/by-sa/3.0/de/deed.en)], via Wikimedia Commons

Potocki

Churchill had pressured General Wladislaw Sikorski, prime minister of the Polish government-in-exile, to withdraw a request for a Red Cross inquiry into the massacre.[11] However the Germans established their own commission of inquiry, which included representatives from the Polish underground, a Polish medical team, and scientists and medical men from twelve occupied and neutral countries, including Switzerland.[12]

Despite the high-level Allied pressure, the Polish government-in-exile charged that 15,000 Polish soldiers and civilians captured by the Russians were missing.[13] *The Washington Post* even ridiculed the Polish government-in-exile as being composed of 'reactionary and feudal' individuals, although most, states Colby, had working-class or peasant backgrounds.[14]

On Easter Day 1983, Geoffrey Potocki de Montalk, writing from Switzerland, reissued his 1943 'Katyn Manifesto', with a preface, and entitled these combined documents the 'Second Katyn Manifesto',[15] in reaction to a letter that had been published in *The Press*, Christchurch, New Zealand, stating that Katyn had been committed by the Germans.

The Polish government-in-exile in regard to Katyn was only permitted to publish the facts about Katyn in Polish, therefore leaving the English-speaking public unaware of the Soviet responsibility for the massacre. It fell to Potocki to correct this.

Writing his preface in 1983 to the 'Katyn Manifesto' that Potocki had distributed forty years earlier, he recounted that he was 'the only person during the war to print and publish the facts in England in English, in Our Katyn Manifesto on 13th May 1943…'[16] Potocki held the 'English government of the time and their Polish lackeys, the so-called Polish government in exile', to have been complicit in the Katyn cover-up. 'The English authorities did everything in their power to prevent the Poles from hiring a hall to discuss the situation', but the Roman Catholic Church 'broke this boycott' and permitted the use of Westminster Cathedral for a public meeting. The authorities were also unable to prevent the hire of Caxton Hall, where a meeting on Katyn was attended by Potocki in 'velvet cap and silver white Eagle', 'scowling' because of the failure of the meeting to have played the Polish anthem'.[17] Potocki continues:

> *No one in the Kingdom except Ourself*[18] *printed anything of the truth about Katyn in English: but the Poles were allowed to print all details in Polish (that is, after Dr Goebbels's broadcast,*

> *13 April, not before) because the English government, being as cunning as they are unwise, could realize that no one could read it except Poles (who knew the truth only too well) and a few spies: and it would and did give the numerous Poles in exile the totally false impression that their so-called government in exile was genuine from a Polish point of view, when in reality they were nothing but a group of highly paid lackeys of the English Secret Service.[19]*

Potocki continued in his scathing attitude towards the compliance of the Polish government-in-exile, calling them 'slaves', 'who had sold their souls for money and for prestige', for not having printed a word in English about Katyn 'to alert the more honest English'.[20] He was contemptuous of their cowardice, asking 'what of it' if they might have been jailed for publishing an expose, as he – 'the Claimant of the Polish Throne' - and his 'inoffensive French wife' had been. As for the possibility of a Katyn expose prejudicing the war, 'what of it?' he asked again.

Potocki had a lifelong involvement with printing limited-edition booklets of his poetry and manifestos on many issues, including a journal called *Right Review*, which he continued to print sporadically for decades after the war. Just as he had circumvented censorship on some of his more risqué poetry, he printed the 'Katyn Manifesto' on his own press, thereby, 'not asking the permission of any English nobody to publish anything'.[21]

In May 1943 Potocki printed thousands of copies of the 'Katyn Manifesto', addressed as a 'Proclamation to the English, the Poles, the Germans and the jews' (sic).[22]

Potocki had shortly before sought out the opinion of the Duke of Bedford, a proponent of a negotiated peace with Germany, in regard to rumours circulating among Polish exiles about the execution of thousands of Poles by the Soviet invaders, which had allegedly taken place in 1940. Bedford replied:

> *Your Majesty*
> *At the moment I am not quite sure where, by reason of my unpopularity, I should really be able to do much to help the Polish cause... What you say is confirmed by what more than one friend has told me of conversations with Poles in the Country.*

> *Very many seem to hate and fear Russia, even more than they hate and fear Germany, and consider that the Russian treatment of Polish prisoners has been more ruthless. Considerably more than a year ago a Polish officer told a friend of mine that the Russians had kept alive the private soldiers among the prisoners captured, but all the officers had disappeared and he believed that they had been murdered. The statement in the German propaganda seems now to confirm his supposition in a rather sinister fashion.*
> *Yours very truly, Bedford.*[23]

Stephanie de Montalk, writing the biography of her cousin sixty years later, recounts in a chapter entitled 'Katyn' that the Count had told her that, 'On 4 May 1943, Poles in London had requested Potocki's help in exposing the atrocity'.[24] Stephanie de Montalk states that on May 13th thousands of copies were run off Potocki's platen press and he went up to London and handed out the manifesto, with the help of Poles.[25]

Potocki was soon placed under surveillance, questions were asked in Parliament, and he was attacked by the press, including the Communist Party's *Daily Worker*, which described the manifesto as 'poisonous filth',[26] calling Potocki a 'crazy Fascist Count'. It was at this time that Potocki was jailed for 'insufficient black-out',[27] recalling that he arrived at the jail 'dressed like Richard II'.[28] After release he was ordered by the Ministry of Labour to serve six months in an agricultural camp in Northumberland, which he attended as a preference to conscription, adorned with his royal attire. After a month he told the camp manager he was leaving, and went.

Katyn Manifesto

Potocki's 'Katyn Manifesto' shows the extent to which the facts were known by the Poles in exile. Potocki in printing the manifesto for wide distribution also took the opportunity to announce his plan for a post-war settlement. This served as a preamble to the Katyn material, beginning:

> *We have consulted a fair number of Poles in London including some of considerable importance and our finding is that they are unanimous in holding that the Bolsheviks*[29] *and not the Germans, murdered the Polish officers at Katyn (and many*

other Poles as well). We have been asked by certain of the Poles we have talked with, to use our influence as a half English Pole to insist that the English look at the facts in the face and recognize that it was the Bolsheviks who committed this loathsome crime.[30]

Potocki was irritated by the insistence of Poles - presumably the government-in-exile – that he should not publish anything that would 'annoy the soviets', (surely an impossible task if one is exposing the Katyn Massacre) or to 'harm the cause of Poland', Potocki explaining: 'by which they plainly mean ("the cause of Poles in England") and in particular we have been begged 1. not to claim any soviet territory and 2. not to demand severance of diplomatic relations with the USSR'.[31] To Potocki the requests were short-sighted and cowardly, and failed to take account of the '30,000,000 Poles in Poland, beside the generations of Poles yet unborn!', stating:

> *We cannot see how the soviets can be regarded otherwise than as the worst possible, and most irreducible enemy of Poland; a soviet Poland would be the same as no Poland and a Poland with a powerful soviet neighbour would live in misery and fear and would be in perpetual risk of ultimate liquidations.*
>
> *Not only the English, but the Poles in England, must look the facts in the face. We wish to know why the bolsheviks may claim Polish lands, while the Poles may not claim lands formerly stolen from Poland by Russians and why the bolsheviks may break off diplomatic relations with Polish officials and these Poles may not retaliate'.*[32]

Potocki next listed his plan for the post-war reorganisation of Europe as it related mainly to Poland and the USSR, reflecting primarily his Royalist principles, beginning with the declaration that there is 'no such thing as soviet land. Russian land belongs to the Tsar'. The lands that are claimed as 'soviet' are 'fundamentally Polish', including those further East, which are 'fiefs of the Polish crown'. Potocki stated that diplomatic relations with the USSR are unacceptable for any 'civilized government' and doubted the 'sanity' of the Germans in regard to the former Russo-German Pact. His final point was that the defeat of England and Poland in the war would be better 'from every point of view, whether spiritual or material', than a victory over Germany won 'in common with the USSR'.[33] After this four-point plan he listed the 'facts about Katyn', which follow verbatim:

1. *Though the USSR occupied half Poland on the pretence of "saving" the Poles from the Germans, they took away vast quantities of the population, terrorised the remainder, and, according to the "Red Star" (17th Sept. 1940) treated 181,000 soldiers as prisoners of war, including about 10,000 officers.*
2. *According to proofs in the hands of the Polish administration in London, in November 1939 the great concentration camps were organised. At the beginning of 1940, the soviet authorities informed the prisoners that the camps were to be liquidated, so that they would be able to return home. For this purpose lists were made. At the time there were in the camps:-*
    At Kozielsk 5000, of whom 4500 were officers.
    At Starobielsk 3920, all officers except about 100 civilians. Nearly 400 were doctors.
    At Otaszków 6570, of whom 380 were officers, the rest largely police.
3. *On the 5th April 1940 the liquidation of the camps began, and every few days from 60 to 300 persons were taken away. From Kozielsk they were taken in the direction of Smolensk.*
4. *According to the Polish-soviet pacts of 30th July 1941 and 14th August 1941, a Polish army was to be formed and it was taken for granted that the above-mentioned officers would form the cadres. By the end of August no officers had turned up from Kozielsk, Starobielsk, or Otaszków, except 400 prisoners who had been removed to Griazowiec, and some who had been removed to common prisons. In all 8300 officers were missing, besides 7000 petty officers, soldiers, and civilians from these three camps.*
5. *On the 6th October 1941 the Polish Ambassador Kot and General Anders applied to the soviet authorities to know what had become of them, and were informed by Wyszinski, Deputy People's Commissar for Foreign Affairs, that all prisoners of war had been liberated and therefore were free.*
6. *In October and November Ambassador Kot repeatedly took up with "Stalin", Molotoff, and Wyszinski, the question of these prisoners and demanded copies of the lists, which had been carefully prepared by the soviets.*
7. *On the 3rd December General Sikorski took up the matter at Moscow in conversation with "Stalin", and in view of the failure of the soviet officials to supply copies of their lists. Handed to "Stalin" a partial list of 3845 names put together*

>   by some of their fellow-prisoners. "Stalin" assured Sikorski
>   that they had all been set free. An additional list of 800 names
>   was handed to "Stalin" by General Anders on the 18th
>   March 1942, but not a single one of these men reached the
>   Polish Army.
>   8. Count Raczynski also took the matter up with "Ambassador"
>   Bogomolow, who, in a note dated 13th March 1942, once
>   more assured that all the prisoners, whether civil or military,
>   had been freed.
>   9. Neither the Polish administration in London, nor the Polish
>   ambassador in Russia, has ever received any answer as to the
>   whereabouts of the officers and other prisoners removed from
>   these three camps aforementioned.
>
>   *These facts were mainly translated from the* Dziennik Polski, *and were confirmed to us personally by a high Polish official. In these circumstances how can any person in his right mind accept the Bolshevik version, to the effect that "the Germans did it"?*
>
>   *We are not aware that the Germans have ever, in their history, done such a thing, whereas the soviets have printed boasts of equally wicked crimes.*
>
>   *How is it the USSR have only now discovered, after the German announcement, that these prisoners were sent to work at Smolensk and were captured by the Germans?*
>
>   *Neither Poland, nor England, have any right to be allied to such a government.*
>
>   *It is high time for a negotiated Peace, in which we hope the Germans will be persuaded to display a proper regard for the rights of Poland. Poland and Hungary to be united according to our map*[34] *(with possible concessions to the Germans); the jews to be helped if they will even at this late hour repent and behave themselves; the Tsar to be restored in Russia and the King in France.*[35]

Inconvenient Poles

The betrayal of Poland by the USA and Britain to the USSR was a standing embarrassment and the public could not be permitted to compare this to the acclaimed war aims of the Allies, and specifically Britain's ostensible reason for declaring war on Germany over the Polish issue. Katyn had to be put down the 'Memory Hole'.

One of the most ignoble actions of Britain towards Poland came after the war when the official Victory Parade was held in London on June

8th 1946. Bernard Smith, (whose book carries a foreword by Irena R Anders, widow of Lieutenant General W Anders, commander of the free Polish Army) states that 'the Polish forces, who had been the first in Europe to fight the Germans, were not asked to take part' in the Victory Parade. Twenty-five airmen, representing the Polish crews who had played a significant part in the Battle of Britain, were invited to take part, but refused, because of the ban on the participation of the Polish Army.[36] Even in 1976, the British Government would not send a representative to attend the unveiling of the Katyn Memorial in London and, moreover, members of the armed forces were forbidden to attend in uniform.[37] Such an enduring attitude towards the Poles and Poland by Britain begs the question, which vested interests do not want asked: was the declaration of war on Germany in 1939, supposedly in defence of Poland, no more than a pretext for going to war, and was intended to hide wider issues?

The facts bought out by Potocki to the English-speaking public in 1943 were not conceded by the USSR until 1990. Stephanie de Montalk, in writing the biography of her cousin, states that when he told her about the Katyn Massacre in 1983, i.e., the year that he republished the 'Katyn Manifesto', she had 'regarded his account with some scepticism', stating that her own efforts at finding out about Katyn were 'inconclusive'.[38] She writes, citing what Potocki told her in 1983:

> *It was not until June 1995 that I discovered from reports in the press the wartime intelligence reports, sealed for fifty years after the war, confirmed not only the full horror of the atrocity, but also Potocki's belief at the time that the British Government had been aware of the massacre. The official line had been 'to pretend that the whole affair had been a fake' and that the Government had believed: 'this is obviously the most convenient attitude to adopt, and, if adopted consistently enough, will doubtless receive universal acceptance'. The reason was that 'any other view would have been most distasteful to the public since it could be inferred that we were allied to a power guilty of the same sort of atrocities as the Germans'. The Soviet Union had also emphatically denied Germany's assertions that it was responsible for the massacre, and continued to do so until 1990, when KGB archives revealed irrefutable evidence that it had been carried out on the direct orders of Stalin.*[39]

While British reluctance to disclose the facts seems to have been as persistent as that of the USSR, the US Congress initiated an enquiry in September 1951. The US authorities had known of the Katyn Massacre in 1943, as two American prisoners of war had been among the team taken by the Germans to inspect the execution site at Katyn Forest. The senior officer, Colonel John H. Van Vliet, handed a report on the matter to Major General Clayton Bissell, assistant chief of staff in charge of Army Intelligence, in May 1945. This was suppressed and Van Vliet was ordered to stay quiet. Van Vliet prepared a second report in 1950. The Congressional enquiry concluded that the report had been removed or destroyed. The Congressional investigation took two years, heard 81 witnesses, and unanimously found that the Poles had been murdered by the Soviets in the spring of 1940. The number of bodies found at Katyn Forest only amounted to 4,143, who had been prisoners at the Kozielsk camp, yet the committee concluded that the total number of Poles taken from the camps and executed amounted to approximately 15,400.[40] Potocki's publication in 1943 of the estimate of '8300 officers ... besides 7000 petty officers, soldiers, and civilians from these three camps',[41] had been accurate.

Why had the USA reversed its position on the Katyn cover-up from 1950 while the British authorities remained mute? Firstly, the primary reason advanced for Britain's having declared war on Germany was over the issue of Polish sovereignty, and the myth had to be maintained that the USSR had been invading 'liberators', otherwise British duplicity would become apparent. Secondly, the USA had entered the war for reasons other than Poland, and in the post-1945 world Stalin had become the 'new Hitler', much like today any number of US obstacles to global hegemony – such as Saddam Hussein or Milosevic – are transformed into 'new Hitlers'. Rather than a 'new world order', as it is now called, emerging in the aftermath of World War II, in which the old empires would be eliminated in the spirit of 'free trade',[42] and the USSR would serve as a junior partner in a US-dominated post-war world, Stalin rebuffed the USA's overtures and he ceased being 'Uncle Joe.' Specifically, the USSR had rejected the two foundations for a US-dominated world order:

- The USSR rejected the American plan for the United Nations General Assembly to serve as a world parliament, in which the USSR would be out-voted, and instead insisted that authority be vested with the UN Security Council, with member states having

the right to veto any decision; thereby making the United Nations Organization null and void as a potential basis for a world government, and
- The USSR rejected the 'Baruch Plan' for the 'internationalisation' of nuclear energy under UN auspices, which the USSR again regarded as giving de facto authority to the USA.[43]

As Benjamin Colby comments in relation to Katyn and the new post-war world situation: 'It was not until the United States found itself fighting a war in Korea against an army trained, equipped and supplied by Russia, that an official effort was made to reveal the facts of Katyn. At long last the whitewash was to be stripped away'.[44] Katyn could now be used as Cold War propaganda against the USA's former wartime ally. As for the Soviet Union's eventual admission of guilt in 1990, this was a time when the new rulers of Russia embarked on an altogether different path: that of de-sovietising the USSR,[45] dismantling the Warsaw Bloc, and bringing Russia into the type of 'brave new world'[46] that Stalin had rejected in 1945. The release of the facts about Katyn was serving a new political agenda in Russia, just as their suppression had served an agenda of a different type during World War II. Katyn shows that, like the recent and present allegations of 'war crimes' in Kosovo and Syria respectively, such allegations are publicized or suppressed selectively, in the cynical pursuit of political agendas, and seldom have any regard for truth.

Notes:

1. Joseph Bishop, 'Katyn: Unanswered Questions', *Inconvenient History*, Vol. 3, No. 2, http://www.inconvenienthistory.com/archive/2010/volume_2/number_3/ katyn_unanswered_questions.php
2. K. R. Bolton, 'Geoffrey Potocki de Montalk: New Zealand Poet, Polish King and "Good European"', *Counter-Currents*, August 2010, Three Parts, http://www.counter-currents.com/2010/08/count-potocki-de-montalk-part-i/
3. ibid., Part II, http://www.counter-currents.com/2010/08/count-potocki-de-montalk-part-ii/
4. Benjamin Colby, *'Twas a Famous Victory: Deception and Propaganda in the War with Germany* (New York: Arlington House Publishers, 1974), p. 65.
5. *Time*, July 17, 1972, cited by Colby, ibid.
6. Colby, ibid.
7. Ibid., p. 68.
8. Ibid., pp. 70-74.
9. *Time*, April 26, 1943, cited by Colby, ibid., p. 71.

10. Colby, ibid.
11. Ibid., p, 68.
12. Ibid.
13. Ibid., p. 71.
14. Ibid., p. 72.
15. Geoffrey Potocki de Montalk, 'Second Katyn Manifesto', Switzerland, 1983.
16. Ibid., p. 2.
17. Ibid.
18. Potocki capitalized references to himself as the claimant to the Polish throne and that of Hungary and Bohemia, and used the 'Royal We'.
19. Geoffrey Potocki de Montalk, 'Second Katyn Manifesto', op. cit., p. 2.
20. Ibid.
21. Ibid.
22. 'Jews' lacked capitalization; an idiosyncrasy that Potocki also later adopted toward the 'english'.
23. Bedford to Potocki, April 29, 1943; cited by Stephanie de Montalk, *Unquiet World: The Life of Count Geoffrey Potocki de Montalk* (Wellington, New Zealand: Victoria University Press, 2001), p. 229.
24. Stephanie de Montalk, ibid., p. 232.
25. Stephanie de Montalk states that Potocki was helped by the Polish government-in-exile, although this seems unlikely, considering what Potocki wrote of the matter in 1983.
26. Stephanie de Montalk, op. cit., p. 232.
27. Ibid., p. 234.
28. Geoffrey Potocki de Montalk, 'Second Katyn Manifesto', op. cit., p. 2.
29. Potocki always distinguished between 'Bolsheviks' and the Russian people.
30. Geoffrey Potocki de Montalk, 'Second Katyn Manifesto', 1983, op. cit.; citing the first 'Katyn Manifesto,' 1943.
31. Ibid.
32. Ibid.
33. Ibid.
34. Included in the original 1943 edition of the 'Katyn Manifesto', but not included in the 1983 reprint.
35. Geoffrey Potocki de Montalk, 'Second Katyn Manifesto', 1983, op. cit.; citing the first Katyn Manifesto, 1943.
36. Bernard Smith, *Poland: A Study in Treachery* (West Sussex, 1984), p. 26.
37. Ibid., p. 18.
38. Stephanie de Montalk, op. cit., p. 231.
39. Ibid.
40. Benjamin Colby, op. cit., pp. 75-77.
41. Geoffrey Potocki de Montalk, 'Katyn Manifesto', 1943, point 4.
42. Franklin D. Roosevelt and Winston S. Churchill, 'The Atlantic Charter' (Point 4) August 14 1941,http://usinfo.org/docs/democracy/53.htm

43. K. R. Bolton, 'Origins of the Cold War and How Stalin Foiled a New World Order', *Foreign Policy Journal*, May 31, 2010, http://www.foreignpolicyjournal.com/2010/05/31/origins-of-the-cold-war-how-stalin-foiled-a-new-world-order/all/1

44. Benjamin Colby, op. cit., p. 76.

45. Mikhail Gorbachev, as the architect of Russia's subjugation to oligarchy, plutocracy and globalisation – albeit short-lived – handed the Soviet archives on Katyn over to Polish president Wojciech Jaruzelski in 1990, stating that the documents showed 'indirectly but convincingly' the Soviet responsibility. See: Esther B. Fein, 'Upheaval in the East; Gorbachev Hands over Katyn Papers', *New York Times*, April 14, 1990, http://www.nytimes.com/1990/04/14/world/upheaval-in-the-east-gorbachev-hands-over-katyn-papers.html?pagewanted=all&src=pm

46. K. R. Bolton, 'Mikhail Gorbachev: Globalist Superstar', *Foreign Policy Journal*, April 3, 2011, http://www.foreignpolicyjournal.com/2011/04/03/mikhail-gorbachev-globalist-super-star/

A Revisionist in Prison

Germar Rudolf

1. Introduction

For more than a decade now, revisionists have been sent to prison in many European countries. And it is to be expected that many more will follow before the legal situation will change. In this essay I want to give an insight into my own time in various U.S. and German prisons. I will abstain from reporting about the daily humdrum reigning in every prison, however, and will instead focus on the more uplifting aspects, the acts of inner restance. I hope that this might inspire others who might find themselves in such an unpleasant spot in the future. May they, too, resist as much as they can!

In various papers, most of which are also posted on my website at www.germarrudolf.com, I have described how I became a revisionist and what impact that had on my life, with the nadir being my eventual arrest and long-term incarceration. I will not here repeat my personal story which got me into the gaol here, so the uninformed curious reader is advised to read those autobiographical essays as a background to the present essay.

2. Arrest

As is known, in 2000 I had applied for political asylum in the U.S. In 2003 the U.S. administration had decided that my asylum application had been unmerited and indeed fraudulent. I was a mere fugitive from justice in their eyes. In 2004, while my asylum case was pending review by a U.S. Federal Court, I married a U.S. citizen and thus asked to be granted permanent residence in the U.S. based on this marriage. The U.S. Immigration Services, however, denied that I even had a right to submit such a request. So that case went to the Federal Court as well.

On October 19, 2005, roughly a year after my wedding, we were invited by the U.S. Immigration Services in Chicago for an interview where they would determine whether our marriage was genuine or of convenience to immigration purposes. That is standard procedure. We went there not only with a plethora of documentation about our shared life, but also with our six-months-old baby in a stroller. We won hands down.

A short while after the interview, the lady who had conducted it approached us, congratulated us, handed us our ornate certificate of our acknowledged-genuine marriage, and told us that we could now go one level lower to apply for permanent legal residence for me.

But then two guys stepped out from behind her and told me that I was under arrest. After a long argument between one of them and my lawyer, I ended up handcuffed and shackled to a chain together with a bunch of convicts in a prison van on the way to Kenosha County Jail in Wisconsin. I got my personal wristband identifying me and stating the reason why I was there. I was the only person in the entire jail that had as a reason given: "non-criminal." Even the prison guards did not believe their eyes. Why the heck do they put a non-criminal person into prison? In Kenosha I loved to discuss with the inmates all kinds of controversial topics, giving them a heads-up about how we all are getting screwed over by the Powers That Be. We had a swell time… to some degree.

I stayed there four weeks, during which my lawyer went all the way up to the Supreme Court in a vain attempt to stop my deportation. My constitutional right to a legal hearing was denied. When the Federal Court ruled three months after my deportation that the U.S. government's refusal to allow me to apply for permanent legal residence was illegal, it was not much more than a bad joke. By that time I was stuck in a German prison for years. They also confirmed that my asylum application had been without merit, stating that it is all right if a respected democracy like Germany persecutes dissidents. Then it is simply called lawful prosecution. So if a respected democracy decided to gas all Jews, that's all right, too? The court also argued that, after a history of jailing dissidents and burning books (during the Third Reich era), Germany today has the right or even the obligation to jail dissidents and burn books. Makes sense to me.

3. Inner Resistance

In Germany I got put into almost solitary confinement, because I was either considered a threat to the other inmates or they were allegedly a threat to me, or both. Since I was considered a "Nazi" and most inmates are immigrants, the prison officials thought that I would either beat them up or vice-versa. Fact is that many immigrants in German prisons are Muslims. When they found out why I was in prison, I had a large community of fans and ardent listeners to my stories. One of them, an Iranian national who thanked me for showing him the proper historico-political way, even offered to organize a personal protection squad for me in 2008 at the Rottenburg prison. But I had no need for it. An athlete of 6'5" can take care of himself pretty well.

Birthday, © Germar Rudolf 2006
At the beginning of the Christmas church service of 2005 in the Stuttgart-Stammheim penitentiary, every inmate received a red rose. Rudolf tied his to a shelf board in his cell so that it would dry. Not quite two months later he drew this rose with a ball point pen based on the now shriveled-up dry rose and sent it to his wife on the occasion of the first birthday of their daughter. This was the start of roughly two years of artistic activities behind bars.

One of the first things the German authorities asked me to do was sign away my constitutional right for privacy of my correspondence. I refused. So a judge had to make a decision to revoke that right, as a consequence of which the prosecution, which normally does the prison censorship, lost that privilege, and the judge himself, with no staff at his disposal, had to censor my letters. He couldn't handle it. I quickly figured out that he wasn't even reading any of my foreign language letters. They went in and out unread. So I tested the waters more and more. For instance, in a letter of Dec. 30, 2005, just 6 weeks after I had arrived in Germany, I wrote a letter to Fredrick Töben discussing revisionist issues and even talking about publishing projects.[1] A while after that I realized that all the instructions I had given while in Kenosha to keep my revisionist publishing empire going were being ignored or handled amateurishly, so I sent out a number of angry letters to several people being very clear as to what I expected them to do. They all arrived unimpeded.

Fortunately I was able to purchase a typewriter in the Stuttgart prison. I decided therefore to use this ultimate weapon of crime for its intended purpose. Some of my lawyers agreed to help me (I won't say which). They got me books that are outlawed in Germany. They agreed to smuggle out publishing projects. So I started translating revisionist works in my prison cell: I translated "The Leuchter Report. Critical Edition" and "Auschwitz: The First Gassing" from English to German, and I also started some other books. The typescripts were then sent to England to my helpers there in order to get them published. Little did I realize that those folks were either too disorganized or inept to pull off a project like this, or else they were too timid, always afraid to harm me (or using this as an excuse, I don't know). Anyway, fact is that I had a zillion cell searches during that time by the prison guards, but they were never suspicious of anything. After all, they were looking only for drugs, weapons, alcoholic beverages, cell phones and objects like that. Paper was not of any interest to them. Hence my piles of papers in my locker, on my desk and in my binders on the floor were always ignored...

It was at the time when I was preparing my defense speech that a correspondence partner contacted me, forwarding a question by Israeli dissident Israel Shamir. The mood I was in during those months prior to my second trial can be gleaned from my response, which is nothing short of a battle cry and which also passed through the enemy lines of censorship unintercepted.[2]

After I had been sentenced to another 30 months due to my opus magnum "Lectures on the Holocaust," I tried to publish my defense speech in German from within. Since censorship had been handed over by the judge to the prison staff after my verdict had become effective, I now had some keen readers of my correspondence among the prison staff itself. Since that publishing project involved sending lots of paper in and out and also was in German, it had to raise red flags. So one of those days I had the police visit me in prison (quite a parade of officers entering my tiny cell; what a spectacle!) in search of a dangerous stack of paper: my defense speech (what a threat to the state!), in which I had committed the crime of using adjectives of doubt in connection with historical claims (how dare I!). Plus I had quoted the indictment (yikes!), which consisted mostly of quotes from my book. Since my book was illegal, quoting it, even though contained in the indictment, was deemed illegal too...[3] Fortunately my lawyer managed to get the case quashed.

One of the highlights was a Bible discussion group at Mannheim Prison. We had some 15 inmates, among them also Ernst Zündel and I. One day we discussed Paul's letter from prison to some Christian congregation. His exhortation to stay true to his beliefs in spite of severe persecution made me comment that this is exactly what Ernst and I are experiencing. That made one of the inmates very angry (a PhD lawyer who had stolen a Spitzweg painting from a museum). He thought I was going to voice my historical views next, which he hated (although he probably didn't know them). But that wasn't what I had in mind. When I kept talking about parallels of those cases, he finally had enough and threatened to beat me up. I stayed very calm and merely argued that this is yet another parallel to Paul and the early Christians, who were also threatened with violence by a mob made rabid by utterly irrational hate propaganda. "Dr. Spitzweg" in turn jumped up, and only the intervention of the prison pastor and the social worker prevented him from getting physical. Both officials granted me freedom of speech, and that was the end of it. Ernst couldn't believe what he had just experienced and that I had stayed so absolutely calm, unimpressed, rational, and cruelly to the point. I loved it!

When a judge had to decide toward the end of my term in mid-2009 whether I should be whacked with "conduct supervision" after my release, he relied on an assessment of my person by the prison authorities: I could not be deemed resocialized since I kept spreading my views among the inmates and because I had even tried to publish my defense speech from within. Bad boy! So I got a probation officer assigned to my side to keep an eye on me for three more years.

4. For Better or Worse

Even though the authorities treated me worse than other inmates because I did not recant my views and showed no signs of remorse, my lot was far better than that of the other inmates from a psychological point of view: being incarcerated did not tarnish my reputation, quite to the contrary. I wear it like a badge of honor, or as the German historian Prof. Dr. Ernst Nolte wrote to me in a letter after my release, I can now count myself among the men of honor who have gone to prison for reasons of conscience. Whereas most inmates lose most of their friends and often even the support of their families, my friends and family have stood firmly by me. Whereas most prisoners struggle financially and get in deep debt during their incarceration, as they lose their jobs and subsequently often also their home and property, I was very fortunate to find many generous supporters.

Most important and in contrast to most inmates, political prisoners don't lose their feeling of meaning; they feel neither guilty nor ashamed of what they have done. Or as David Cole expressed it once: We are loud, we are proud, and the best of all: we are right!

This attitude, more than anything else, makes you wing even the toughest of times, and it keeps you going afterwards as well, as the *New York Times* correctly observed in an article entitled "Why Freed Dissidents Pick Path of Most Resistance." This article, which was fittingly published five weeks prior to my release from prison, describes how Arab dissidents who were incarcerated for their peaceful political views went right back to their acts of civil disobedience once released from prison.[4] As one of them expressed it:

> *"It is a matter not only of dignity, it is the sense of your life. It's your choice of life, and if you give up, you will lose your sense of your life."*

He said he had no choice but to go right back to where he had left off.

Right-o!

Notes:

1. Online: http://germarrudolf.com/persecution/germars-persecution/letters-from-the-dungeon/december-30-2005/
2. Online: http://germarrudolf.com/persecution/germars-persecution/letters-from-the-dungeon/august-27-2006/
3. See the document at the very end of my book Resistance Is Obligatory, Castle Hill Publishers, Uckfield 2012.
4. Published online at www.nytimes.com/2009/05/27/world/middleeast/27egypt.html on 26 May 2009. A version of this article appeared in print on 27 May 2009, on page A6 of the New York edition under the headline "Once Freed from Prison, Dissidents Often Continue to Resist."

Three Books on Treblinka

Thomas Kues

During recent years there have appeared from time to time new books on the Treblinka "death camp". Compared with the vast number of Auschwitz-related publications, and considering the fact that according to the exterminationist point of view Treblinka claimed the second-highest number of victims among the six "death camps" (the victim figure given usually varies between 750,000 and 900,000) this is only a small trickle. One might expect then that the contents of these few books would at least be partially fresh, offering us new insights and new material. Unfortunately this is not the case: from the publication of Yitzhak Arad's *Belzec, Sobibor, Treblinka* in 1987 the exterminationist literature on the Treblinka camp has very much been treading old ground. In the following review I will briefly discuss three books relating to the camp which were published between 2003 and 2012. It will be not so much a comprehensive review as a presentation of what these books have to offer which is not a rehash of Arad, Sereny et al – pitifully little, as we will see.

Torben Jørgensen's Book on the Aktion Reinhardt Staff

Let us begin with a book by Danish historian Torben Jørgensen, *Stiftelsen. Bødlerne fra Aktion Reinhardt* (*The Foundation. The Executioners of Aktion Reinhardt*, Lindhardt og Ringhof, Copenhagen 2003). This concerns the Aktion Reinhardt personnel as a whole, but as can be expected a significant portion of it concerns Treblinka.

The book contains very little information of interest, despite the fact that the author had reportedly surveyed 3,000–4,000 pages of court material. Remarkably, there are almost no quotations in this book that have not already appeared in Arad, Jules Schelvis, Adalbert Rückerl or Ernst Klee et al. There is also virtually nil information provided on the interrogations themselves. We learn some more, however, on the astoundingly lax security reportedly prevailing at Treblinka during the tour of its first commandant, Dr. Irmfried Eberl (p. 75):

> "Prostitutes and blackmarketeers from Warsaw erected regular shops in the woods around Treblinka. The personnel, Ukrainians as well as Germans, were in a permanent state of inebriation. In addition to this, a number of unauthorized people visited the camp. Those were, among others, German soldiers

> *who were stationed in Warsaw, among them personnel from a Panzerkorps, that is, the Wehrmacht. Members of these units made excursions to Treblinka, which was not sealed off; here they went about taking photographs and observing the fate of the transports."*

This description should probably be regarded with some caution, since it is based on a court statement made by the second commandant, Franz Stangl, who arrived at Treblinka only after Irmfried Eberl had been sacked for incompetence; the information that Wehrmacht soldiers visited Treblinka is therefore from a second-hand source. Nevertheless it is worth noting: If an indeterminate number of German soldiers went around taking photos at the camp, how come none of these has ever been discovered? Could it be that photographs were indeed taken, but that what they showed did not conform to the "death camp" allegation, so that the person(s) in possession of the photo(s) either hesitated to come forward with it, or simply did not connect it with Treblinka?

We also learn that the protocols from the interrogations of Irmfried Eberl, Franz Hödl, Heinrich Barbl, Ernst Lerch, Hermann Hoefle and others are kept in the *Österreichische Widerstandsarchiv* in Vienna. No further details are given, however (in the case of Eberl the interrogation may not be relevant to the "death camp" issue, since he was arrested because of his involvement in the euthanasia program and supposedly committed suicide before his role at Treblinka had been discovered).

Unrelated to Treblinka we are informed (in a footnote on page 215) that two (unnamed) Bełżec survivors were found living in Israel several decades after the war. This claim, which is noted to derive from Michael Tregenza, is rather sensational considering that only 7 inmates are alleged to have survived Bełżec, only two – Rudolf Reder alias Roman Robak and Chaim Hirszman[1] – of whom left any testimony on their supposed experiences. Why, we may ask, has Tregenza not furnished any information on these two hitherto unknown Bełżec survivors?

Dr. Irmfried Eberl, the first commandant of Treblinka. Eberl was a trained psychiatrist, Public Domain. Wikipedia.org

Some new light is also shed on the mysterious death of the former Sobibór SS man Gustav Wagner in Brazil in 1980 (p. 225):

> "During a conversation with the author in Lublin in the summer of 2001, Thomas Blatt [a prominent Sobibór eyewitness] told that another survivor from Sobibór who lived in Brazil in 1980 killed Wagner together with some other former prisoners."

Only two former Sobibór inmates are known to have settled in Brazil after the war: Chaim Korenfeld and Stanislaw Szmajzner. Since Jules Schelvis[2] and others have noted that Szmajzner himself had hinted that he was involved in the murder, and since Blatt was close to Szmajzner, this pretty much settles who was behind Wagner's death, which (according to most sources) was officially ruled as a suicide.

The Testimony of Hershl Sperling

Mark S. Smith's *Treblinka Survivor. The Life and Death of Hershl Sperling* (The History Press, Stroud 2010) is an attempt to trace the life and fate of Hershl Sperling, a former inmate of Treblinka *and* Auschwitz-Birkenau (!) who committed suicide by drowning in Glasgow in 1989. The book mostly consists of interviews with Sperling's son, psychological ruminations and descriptions of Smith's travels in Sperling's footsteps to Treblinka and other places in Poland and Germany, interspersed with rehashings from well-known exterminationist publications on the subject and excerpts from Sperling's only testimony on Treblinka (he left none regarding his time at Auschwitz, to where he was sent in the autumn of 1943), a brief account simply entitled "Treblinka" which was published in 1947 in issue 6 of the obscure Yiddish-language journal *Fun letzter Churbn (Since the Recent Catastrophe)*. Fortunately Smith presents a complete English translation of this testimony as an appendix to his book. This is pretty much the only part of the book which is of any real interest, however meager it is. Below I will briefly discuss the most interesting parts of it.

Sperling was deported to Treblinka from Czestochowa "almost at the end of the period of deportations" from that city (pp. 243–244). According to the transport lists presented in Yitzhak Arad's book on the Reinhardt camps, the last deportation from Czestochowa to Treblinka took place on 5 October 1942. Sperling informs us (p. 244) that the "disinfectant calcium chloride" was "scattered liberally into each wagon" of the convoy. This practice is likely the origin of the early holocaust claim (found in the writings of Jan Karski and others) that the Germans were killing the Jews not in gas chambers but in transport trains, using chloride or unslaked lime. Sperling also reveals that Polish workers which the Jews of the convoy encountered during the drawn-out railway travel spread atrocity stories causing great fear among the deportees (p. 245):

> *"One of the Polish workers mentions burnings, another, shootings, and a third – gassings. Another tells of inhuman, unbelievable tortures. An unbearable state of tension mounts among us, which in some cases even leads to outbreaks of hysteria."*

At the camp Sperling was selected for work and made a member of the "sorting squad" working in the "reception camp". He never set foot in the "upper camp" or "death camp proper", where the alleged gas chambers and the mass graves were located, so his description of that area is based only on second-hand sources. The details of the alleged killing method were relayed to Sperling and his fellow inmates in Camp I by prisoners assigned to carry food between the different parts of the camp (p. 247-248):

> "It was strictly forbidden to cross from one camp to the other. In the early period the food carriers used to come to us from Camp II and bring us all the minute details of the cruel deeds that were being perpetrated there.(...)

The food-carriers describe to us how the path to the death camp goes through a garden. Just before you come to the death-shower there is a hut, where everyone is instructed once again to relinquish money and gold. (...). At the shower room of death, which is adorned only by a Star of David, the victims are received with bayonets. They are driven into these shower rooms, prodded with these bayonets. (...). When all the wretched victims have been forced into the showers, the doors are hermetically sealed. After a few seconds, uncanny, horrifying screams are heard through the walls. (...). The screaming becomes weaker and weaker, finally dying away. At last everything is completely silent. Then the doors are opened, and the corpses are thrown into huge mass graves, which hold about 60 to 70 thousand people. When there was no room for any new victims in the mass graves, there came a new command to burn the dead bodies. They would dig out a deep trench, and throw in a few old trunks, boxes, wood and things like that. All is set alight, and a layer of corpses is thrown onto it, then more branches, and more corpses, and so on. Later the order was given to dig out the dead in the mass graves, and burn them too."

While this is merely a second-hand description of the "death camp proper", three aspects of it are worthy of note.

First, we have the fact that nowhere in the above description do we find any hint as to what the actual killing agent was. According to the official version of events it was the exhaust fumes from a large engine mounted in a separate room in the "gas chamber" building. Considering the short distance between this building and the fence to Camp I (some 50 meters in the case of the new building) one would expect that the inmates of Camp I soon would connect the purported mass murder of the deportees with the sound from this engine. As I have pointed out in the study on Sobibór which I co-wrote with

Jürgen Graf and Carlo Mattogno[3] the earliest testimonies about the alleged death chambers at that camp – which supposedly functioned in the same way as at Treblinka – mention murder methods used in these chambers which strongly imply that these witnesses did *not* connect the alleged gassings with the sound of an engine. Sperling's testimony very much fits into this picture.

Secondly we have the ridiculous notion that the cremations were carried out using as fuel "a few old trunks, boxes, wood and things like that". If the vast amount of firewood required for the cremation of some 800,000 corpses – some 139,200 metric tons[4] – had actually been brought into Treblinka, either by train or truck or from the nearby forested areas Sperling would inescapably have observed and taken note of this – that he did not is yet another hint that the amount of firewood used in the cremations at Treblinka was much smaller, corresponding to a number of corpses much smaller than alleged by mainstream historiography.[5]

Third and last we have the emphasis on the word "shower". Compare this with the statement of Polish prisoner Jan Sulkowski (quoted in Arad's book on the Reinhardt camps): "I was told by the SS men that we were building a bath-house and it was after a considerable time that I realized that we were constructing gas-chambers." This implies that the Germans either went to extreme lengths to disguise homicidal gas chambers as shower rooms, or that they actually built shower rooms for a delousing facility. In this context it is worth mentioning a letter sent from Treblinka commandant Irmfried Eberl to the commissar for the ghetto in Warsaw, Dr. Heinz Auerswald, on 19 June 1942 (i.e. some 1 month before the opening of the camp), in which he ordered the following "still needed" items for the Treblinka camp:[6]

>*"10 m copper pipes 1/4 inch*
>*5–10 kg filler wire stacks*
>*2 kg brass wire for brazing*
>*50 m iron pipes of each of the sizes: 1 inch, 3/4 inch, 1/2 inch*
>*20 iron pipe T-fittings of each of the sizes: 1 inch, 3/4 inch, 1/2 inch*
>*30 iron pipe elbow joints of each of the sizes: 1 inch, 3/4 inch, 1/2 inch*
>*20 double nipples (connection pieces) of each of the sizes: 1 inch, 3/4 inch, 1/2 inch*

6 waterproof lighting fixtures with sockets, enclosed with cages
10 water-taps 3/4 inch with hose connection
10 water-taps 1/2 inch with hose connection
Electric light bulbs 120 Volt: 30 items 25 Watt
20 items 60 Watt
20 items 75 Watt
20 items 100 Watt
300 m two-conductor G.A. flexible wire
1000 m for overhead lines 2.5 sq. mm diameter"

On 7 July Eberl wrote again to the commissar, notifying him that the camp would be ready for operation on 11 July and ordering additional items for the camp.[7] Most of these were related to lighting but among them were also "3 intake strainers [*Saugkörbe*] for wells with check valves [*Rückschlagventil*] 1 1/2 inch". From testimonial evidence we know that a Polish construction worker named Grzegorz Wozniak worked on coordinating the piping and trenching during the camp's construction phase.[8]

For what purpose would the small Treblinka camp, supposedly a "pure extermination camp", need *at least* 160 meters of piping? From an exterminationist viewpoint the apparent conclusion is that they were used for a fake shower installation that was part of the murder weapon. Yitzhak Arad describes the alleged first gas chambers at Treblinka as follows:

> *"During the camp's first months of operation, there were three gas chambers, each 4 x 4 meters and 2.6 meters high (...). A room attached to the building contained a diesel engine, which introduced the poisonous carbon monoxide gas through pipes into the chambers, and a generator, which supplied electricity to the entire camp.[...]. Inside the chambers the walls were covered with white tiles up to a certain height, and shower heads and piping crisscrossed the ceiling – all designed to maintain the illusion of a shower room. The piping actually served to carry the poison gas into the chambers. When the doors were closed, there was no lighting in the chambers."*[9]

But is this setup really believable? Given a room height of 2.6 m, the shower heads would have been placed some 2.3–2.4 m above the floor – clearly within reach of the taller of the alleged victims, as well as shorter ones lifted up by or standing on others. According to the verdict from the Treblinka trial, each of the three chambers in the old gas chamber building could hold 200-350 victims, i.e. a capacity 600–1,050 victims per gassing.[10] Considering that during the first month of the camp's operation some 6–8,000 Jews were sent daily to the camp from the Warsaw ghetto,[11] this would mean that some 6–14 gassings would have to be carried out daily. Considering the design usually employed for the shower installations in the German concentration camps,[12] it seems inevitable that the "fake" piping and shower heads would have been damaged by panicking, desperate victims on a daily basis – if lethal exhaust gas had been indeed been streaming out from these showers, that is. The notion that it would have been feasible to feed the gas into the chambers using a fake shower installation is therefore, at closer glance, absurd. Another hint that the piping, if indeed used for the "bath house" described by Sulkowski et al (something for which we have no conclusive proof but which seems likely in the absence of other known installations at the camp that would have utilized such piping) formed part of an actual shower installation is the fact that Eberl together with the piping ordered *"waterproof* lighting fixtures with sockets" (emphasis added).

Even more significant are the "3 intake strainers [*Saugkörbe*] for wells with check valves" ordered on 7 July 1942. A "*Saugkorb*" is a large strainer, sometimes suspended in a float to hold it near the surface of the water and containing a check valve or setback valve, which is placed at the intake end of a suction hose, which in turn is connected to a pump. Its function is to filter the water and to see to that the suction hose is kept filled with water. [13] Intake strainers are usually employed by fire fighters as a means to obtain the large amounts of water needed for their fire hoses from dirty waters (such as ponds or lakes), but they can also be used in wells as part of a pump device.

According to the most ambitious exterminationist attempt to visually reconstruct Treblinka, the Peter Laponder maps from the early 2000s,[14] there existed a total of five wells in the camp: one well for the German staff in the northernmost part of the camp, one near the kitchen of the Ukrainian guards, one west of the living quarters of the Jewish prisoners and south of the "zoo", one in the "reception camp" near the railway siding, where the arrivals disembarked their trains, and finally one in the "death camp proper", in the immediate vicinity of the original "gas chamber building". The third of these wells is visible in one of Kurt Franz's photographs of the "zoo".[15] It is clear that this well was manually operated, and no suction hose or similar device is in sight. So far I have not been able to find any detailed descriptions of the other four wells, but it appears that the first three were all used in connection with the kitchens for the guards and prisoners, so that it is likely that they all resembled the one seen on the Kurt Franz photo. The presence of three intake strainers at the camp however indicates that one needed to draw a considerable amount of water from possibly as many as three wells (although one of the intake strainers may have been for spare use). Such a need may possibly have applied to the well in the reception camp, where water under pressure may have been used for cleaning the emptied rail wagons, but I have found no testimonial evidence stating that this well was equipped with a suction system. This would seem to indicate that one or more of the intake strainers were used in the "death camp proper". From an exterminationist viewpoint such an installation would be rather pointless, but from a revisionist viewpoint it is perfectly explainable, as a shower installation used by hundreds of deportees at a time would have required the drawing of large amounts of water. If the pump system was powered by an engine (as is often the case) this might help explain the origin of the allegation that engine-exhaust gas was used for homicidal gassings. In this context it is worth pointing out that the ARC website displays a photo, apparently taken at some museum exhibition, of what is purported to be a "Gassing pipe used in the Belzec gas chambers".[16] This rusty item, however, with its perforated basket-like lower part, resembles nothing so much as a strainer with a dual intake.

Sperling has the following to say on the number of deportees arriving at the camp (p. 249):

> "New transports arrived at Treblinka all the time. Sometime there is a break of a few days. But on the average ten thousand people per day are murdered in Treblinka. There was one day in fact when the human transport reached the figure of twenty-four thousand."

Between 22 July 1942 and the end of the same year – a period of 163 days – a total of 713,555 Jews were brought to Treblinka, which means an average of 4,378 arrivals per day. An average of 10,000 per day would mean 1,630,000 arrivals during the same period, so Sperling is clearly exaggerating rather than just misestimating.

In connection with the discussion of the number of arrivals, Sperling shares with his readers the following bizarre anecdote (p. 249):

> "Only once did Jews leave the camp alive. The Front had demanded women. So one hundred and ten of the most beautiful Jewish girls, accompanied by a Jewish doctor, were sent off."

Besides the preposterous claim that Jewish women would have been sent to the frontlines to be used as prostitutes – something which would be in violation of the National Socialist racial laws (on "*Rassenschande*", defilement of the race) we may compare Sperling's assertion that Jews were able to leave the camp "only once" with witness Israel Cymlich's statement that groups of Jews from the extermination camp were *regularly* transferred to the Treblinka I labor camp to replenish its labor force,[17] and the verdict of the Düsseldorf Treblinka trial, according to which "coming from Treblinka, several thousand people are said to have arrived at other camps".[18]

The Smoke and Mirrors of Ian Baxter

Finally I will take a brief look at Ian Baxter's *The SS of Treblinka* (Spellmount, Stroud 2012). A search at Amazon or any other online book will reveal that Baxter is not a Holocaust historian, but a military historian and author of a number of photography-focused books dealing with the European theatre of WWII, in particular the Eastern front. A common thread in the online reviews of his book is that the layout and photos are high quality, but that the writing is "history light" or even display examples of poor scholarship. The latter unfortunately applies to his recent book focusing on the German and Austrian staff employed at the Treblinka "extermination camp".

This book is mainly a rehash of Arad, Sereny, Chrostowski, Steiner and Rückerl (as well as material from the H.E.A.R.T., Holocaust Research Project and ARC websites, from which most of the illustrations are taken), with most of the usual quotes from Wiernik et al. It follows from this that the book is mostly for those seeking exhaustive coverage; if you are buying only one book this summer, save the money for something better...

It should first of all be pointed out that, despite the title, the book contains next to no new material on the lives of the men stationed at Treblinka. One might expect that Baxter would have dug deeper in the interrogation and investigation files and perhaps even tried to interview relatives or acquaintances of them in order to shed more light on their activities before and during the war as well as their post-war fates, but unfortunately no such research seems to have been carried out.

As for poor scholarship, Baxter recycles the claim that John (Ivan) Demjanjuk served as a guard in the "extermination area" (p. 68), despite the fact there exists no solid evidence whatsoever for Demjanjuk being posted to Treblinka. That Demjanjuk has now passed away is, unfortunately, unlikely to stop the frequent repetition of this accusation, we suspect. We further find claims that transports of Dutch Jews were sent to Treblinka in 1943 (p. 91), something which can be ruled out from readily available statistics and transport data. Baxter's sloppiness in the field of research is also revealed by the fact that he gives the victim figure for Sobibór as "approximately 250,000" (p. 159) – an estimate which was rendered impossible by the discovery of the Höfle document in 2000 – despite listing in his bibliography the 2003 German edition of Jules Schelvis's Sobibór study, which gives the number of Jewish arrivals at that camp as some 170,000.

As for small but interesting fresh tidbits, Baxter asserts (p. 81) that during the latter phase of operations, killing of sick deportees and inmates were carried out not only by shooting but also by lethal injections; the source for this, however, goes unstated. We also learn a little more about the supposed "deception" of the arriving Jewish deportees. The testimony of SS-*Unterscharführer* Willi Mentz is quoted as follows (p. 71):

> *"When the Jews had got off, Stadie or Matzig would have a short word with them. They were told something to the effect that they were a resettlement transport and that they would be given a bath and that they would receive new clothes. They were also instructed to maintain quiet and disciplined. They would continue their journey the following day."*

The by-far-most-interesting part of Baxter's book consists of three brief diary excerpts. The first one of them, reproduced without a date of writing or name of the author, except for the information that he was a "staff officer attached to [Christian] Wirth's office", reads as follows (p. 103):

> "*I frequently visited TII in the summer of 1943 and regularly reported back to Wirth with a progress report on the dismantling of the camp. Whilst the commandant [Stangl] was on leave I came to Treblinka and was given a guided tour by Deputy Franz and another officer. Here I was shown the cremation areas and the pits where the corpses were being exhumed by prisoners. I had my briefcase with me and I got my assistant to write down notes on the calculation Franz gave me on the total number of bodies exhumed thus far. I was not chiefly interested in the quantity or condition of the prisoners working inside these pits, but more anxious about how the job was going to be completed in the specified time.*"

The endnote to this quote gives the source as "Extract from Ernst Reuss to Author. November 2008. Diary Catalogued 43216/A/2 ER". Ernst Reuss is possibly identical with the German expert witness and author of the study *Kriegsgefangen im 2. Weltkrieg* (Augsburg 2011). It is not made clear to which archive the document number refers. From the contents of the quote it is clear that it was written in retrospect in 1944 or later, as the unnamed author would hardly have written "in the summer of 1943" in 1943. For the second quote we are presented with at least a modicum of background: "A Staff officer named Kratzer visiting Treblinka with one of Globocnik's representatives found Floss to be a 'determined fellow' who displayed versatility 'and much relish for the mission'." Is this Kratzer the same person as the author of the first quoted text written in 1944 or later? The reader has no way of knowing. In any case the second quote reads as follows (p. 104, ellipsis by Baxter):

> "*I admire the way in which our men are dealing with cremating the corpses. I have been informed by the cremation expert Floss that the burnings will be terminated by the end of August or September ... There is much activity in the camp and the staff here are working exceptionally hard to bring about a conclusion to this dirty work. TII is certainly being run effectively and my report on its decommissioning will be presented in due course.*"

Again no date is given, although we are told by Baxter that Kratzer's visit took place "some time at the end of July or early August 1943" (the Treblinka prisoner revolt, we should keep in mind, took place on 2 August 1943) – a vagueness which implies that this passage is either written in retrospect or not part of a regular diary, but rather some form of memoir. The source for the second quote is given as "Extract from Ernst Reuss to Author. November 2008. Diary Catalogued 43217/B/3 ER". The third quote reads (p. 106):

> *"After my tour I made specific notes and a sketch of the camp so that my boss had an overall idea of the general layout of the camp This was undertaken in order to make preparations for the installation's decommissioning."*

The source is given as "Extract from Ernst Reuss to Author. November 2008. Diary Catalogued 43218/C/4 ER".

We will observe here first of all that none of these quotes supports the allegation that Treblinka served as a "pure extermination camp", only that an unspecified number of corpses were burnt there. Baxter tells his readers (p. 104) that Kratzer "visited the 'Upper Camp' and saw for himself the gas chambers, the installations for the disposal of the corpses and the huge iron grills, and the barracks for the Jewish workgroups." This description, however, is completely unsourced, and no further quotations are presented which allow us to verify to what degree (if at all) it corresponds to what Kratzer actually wrote, and to what degree it is just Baxter's conjecture. This in itself is extremely revealing, because Baxter must certainly be aware of the fact that, since virtually no war-time documents on Treblinka have been preserved (or rather: are known to exist) the discovery of an authentic contemporary diary text describing the camp, and moreover one written by a German staff officer (or possibly two different officers) with access to all parts of the camp, is something no less than sensational. One would expect that Baxter, instead of rehashing old material, would present these texts in full with commentaries – or at least any passages confirming the existence of homicidal gas chambers at the camp, thus refuting the "deniers" once and for all. In the introduction (p. 9) he in fact speaks of "recently discovered material, some of which has never been published before". The latter can, as far as I am able to tell, only relate to the above discussed diary entries. One would thus expect Baxter to reproduce the entries in full (perhaps even in facsimile) instead of devoting five pages (pp. 151–155) to an irrelevant general list of concentration camps, eight pages to reproducing the transport lists from the appendices to Arad's *Belzec, Sobibor, Treblinka*, or 16 pages to miniature biographies of camp staff lifted almost verbatim from the ARC website (which, to Baxter's credit, he at least attributed). But no, Baxter is content with presenting only the three quotes above. We may safely assume that

Baxter (or his colleague Reuss) would have jumped eagerly at the opportunity to publish a contemporary German document (be it a memorandum or a diary) describing homicidal gas chambers and/or mass graves filled to the brim with hundreds of thousands of Jewish corpses at Treblinka if he had in fact access to such a document, which means with almost 100 % certainty that he (or Reuss) does *not* have such a document in his hands. This in effect leaves only two possible conclusions:

1.The descriptions of the camp found in these diary entries are so vague that they neither confirm nor refute the official version of events.

2.The descriptions of the camp are incongruent with the official version of events.

Whatever the facts may be on this issue, it is imperative that this potentially extremely important historical document is appropriately presented to the public, be it in another book, an article or online. Since it is unlikely that Baxter will respond to an appeal voiced by revisionists, I await exterminationist Holocaust historians and anti-revisionists to do their best to get Baxter or Reuss to publish the document(s). Surely here they have an excellent opportunity to finally prove with documentary evidence the existence of homicidal gas chambers at Treblinka?

Notes:

1.   I have discussed the short and not very well-known testimony of this witness in my article "Belzec – The Testimony of Chaim Hirszman," *Smith's Report* no. 169 (February 2010), pp. 7–10.
2.   Cf. Jules Schelvis, *Sobibor. A History of a Nazi Death Camp*, Berg, Oxford/New York 2007, p. 264.
3.   J. Graf, T. Kues, C. Mattogno, *Sobibór. Holocaust Propaganda and Reality*, TBR Books, Washington D.C. 2010, pp. 94–95
4.   Cf. Carlo Mattogno, Jürgen Graf, *Treblinka. Extermination Camp or Transit Camp?*, Theses & Dissertations Press, Chicago 2004, p. 150.
5.   See my article "Tree-felling at Treblinka", *Inconvenient History*, vol. 1, no. 2 (Fall 2009), online: http://www.inconvenienthistory.com/archive/20 09/volume_1/number_2/tree_felling_at_treblinka.php
6.   This document is reproduced online at http://www.holocaustresearchproject.org/ar/treblinka/docs/Treblinka%20-%20eberl%20letter.jpg and also in Ian Baxter's Treblinka book (unpaginated section with photographs). This as well as the following letter from Eberl

can also be found in facsimile in J. Gumkowski, A. Rutkowski, *Treblinka*, Council for Protection of Fight and Martyrdom Monuments, Warsaw 1961, reproductions on unnumbered pages.

7. Reproduced online at: http://www.deathcamps.org/treblinka/pic/bigeberl.jpg

8. Cf. Ian Baxter's book on Treblinka reviewed below, pp. 33–34.

9. Y. Arad, *Belzec, Sobibor, Treblinka. The Operation Reinhard Death Camps*, Indiana University Press, Bloomington/Indianapolis 1987, p. 42.

10. Cf. C. Mattogno, J. Graf, *Treblinka. Extermination Camp or Transit Camp?*, op.cit., p. 117.

11. Ibid., pp. 275–276.

12 Cf. photos of such showers at Dachau and Majdanek online at: http://v1.cache7.c.bigcache.googleapis.com/static.panoramio.com/photos/original/32565498.jpg? ir=1&redirect_counter=2 and http://www.whale.to/b/DachauShowers.jpg

13. Cf. http://de.wikipedia.org/wiki/Saugkorb and also https://store.primopumps.com/Suction-Hose/products/18/

14. Online at: http://www.deathcamps.org/treblinka/maps.html

15. Online at: http://www.holocaustresearchproject.org/ar/treblinka/treblinkagallery/Treblinka%20zoo%20and%20well%20.html

16. http://www.deathcamps.org/belzec/photos.html

17. Israel Cymlich & Oskar Strawczynski, *Escaping Hell in Treblinka*, Yad Vashem, New York/Jerusalem 2007, p. 40.

18. Cf. C. Mattogno, J. Graf, *Treblinka. Extermination Camp or Transit Camp?*, op.cit., p. 287.

The Number of Victims of Sachsenhausen Concentration Camp (1936-1945)

Klaus Schwensen

Every year on 22 April the liberation of Sachsenhausen Concentration Camp is duly commemorated. On this occasion, the press sometimes still mentions the figure of 100,000 victims who allegedly perished or were murdered at this camp. Although Sachsenhausen does not belong to the six "classic" extermination camps (Chelmno, Majdanek, Auschwitz, Belzec, Sobibor, Treblinka), the epithet of a "death camp" which was given to it by Soviet propaganda is sometimes still used. While the Sachsenhausen Memorial Site today contents itself with a death toll of "tens of thousands", it has never publicly disavowed the propagandistic figure of 100,000 victims. One might speak of a "silent revision": Certain Allied propaganda figures which arose during or shortly after the war are quietly jettisoned, but this fact is never publicly admitted, nor is there any discussion about the way these wildly exaggerated numbers arose.

So, how many people *really* perished at Sachsenhausen?

The conclusions of the Soviet Investigating Commission

As early as 1942 the Soviet authorities had founded an "Extraordinary State Commission" (ESC) aiming at ascertaining "crimes" committed by the "German fascist occupiers" and the damage caused by them. The activities of the ESC naturally extended to the German concentration camps that had been liberated by the Red Army. Thus a Soviet commission carried out an investigation at Sachsenhausen in May/June 1945, one of its tasks being the ascertainment of the number of victims of the camp.

Members of the Soviet Investigating Commission at Sachsenhausen (May/June 1945). Source: GARF 7021-104-10

While the death books had been largely lost during the evacuation of the camp, the daily figures of prisoners present at roll call (*Veränderungsmeldungen*) has survived. With a few gaps, these documents covered the period from 1 January 1940 to 17 April 1945. Based on these figures, the Prisoner Records Office (*Häftlingsschreibstube*), which answered to the SS, had compiled monthly statistics of Prisoner Movement (*Häftlingsbewegung*). These documents, which were also captured by the Soviets, are now exhibited at the Sachsenhausen Memorial Site (Barracks 38), however they are falsely presented as statistics drawn up by former prisoners after the end of the war. As a matter of fact, the tables are contemporaneous with the camp's operation and compiled at the Prisoner Records Office , which was subordinated to the Political Section (*Politische Abteilung*) of the SS.[1]

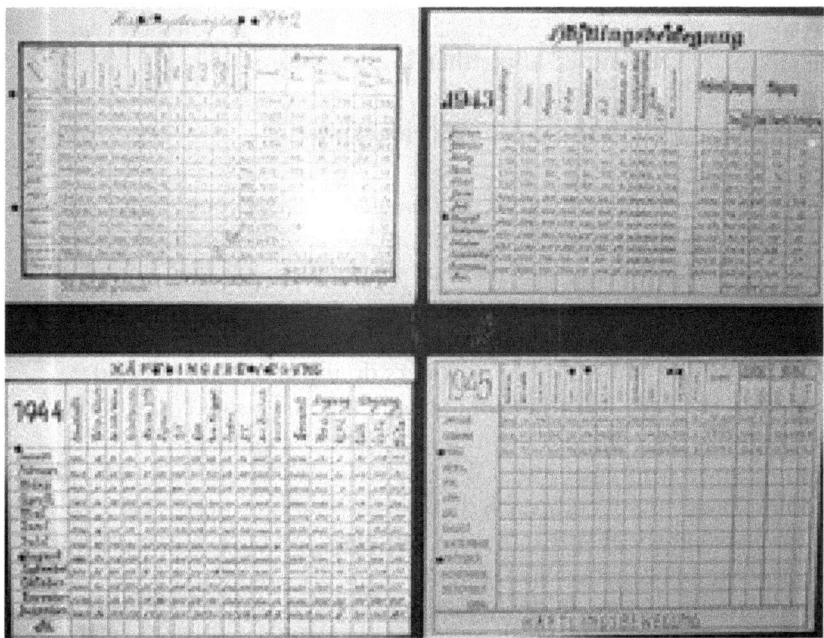

The authentic Häftlingsbewegung reports. Source: Sachsenhausen Memorial Site (permanent exhibition in Barracks 38)

The Soviet investigators ordered three former prisoners, the Communists Walter Engemann, Gustav Schöning and Hellmut Bock, to audit the statistics. This was undoubtedly done in order to prove that the SS had falsified the statistics to "cover up their crimes". The group, headed by Engemann, performed its task conscientiously, paying special attention to "exits without information" (*Abgänge ohne Angaben*). Altogether 3,733 such unaccounted "exits" were found, 2,448 of them concerning Soviet POWs, who had disappeared from the statistics of the camp on 22 October 1941. Of course this does not prove in any way that these POWs were shot.

For the years 1940-1945, Engemann, Schöning and Bock, based on the *Veränderungsmeldungen*, ascertained a figure of 19,900 prisoners who had died in the camp. This result largely confirmed the death toll reported by the SS. In a report he produced for the ESC in Moscow, the head of the Sachsenhausen Commission, Lieutenant Colonel A. Sharitch, adopted this figure. In 2003, Carlo Mattogno arrived at a slightly higher number (20,173).[2] This author (K.S.), who based his analysis on the *Häftlingsbewegung* data rather than the *Veränderungsmeldungen* and considered the whole period of existence of the camp (1936-1945), comes to the conclusion that Sachsenhausen claimed altogether 21,999 victims.

Which figures are these reports referring to?

In addition to the main camp, Sachsenhausen Concentration Camp comprised about 15 satellite camps and dozens of small outstations. In the pre-war period, only male prisoners were interned here, but during the war, thousands of female prisoners were deported to Sachsenhausen as well. Another category of detainees was the Soviet POWs. Which categories of prisoners do the above-mentioned statistics refer to: All prisoners, or only the male ones? The entire Sachsenhausen complex including the satellite camps or only the main camp? And what about the Soviet POWs? Engemann and his comrades do not even broach these important questions, and historians hardly ever discuss them either. However, a comparison with contemporaneous SS statistics of *all* prisoners in *all* concentration camps (a document dating from January 1945) allows us to conclude that the *Veränderungsmeldungen* and the *Häftlingsbewegung* referred to the entire camp including the satellite camps, but only to the male inmates.[3]

How did the figure of 100,000 victims arise?

The man in the Kremlin, who was responsible for millions of deaths in the GULAG and who had his propagandist Ilya Ehrenburg claim 4 million victims of Auschwitz before the Red Army had even entered that camp, was apparently not sufficiently impressed by the Sachsenhausen death toll. For this reason, the figure of 19,900 (or slightly more) victims never appeared in Soviet propaganda. Instead the number of 100,000 first appeared in October 1945 in a letter Professor I. P. Traynin, a member of the ESC, wrote to Foreign Minister V. Molotov. The letter begins abruptly as follows[4]:

> "At the Sachsenhausen concentration camp near Berlin, the German authorities have annihilated more than 100,000 citizens of the USSR, England, France, Poland, Holland, Belgium, Hungary and other states."

No explanation whatsoever is given for this laconic assertion. It is highly improbable that Traynin would have undertaken to issue such a statement without a hint from the very top – in other words, from

Stalin himself. The figure of 100,000 victims was immediately spread by Soviet propaganda.

In late 1946 and early 1947, a "forensic commission" headed by one of Russia's most illustrious pathologists, Professor V. I. Prosorovski, visited Sachsenhausen, but apparently did not carry out any further investigations. Prosorovski was no newcomer to this kind of activity: He had served as an expert for the ESC at the "war crimes trials" at Krasnodar[5] and Kharkov[6],[7] (1943), co-authored the Soviet counter-expertise at Katyn[8] (January 1944) and acted in the Katyn case as a witness for the prosecution at Nuremberg. It goes without saying that his forensic reports invariably confirmed the version of the ESC. As a citizen of the Stalinist Soviet Union, he had of course no other choice.

While the commission headed by Prosorovski adopted the figure of 21,700 victims which was based on the SS *Häftlingsbewegung* records and had been confirmed by Engemann and his team, they invented a plethora of additional groups of victims, making no attempt whatsoever to justify the figures adduced. The final death toll given by the commission was 100,000. This figure was adopted without any further ado by the Soviet military court that conducted the so-called "Berlin Trial", where several members of the former SS garrison of Sachsenhausen were put on trial in Berlin-Pankow (October 1947). In 1961, when the "Sachsenhausen National Commemoration Site" was inaugurated by the East German authorities, a Book of Commemoration was published, where the 100,000 figure appeared three times: in the introduction, in a speech by Walter Ulbricht and in the "Cry of Sachsenhausen". In the German Democratic Republic, this figure thus became a dogma nobody would dare to question.

The Soviet Prisoners of War at Sachsenhausen Concentration Camp

The number of Soviet POWs who perished at Sachsenhausen is still an unanswered question. Why were these POWs sent to a concentration camp in the first place and not to a "normal" POW camp - in their case, a "Russian camp"?

After their invasion of the Soviet Union, the Germans took hundreds of thousands of prisoners within the first few months (the exact number is still disputed). Sheltering and feeding this huge mass of people confronted the Wehrmacht with enormous problems. Those Soviet POWs who were sent to the territory of the Reich before the onset of winter were relatively lucky. Since the capacity of the existing POW camps was insufficient to lodge them all, a considerable number of Soviet prisoners were sent to farms to perform agricultural work or to German towns to perform communal work. Thousands more were interned in concentration camps – not for annihilation, but in order to work in industrial plants situated in the neighborhood of the camps. The "normal" camp inmates had to evacuate some of their barracks for the newcomers, which led to serious overcrowding.

Soviet POW's arriving in Sachsenhausen Concentration Camp (Fall 1941) Bundesarchiv, Bild 183-K0901-014 / CC-BY-SA [CC-BY-SA-3.0-de (http://creativecommons.org/licenses/by-sa/3.0/de/deed.en)], via Wikimedia Commons

Typhus

The six "Russian barracks" designated for the Soviet POWs at Sachsenhausen were named *Kriegsgefangenen-Arbeitslager* and strictly separated from the rest of the camp (*Russen-isolierung*). From an administrative point of view this sector was not a part of the concentration camp but became part of *Kriegsgefangenen-Stalag Oranienburg* instead.[9] Owing to the massive influx of POWs, the usual registration procedure which included delousing and 14 days of quarantine was apparently not observed, and within a short period of time typhus was rampant in the camp.

A separate register of deceased prisoners seems to have been maintained for the *Stalag* (*Stammlager für Kriegsgefangene*) since 22 October 1941. This document has not survived. The mortality among the Soviet POWs was staggeringly high. A surviving list[10] about the (presumably) first two Russian transports reveals a horrific death toll: In the period from 18 October to 30 December 1941 altogether 2,508 Soviet POWs had been admitted to Sachsenhausen; however on 30 December 1941 only 1,360 of them were still alive. In other words: 1,148 prisoners (46% of the total) had died within these two and a half months, most of them undoubtedly from typhus.

The "Russenaktion"

Communist functionaries, especially Political Commissars (*Politruks*), of which at least one was attached to every unit of the Red Army, were meted out a far worse treatment than "normal" Russian prisoners (*Arbeitsrussen*) because from the National Socialist point of view, these functionaries were "carriers of the Soviet regime". According to the *Kommissarbefehl* issued by the *Oberkommando der Wehrmacht* on 6 June 1941 at Hitler's instigation, commissars were not recognized as combatants and were denied the protection they would be entitled to as POWs in accordance with international law. They were ordered to be shot after capture. To its credit, the Wehrmacht disapproved of the *Kommissarbefehl* from the very beginning and largely failed to implement it so that only a minority of the captured commissars were actually shot. With Hitler's agreement, this order was effectively revoked on 6 May 1942.[11]

While the *Kommissarbefehl* concerned primarily the combat units, two special orders (*Einsatzbefehle*) issued in July 1941 by Reinhard Heydrich, chief of the *Sicherheitspolizei* and the SD, provided for the screening of the inmates of POW camps. The Germans had become aware of the fact that many commissars had mingled with the great mass of prisoners, their uniforms being indistinguishable from the ones of military officers or common soldiers but for a red star on the sleeve (which could easily be removed). Therefore the POWs in the camps were subjected to systematic interrogation. Those identified as commissars were "singled out" and sent to the nearest concentration camp to be shot. Both the *Kommissarbefehl* and Heydrich's

Einsatzbefehle were highly questionable measures and most likely illegal from the point of view of international law. As early as 15 November 1941, the two *Einsatzbefehle* were somewhat mitigated with Himmler's approval: From now on, those singled out as commissars could be used for hard physical labor in the quarries instead of being shot.

It is not known when the shooting of Soviet POWs (*Russenaktion*) at Sachsenhausen began; the earliest date mentioned is late August 1941. Our knowledge is exclusively based on the statements of former prisoners (Büge, Sakowski etc.) which often contradict each other and were probably made under duress. In mid-November 1941 the *Russenaktion* was allegedly stopped, presumably for two reasons: The revocation of Heydrich's *Einsatzbefehle* (15 November 1941) and the recent outbreak of typhus. Incidentally several German prisoners employed at the crematorium were among the first victims of the dread disease. During the *Russenaktion* they had sat on a heap of clothes belonging to shot Soviet soldiers and been infected by lice. Subsequently the camp was subject to a quarantine that lasted several weeks.

Soviet Propaganda

Efficiently exploiting the *Russenaktion*, the relatively bad living conditions in the camps and the frighteningly high mortality among "normal" Soviet POWs, Soviet propaganda insinuated that the NS regime deliberately exterminated its captured soldiers of the Red Army. Of course Moscow's propagandists remained silent about the fact that the treatment of the Russian prisoners, who fared indeed much worse than Western POWs, was a direct consequence of Soviet policy. As early as 1919, the USSR had withdrawn from the 1907 Hague Convention, and the Soviet government never signed the 1929 Geneva Convention about the protection of prisoners of war. For this reason, the captured soldiers of the Red Army were not protected by these conventions, even if the universally recognized laws of humanity did apply to them.

After the liberation of the Sachsenhausen Camp, Soviet operatives "fed" the former inmates with disinformation and atrocity propaganda about a huge slaughter of Soviet POWs. Rumors which had arisen during the war were now "confirmed" by "knowledgeable" former prisoners. German prisoners of war and prisoners of the NKVD were forced to make statements that they would never have made voluntarily. To what extent Soviet propaganda distorted the facts is demonstrated by the immensely exaggerated figures of victims bandied about by Moscow's propagandists.

The number of allegedly shot Russian POWs according to the witnesses

The *Russenaktion* was carried out in the northern sector of the *Industriehof* (industrial court) which was situated outside the camp triangle. A special part of the *Industriehof* was the so-called *Holz- und Kohleplatz* (wood and coal yard), which was protected from prying eyes by walls and buildings. According to the official history (which was later confirmed by former SS men before West-German Courts), the unsuspecting prisoners were marched into the barracks where they were placed in front of a supposed height-measuring device. Through an opening in the wall behind this device, the victim was killed with a shot in the back of his neck by a man standing in the adjacent room, various SS-*Blockführer* acting as executioners.

The bodies of the victims were incinerated in four field crematoria that had been installed in front of the barracks and were surrounded by a wooden fence. This grisly work was carried out by about eight German prisoners. The overwhelming majority of the inmates were not allowed to enter the northern sector of the *Industriehof* and had no possibility whatsoever to witness the killings: Whatever they knew was based upon rumors. As is to be expected under these circumstances, the "eyewitness reports" are literally teeming with improbabilities and contradictions. Nearly all "witnesses" claimed between 14,000 and 18,000 shooting victims, and some of them ventured even higher figures. In all likelihood, these "witnesses" had been instructed by Soviet operatives.

After the end of the war, at least two former prisoners seemed very well informed about the *Russenaktion*: Emil Büge, who had worked at the Prisoner Records Office where he had to register the admittees, and Paul Sakowski, who had been one of the crematorium workers. Both men left very detailed written reports about what had transpired at the camp, and Sakowski entered the witness stand at the Berlin Sachsenhausen trial. Both of them mentioned the usual figure of 14,000 or more shot Russian POWs. It stands to reason that they had no choice, each of them subject to the mercies of one of the victorious powers. According to his own statements, Büge had worked "for the Americans", which most probably means the Augsburg-based U.S.

War Crimes Commission. Lonely, impoverished and no longer needed by the Americans, Emil Büge committed suicide in 1950.

Paul Sakowski (born 1920), whom East German propaganda christened "the hangman of Sachsenhausen", was arrested by the NKVD shortly after his liberation from the camp. In October 1947, he was among the defendants at the Sachsenhausen trial at Berlin-Pankow. Sakowski was sentenced to 25 years, which he served until the very last day, first at Workuta and later in East Germany. As he had been previously interned at Sachsenhausen for six years, this man spent more than 31 years of his life behind prison bars.

The case of SS-*Scharführer* (Second Sergeant) Paul Waldmann starkly illustrates the means the Soviet agents resorted to in order to "prove" imaginary figures of victims. Waldmann, who had been a driver for the Oranienburg SS, was sent to the Eastern Front in December 1941 where he uninterruptedly served until the retreat of the German forces to Berlin. On 2 May 1945 he was taken prisoner by the Red Army near the "Zoo" Train Station[12] and transferred to Posen, where he was subjected to routine questioning. The fact that he had served at Sachsenhausen obviously aroused the interest of his interrogators. On 10 June 1945, Waldmann signed a "confession", stating that the *Russenaktion*, in which he had allegedly participated, had claimed the lives of no fewer than 840,000 (!) Soviet prisoners. Although this preposterous figure was never put about by Soviet propaganda, it has survived because owing to an obvious error of the clerks in Moscow, it was filed among the Auschwitz documents (IMT Doc USSR-52) where it was rediscovered by Carlo Mattogno in 2003. Paul Waldmann disappeared without leaving any trace; presumably he met his fate in the GULAG. In February 1946, the clerks in Moscow had apparently not yet become aware of their error, because excerpts from Waldmann's "confession" were read by Soviet prosecutors Pokrovski and Smirnov at Nuremberg and thus became part of the protocols of the Nuremberg trial as well.[13]

The number of shooting victims – official statements

One of the earliest post-war documents about Sachsenhausen Concentration Camp is the so-called prisoners' report (*Häftlingsbericht*) authored by Hellmut Bock. The report exists in seven or eight – more or less different – versions. The first version which was presumably completed on 7 May 1945 is now lost, but an English translation has remained.[14] There we read:

> *September – December 1941. 16,000 Russian prisoners, driven together like cattle, were slaughtered. On the grounds of the industry-department four riding furnaces were standing so that the corpses could be cleared away uninterruptedly. Their ashes became the site for the new crematory. Before these people were murdered they were beastly ill-treated. Music out of big loudspeakers deafened the shrieking of the victims.*

Although this earliest version of the report was modified several times, the number of 16,000 murdered Soviet POWs was still the same when Hellmut Bock submitted the final, seventh version of the report to the Soviet Investigation Commission.[15]

The head of the commission, Sharitch, slightly reduced this figure; on 30 June 1945 he wrote in his report[16]: "In September/October 1941, 13,000 to 14,000 Soviet prisoners of war were shot."

In the various drafts of the ESC about Sachsenhausen the figure of 14,000 shot Soviet POWs regularly recurs.[17] On the other hand, the commission headed by Professor Prosorovski[18] mentioned 20,000 shooting victims (January 1947), and in April 1961, when East Germany dedicated a National Memorial Site at Sachsenhausen, yet another figure (18,000) was claimed.

Since the collapse of East Germany, these figures have been somewhat reduced. On the occasion of the 56th anniversary of the camp's liberation it was declared[19]:

> *"The so-called 'Station Z', called so by the Nazis, was the annihilation site of the Concentration Camp with a neck-shot facility, gas chamber and crematorium. In Fall 1941 at least 12,000 Soviet POWs were shot here."*

Only four years later (2005) the Sachsenhausen Memorial Site wrote[20]:

> *"In the months from September to November 1941, the Wehrmacht transported at least thirteen thousand Soviet prisoners-of-war to Oranienburg, where the Concentration Camps' Inspectorate organized the entire operation for the murder of Soviet prisoners-of-war. More than ten thousand of*

these were murdered within only ten weeks in an automated 'head shot' facility."

All these sources remained silent about the factual basis of their figures. Today, the official figures are obviously still based on the Soviet view of history as it was imposed after the War.

To the best of our knowledge, the only attempt to determine the number of Soviet POWs shot at Sachsenhausen with any degree of accuracy was made by the district court of Cologne (Köln) at the trial of Kaiser, et al. (1965).[21] However, the verdict freely admitted: "It was not possible to ascertain the number of the shot Russians. There were no documents about this question." All the same, the court quoted two sources it considered relatively trustworthy: A compilation by the former *Arbeits- und Rapportführer* Gustav Sorge and a statement made by the former camp elder (*Lagerälteste*) Harry Naujoks who had been assigned to collect the identification tags of the Russian soldiers. Despite its initial reluctance to name a concrete figure, the court finally concluded:

> *"Considering the possibility of further imprecisions, we can assume now as certain, that during the action from begin of September to mid of November 1941 at least 6,500 Russian POWs have been shot in Sachsenhausen Concentration Camp."*

The Russian commemorative stone

In November 2000 a relatively modest monument consisting of two black granite blocks was dedicated on the grounds of the former Sachsenhausen concentration camp by the foreign ministers of Russia and Germany, Igor Ivanov and Joschka Fischer. One of the stones bears a bronze plaque with the following inscription in Russian and German:

> *"1941-1945. Remember every single one of the thousands of sons and daughters of the fatherland who were tortured to death at Sachsenhausen Concentration Camp. The Government of Russia."*

Thus no explicit figure was mentioned, apparently because neither side desired to identify with the propagandistic figures still publicized by the media (10,000 to 18,000). Whether authentic German documents about the real number of victims of the *Russenaktion* still exist today (in Moscow or elsewhere) remains to be seen.

Summary

In the nine years of its existence, Sachsenhausen Concentration Camp (including all satellite camps and outstations) claimed the lives of about 22,000 male prisoners. In view of the fact that approximately 140,000 male deportees were sent (and registered) to this camp, this means that 15.7% of the prisoners perished. Compared to prison camps of other states, other wars and other times, such a percentage is unfortunately nothing extraordinary.

This number does not comprise the female detainees who died in the satellite camps and the Soviet POWs who perished from "natural causes" or were shot. The real number of these victims deserves further research. It bears mentioning that 533 prisoners were killed during Allied air raids in 1944/1945. After the Auer factories at Oranienburg had been bombed on 15 March 1945, the dead bodies of 282 female prisoners were retrieved.[22] However, these tragic losses do not even remotely justify the propagandistic figure of 100,000 victims. As to the number of prisoners who perished during the evacuation of the camp (the inmates were marched away in various columns), the existing information is very incomplete. Obviously these deaths cannot be ascribed to the conditions in the camp. Just like the German refugees who died on their flight from the Eastern provinces to the West, these victims succumbed to the horrible conditions prevailing as a consequence of the invasion and conquest of Germany.

Abbreviations

AS   Sachsenhausen Archive

BArch   Bundesarchiv Berlin (Federal Archive, Berlin-Lichterfelde)

FSB RF   Federal Security Service of the Russian Federation

GARF   *Gosudarstvenniy Archiv Rossiskoy Federatsij* (State Archive of the Russian Federation)

GULAG   *Gosudarstvennaj Upravleniye Lagerej* (State Administration of Camps)

IfZ   *Institut für Zeitgeschichte*, Munich (Institute for Contemporary History, Munich)

NKGB   *Narodniy Kommisariat Gosudarstvennoy Besopasnosti* (People's Commission for State Security)

Notes:

1. Klaus Schwensen, "Zur Opferzahl des KZ Sachsenhausen (1936-1945)," unpublished.
2. Carlo Mattogno, "KL Sachsenhausen – Stärkemeldungen und 'Vernichtungsaktionen' 1940 bis 1945," in: *Vierteljahreshefte für freie Geschichtsforschung (VffG)*, vol. 7 (2003), no. 2, pp. 173-185 http://vho.org/VffG/2003/2/2_03.html.
3. Administration [*Inspektion*] of the Concentration Camps, List of Number of Prisoners in All the Camps (Bestandsliste der deutschen Konzentrationslager), Status 1. Jan. and 15. Jan. 1945; in: IfZ-Archiv, Sign. Fa 183; BArch NS3/439.
4. Letter from I.P. Traynin to Molotov, GARF 7021-116-177, p. 67. Handwritten date 8. X. 45, Reg. No. 189.
5. Forensic Expertise on German War Crimes in Krasnodar, dated 29 June 1943 (quoted in the Trial of Kharkov).
6. Expertise of the Forensic Expert Commission, dated 15 September 1943; quoted in the Trial of Kharkov, see *FN* 7, pp. 12 and 77-81.
7. N.N., Deutsche Greuel in Rußland. Gerichtstag in Charkow (German Atrocities in Russia. The Trial of Kharkov) [Official Protocol of the Kharkov Trial], Stern-Verlag, Vienna undated [1945].
8. IMT-Document USSR-54, *Report of a Special Commission for the examination and investigation of the circumstances of the shooting of Polish prisoners of war in the Katyn Forest* by the German fascist invaders, Smolensk, 24 January 1944.
9. Mikas Šlaža, *Bestien in Menschengestalt (Beasts in Human Shape)*, Vilnius (Wilna), Vaga Verlag 1995. The book contains Šlaža's complete Sachsenhausen Report in German and Lithuanian with an afterword by Domas Kaunas.
10. German list (Mimeograph) „Russische Kriegsgefangene" (Russian POWs), dating from 18.10. - 30.12.1941; in: GARF 7021-104-4, p. 149-150.
11. Walter Post, "Erschiessung sowjetischer Kommissare," in: Franz W. Seidler und Alfred M. de Zayas (Ed.), *Kriegsverbrechen in Europa und im Nahen Osten im 20. Jahrhundert*, Verlag Mittler, Hamburg 2002, pp. 76-82.
12. There was a huge air-raid shelter (Zoo-Bunker) in the area of the Berlin Zoo and close to the "Zoo" S-Bahn station. The bunker was equipped with anti-aircraft guns (Flak) and was one of the last strongholds of the defenders.

13. Soviet Prosecutor L.N. Smirnow on Tuesday, 19. Feb. 1946 (62nd day, forenoon), IMT Vol. VII, p. 635 ff.
14. N.N., *REPORT ON CONCENTRATION CAMP SACHSENHAUSEN AT ORANIENBURG*, [as Part 1 of a more extended report of Dutch ex-prisoners Frederik Willem Bischoff van Heemskerck and Johann Hers, translation into English by Bischoff]. Archives: Zentralnyj archive FSB RF or Rijksinstituut voor Oorlogsdocumentatie, Karton 27 Sachsenhausen, Nr. 59, Mappe 3 or AS Ordner 7 (Netherlands).
15. Hellmut Bock, *Bericht Konzentrationslager Sachsenhausen*, presented to the Commission of the USSR to Investigate the Crimes of the German Fascists in Sachsenhausen Concentration Camp, Oranienburg, 12 June 1945. Archives: GARF, 1525-1-340, T. 3, p. 31350 – 31382 (or sheet 351-383); Copy in AS 235 M. 173 Bd. 3, Bl. 148 -181.
16. A. Sharitch, Investigation Report [to the ESC in Moscow], Berlin, 29 June 1945; in GARF 7021-104-2, p. 29 (handwritten archive number).
17. Klaus Schwensen, "The Report of the Soviet Extraordinary State Commission on the Sachsenhausen Concentration Camp," *Inconvenient History*, Vol. 3 No. 4 (Winter 2011) or http://www.inconvenienthistory.com/archive/2011/volume_3/number_4/the_report_of_the_soviet_extraordinary_state_commission.php
18. Expertise of the Forensic Expert Commission, on behalf of the Investigation Group of the NKGB, [Jan. 1947]. German Translation: Staatsanwaltschaft Köln, 24 Ks 2/68 (Z), Sonderakten, Bd. 8, Bl. 1-28. Today in Hauptstaatsarchiv Düsseldorf, Bestand Gerichte, Rep. 267 Nr. 1683.
19. International Sachsenhausen Committee, official Statement, 22 April 2001.
20. Günter Morsch (Ed.) [Director of Sachsenhausen Memorial Site], Mord und Massenmord im Konzentrationslager Sachsenhausen 1936–1945 [Murder and Mass Murder in Sachsenhausen CC], Metropol-Verlag, Berlin 2005, p. 166.
21. Irene Sagel-Grande, H. H. Fuchs und C. F. Rüter, *Justiz und NS-Verbrechen*, University Press Amsterdam, Amsterdam 1979, Urteil 591, p. 64 – 139 ff.
22. Wolff, Georg, *Kalendarium der Geschichte des KZ Sachsenhausen*, Herausgegeben von der Nationale Mahn- und Gedenkstätte Sachsenhausen, Oranienburg 1987.

REVIEW

The Black Swan (Revised Edition)

by Nassim Nicholas Taleb. Penguin Group, New York, 2010, 379 pp.

Ezra MacVie

This book is about the profound subjects of thinking, knowing, understanding, and then acting (or just as often, refraining from acting) on understanding. While it concentrates on *how* to think, know, and understand, it necessarily, and very valuably, strays occasionally into *what* to think and know about. Its attainment of bestseller status is, according to the narrative I have constructed, based on its promises in the domain of prediction. But in its contemplations of prediction or, more accurately, preparedness, it (again, necessarily and most valuably) delves into prediction's mirror-image—understanding the past—in ways that will gladden the heart and enrich the mind of every revisionist who engages in revision as a search for the truth.

From its pages, an analogy of reverse-prediction, that is, understanding of *what happened*, or *how things were* (and no longer are) stands out among all the other recollections that ensue from reading this book. And that is the Story (my capitalization) of the Ice Cube.

It posits the presence of a puddle of water, somehow known to the observer to be the runoff from the melting of a piece of ice—perhaps the consequence of a recent period. Gratuitously, I have added to the situation the specifications that what is known encompasses the exact period of time (in the past) that the ice cube melted, and even (from the volume of water observed) the amount of water the (somehow known-to-have-existed) ice cube contained, and even *where* the ice cube was—an amount of knowledge seldom available in situations of observed moisture. What Taleb irrefutably points out is that even someone possessing all this unlikely knowledge would *still* remain utterly unable to reconstruct, even approximately, the specific *shape* of the piece of ice—where it protruded, and how much, and where it had recesses, and how deep these were, and so on and on in an infinitude of impossible specifications.

Nassim Nicholas Taleb. Photo available for public use.
http://www.fooledbyrandomness.com/pictures.htm

And yet, pundits, seers, experts, and charlatans regularly attain high incomes in our society from propounding just such "information" concerning the factors and causes of recent past events, even while in many cases venturing with varying degrees of assurance predictions as to what the purported present set of circumstances portends for those of us who managed to survive the just-past debacle. Taleb explores such mass—and massive—gullibility somewhat tentatively, likely because Taleb is not a psychologist (nor a pundit, seer, expert, nor charlatan), but rather, a former securities trader who first hit it big in 1987 with contrarian positions that paid off enormously on the 23% swoon of the stock market that occurred in that year. It appears Taleb may again have scored in the 2008 financial crisis, if on no other evidence than that, in this book's first edition (2007), he very clearly anticipated those developments in telling detail. This review concerns the book's second edition (2010), which includes a 96-page

"Postscript Essay" that to my reckoning embodies something close to half the value of the overall work, at least for revisionists. In it, Taleb dwells but little on past events that he can well claim to have predicted (he sniffs that he is more interested in future events than in past events, but this still leaves over a good deal of useful insight as to the less-favored direction of the arrow of time—the one of primary interest to revisionists).

History, indeed, gains some very special treatment at the hands of this master of time and events, though he directs considerable opprobrium also to the fields of economics, monetary policy, regulation, the social sciences in general, and indeed academia en toto, to which he affixed the indelible label "organized knowledge," echoing the term "organized religion." History, and many of the other "narrative disciplines" such as economics and the social sciences, are subject to what he styles the "narrative fallacy," this being the complementary propensities of consumers (the public) and suppliers (experts) to produce and accept explanations of past and present conditions that: (a) accord well, or even perfectly, with the known conditions of the present; and (b) are but one or another among potentially millions of narratives that could, with equal plausibility, explain those few known results observable in the present day. That the favored narratives might have been selected by, or concocted for, any of numerous predispositions to believe, or persuade, is so irresistible as not even to require mention.

On Page 309 (of the paperback second edition), he reports first under the heading of "My Mistakes" (committed in the first edition):

> *The first fault was pointed out to me by Jon Elster. I had written that the narrative fallacy pervades historical analyses, since I believed that there was no such thing as a test of a historical statement by forecasting and falsification. Elster explained to me that there are situations in which historical theory can escape the narrative fallacy and be subjected to empirical rejection—areas in which we are discovering documents or archeological sites yielding information capable of countering a certain narrative.*

Indeed. Any revisionist might have told him the same thing, and Jon Elster turns out to be a Norwegian social and political theorist who has authored works in the philosophy of social science and rational choice theory. He evidently is not primarily known as any sort of revisionist, though for obvious reasons, I suspect he harbors a specific revisionist notion or two—among which, no doubt, are notions that he finds it best for his career not to announce or admit too noticeably, things being as they are.

Taleb concludes the first section of his "My Mistakes" with the sentence, "Once again, beware of history." This options-trader-turned-philosopher is showing a good hand indeed in the central issues that engage readers of INCONVENIENT HISTORY. He shows this good hand in many other matters of vital importance, as readers of his book will discover.

But returning to the matter of history, or of the "just what really happened here?" line of inquiry, Taleb adduces one other item that attracted the attention of this revisionist: the existence of one Helenus of Troy. This Helenus's face most definitely did not launch any ships, as the famed Helen's was said to have done, as Helenus was the son (not daughter) of King Priam and Queen Hecuba. In his own right, Helenus was a warrior of ability befitting a prince, and of importance, too, as at one point the besieging Greeks captured him, and apparently tortured him for information. But Taleb ascribed to Helenus an ability of positively riveting interest: he was a *reverse prophet*. That is, according to Taleb, he possessed a gods-given ability to discern and report what happened *in the past*—in answer, no doubt, to the torrent of questions eternally arising in the minds of people who wonder just how things got to be the way they are.

I have been unable via other (secondary) sources to confirm Taleb's report of Helenus's special gift, but apparently it is described in *The Iliad*, which may in fact be the entire corpus of information about this figure of the ancient past. Taleb enjoys a reputation as a formidable scholar and as a polyglot to boot, being as he is fluent in French, English, Arabic (he is from Lebanon), Italian, and Spanish, and able to read texts in Greek, Latin, Aramaic, Hebrew, and the Canaanite script. No doubt, his information concerning Helenus is derived directly from text rendered in the original ancient Greek, and its absence from Wikipedia articles is a reflection on the "free encyclopedia" rather than on the veracity of Taleb's disclosures.

As the author noted, a Helenus in this present day would be a fine thing for us all to have—if some of us didn't kill or otherwise silence him for saying things that displeased them, anyway. Wikileaks, among many other institutions, would instantly become very small potatoes, indeed.

The Black Swan is about what we (think we) know, and how we get to thinking so—a subject known by the fancy name of epistemology. For the revisionist interested in the theory and mechanics of such vital processes—in which perforce every revisionist is in fact deeply involved—this book provides a profoundly rich reward of understanding.

REVIEW

The Gas Vans: A Critical Investigation

by Santiago Alvarez and Pierre Marais, The Barnes Review, Washington, D.C., 2011, 390 pp., illustrated, with notes, bibliography, indexed.

Richard A. Widmann

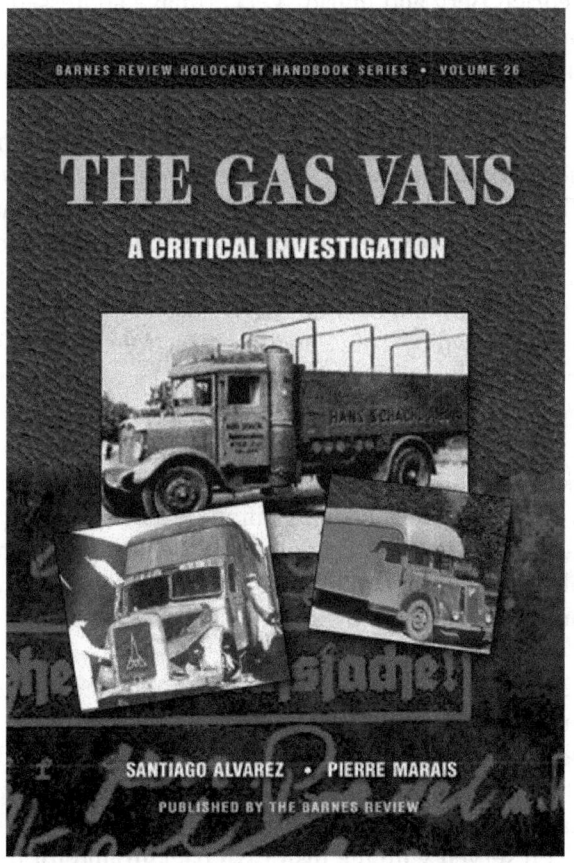

Cover reproduced with permission of Santiago Alvarez

The Gas Vans fills a significant gap in Holocaust literature. Often forgotten in the public mind and limited to minor entries in the most important Holocaust tomes, (gas vans are mentioned on 4 pages out of 790 in Hilberg's *The Destruction of the European Jews* and on 7 pages out of 622 in Reitlinger's *The Final Solution*). While they may seem unimportant to the broader Holocaust story, one must pause when one realizes that the Holocaust fundamentalists charge that as many as 700,000 fell victim to these wheeled killing machines. Recognizing that the gas vans were charged with something greater than 10% of claimed Jewish Holocaust deaths, and with formerly key elements of the traditional story like the extermination camp at Majdanek being whittled away (total deaths have been reduced since 1944 from 1.7 million to some 60,000), it is a wonder that greater emphasis has not been placed on the gas van story. Revisionists, most notably Friedrich Berg and Ingrid Weckert have addressed the subject in various articles, but this volume represents the first book-length treatment in English from either camp in the Holocaust controversy.

According to the Preface of this edition, Alvarez had only intended to translate Pierre Marais's French study *Les camions a gaz en question* (*The Gas Trucks Scrutinized*) (1994) into English. Apparently while translating Marais's work, the author noticed numerous errors as well as flawed and missing arguments. Also omitted, of course, was documentary material that only surfaced post-1994. The resulting manuscript had grown by 100% and large sections of Marais's text were either rewritten or replaced and in some cases even deleted.

The Gas Vans is Volume 26 in the Holocaust Handbook Series. It is arranged like many other volumes in the series — in a very detailed format that appears exhaustive and can indeed be quite exhausting to the reader. Alvarez, by the way, notes that the current volume is far from complete as additional materials are held by the *Zentralstelle* in Germany and are inaccessible due to German censorship laws.

While more readable than many of the other volumes in this series, it suffers from similar flaws. While technically there is an "Introduction," the four pages labeled some as such really do not introduce the topic historically. As the book begins we are provided with criteria for a legal and a scientific investigation. The book would have been well served with the historical background for the subject, especially in this case, where so little is generally known about gas vans. The book begins in a way that suggests that the author assumes that his readership is already fairly familiar with the literature.

Abb. 1. Saurer 5 BHw. mit Holzgasantrieb.

A German wartime producer-gas truck from Saurer (Type 5 BHw, produced until 1935. It is argued that had the Germans intended to commit mass murder with carbon monoxide, they would have employed this gas technology rather than the alleged diesel exhaust.

Before the reader knows it, they are on a rollercoaster ride of lengthy quotes and the debunking of the same. Before long we are already being treated to the topic of the toxicity of diesel exhaust gas. While important to the overall claims, the technical nature of this topic hardly seems to be something that would kick off such a volume. A long section follows which reviews relevant documents. Without much context, the documents are reviewed, oftentimes with reference to key revisionist arguments.

The book continues with a consideration of court records from both the war and post-war period. Finally the author addresses witness testimonies before reaching his conclusion. Essentially echoing an argument made by Friedrich Berg many years prior, Alvarez argues that the Germans were too sophisticated to use such a crude makeshift solution for murdering people *en masse* as the gas vans. He goes on to discuss so-called producer-gas vehicles that were equipped with wood gas generators as a much "better" alternative than what is asserted to have been used. It is interesting to consider whether such vehicles may have been created by the decidedly less sophisticated Soviets for the torture and murder of their political enemies. While there is some evidence that this may be the case, it remains inconclusive whether the Soviets retroactively charged their own crimes, like the murder of Polish officers at Katyn, to their German enemies.

Ultimately Alvarez and Marais conclude "there are ...no material traces of these vehicles and no photos." There is little doubt that gas vans are simply one more evil Holocaust fairy-tale like the soap made from human cadavers and lampshades made of human skin. Revisionists have thought this as early as 1948 when Francis Parker Yockey quipped, "a 'gasmobile' was invented to titillate the mechanically-minded." Forty-five years later, Ingrid Weckert came to a similar conclusion in her treatment of the subject, "The Gas Vans: A Critical Assessment of the Evidence"

> *"On the whole, the evidence submitted for the 'gas vans' cannot be accorded any evidential value, and the claim that Germans had murdered thousands of human beings in 'gas vans' must be regarded strictly as rumor."*

There is little chance that this book will find new converts to Holocaust revisionism. Unfortunately even that hardcore group of revisionist completionists who seek out this handsome and well-made volume will likely let this one sit on the shelf and gather dust after perusing the photos and pictures. Alvarez has made an in-depth analysis of an important topic; one almost completely ignored by both sides of the Holocaust debate, but has done so in a style that will likely result in its neglect. That is unfortunate, because the fall of this pillar of Holocaust mythology is long overdue.

The Gas Vans may be purchased through The Barnes Review.

COMMENT

Revisionism's Final Victories

Jett Rucker

Perhaps France fell first, in 1991, with its *loi Gayssot*. Then (or slightly before) fell Switzerland, Germany, Austria, Belgium, not necessarily in that order. All these countries, and of course Israel, have capitulated to historical revisionism in the most abjectly desperate manner imaginable: they now officially, *with laws*, threaten people who express certain views of recent history with fines and imprisonment for so doing. Specifically, these countries, and other countries by various devices, punish "Holocaust Denial" with the mechanisms originally emplaced for dealing with rapists, murderers, thieves, and other such perpetrators of death and destruction.

They've all given up. They've given up on social disapprobation, they've given up on the wisdom of crowds, and they've given up on all pretense, otherwise dear to their regimes, of freedom of expression. They've fallen back on the scoundrel's last recourse: legal prohibition—the very same device with which once the United States sought to contain Demon Alcohol, and with which it, and other countries, continue to assault what might be styled "freedom to ingest."

Of course, it fails. It fails frequently and widely, and ironically, it exacerbates its own failure in inciting, and even rewarding, those who contrive by various means—nowadays often the Internet—to circumvent and overcome its ostensibly intended effects. And, with regularity, it claims victims—examples for The Rest to behold—in the form of transgressors who are investigated, raided, accused, stripped of honors and degrees and livelihoods and even citizenships, and fined, and jailed, and publicly excoriated. In doing this, it creates not only opponents with massively reinforced wills to resist, but public martyrs as well—prisoners of conscience whose antecedent is none less than Jesus Christ himself, and the long trains of succeeding martyrs in both Christianity and in other religions and causes, who form the panoply with which ultimately the rectitude of their causes can be more brilliantly illuminated for the inspiration of new recruits.

Drug dealers thrown into prison could avail themselves of an idealistic basis for refuting the legitimacy of their incarceration by asserting their support for the right of people to acquire the substances of their choice for introduction into their own bodies, but drug dealers seem not to do this. One reason for this might be the enormous profits that successful dealers enjoy from plying their trade, though in honest contemplation, this factor does not in the slightest diminish the point. Those espousing a disapproved understanding of history, on the other hand, serve a small and rather parsimonious "market" of truth-seekers who, in the event, fail notably to enrich their purveyors. While, like drug dealers, revisionists may be marginalized and dispossessed by any of many means, they never attain anything resembling the wealth and opulent lifestyles often seen among the purveyors of chemical freedoms.

And one other critical difference: although often themselves the victims of violence, the purveyors of intellectual freedom as regards history never themselves employ violence—not even, in many recorded cases, the sorts of defensive violence that could protect their persons and their (meager) properties from assault by their violent detractors. In this, all revisionists of record resemble not only the Christian Son of God, but Gandhi, The Buddha, and many others whose influence ultimately has pervaded both consciences and institutions to an extent that should give pause to those who undertake to oppose them.

Those who oppose them, particularly in the ambit of this Holocaust matter, may have managed, indeed, to disguise themselves in the various cloaks under which the casual observer might infer, however indistinctly, the forces of righteousness, or of opposition to racism, or discrimination, or some other of the principles of civilization to which the virtuously inclined might fancy themselves to be devoted.

This distinction—between those moved, on the one hand, by the implications of tangible evidence and, on the other, by the interested confabulations of those who say they were there at that time—should be made by those who wish to learn what might have been done to whom, by whom, when, where, how, and even, in the best of worlds, exactly why.

But, in numerous regulated regions, this is not to be. Superior forces—forces superior to the common man (or woman)—will stipulate what may be uttered to the public ear, and what may not. The rationales for such control of thoughts are numerous. They encompass suppressing the re-emergence of a doctrine advanced by a political party under which Germany disastrously lost a genocidal war, spreading "false history," "offending" various groups apparent within the polity, inciting intergroup disaffection, and on and on in such manner.

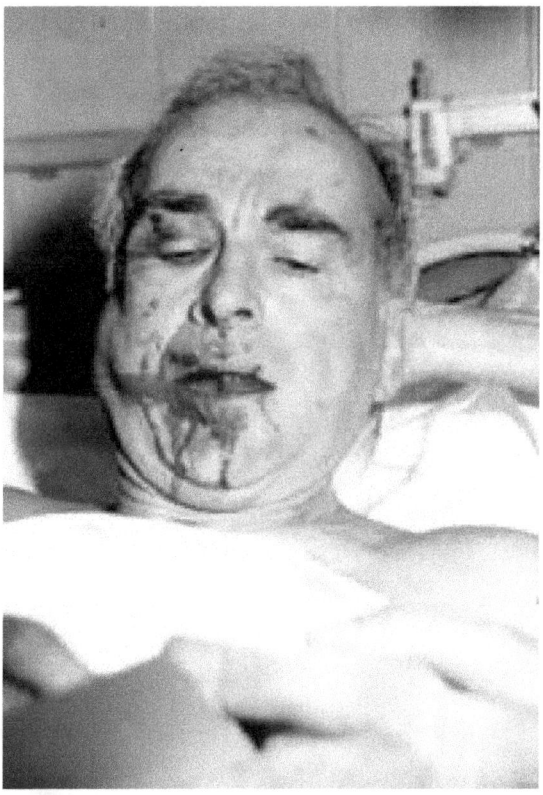

Professor Robert Faurisson in a hospital bed following a near fatal attack by Zionist thugs on 16 September 1989.

They are all—as such measures always are—driven by an ulterior agenda. The agenda in this case encompasses not only the desire of a cohesive group to eternally wrap itself in the mantle of victimhood, but far more urgently, to enshroud in the same mantle the depredations that Israel has long visited on the natives of Palestine, the taxpayers of Germany and the United States, and, with the attainment of the capability to launch missiles with nuclear warheads from long-range submarines, the entirety of humanity that lives within 500 miles of any ocean.

True history has its opponents, everywhere and always. It may, here and there, and now and then, also have its would-be adherents. These two communities, such as they may respectively be empowered, and motivated, and suppressed, and successful, eke out between their contentions, what is "known" and understood by those many whose interests place them between the poles represented by the opposing camps.

The intervention of law in favor of one side in this contest announces defeat on the part of the group so favored.

Victory is documentably theirs.

And inevitable defeat.

Volume IV

Number 4, Winter 2012

COMMENT

Uncle Sam, May I?

Jett Rucker

The US elections this past November 6 were dominated by a close presidential race whose partisans, if not the candidates themselves, seemed to entertain mutually hostile visions of how government should proceed into the future. As is the American custom, however, myriad issues and candidates went before the electorate under the guise of "local" issues on the same occasion and, in fact, on the same ballots. And inevitably, a few of these contests were actually bellwethers of issues of not just national, but in fact global import.

Of these, the initiatives to legalize the possession and production of marijuana stands out, not just in terms of its social/political/economic importance, but in the fact that in two states—Colorado and Washington—the private growing and use of marijuana has been decriminalized, at least so far as those two states' law-enforcement apparatuses are concerned.

The movement to legalize marijuana invites comparison with an American project of almost a hundred years ago to prohibit the sale and consumption of alcoholic beverages, while at the same time it illuminates a panoply of profound human-rights issues as well the political maelstroms that occasionally arise in the ambit of the United States' distinctive "federal" system of quaintly mischaracterized "sovereign states."

It has been little noted that the impetus for Franklin D. Roosevelt's famous emancipation of America's tipplers was driven by his government's desperate need for revenues, these having been deeply reduced by the ravages of the Depression that entered its third year in FDR's first year (1933) in office. Repeal (of Prohibition) had been pushed since Prohibition's first day by two groups, membership in both of which was claimed by many of the so-called "Wets." The first group, the smaller, held that regulation of what people could ingest—or of alcohol, at any rate—was not a fit office of government; that people should be free in this as well as all other respects in which their actions did not hurt others. The numbers of this group became vastly greater as experience developed with the extensive evils and destruction that attended the enforcement of Prohibition.

**Prohibition agents destroying barrels of alcohol 1921. Public Domain.
Wikipedia.org**

The second group, far larger, even, than its considerable confessing membership, simply wanted to be able to drink, and/or or to purvey drinks, without breaking the law. Those advocating Prohibition, of course, likewise fell into disparate categories celebrated even to the present day by contemporary analogies with the "Baptists and bootleggers" whose incongruous alliance sustained Prohibition long after its insufferable costs became apparent even to those who were happy if no drop of alcohol ever passed their lips.

But this battle, not unlike today's prohibition of marijuana and other recreational drugs, raged on endlessly until the federal government's revenues were ravaged by the Depression, and Prohibition tumbled as wheat before the scythe of the government's ravenous appetite for the people's pelf. America's federal system at that time displayed a spectacle that it has manifested on a number of occasions: various states anticipated the federal government's Prohibition by voting themselves "dry" in considerable numbers before the national drought struck in 1933. This pattern also appeared, among other times, in states including women in their electorates before the 1920 Constitutional amendment requiring all states to do so, and in states liberalizing permission for women to have abortions prior to the 1973 Supreme Court decision striking down the laws in the laggard states that still restricted abortion in ways the Court deemed contrary to the dictates of the Constitution.

Today, in a tax-revenue context not unlike that of the early Thirties, it appears that America's rambunctious states are leading the charge for repeal, a rolling-back of America's long-standing War on Drugs that, compared with movement toward prohibition, is like driving a vehicle in reverse compared with driving it forward. Or perhaps even a tractor-trailer (truck). Or a ship—it's awkward, hazardous, and the driver's ability to go exactly where he would like to is greatly impaired.

This labored analogy arises from the fact that federal law applies throughout every state, including states that have vacated penalties on possession and use of marijuana from their statute books. And the War on Drugs has been a federal (as well as state) war at least since the Harrison Narcotics Tax Act of 1914. This means that possession and use of marijuana continues to be (only) a federal crime in Colorado and Washington.

And this, in turn, augurs for stand-offs such as did not attend the repeal of Prohibition, where sentiment for repeal seems to have been concentrated in cities, rather than having the statewide appeal demonstrated in the two "free" states mentioned, as well as a number of other states, notably California, in which production and use of marijuana is licensed for certain "medical" purposes and remains under the control of the practitioners (chiefly doctors) who currently are licensed to authorize the purchase of prescription drugs. Although many states had their own Prohibitions, most predating the federal one, none of these repealed its Prohibition prior to the federal repeal, and Prohibition remained the de jure situation throughout all states, including those that had never prohibited alcohol in the first place.

Today's developments would not seem to presage an actual civil war between the federal government and those who wish to banish the federal War on Drugs from their territories. Armed confrontations between state and federal law-enforcement officers in the "free" states have been mooted, though, as the analogy of backing up a tractor-trailer rig was meant to illuminate, the specific directions this conflict may take seem very hard to predict. Federal invasions of "free" states would seem hard to imagine, but the analogy holds.

This is an official government document from the 1920s, a Medicinal Alcohol form. This form was used during the American Prohibition to acquire prescription alcohol, usually whiskey, for strictly medicinal purposes. Public Domain. Wikipedia.org [Click for larger image]

Federal Prohibition of alcohol was but 14 years old at its death, while the federal War on Drugs is almost 100 years old at this point. The alcohol, pharmaceuticals, and incarceration industries are fighting repeal tooth and nail, along with the "Baptists," who continue to feel that the tragic destruction and injustice of the War on Drugs is still justified to forfend the chaos that must arise if it is not waged with ever-mounting ferocity.

And that's the interesting thing about history: it keeps happening.

The Rumbula Massacre – A Critical Examination of the Facts, Part 1

Thomas Kues

1. The Rumbula Massacre in Mainstream Historiography

Of the individual mass shootings of Jews perpetrated by German special units together with local auxiliary forces in the occupied parts of the Soviet Union and the Baltic countries in 1941–1944, the one at Babi Yar near Kiev on 29–30 September 1941 is undoubtedly the best known. This massacre reportedly claimed the lives of 33,771 Jews, although the evidentiary basis for this figure has been disputed.[1] In the shadow of Babi Yar, Holocaust historians list a number of five-figure mass shootings or repeated shootings at special "extermination sites", such as Paneriai (Ponary) near Vilnius, Fort IX in Kaunas, Maly Trostenets near Minsk (sometimes referred to as an "extermination camp"),[2] the Drobitski Yar ravine near Kharkov, Bronnaya Gora near Baranovichi, and the Rumbula site on the outskirts of Riga, where during two mass shootings, one on 30 November 1941 and another on 8 December 1941, the vast majority of the Jews in the Riga ghetto, a total of some 25,000 people, were reportedly massacred by police units under the command of the Higher Leader of the SS and Police (*HSSPF*) in *Reichskommissariat* Ostland, Friedrich Jeckeln. Jeckeln is accused of having previously carried out the mass shooting at Babi Yar, and on 27–28 August 1941 before that the Kamenets-Podolsky massacre which, with 23,600 reported victims, is claimed to be the first of the several purported five-figure massacres of Jews during the German occupation of Soviet territory.

In this study, I will focus on the Rumbula incidents, which have hitherto received no attention from revisionist historians. I will examine the reported events at Rumbula in light of the available documentary sources, the demographic evidence, and, most important, the material evidence. In connection with the demographic-statistical aspect as well as the discussion of certain German documents I have also found it necessary to include longer forays into the fates of the Jews in the rest of Latvia.

What then have the Holocaust historians to say about the events at Rumbula? The entry on the Riga ghetto in a voluminous encyclopedia of ghettos and camps which appeared in the United States in 2012 sums up the events as follows:

> *"On the order of the Higher SS and Police Leader Ostland, Friedrich Jeckeln, almost half of the ghetto inhabitants, more than 11,000 people, were murdered on November 30, 1941, by units of the German Order Police in Rumbula in a wooded area about 10 kilometers (6 miles) from the ghetto. Jeckeln and his staff planned this mass killing. The Jews residing at those addresses selected for the* Aktion *received instructions to gather at the ghetto's central square early in the morning; from there they were escorted to the killing site.*
>
> *During this* Aktion *a rather unexpected incident happened. By this time the deportations of Jews from Germany to the Riga ghetto had already commenced. The first transport of 1,000 Berlin Jews arrived in Riga on the morning of November 30, 1941. Jeckeln decided to kill these individuals together with the Latvian Jews on his authority, without orders from Berlin. Dr. Rudolf Lange, the head of the Security Police in Latvia, refused to participate in the killing of German Jews without a specific order from the Reich Security Main Office (RSHA), and he withdrew his men from the* Aktion. *The first part of the extermination of the inmates of the Riga ghetto therefore took place solely under Jeckeln's direction. The Order Police carried out the shooting without the support of the Security Police.*
>
> *The second* Aktion, *aimed at killing most of the remainder of the Riga ghetto Jews, followed on December 8, 1941, again at the Rumbula Forest site. This time no German Jews were among the victims, and the Security Police actively participated in the massacre. The victims of this shooting numbered more than 14,000 people, and the total number of Latvian Jews killed in these two* Aktions *was at least 25,500. Those spared were mostly men and some younger women who were healthy enough to work and had been moved to a separate part of the ghetto on the evening of December 7, just before the second* Aktion. *"*[3]

Bernhard Press briefly describes the events of 30 November 1941 as follows:

> *"The people were driven down Sadovnikova Street and Ludzas Street and then out of the ghetto along Maskavas Street, kilometer after kilometer upstream [the Daugava River], until they finally reached their destination, which was named Rumbula*

> (...). *Rumbula, which until that day had been only a tiny railroad station, a point on the map, became during those days a meaningful name in the history of the extermination of the Jews, just as the forest of Bikernieki had been previously and the Kaiserwald concentration camp was to be subsequently. Here mass graves had been dug in the forest, which was surrounded by soldiers. Anyone who had reached this place alive suddenly realized in a flash what awaited him or her. In the bitter frost, everyone had to undress, lay their clothes in separate piles, and wait for the bullet that was destined for them, while in the meantime new columns were arriving constantly and the buses driving back and forth brought in new victims. According to the eyewitness A. Baranovskis, the Rumbula station chief, the action began at 8:15 A.M. on November 30 and ended at 7:45 P.M. the same day. On that day more than 15,000 people were slaughtered by the Gestapo and the Latvian police. [...].*
>
> *The arrival of the transports [of Reich Jews] was not at all convenient for the Gestapo, because the reception camps at Salaspils (Kurtenhof) and Jumpravmuiza (Jungfernhof) were still not finished and there were still Latvian Jews in the Riga ghetto. The first of these transports arrived in Riga on November 29, 1941, and the Gestapo decided to liquidate it immediately in view of the aforementioned difficulties it would have had lodging it. The same night the German Jews, about 1,000 people, were brought to Rumbula, where preparations for exterminating the Jews of Riga had already begun, and shot on November 30 before the execution of the Riga Jews had started. This unforeseen operation led to a delay in the execution of the first Jews who arrived (...).*"[4]

Latvian-American historian Andrew Ezergailis stresses the particular "Jeckeln method" allegedly used to implement the mass killing:

> "*In planning the massacre, Jeckeln adapted the system he had devised in Ukraine for the specific conditions in Riga. The system involved detailed planning, subdividing the assignment into manageable parts, and then selecting a specialist in each area. As Jeckeln's aide Paul Degenhart testified, there were nine aspects to the system: 1) SD men inside the ghetto drove the people out of the houses; 2) the Jews were organized in 500-person columns and brought by train to the killing grounds (actually they were driven on foot in 1,000-person columns); 3) the Order Police led the column to Rumbula; 4) the killing was*

done simultaneously in three pits; 5) the victims were undressed and their the valuables collected on the way to the pits; 6) an inner and an outer gauntlet were formed to drive the people to the pits; 7) the victims were be driven [sic] directly into the pits, saving the labor of moving the bodies; 8) Russian submachine guns were used, because the clip had fifty bullets and could be set on single shots; 9) the victims lay face down in layers, after which the marksman would kill them with a bullet in the back of the head. This method has been referred to as Sardinenpackung ('sardine packing'), and even some of the EG operatives were horrified by its cruelty."[5]

We will return later to the issue of Jeckeln's "sardine packing" method. The "Jeckeln method" presumably ensured a killing rate that was nothing less than astonishing, as described by Ezergailis in another study:

"The killing was done by a twelve-man team that Jeckeln personally selected from his retinue, drivers, and bodyguards. While six men rested, the other six worked both sides of the pits. The killing was done with Russian (according to some witnesses Finnish) submachine guns set to fire single shots. (...).

The killing started at 8:00 in the morning and lasted until 7:00 at night, three hours after nightfall. Remarkably, the twelve-man killing unit managed to murder 12,000 people per day. The Jeckeln method of killing even surpassed the killing rates in the death-camp factories. To kill 25,000 people in two 10-hour days, it meant that 1,250 were killed per hour; or 21 per minute, or one person every three seconds. Each marksman killed more than 2,000 people during the two days. In comparison, using the Stahlecker method [of Einsatzgruppe A] in Liepāja, it took three days, from 13–17 December, to kill 2,749 people. At Rumbula more people were killed every three hours."[6]

Most remarkable indeed. Not only must each of the twelve marksmen have been a virtual killer robot, able to murder men, women and children for hours on end, at least 200 victims per hour or 3.3 victims per minute or 1 victim every 18 seconds (assuming that each marksman rested for half of the "working day"), reloading his gun after every fifty shots, rarely or never missing a shot, and apparently remaining unaffected by the noise from the weapons and screams of the victims as well as the recoils from his weapon, but the victims must have acted like a uniform mass of drugged sheep, not putting up any resistance in the face of death, or even behaving in a panicky manner. Can the scenario painted by Ezergailis really be believed?

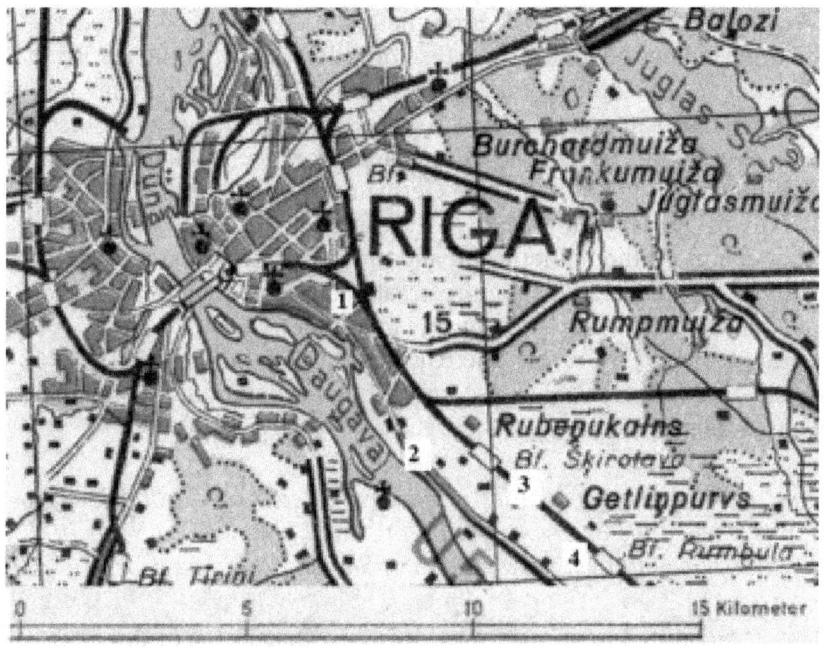

Figure 1. Riga during World War II. Detail from *Deutsche Heereskarte, Osteuropa 1:300 000*, 2nd ed. (1944), Blatt-Nr. S 57, Riga, with numbers added by the author. Legend: 1) Location of the Riga ghetto; 2) Maskavas iela (Moscow Street); 3) Railway line to Daugavpils (and further to Polotsk, Vitebsk and Smolensk); 4) Mass shooting site (*Bf.* = *Bahnhof* = railway station)

2. Early Reports on the Massacre

Before we begin our analysis of the demographic and statistical aspects of the Rumbula massacre we will take a brief look at what was reported of it during the war years. It is indeed quite remarkable how little, if anything, was reported. Take for example the *Contemporary Jewish Record*, an ambitious American-Jewish journal issued six times a year which in each issue presented a lengthy chronicle of news concerning Jewry worldwide during the preceding two months, drawing its sources from press and news bureaus the world over as well as reports from various Jewish organizations. In its issue of February 1942, chronicling the period November–December 1941, the journal merely noted that in early November the Germans had canceled all labor permits held by Jews, that Jews attempting to leave the Riga ghetto would be executed and that the Riga Jews were allowed only half the quantity of food allotted to the rest of the city's inhabitants.[7] In the issue of April 1942 it was reported that the Germans had placed a number of ghettos in the occupied eastern territories under quarantine because of failure to check the spread of epidemics, and that they "had ceased taking Jews from Kaunas, Wilno, Riga, Tallin and Dwinsk to forced labor". It was also noted that "over 30,000 Jews" had disappeared from the Lithuanian capital of Vilnius (Wilno/Vilna) "since German occupation last summer" and that it was "believed that half [of the disappeared Jews] are now in labor camps on the Soviet front, and the remainder have either been interned or executed" – a picture greatly at odds with the original version of events – but nothing was mentioned of the similar "disappearance" of most of the Riga Jews.[8] Only in the August 1942 issue was there a hint of massacres of Latvian Jews, although Riga went unmentioned:

> *"In Latvia, a June 15 release revealed, over 25,000 Jews, a quarter of the pre-war population, had been slain by Nazis in the four days following evacuation of Soviet forces last year."*[9]

This "revelation" is, as shown below in my discussion of the *Einsatzgruppen* and Stahlecker reports, completely at odds with the official version of events, which would have it that less than 1,000 Latvian Jews were killed during the first week of occupation. Moreover, since the events at Rumbula took place in late November/early December 1941 they could hardly have been confused with any events which took place in the preceding summer.

In the issue of December 1942 it was reported:

> *"The situation of the Latvian Jews was reported increasingly difficult, while a portion of the Jews from the Riga ghetto have been deported to south-eastern Poland. A second ghetto was recently opened in Widau."*[10]

Mainstream Holocaust historiography needless to say knows nothing of deportations of Latvian Jews to "south-eastern Poland" – which, based on the map of Poland before the war, could well be taken to mean Galicia or Volhynia (both in present-day Ukraine). The mention of the opening of a "second ghetto"[11] in "Widau" – no doubt a misprint for Windau, the German name of Ventspils, a town in western Latvia, is also highly curious, given that the Jewish population of this town and the surrounding region are claimed to have been exterminated in the autumn of 1941.

The issue of February 1943 carried the following highly interesting notice:

> *"Systematic deportation of all Jews who remained in Latvia, including those brought from Germany, Holland and Belgium was reported Nov. 19. The first step in the policy of extermination was taken Nov. 28, 1941, according to the Manchester Guardian (Oct. 30), when the Nazis established an 'inner ghetto' in Riga, and began to use the main ghetto as a transit camp for Jews from Central Europe."*[12]

Holocaust historians of course know nothing of deportation of Dutch and Belgian Jews to Latvia or any other location in the occupied eastern territories. What is most important to us here, however, is the date on which the "first step in the policy of extermination", consisting of the establishment of an "inner ghetto" in Riga, took place according to the British newspaper: 28 November 1941. This is indeed the date on which the liquidation of the western section of the Riga ghetto began,[13] followed just a few days later by the reported first mass shooting at Rumbula. Following this event, the remaining Latvian Jews were housed in the northern section of the ghetto, between the streets of Kalna and Ludzas, whereas the southern section, between the streets Ludzas and Maskavas, came to be inhabited by Jewish deportees from the Reich and the Protectorate of Bohemia and Moravia.[14]

The *Manchester Guardian* article was also referenced by the following notice in the *JTA Daily News Bulletin* on 20 November 1942 (datelined "London, Nov. 19") :

> *"Jewish relief organizations here today received information that all Jews living in the ghetto in Riga, Latvia, are being deported to Nazi-held Russian territory and that the Nazi administration has decided to make Latvia 'judenrein' within the next few weeks.*
> *Jews from Holland, Belgium and Germany who were deported to the Riga ghetto are among those being sent further east. Neutral non-Jews who visited the Baltic States recently*

attempted to ascertain to where the Jews from the Riga ghetto were being exiled, but no information could be secured from the local non-Jewish population which is afraid to furnish any information about the fate of their former Jewish neighbors. Letters sent to Jews in the Riga ghetto from neutral countries have been returned recently stamped with a notice from the postal authorities that the recipient has 'left for the East.'

The Manchester Guardian publishes a comprehensive survey of the Jewish situation in Latvia revealing that large transports of Jews were sent to the Riga ghetto from Berlin, Cologne, Dusseldorf and other German cities. 'The fate of these German Jews is not known since they were also deported recently from the ghetto in Riga to some unknown destination,' the English paper writes. It estimates that only 4,000 Riga Jews were still left in the ghetto after the terrible massacres carried out by the Nazis in the Latvian capital. Before the Nazi occupation there were about 50,000 Jews in Riga, constituting one-half of the entire Jewish population in Latvia."[15]

Due to its importance I will here reproduce the 30 October 1942 *Manchester Guardian* article in full:

> "FATE OF THE JEWS IN LATVIA
> Another Chapter in the Record of Nazi Savagery
> From our Special Correspondent
> Since the occupation of Latvia by the Germans at the beginning of the Russian campaign in June and July, 1941, the Jews of that country have been known to be in acute danger. Owing largely to the extraordinary precautions taken by the invaders to prevent the leakage of information, reliable details about the fate of the Jewish population have only recently become available. The facts now revealed conform in every particular to the all-too-familiar pattern of German persecution.
> On June 16, 1941, the retreating Russians collected together between two and three thousand Jews and sent them to the Russian interior. These, however, represented but a small proportion of the total Jewish population of Latvia, which was estimated at approximately 100,000 persons. Of these about 32,000 lived in Riga. The Germans entered Riga on July 1 and forthwith laid hands on Jews and compelled them to do various menial tasks. This continued for several days, the Jews being seized upon wherever they appeared. With one exception there was as yet no organised anti-Semitic drive. The exception was

provided by the Latvian auxiliary police, a body evidently open to German influence even before the invasion. Members of this band on the night of July 3–4 forced their way into numerous Jewish houses and flats in Riga, looting wherever they went.

MIGRATION AFTER POGROM

By the end of July the 'system' had begun to work and most of the male Jews of Riga had been herded into labour groups. During August large numbers of women were also conscripted to work for the Germans. Meanwhile an organised pogrom in the provinces had caused the deaths of literally thousands of Jews. There were frequent instances of the only Jewish family in a particular village being completely wiped out either by the Germans or by their Latvian auxiliaries. Consequently there began a great migration towards Riga, evidently inspired by the hope that conditions might be better in a more densely populated area.

Large numbers of those who set out never reached their goal and those who did were doomed to bitter disillusionment, for at the beginning of September the Germans announced their intention of setting up a ghetto in the Moscower suburb, into which all the Jews in Riga would have to go. They were evicted from their homes during the first three weeks of October and on the 25th of that month the ghetto was sealed with a fence of wood and barbed wire.

GHETTO OVERCROWDING

Terrible scenes accompanied this mass 'evacuation'. The victims were allowed to bring with them from their homes one chair per person, one bed for every two persons, a table and a cupboard per family. Accommodation in the ghetto was theoretically allotted on the basis of three square yards of ground room to each person but it did not work out in practice. As a rule about sixteen persons had to share a comparatively small room, sleeping five in a bed. Foodstuff and rations, such as they were, were distributed from seventeen shops. The administration of the ghetto was placed in the hands of a council, selected from prominent members of the Jewish community in Latvia. (The names of those comprising the council are in the possession of your correspondent.) In addition to their own and the Latvian police the Germans installed a corps of Jewish police in the ghetto.

Every morning 16,000 Jews left the ghetto in columns for their place of labour. Some did restoration work, some worked for units of the German Army or the S.S., while others were

> *employed in the industry. They received no recompense whatever, and as all the inmates of the ghetto had to pay for their own food their physical condition deteriorated as time went on.*
>
> *On November 28 the Germans decreed that a section of the ghetto was to be reserved for occupation by some 4,000 Jews engaged on work for the Army and the S.S. These were duly separated from their families, incarcerated in the 'inner ghetto' and surrounded by additional barbed wire entanglements. A further order was issued on November 29 by which only able-bodied men between the ages of 18 and 60 were to remain in the camp, the others being transferred over a period to separate 'lagers.'*
>
> *The four thousand of the 'inner ghetto' were still there in June of this year. As for the main ghetto, it remained empty for a few days only, after which came new arrivals – Jewish deportees from Germany, including many from Berlin, Cologne, and Düsseldorf. By the end of June they too had departed no one knows whither. The gates of the ghetto were open again in readiness for more human victims."*[16]

Aside from the claim that only 2–3,000 Jews had left the country by the time Latvia was occupied, the historiographically unknown – and rather improbable – assertion about a "great migration" of provincial Latvian Jews to Riga in August 1941, and the factually incorrect claim that the Jews deported to Latvia from the Reich had all been evacuated from the Riga ghetto by June 1942, the "special correspondent" of the *Manchester Guardian* displays a remarkably detailed and accurate knowledge of the Riga ghetto: he is aware not only of the Jewish ghetto police, but of the approximate number of Latvian Jews remaining in the "inner ghetto" (their actual number as of February 1942 was 4,358, see Section 2 below), that many of the Reich Jewish deportees came from Berlin, Cologne, and Düsseldorf,[17] and that some 16,000 Riga Jews were employed as forced labor prior to the partial liquidation of the ghetto (in October 1941 a total of 15,650 Jews in the ghetto were classified as "able to work").[18]

Therefore the fact that the correspondent does not state that the Jews evacuated from the ghetto at the end of December were murdered is all the more extraordinary. While they are spoken of as "victims", their fate is portrayed as the same as that supposedly suffered by the Reich Jews ("they *too* had departed no one knows whither") – that is, deportation to an unknown destination. While one may, by help of the usual Holocaust exegesis, detect here an implication that evacuation from the ghetto equalled death, the most important issue remains: How could the correspondent know so much about the history of the ghetto up to at least spring 1942, but then know nothing whatsoever about the Rumbula massacre nearly a year after the alleged event?

In the *Contemporary Jewish Record* issue of August 1943 it was noted that from "London word came on June 9 that [the famous Jewish historian] Simon Dubnow, 81, was executed in Riga, Latvia, on Dec. 1, 1941",[19] but this is not mentioned in the context of a larger massacre of Riga Jews.

Only in the issue of December 1943 was it first reported by the *Contemporary Jewish Record* that a large part of the Jews in occupied Latvia had been exterminated by the Germans:

> *"Earlier reports that wholesale slaughter by the Nazis had wiped out huge numbers of the Jewish population of Latvia, estimated at 94,000 in prewar days, were confirmed by an eyewitness account published in the Swedish paper Ny Dag, on Sept. 1. Surviving Jews were working in war industries on starvation rations, but mass executions still continued among deportees from abroad.*
>
> *Some 80,000 Jews were said to have been murdered near Chiube, in the woods between Rumbula and Alaspile. Only a few Jews out of 44,000 remained in Riga, and none at all in Daugavpils, Rezekne or Ludza."*

The "earlier reports" had not been reproduced by *Contemporary Jewish Record*, probably because they were not deemed sufficiently reliable. Here the name of Rumbula is mentioned for the first time by the journal. "Alaspile" is most likely a corruption of Salaspils, which is located some kilometers to the east of Rumbula. The article from the Swedish Communist newspaper *Ny Dag*, published on 26 August 1943, stated:

> *"During the winter 1941–1942 the Germans deported to Riga Jews from Austria, Czechoslovakia, France, and other occupied countries and executed them together with Jews from Riga in the pine forest at Čuibe, between the stations of Rumbula and Salaspils."*[20]

On 24 July 1944 the *JTA Daily News Bulletin* carried the following notice:

> *"A Latvian Jewish woman, who arrived in Sweden recently after hiding from the Gestapo for a year-and-a-half, gave an eye-witness account today of the massacre of Latvian Jews by the Germans and also submitted a list of the 24 persons responsible for the atrocities.*
>
> *The woman, Selma Anderson, whose family name before her marriage was Shebshelovitz, was saved from the Riga ghetto in November, 1941, on the eve of a wide-spread massacre, by Alexander Anderson, whom she subsequently married. They lived in Latvia for more than a year, under the noses of the Gestapo.*
>
> *At the outbreak of the war, Mrs. Anderson was a student at the English College in Riga. After the German occupation she was forced to work in the ruins of the bombed sections of Riga, and later as a kitchen maid in S.S. headquarters. In October, 1941, she was placed in a ghetto together with her parents, Josif and Emma. Here, seven persons had to live in a room nine yards square.*
>
> *She reveals that in the first weeks of the occupation 26,000 Jews were murdered in the provinces, and the rest fled to Riga where further thousands were killed. Latvian guards fired into the ghetto houses at random, daily, killing hundreds. Many were beaten to death. Women were raped. Some Latvian policemen, students, hooligans and dregs from the Riga underworld participated in the atrocities.*
>
> *About 15,000 Jews were killed in the first wholesale massacre in Riga, in the courtyard of the Qadrat [sic] Rubber Co. factory outside the city, on November 27, 1941. Several thousand were murdered in a second massacre on December 7. After that only Jews employed in the German war factories remained in the ghetto, which was finally liquidated in the autumn of 1943, when the survivors were taken to Kaizerwald. Their fate is not known."*[21]

This "Selma Anderson" is Selma or Selda Šebšelovicz (also transliterated Schepschelovitz), a young Latvian Jewess who, after living under a false identity in the home of a Latvian officer, Jānis Vabulis, and working in the offices of the Arājs Commando – which functioned as an auxiliary unit under *Einsatzkommando* 2 – escaped to Sweden in April 1944.[22] Both Šebšelovicz and Vabulis, who had married the former and escaped with her to Sweden, had contacts with pro-Soviet elements in Sweden.[23] It is highly remarkable that Šebšelovicz did not place the massacre of the Riga ghetto Jews in the forest at Rumbula, or in any other of the forests surrounding Riga, but in a factory courtyard. Kvadrāts is an industrial area in the Kengarags city district housing the factory of the Baltijas Gumijas Fabrika (Baltic Rubber Factory). It is located on the right side of Maskavas Street facing south and by the Daugava River, some 2.5 km west-north-west of the Rumbula mass-shooting site.

The propagandists of the Soviet Union also made a few statements on massacres of Riga Jews during the war. In a "Statement issued on December 19, 1942, by the Information Bureau of the People's Commissariat for Foreign Affairs of the U.S.S.R. on 'The execution by Hitlerite authorities of the plan to exterminate the Jewish population in the occupied territory of Europe'" we read the following:

> "Soon after their invasion the Hitlerites shot more than 60,000 Jews in Riga, including many who had been brought from Germany, carrying out the shootings almost continuously. Parties of 300 to 400 persons were taken to an island in the western Dvina River (Drucava), eight miles from Riga, and also to the highway leading from Riga to Daugavpils.
> Whole families were shot. Children were snatched from their mothers' arms and murdered before their eyes or thrown alive into pits and ditches dug beforehand. There are now no more than 400 Jews in Riga, living in a ghetto surrounded by barbed wire, access to which is prohibited. This group of Jews is doomed to death by starvation and is slowly dying out."[24]

The "highway leading from Riga to Daugavpils" is Maskavas Street, whereas Dvina is the Russian name for the Daugava River, which flows through Riga. "Drucava" is most likely a corruption of Daugava, as there exists no other island in the river in the Riga region with a similar name.

One of the earliest sources on the liquidation of the Riga ghetto was a report left in Geneva on 1 October 1942 by Gabriel Ziwjan (Ziwian), a young Jew (b. 1923) who had escaped from the ghetto in December 1941. The reported was drafted for representatives of the World Jewish Congress in Bern, which subsequently submitted it to the US Consul in Geneva. The relevant part of it reads:

"Such was the situation until November 28th. On that date an order was issued according to which a certain part of the Ghetto was to be cleared from its inhabitants. All Jews who had been living so far in this part of the Ghetto were to be placed in the other part. The district thus cleared was again separated by a fence and was called the 'small Ghetto.' The intention was that all men working for the German authorities outside the Ghetto should live in [the] future in this newly established 'small Ghetto.' The women and families of these men were to remain in the old, so-called 'large Ghetto' which of course was now smaller than before.

On November 29th, an additional order was issued, saying that all men able for work and between the age of 18 and 60 years had to line up in a street near the newly established small Ghetto on November 30th, while the rest of the population would be sent to camps. Each person was allowed to take along 20 kg. of luggage. On November 30th, the announced selection among the male population took place. All people over 60 and all people ill or disabled were sent home to the Large Ghetto and also all doctors were sent home. The result of the selection was that as from November 20th, about 4,000 men were settled in the 'Small Ghetto.' (...).

In the night of November 30th, all people living in one part of the Large Ghetto, numbering 8,000, were assembled. They had their luggage of 20 kg with them. They had to stand there during the whole night without shelter and in the early hours of the morning of December 1st, they were led away by Latvian auxiliary police under German supervision. They had to pass along the fence which separated the Large Ghetto from the 'Small Ghetto,' so that the men inside the 'small Ghetto' were seeing what was going on. During their march, the group of 8,000 was treated with the utmost brutality. Those who were unable to keep pace were shot. The group of 8,000 was led to the woods, the so-called wood of Bickern and the wood near Zarnikau and there all the 8,000 were shot.

After this mass-execution, only 16,000 Jews remained in the old Ghetto. In the following week nothing special happened. Only 800 women were arrested some day, 400 were imprisoned while the other 400 returned some time later to the Ghetto.

On December 7th, an order was issued that all women had to be at home by 7 o'clock in the evening. In the night of December 7th to December 8th, the 16,000 people still in the old Ghetto

> were assembled and taken away, just like the 8,000 a week before.
>
> According to a statement of the commander of the Latvian Ghetto-guard who later told about these things to some people with whom he took drinks, the 16,000 people were led to the woods. Russian prisoners of war had to dig trenches 3 to 4 meters deep. Then the men were separated from the women and children, each group standing to one side of the trenches. Anything of any value they possessed had to be laid down at a certain spot. Then the 16,000 had to undress so that the men were completely naked while the women were allowed to keep their shirt. All the clothes had to be put down and were collected by the police. Then the naked men were ordered to lie down in the trenches after which 5 or 6 German soldiers with machine-guns arrived and shot the men lying in the trenches. The next group had to lie down on the bodies and was shot in the same way. Women and children suffered the same fate.
>
> That is how the rest of the population of the larger Ghetto of Riga was killed in the night from December 7th to December 8th, 1941. This report coming from the Latvian Ghetto-commander was later confirmed by a number of members of the Latvian police who were present."[25]

In an attachment to his report Ziwjan further stated:

> "The statement concerning the execution of the Jews of Riga, who were taken away from Riga in the nights of November 30th to December 1st and from December 7th to December 9th (...) is based on a conversation I have had personally at the end of December 1941, with Captain OZOLIN, Commander of the Latvian Ghetto guard, to whom I had been introduced as a Latvian by Mr. Janis Dulebo of Riga, who has helped me in hiding outside the Ghetto. All the facts I have mentioned in the report with regard to the execution of the Jews of Riga have been communicated to me by Mr. Ozolin."[26]

It is rather remarkable that Ziwjan and, supposedly, his informer Ozolin, identified the site of the massacre as the Biķiernieku Forest, since this is located some 5–6 km north-north-west of Rumbula. "Zarnikau" is most likely a corruption[27] of Carnikava, a municipality immediately to the north-east of the Riga city limits,[28] more than 11 km to the north of Rumbula. As for Biķiernieku, this forest (called Bickern or Hochwald in German) was reportedly used as a site for smaller mass shootings of Jews before as well as after the events at Rumbula, but bringing tens of thousands of Jews there at the same time would not only have been logistically more challenging, but also attracted considerable attention from the civilian population, as noted by Angrick and Klein:

> *"It is to be assumed, however, that from the start Bikernieki was clearly not an option. This location had already achieved a notorious 'renown' among Riga's population and could no longer be used, for reasons of secrecy. Moreover, due to the ghetto's location, a southern solution was to be preferred so as to avoid marching the Jews through the heart of Riga in the process of 'resettling' them."*[29]

According to Bert Hoppe and Hildrun Glass, the commander of the Latvian ghetto guard was in fact named Alberts Danskops. They conclude that the actual informant was Eduard Ozoliņš, a railway worker posted at the Šķirotava station, which is the station before Rumbula station travelling from Riga central station (cf. Figure 1 above).[30] If this identification is correct, then Ziwjan's identification of the mass killing site becomes fully incomprehensible, as someone who worked so close to the Rumbula site could not have possibly confused it with Biķiernieku!

Finally I will take note of an example of brazen forgery in connection with Rumbula. In the supposedly contemporary diary entries of the Baltic-German Riga resident Jürgen E. Kroeger, the Rumbula massacre appears in the following way:

> *"1 December 1941. Today 30,000 Jews, mainly Jews from Vienna and the Altreich, were killed by the Security Police with the active help of Latvian execution commandos near Salaspils. Even though the operation was kept secret the horrible truth soon got out. The city is transfixed."*[31]

What is remarkable here is of course the claim that the majority of the victims were Reich Jews, in contrast to mainstream historiography which has it that only 1,000 of the 25,000–28,000 victims were Reich Jews – moreover Jews from Berlin, not Vienna. Also, if the massacre had already become common knowledge on 1 December 1941, then it would certainly have been known that a large portion of the ghetto inhabitants had been marched out of the city (since this could easily have been observed by residents living along Maskavas Street), making it unlikely that anyone would have believed the majority of the victims to be Reich Jews. It is also suspicious that the victim figure mentioned (30,000) is very close to the officially held one, despite the fact that the reported second mass shooting on 8 December had still not occurred.

Kroeger's assertion that the "horrible truth soon got out" can be contrasted with what Andrew Ezergailis writes on the public's knowledge of the massacre:

> *"Of course many Latvians knew about the Rumbula Action because many Latvian policemen participated in it. But it is surprising how many Riga inhabitants did not. The police appear not to have gossiped as widely about it as the Germans thought they would. The burning of the corpses Himmler ordered in 1943 attracted more attention because of the smoke and the stench."*[32]

He adds in a note to this passage:

> *"From my own survey of Riga inhabitants who live in exile, I would have to say that half of them know nothing of Rumbula; they hardly knew that a ghetto existed. The ones who know something about Rumbula know it from some friend or family member who had police connections."*[33]

I will return later in this study to the problem of keeping the reported mass murder of nearly 30,000 people a secret.

What definitely exposes Kroeger's reports on this issue as fraudulent is his entry for 19 December 1941. Here he describes a supposed personal meeting with the *Gebietskommissar* of the City of Riga, Hugo Wittrock, during which the latter tells him about the mass shootings:

> *"The truth is awful! A minority of Latvian right-wing extremists have, with the approval and leadership of German SS, exterminated the Jews in the countryside and in the district cities. Later nearly 100,000 Jews, part of them evacuated here from the Altreich and Vienna, have been murdered by the SS with Latvian assistance in the vicinity of Riga."*[34]

As we will see below, the official version of events has it that less than 40,000 Jews had been killed in or near Riga by this point in time, of whom only 1,000 were non-Latvian Jews, all deported from Berlin. Considering moreover that 100,000 is in excess of the total pre-war Jewish population of Latvia in its entirety, the statement attributed to Wittrock (who at the time of the publication of Kroeger's diary in 1973 had conveniently been dead for fifteen years) is patent nonsense. As it is impossible that Wittrock could have been so misinformed, and since he would have had no reason to make up such lies, it is clear that Kroeger must have forged this and most likely also the 1 December 1941 entry.

2. The Victims – Their Theoretical Maximum Number and Demography

Andrew Ezergailis has the following to say on the Rumbula victims figure:

> *"In general there is little dispute about the numbers killed at Rumbula. The numbers have ranged from the 20,000 mentioned as a minimum by Jeckeln at his trial to about 30,000 claimed by Max Kaufmann. Certainly almost 25,000 people perished on November 30 and December 8, of whom 24,000 were Latvian Jews.*
>   *There are various ways of calculating this: 1) Prior to the killings of Rumbula there were about 29,000 Jews in the ghetto. About 5,000 (more than 4,500 men and about 500 women) were held back for labor; the number comes to about 24,000; 2) A thousand persons per column every half hour on both killing days, from 6:00 in the morning to 12:00 noon, were sent out from the ghetto to Rumbula—the number again comes out to about 24,000. 3) After the killings Jeckeln had told Degenhart that 22,000 rounds of ammunition had been used at Rumbula. Noting that on the two days over 1,000 people were killed within the ghetto and on the road to Rumbula, the number adds up to just below 24,000. In addition to the 24,000 Latvian Jews killed, one must add 1,000 German Jews who were liquidated there on the morning of November 30."*[35]

As we will see below, Ezergailis's contention that "in general there is little dispute about the numbers killed at Rumbula" is refuted by what one would expect to be the most authoritative source on this issue, namely German documents. Besides these, early post-war Soviet investigators came to the conclusion that no fewer than 38,000 victims of mass murder had been buried at the Rumbula site.[36]

The particular issue of the convoy of German Jews will be discussed in full in the next part of this study.

Let us begin by pointing out that Ezergailis's method for establishing the number of victims is clearly flawed, because judging by his notes there exists no document regarding any amount of ammunition ordered or used at this point in time, only a witness statement (apparently from Jeckeln's Chief of Staff, SS-*Obersturmbannführer* Herbert Degenhardt[37]), and moreover it is absurd to use such a statement as a criterion of judgement, as it is well-known among soldiers that shots to the head or neck are far from always certainly fatal – even if keeping to a "one person – one bullet" policy (as claimed for Jeckeln) the person in charge of the mass murder would have ordered a considerable surplus of ammunition (say 10 % or more), and a large part of this surplus ammunition would almost certainly have been used.

How many Jews were then evacuated from the Riga ghetto on 30 November and 8 December 1941, and how many of these reached the Rumbula site? The establishment of the Riga ghetto began in early August 1941 but was not completed until the beginning of October that same year. The "Resettlement Office" in charge of organizing the resettlement of Riga's Jews within the ghetto's borders was informed in early August that the ghetto was to offer space for just under 30,000 people, and according to a census of the civilian administration undertaken at around the same time "approximately 27,000" were to be relocated to the ghetto, which was located in the poor district of Maskavas Vorštate south-east of the Riga central railway station, where 1,700 Jews were already residing, making for a total of some 28,700 ghetto inhabitants.[38]

Once the settlement had been completed in early October 1941, the Labor Office compiled statistics showing the population of the ghetto to amount to 29,602 Jews.[39] A census from 16 February 1942, two and a half months after the liquidation of the "Large ghetto", gave the number of Jews in the "Latvian ghetto" as 4,717, of whom 524 were women.[40] This figure, however, explicitly included also Lithuanian Jews. 359 Jewish workers were deported from Kaunas to Riga on 6 February 1942.[41] This brings down the number of remaining Latvian Jews in Riga to 4,358, including apparently some 300 women.[42] The relevant difference between the October and February figures is thus (29,602-4,358=) 25,244. From this we must subtract some further categories. First, it is stated by witnesses that in all some 300 Jews who had either committed suicide during the evacuation or been shot while trying to escape or for being perceived as causing problems during the long walk to Rumbula were buried in the Jewish Cemetery on 30 November.[43] During the second evacuation on 8 December many of the remaining ghetto inhabitants tried to delay the operation for as long as possible; as a result units of Latvian militia auxiliaries (the"Arājs Commando") were sent into the ghetto to force the evacuation; it is further reported that Jews unable to be transported were shot in their apartments or in the ghetto hospital. According to Angrick and Klein, "around 900 corpses were taken to the Jewish cemetery by the Jewish labor commandos, while scores of corpses were left lying in their apartments".[44]

Andrew Ezergailis on the other hand estimates the number of Jews killed in the ghetto during the second evacuation at only some 300.[45] Finally, Jews who had been hiding in the liquidated part of the "Large ghetto" after the operation were taken to be shot at the Jewish cemetery – although some eyewitnesses assert that they were taken instead in buses to the mass shooting site in the Biķiernieki forest.[46] Angrick and Klein in this case give as a minimum 200 victims but mention a witness (Max Kaufmann) speaking of a total of 500 victims. While the above figures are all primarily derived from Jewish eye-witness testimony and therefore likely to be at least somewhat exaggerated, there can be little doubt that they are at least partially based on reality. I will here use a rough estimate of 800–1,200 deaths outside of the Rumbula site. This leaves a maximum victim figure of 24,044–24,444. To this should then be added the 1,000 Berlin Jews reportedly murdered at Rumbula on 30 November, bringing the maximum total victim figure at Rumbula to approximately 25,000–25,400.

What then do we know about the demographic makeup of this group of alleged Latvian-Jewish Rumbula victims? In the already mentioned October 1941 Labor Office report on the ghetto population we find the following demographic breakdown:[47]

Table 1: Labor Office statistics on the Riga ghetto population, October 1941		
1. Children up to 14 years of age		
Boys	2,794	
Girls	2,858	
Total		5,652
• Those able to work, age 14–65		
Men	6,143	
Women	9,507	
Total		15,650
• Those unable to work, age 14-65		
Men	2,069	
Women	6,231	
Total		8,300
	Total	29,602

From another German report we know that there were 2,660 Jews in the ghetto categorized as skilled workers, including 1,300 female tailors.[48] Since as already mentioned only some 300 female Latvian Jews, like the remaining men all workers, remained in Riga after 8 December, and since this group included not only female tailors but also an unknown number of seamstresses and furriers,[49] we have to estimate that some 1,100 skilled female workers were among the Jews brought to Rumbula, and moreover that only about a third of the male Latvian Jews remaining after the evacuations had previously been classified as skilled workers. In addition to the 1,100 skilled female workers the alleged victim group would have included approximately (9,507-1,100=) 8,407 unskilled female workers as well as 6,231 elderly women or women otherwise deemed unfit for work.

As for the 5,652 children, we know little about their internal demographics. It is merely known that four schools, three kindergartens, and one nursery were established in the ghetto.[50] From this we may infer that small children and toddlers as well as school children were present in the ghetto – which should hardly surprise. Since up until the end of November 1941 virtually only adult Jewish men had been targeted for mass shootings (real or alleged), it seems most reasonable to assume that the number of children (0–13 years of age) was roughly evenly divided among each year of birth, so that there were (5,652/13=) 435 children aged 0–1 years, and so on. It seems likely that the figures were somewhat lower for the 0–2 age span due to the lower natality normally coinciding with the unrest of wartime, but I will nevertheless use the 435 figure to strengthen conclusions from my argument.

Next we must subtract the rough estimate of 800–1,200 deaths outside of the Rumbula site from the respective demographic categories. As already mentioned, this estimate consists of suicides, people who were shot during the some 10-km-long walk from the ghetto for attempting to escape or who broke down from exhaustion during said march, as well as people who kept themselves hidden in the liquidated "Large ghetto" but were ferreted out and executed on 9 December. We have no means of telling if any demographic category was under- or overrepresented among these victims. One might suspect that children would be underrepresented among the suicides, but on the other hand we learn of cases of "family suicides", where a mother or grandmother killed her children or grandchildren and then herself, usually by poison.[51] Such child victims would not technically be suicides but for the sake of simplicity I would count them as such. One might similarly expect that the elderly would be overrepresented among those who died along the wayside, yet it is claimed that at least a large portion of the elderly were taken to the Rumbula site in trucks or in blue city buses borrowed from the Riga city traffic administration.[52] Accordingly, the only reasonable way to proceed is to distribute these deaths proportionally. This results in the following break-down of the Jews said to have reached the Rumbula site on 30 November and 8 December.

Table 2: Demographic estimates for the Latvian Jews said to have reached the Rumbula site		
• **Children up to 14 years of age**		
Boys	2,661–2,706	
Girls	2,722–2,767	
Total:		5,383 – 5,473
• **Those able to work, age 14–65:**		
Men	1,985–2,019	
Skilled female workers	1,048–1,065	
Unskilled female workers	7,722–7,850	
Total:		10,755–10,934
• **Those unable to work**		
Men	1,971–2,003	
Women	5,935–6,034	
Total:		7,906 – 8,037
	Total:	24,044–24,444

From this table, it is clear that the number of Jews arriving at Rumbula would have included a considerable percentage of people – some 45%, in fact – who were able to work or even skilled workers. Aside from the some 1,050 skilled female workers there were also Jewish males who might be considered skilled in a very particular way, namely members of the Jewish ghetto police (*Ordnungsdienst*). We will return to this particular group later on.

3. The Documents

3.1. Rumbula in the Einsatzgruppen incident reports

The most important contemporary documentary source on the Rumbula Massacre is the reporting of the *Einsatzgruppen* of the Security Police and the SD. Here I will not dwell on the larger issue of the reliability and authenticity of these reports, but will simply present and analyze what they have to say about the events in Riga at the end of November and beginning of December 1941.

Rather remarkably, the event later known as the Rumbula Massacre was not mentioned in the very frequent "incident reports" (*Ereignismeldungen*, hereafter *EM*) of the *Einsatzgruppen* until more than a month after the alleged incident. In *EM* No. 151 of 5 January 1942 may be read:

> *"The Higher SS and Police Leader in Riga, SS Obergruppenführer Jeckeln, has meanwhile embarked on a shooting action [Erschießungsaktion] and on Sunday, 30 November 1941, about 4,000 Jews from the Riga ghetto and an evacuation transport from the Reich were disposed of [beseitigt]. The action was originally to have been carried out by the Higher SS and Police leader's own forces, but after a few hours the 20 men of EK 2 who had been detached for security purposes were nevertheless employed in the action."*[53]

In *EM* No. 155 of 14 January 1942 the event was again mentioned:

> *"In Latvia there remain Jews only in Riga and Dünaburg. The number of Jews left in Riga – 29,500 – was reduced to 2,500 by an action carried out by the Higher SS and Police Leader Ostland. In Dünaburg there still live 962 Jews who are urgently needed for the labor deployment [Arbeitseinsatz]."*[54]

It must be pointed out that "reduced" is not synonymous with "killed" – this entry thus only states that 27,000 Jews were removed from the city. Nevertheless we will here, for the sake of argument, view the report from an exterminationist viewpoint which assumes that reduction = murder. The victim figure reported on 14 January – (29,500 – 2,500 =) 27,000, not including German-Jewish deportees – is thus (27,000 - 4,000 =) 23,000 victims or 6.75 times higher than the number of killed Riga Jews claimed by the report from 5 January! The statement that the Jewish population of Riga had been reduced from 29,500 to 2,500 was repeated in the summary "Activity and Situation Report"(*Tätigkeits- und Lageberichte*) No. 9 covering the period 1–31 January 1941 (there is no mention of the Riga Jews in the corresponding report for December 1941).[55] The statement that Jews at this point in time remained only in Riga and Daugavpils is incorrect, since the ghetto in Liepāja still existed (see below).

In the following report, *EM* No. 156 of 16 January 1942, the event was mentioned a third time, with a victim figure drastically lower than the number of removed Jews implied by the 14 August report:

> "*On 30 November 1941, 10,600 Jews were shot in Riga. The action took place under the command of the Higher SS and Police Leader Ostland. In the execution [of this action] Einsatzkommando 2 participated with 1/20 [i.e. one officer and twenty enlisted 20 men].*"[56]

It is not stated whether this included the (unspecified) number of German-Jewish deportees mentioned in the report from 5 January. Assuming that it is not included, the victim figure drops by 16,400, i.e. some 60% between *EM* No. 155 and *EM* No. 156. Thus between 5 January and 16 January 1942 the Latvian-Jewish Rumbula "victim figure" reported by *Einsatzgruppe* A shifted from 4,000 to 27,000 to 10,600. Besides this astounding fluctuation in numbers we have the fact that none of the reports mentions the second mass shooting on 8 December 1941.

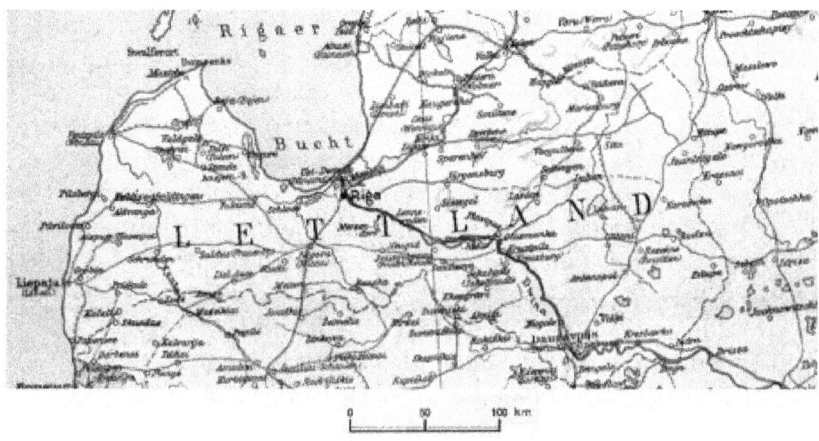

Figure 2: Latvia during World War II. Detail from *GEA-Übersichtskarte Europäisches Rußland* 1:3 300 000, GEA-Verlag/Berliner Lithographisches Institut, Berlin 1943. (The borders of the former Republic of Latvia are marked with a dotted blue line).

3.2. The murder of the Jews of Riga, Daugavpils and Liepāja according to the Stahlecker Reports

In the so-called "Second Stahlecker Report", a general report on the activities of *Einsatzgruppe* A in the Baltic states and White Ruthenia from mid-October 1941 to the end of January 1942 may be read the following about mass shootings of Latvian Jews:

> "*The total number of Jews in Latvia in the year 1935 was: 93,479 or 4.79% of the whole population. [...]*
> *At the entry of German troops there were still 70,000 Jews in Latvia. The rest had fled with the Bolshevists. The remaining Jews were very active as saboteurs and arsonists. Thus in Dünaburg [Daugavpils] the Jews set so many fires that a large part of the city was destroyed. [...].*
> *After the terror of the Jewish-Bolshevist rule – in total 33,038 Latvians were deported, arrested or murdered – a large-scale pogrom was to be expected from the population. However, only some thousands of Jews were disposed of by local forces at their own initiative. It was therefore necessary in Latvia to carry out extensive cleansing operations [Säuberungsaktionen] using special units [Sonderkommandos] with the help of selected forces from the Latvian auxiliary police (mostly relatives of deported or murdered Latvians).*

> *Up until October 1941, about 30,000 Jews were executed by these special units. The remaining Jews, still indispensable due to economic importance, were collected in ghettos that were established in Riga, Dünaburg and Libau [Liepāja]. Following the processing of criminal cases on the basis of not wearing the Jewish star, black marketing, theft, fraud, but also on account of preventing danger of epidemics in the ghettos, further executions were carried out afterwards. Thus, on 9 November 1941, 11,034 were executed in Dünaburg, 27,800 in Riga at the beginning of December 1941 by an operation ordered and carried out by the Higher SS and Police Leader, and 2,350 in Libau in mid-December 1941. At this time there are Latvian Jews in the ghettos (aside from the Jews from the Reich) in:*
> Riga   approximately 2,500
> Dünaburg   "   95
> Libau   "   300.*"*[57]

In the first Stahlecker Report, describing the activities of *Einsatzgruppe* A up until 15 October 1941, it is claimed that up until then a total of 30,025 Jews had been executed in Latvia, of whom roughly 6,000 were in the Riga district, over 11,000 in the Liepāja (Libau) district, 9,256 in the Daugavpils (Dünaburg) district, some 3,000 in the Jelgava (Mitau) district, and finally a small number, about 100–200, in the Valmiera (Wolmar) district.[58] These "districts" are clearly identical to the four *Gebietskommissariate* constituting *Generalbezirk Lettland*.[59] In addition to this, some 500 Riga Jews had been killed in pogroms during the initial period of the occupation, giving a total of 30,525 killed Jews.[60] The document further states that "[o]f the in total some 28,000 Jews remaining in Riga 24,000 have up until now been transferred to the ghetto."[61] This brings us to yet another statistical contradiction: if only 28,000 Jews remained in Riga on 15 October 1941, how could 27,800 of them have been murdered at the beginning of December, with 2,500 remaining (27,800 + 2,500 = 30,300)?

As has already been pointed out by Carlo Mattogno and Jürgen Graf, the figures mentioned in the second Stahlecker Report are internally contradictory: If one adds the number of Jews killed up to 15 October 1941 (30,525) to the number of ghetto Jews shot (11,034 + 27,800 + 2,350 = 41,184) and the number of Jews still remaining in the three ghettos (2,500 + 950 + 300 = 3,750) one gets a total of 75,459, a number that is higher than that of the Jews reportedly still remaining at the time of the entry of German troops into Latvia (70,000).[62] The unreliability of Stahlecker's figures is aggravated by the fact that, as mentioned above, there remained 4,358 Latvian Jews in Riga on 16 February 1942, not a mere 2,500.

As for the ghetto in Daugavpils (in German Dünaburg, in Russian Dvinsk) in eastern Latvia, a report from Department II of the General Commissariat of Latvia dated 20 November 1941 stated the number of Jews still present in Daugavpils as 935 (including 173 children, 719 adults able to work, 25 adults unable to work and 18 over 65 years of age).[63] A list of the Daugavpils ghetto inmates dated 5 December 1941 gives the number as 962, a figure which is repeated in *EM* No. 155 from 14 January 1942.[64] This would confirm Stahlecker's estimate of some 950 Jews remaining in that ghetto, yet it must be pointed out that his claim that 11,034 Daugavpils Jews were executed on 9 November 1941 is contradicted by other statistics. In 1935 there lived 11,106 Jews in Daugavpils.[65] According to reports in the local press from mid-July 1941, at the time of the establishment of the ghetto, the Jews remaining in Daugavpils, including refugees from other parts of Latvia, amounted to some 14,000.[66] The same figure was supposedly reported by the Daugavpils Jewish council at the end of July.[67]

In the so-called Jäger Report on mass shootings carried out by *Einsatzkommando* 3 of *Einsatzgruppe* A, predominantly in Lithuania, up until 1 December 1941, we find an entry according to which a subunit of *Einsatzkommando* 3 had executed "9,012 Jews, Jewesses and Jewish children" in Daugavpils in the period from 13 July 1941 to 21 August 1941.[68] According to the recollections of Daugavpils ghetto inmate Sidney Iwens, several hundreds of elderly and sick Jews had been taken from the ghetto to the nearby forest of Pogulianka some 8 km north-west of the city and murdered there on 28 July 1941,[69] some 2,000 Jews on 1 August,[70] a group of 2,000–3,000 people on 6 August 1941,[71] and another large group on 18–19 August 1941.[72] In *EM* No. 21 from 16 July 1941 one may further read that up until then a total of 1,150 Jews had been executed in Daugavpils by another unit of *Einsatzgruppe* A, *Einsatzkommando* 1b.[73] While it was asserted by a post-war indictment that these 1,150 Jews were for the most part not from Daugavpils itself but from surrounding communities,[74] it is claimed that another group of 1,150 male Jews from Daugavpils were brought to the city prison on 30 June 1941 and executed soon thereafter.[75]

But if there were approximately 14,000 Jews in Daugavpils when the ghetto was established, and if some 10,000 Jews were been killed between the end of June and the end of August, how then could 11,106 Jews from the Daugavpils ghetto be murdered on 9 November 1941[76] and there still be 935 Jews left in the city on 20 November? It is worth noting that one of the major Holocaust historians to have written on the subject of the Holocaust in the Soviet Union, Yitzhak Arad, disregards the figure in the second Stahlecker Report and gives the number of victims as 5,000–6,000.[77] Moreover, as seen above, the first Stahlecker Report gave the number of Jews executed in the Daugavpils district up until 15 October 1941 as 9,256. This figure could include the 9,012 Jews shot in Daugavpils according to the Jäger Report, but *not also* the 1,150 Jews reportedly executed by *Einsatzkommando* 1b.

The Daugavpils demographics incongruities get even worse in the light of the fact in early October 1941, i.e. after the reported period of activity of *Einsatzkommando* 3 but before the alleged mass shooting on 9 November, the General Commissar of Latvia, Otto-Heinrich Drechsler, wrote a letter to the Reich Commissar of Ostland, Hinrich Lohse, in which the number of Jews in the Daugavpils ghetto is given as merely 2,185.[78] This figure is echoed by an article published in the 12 October 1941 issue of the local newspaper *Daugavas Vēstnesis*, according to which the ghetto population numbered 2,175.[79] But if only some 2,000 Jews lived in the Daugavpils ghetto in October 1941, how then could some 11,000 Jews from the same ghetto have been murdered in November 1941? It must be stressed here that Holocaust historiography knows of no transports of Jews to Daugavpils between October and November 1941.

As for Liepāja (Libau), its Jewish population in 1935 amounted to 7,379. Some additional 300 Jews lived in nearby towns.[80] By June 1941 the number of the Liepāja Jews had decreased to an estimated 7,140. On 14 June 1941 Soviet authorities deported 209 Jews from the city to Siberia, and in the following two weeks about 300 Jews fled to the USSR to escape the German invasion; another 160 local Jewish soldiers and guards retreated with the Red Army, so that some 6,589 Jews remained in Liepāja when the city was captured by German forces on 29 June 1941.[81] In the aforementioned letter of Drechsler's from early October 1941 it is stated that some 5,500 Jews remained in the province of Courland (Latvian. Kurzeme, the western part of Latvia) whose capital is Liepāja, and that these Jews were to be concentrated in a ghetto in Liepāja. In the also abovementioned report of Department II of the General Commissariat of Latvia from 20 November 1941 the number of Jews registered in Liepāja is given as 3,890, of whom 3,002 were adults able to work, 106 adults unable to work and 782 children. According to Holocaust historian Katrin Reichelt the Jews of Liepāja were subjected to the following massacres during 1941:[82]

- Some 100 male Jews shot by *Sonderkommando* 1a and members of the navy on 4 or 5 July;
- Some 1,430 Jews shot in Rainis Park – right in the middle of the city![83] – from 29/30 June to around 5 July;
- 1,100 male Jews shot by the "Arājs *Kommando*" on 24 and 25 July;
- Some 600 people shot in September, unclear how many of them Jews;
- 500 Jews in October;
- 2,749 Jewish men, women and children on Šķēde Beach between 15 and 17 December.

For the September massacre Reichelt gives no indication of the number of Jewish victims. Another exterminationist source gives the number of September victims as 300 (elderly) Jews.[84] The above-listed mass shootings thus add up to approximately 6,179 victims. Available documentation shows that on 1 July 1942 there still remained 864 Jews in the Liepāja ghetto,[85] not 300 as indicated by the second Stahlecker Report. If we add the 864 remaining Jews to the some 6,179 alleged victims we get 7,043, a figure that is some 500 higher than the number of Liepāja Jews that originally fell into German hands (approx. 6,589). Yet it would appear that the number of Jews remaining in the city after mid-December 1941 was in fact higher than 864. Subtracting the 2,749 reported victims of the mid-December massacre from 3,890 registered Liepāja Jews at the end of November one gets 1,141, a number which may well have been reduced by "natural" mortality to 864 by July 1942, although Arad (but not Reichelt) asserts that some 200 Liepāja Jews were killed "between February and April 1942."[86] 1,141 added to the 6,179 alleged victims makes a total of 7,320. It must be pointed out, however, that the figure of 2,749 victims (as opposed to the Stahlecker figure of 2,350) is derived from an activity report of the *SS-und-Polizeistandortführer Libau* dated 29 December 1941, in which it is stated that "2,749 Jews were *evacuated* in the period from 14 to 17 December 1941" (emphasis added).[87]

Latvian Holocaust historians Edward Anders and Juris Dubrovskis have written as follows on their attempt to identify the Jewish victims of the Liepāja massacres (emphasis in original):

> *"Nearly all [of the 6,589 Jews estimated to have remained in the city] were killed, but even after checking more than a dozen sources, we have direct evidence for the death of only 3,534. For the remaining 3000+ people, we will have to use an indirect method: given a complete list of Holocaust survivors, we would be able to infer that anyone not on this list had perished.*
>
> Alas, the survivor's lists are *not* complete."[88]

The authors have nonetheless identified through the use of various sources a total of 958 Liepāja Jews who still remained in the city in early 1942, while noting that the real number of Jews surviving at this point likely amounted to approximately 1,050. They further conclude that some 800 of these Jews were still alive in the Liepāja ghetto on the eve of its liquidation in early October 1943.[89] Subtracting 1,050 from 6,589 we get 5,539 hypothetical victims for the massacres in 1941, of which at least (5,539 - [2,749 + 500] =) 2,290 pertain to the period before mid-October 1941. Anders and Dubrovskis estimate the number of Liepāja Jews shot during the period July–December 1941 at approximately 5,470.[90]

To summarize: While the second Stahlecker Report claims that only 3,750 Latvian Jews remained at the end of January 1942, reliable documentation shows that this figure in reality amounted to at least 6,184 (4,358 in Riga in mid-February 1942, 962 in Daugavpils in December 1941, and 864 Jews in Liepāja in July 1942).

The unreliability of the figures in the second Stahlecker Report becomes clearly exposed when we examine an appendix to the report containing a breakdown of the "number of executions carried out by *Einsatzgruppe* A up to 1 February 1942"[91], reproduced below (Figure 3).

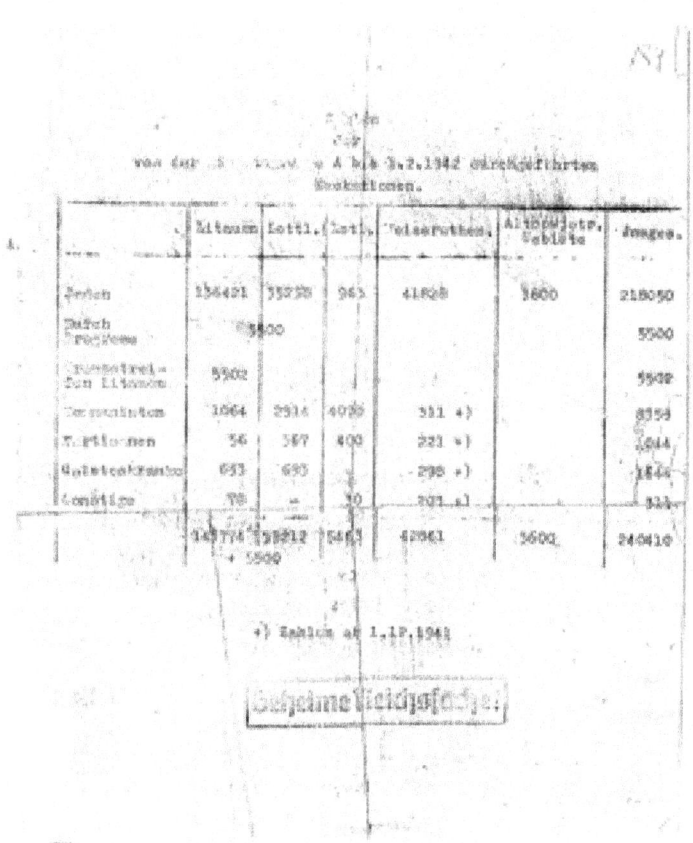

Figure 3: Number of executions carried out by *Einsatzgruppe* A up to 1 February 1942

Here the number of Latvian Jews executed by *Einsatzgruppe* A up until this date is given as 35,238, which would mean that since 15 October 1941 it had executed only an additional (35,238-30,025 =) 5,213 Jews. The figure of 5,500 Latvian and Lithuanian Jews killed through pogroms is identical with the corresponding figure given in the first Stahlecker Report, where it was made clear that only 500 of these pertained to Latvia[92] (as opposed to the statement in the second report that "some thousands" of Latvian Jews had been eliminated through pogroms).

One might argue that the 1 February 1942 total refers only to Jews liquidated by *Einsatzgruppe* A and forces placed at its command, but leaves out killings carried out by, to name the most obvious culprit, the Higher Leader of the SS and Police Ostland (*HSSPF* Ostland, i.e. Jeckeln). This line of reasoning would mean that, based on the figures found in the second Stahlecker Report proper, (70,000 − (2,500 + 950 + 300) =) 66,250 − 35,738 = 30,512 Jews were killed by German forces other than those attached to *Einsatzgruppe* A in the period from the beginning of the occupation to 1 February 1942. Since the Rumbula Massacre, with a reported total victims of some 27,800 is stated to have been carried out by *HSSPF*, one might suppose that the figures add up, at least roughly[93] – but is this really so? In order to arrive at an answer we will have to see first what exactly the *Ereignismeldungen* have to say about killings of Latvian Jews up until February 1942, and then embark on a brief excursus relating to the demographics and fates of the provincial Jews.

3.3. The murder of Latvia's Jews according to the Ereignismeldungen *and the Jäger Report*

In *EM* No. 15 from 7 July 1941 we read that 400 Jews had been liquidated in Riga through pogroms,[94] whereas another 100 Jews were shot in Riga by a commando of the Security Police and SD as reprisal for the killing of 20 German POWs.[95]

In *EM* No. 24 from 16 July 1941 it is reported that 5 Jews were shot for arson in Daugavpils;[96] moreover 1,125 male Jews were at present imprisoned in the same city and "were to be shot within a short time and in already prepared graves", whereas 1,150 Jews had already been shot by *Einsatzkommando* 1 b in Dünaburg [Daugavpils]".[97] As for Riga the same report states that 2,000 Jews (as well as 600 Communists) had been placed in the city's prison. It repeats the figure of 400 Riga Jews killed through pogroms, adding that 2,300 Riga Jews had been executed since *EK2*'s arrival in the city, "partially by Latvian auxiliary police, partially by own forces", and that "the prisons will be completely cleared out in the following days". In "Latvia outside of Riga" another 1,600 Jews had been executed.[98]

In *EM* No. 26 from 18 July 1941 one reads about Rezekne (German: Rositten), a town in northeastern Latvia:

> "*The larger part of the Jews had escaped to Russia and to the surrounding forests at the time of the entry of the German troops. The arson carried out in the town is for the most part perpetrated by the Jews. At the entry of the German troops some 60 leading*

> Latvians were found in a completely mutilated state. Following this 80 Jews were liquidated. Police Prefect Matsch has taken over the liquidation of the Jews."[99]

The local Jews were claimed to constitute a "key element of the Communist Party" ("*tragende Element der Kommunistischen Partei*").[100]

In *EM* No. 40 of 1 August 1941 one reads that "[d]uring the self-cleansing [*Selbstreinigung*] in the territories of Lithuania, Latvia and Estonia a total of far more than 20,000 Communists and Jews have up until now been liquidated by self-defense organizations [*Selbstschutzorganisationen*]".[101]

In *EM* No. 48 of 10 August 1941 *EG* A reports that "[t]he cleansing of the rear army zone, partially with the assistance of Lithuanian and Latvian auxiliary commandos, continues according to plan. In total 29,000 people have been liquidated in these territories."[102]

In *EM* No. 88 of 19 September 1941 it is mentioned that 172 Jews are currently held in the central prison in Riga and that the clearing-out of the prison is being carried out continuously.[103]

In *EM* No. 96, dated 27 September 1941, it is stated that 459 people had been executed during the period 30 August to 5 September, of whom "237 mentally ill Jews from the lunatic asylums in Riga and Mitau"; it is further stated that the "preliminary total result in the area of *EK* 2 [=Latvia] has at this point reached 29,246 people".[104] There is also mention that the number of Jews currently held in the Riga prison amount to 195 (as compared to 3,462 Communists),[105] and that "[a]t the time, all Jews in Libau are being registered."[106]

In *EM* No. 131 of 10 November 1941, *Einsatzgruppe* A reports that the "preliminary total result in the area of *Einsatzkommando* 2 has hereby reached 31,598."[107] It is also mentioned that in the period 18–25 October, 6 Jews were executed in Riga (as against 115 Communists), 15 in Valmiera and 18 in Liepāja.

Following *EM* No. 131 there are only the three reports relating to the Riga/Rumbula operation, which have already been discussed (with the exception that *EM* No. 156 also mentions the shooting of 1 (one) Jew in Liepāja).

The so-called Jäger Report, chronicling mass shootings carried out by *Einsatzgruppe* A's *Einsatzkommando* 3 and its subunits and auxiliaries up until the end of 1941, chiefly concerns Lithuania, but there is listed the killing of a total of 212 Jews in the Latvian towns of Dagda and Kraslava (not far from Daugavpils) on 27 August, and the abovementioned execution of 9,012 Jews in Daugavpils between 13 July and 21 August 1941.[108]

Based on the above-listed documentary mentions, one would have to draw the conclusion that out of the 35,238 Jews reported as killed by *Einsatzgruppe* A during the period in question, at least (100 + 1,150 + 2,200 + 6 + 18 + 1 + 212 + 9,012 =) 12,487 refer to the three cities of Riga, Daugavpils and Liepāja, leaving a hypothetical maximum of (35,238 − 12,487 =) 22,751 Jews who could have been executed by *Einsatzgruppe* A and its auxiliaries in the provincial towns and villages.

Excursus I: The Jews in Provincial Latvia

In order to better grasp the demographic context of the events at Rumbula and the figures mentioned in the Stahlecker Reports it is beneficial to take a closer look at data concerning the Jewish population of Latvia as a whole. The last census in Latvia before the outbreak of the war took place in 1935. In this year the Jewish population of the country amounted to 93,479. This figure can be broken down as follows in order of the individual populations (German names of the locations in parentheses):[109]

Table 3: The Jewish Population of Latvia according to the 1935 census	
City, town or rural district	Number of Jewish inhabitants
Riga	43,672
Daugavpils (Dünaburg)	11,106
Liepāja (Libau)	7,379
Rēzekne (Rositten)	3,342
Jelgava (Mitau)	2,039
Ludza (Ludsen)	1,518
Krāslava (Kraslau)	1,444
Ventspils (Windau)	1,246
Krustpils (Kreuzburg)	1,043

Table 3: The Jewish Population of Latvia according to the 1935 census	
City, town or rural district	Number of Jewish inhabitants
Līvāni (Lievenhof)	981
Tukums (Tuckum)	953
Varakļāni (Warkland)	952
Preiļi (Prelen)	847
Jēkabpils (Jakobstadt)	793
Kārsava (Karsau)	785
Bauska (Bausk)	778
Kuldīga (Goldingen)	646
Jaunjelgava (Friedrichstadt)	561
Aizpute (Hasenpoth)	543
Gostiņi (Trentelberg)	504
Talsi (Talsen)	499
Zilupe (Rosenhof)	471
Viļeni (Wilon)	396
Subate (Subbath)	387
Balva (Bolwa)	379
Saldus (Frauenburg)	329
Sabile (Zabeln)	281
Grīva (Griwa)	234
Smiltene (Smilten)	221
Priekule (Preekuln)	193
Jūrmala (Riga-Strand)	181
Cēsis (Wenden)	180
Alūksne (Marienburg)	176
Valdemārpils/Sasmaka (Sassmacken)	159
Auce (Autz)	143
Madona (Modohn)	115
Limbaži (Lemsal)	100
Grobiņa (Grobin)	95
Valmiera (Wolmar)	93
Gulbene (Schwanenburg)	84
Ape (Hoppenhof)	82
Dobele (Doblen)	72
Ilūkste (Illuxt)	71
Kandava (Kandau)	68

Table 3: The Jewish Population of Latvia according to the 1935 census	
City, town or rural district	Number of Jewish inhabitants
Rūjiena (Rujen)	62
Abrene (Abrehnen)	61
Valka (Walk)	57
Ogre (Oger)	50
Piltene (Pilten)	45
Plaviņas (Stockmannshof)	35
Strenči (Stackeln)	27
Sigulda (Segewold)	15
Sloka (Schlock)	10
Ķemeri (Kemmern)	9
Durbe (Durben)	8
Mazsalaca (Salisburg[110])	4
Ainaži (Haynasch)	1
Total for above cities, towns and rural districts	**86,554**
Other locations	6,925
Total	**93,479**

As seen above the three largest communities – Riga, Daugavpils and Liepāja – accounted for 62,157 Jews or 66.5% of Latvian Jewry. Of the remaining 31,322 Latvian Jews, 10,632 lived in the six towns of Rēzekne, Jelgava, Ludza, Krāslava, Ventspils and Krustpils, while the rest were dispersed in smaller numbers among a large number of towns and villages.

In Table 4 below I present for reference a *non-exhaustive* list of reported or alleged mass killings of Latvian Jews in rural communities up until mid-October 1941, by which time, according to the first Stahleckecker Report, *Einsatzgruppe* A had killed a total of 30,025 Latvian Jews. For many of the smaller provincial Jewish communities the available sources simply state that they were exterminated in the "summer of 1941" or "fall of 1941" or simply "in the second half of 1941". The survey is based mainly on five scholarly sources published after the year 2000: Geoffrey P. Megargee, Martin Dean (eds.), *The United States Holocaust Memorial Museum Encyclopedia of Camps and Ghettos 1933–1945, Volume II: Ghettos in German-Occupied Eastern Europe, Part B* (op.cit.), which I will abbreviate in the table below as "UE"; Shmuel Spector, Geoffrey Wigoder (eds.), *The Encyclopedia of Jewish Life before and during the Holocaust* (New York University Press, New York 2001), in three volumes with running pagination, abbreviated below as "EJL"; and three volumes collecting papers from conferences held by the Commission of the Historians of Latvia, abbreviated below as "LV1",[111] "LV2"[112] and "LV3"[113] respectively. Only a few massacres of provincial Latvian Jews are alleged to have taken place later than October 1941. 386 Jews are alleged to have been killed in Aizpute on 27 October (EJL, p. 24), whereas, remarkably enough, 26 Jews in Ludza were killed as late as 2 April 1942 (LV1, p. 253).

Table 4: Alleged or reported mass killings of Latvian Jews in rural communities up until mid-October 1941

Date	Victims ~estimate	Location/community	Source
Late June	~ 135	Skaitskalne	EJL (p. 1188)
4 July	10	Rēzekne	UE (p. 1018)
11 July	80	Jaunjelgava	UE (p. 1005)
12 or 13 July	48	Dobele	UE (p. 1003)
15 July	120	Rēzekne	UE (p. 1018)
16–18 July	300	Ventspils	EJL (p. 1386); M. Deland 2010 (p. 47)
19 July	~ 190	Viesīte	EJL (p. 1395)
24 July	39	Aizpute	EJL (p. 24)
July	~ 600	Kuldīga	UE (pp. 1010–1011)
July	~ 200	Aknīste	EJL (p. 25)
July	~ 46	Iecava	EJL (p. 543)
July	150–200	Saldus	LV2 (p. 136)
July	~ 600	Tukums	EJL (p. 1339)
July	1,550	Jelgava and surroundings	*EM* No. 40 (1 August 1941)
Second half July	25	Krustpils	UE (p. 1010)
1 August	~ 400	Krustpils	UE (p. 1010)
1 August	~ 200	Rēzekne	UE (p. 1018)
2 August	350	Jaunjelgava	UE (p. 1005)
3 August	50	Bauska	EJL (p. 93)
4 August	~ 300	Viļāni	EJL (p. 1396)
4 August	540	Varakļāni	EJL (p. 1375)
8 August	200	Smiltene	EJL (p. 1204)

Table 4: Alleged or reported mass killings of Latvian Jews in rural communities up until mid-October 1941

Date	Victims ~estimate	Location/community	Source
9 August	~ 500	Balvi	EJL (p. 83)
9 August	~ 200	Gulbene/Litene	UE (p. 1005)
12 August	182	Alūksne	EJL (p. 36)
Early August	~ 400–500	Viļaka	EJL (p. 1396); LV3 (p. 94)
20 or 21 August	350–500	Karsava	UE (p. 1009); LV1 (p. 253)
27 August	212	Dagda/Krāslava	Jäger report
July–August	~ 160	Baltinava	EJL (p. 83)
July–August	~ 150	Valdemārpils	LV1 (p. 277)
July–August	157	Nereta and surroundings	LV2 (p. 310)
July–August	~ 700	Preiļi	LV3 (pp. 257–258)
July–August	~ 150	Madona	LV3 (p. 117)
July–August	~ 1,200	Ludza	LV1 (p. 59)
August	~ 2,500	Rēzekne	UE (p. 1018)
August	~ 100	Šķaune	LV1 (p. 254)
Mid-to-late August	~ 70	Jaunjelgava	UE (p. 1005)
Late Summer	~ 125	Vaiņode	EJL (p. 1372)
August–September	150–200	Zilupe	LV1 (p. 254)
12 September	~ 470	Jekabpils	UE (p. 1006)
30 September	~ 800	Bauska	EJL (p. 93)
July, September	~ 80	Limbaži	LV1 (p. pp. 194–195)
September	200	Ventspils	EJL (p. 1386)
End September	~ 400	Talsi	EJL (p. 1287)
3–17 October	533	Ventspils	EJL (p. 1386)
Total:	**~ 15,922–16,272**		

At the onset of the German occupation there lived approximately 34,600 Jews in Riga,[114] 14,000 in Daugavpils, and some 6,500 in Liepāja, making for a total of approximately 55,100, i.e. 7,057 less than the combined 1935 population, suggesting an evacuation ratio of some 11%. If the estimate in the second Stahlecker Report that 70,000 Latvian Jews had remained behind in the country is correct, then there would have remained a mere 14,900 Jews outside of the three main cities, out of the original 31,322, a reduction of more than 50%. One has to consider, however, that at least some thousands of the Jews who found themselves in Riga, Liepāja and Daugavpils in July 1941 were refugees from neighboring provincial settlements. In Daugavpils the number of refugees in the city's ghetto must have numbered at least some 4,000 (assuming that the estimate of 14,000 ghetto inmates is reliable) considering the 1935 Jewish population (11,106) and the city's proximity to the Russian border.

One might argue that changes in population between 1935 and 1941 would make the above estimates unreliable. This, however, is only partially correct. According to demographer Mordechai Altshuler, the Jewish population decreased between 1935 and 1941 by some 3,080 persons due to net emigration and declining birth rate reflected by aging of the population. Altshuler's estimate should be considered conservative, as by his own admission he does not take into account Jewish emigration to countries other than Palestine and the United States, as well as clandestine emigration to Palestine. It follows that the Latvian-Jewish population by June 1941 amounted to 90,400 at the most.[115]

Is, then, Stahlecker's estimate of 70,000 remaining Jews reliable? In a paper presented in 2000 the two Latvian historians Edward Anders and Juris Dubrovskis estimate that 1,771 Latvian Jews had been deported to the Soviet interior shortly prior to the outbreak of the war, on 14 June 1941, while another 11,000 Jews were evacuated between 22 and 30 June (the latter figure includes retreating soldiers of Jewish ethnicity). Both of the figures (totalling 12,771) are marked by the authors as "uncertain".[116] As Anders and Dubrovskis accept Altshuler's estimate that the Latvian-Jewish population had declined to 90,400 by mid-1941 they find that some 88,600 Jews remained in Latvia after the deportations on 14 June. They admit, however, that

> "The number of Jews who fled to the USSR is very poorly known. Einsatzgruppe A figures for the number of Latvian Jews killed (63,238) and still alive (3,750) by early 1942 total only 67,000, considerably less than the 22 June 1941 population of about 88,600. (Actually, the numbers alive were seriously underestimated, e.g. 350 rather than 1,050 for Liepaja.) Some historians have tried to balance the numbers by assuming that some 20,000 Latvian Jews fled to the USSR. That is clearly too high: in 1944, many Aktionen and Selektionen later, some 4,500 Jews were still left for deportation to Stutthof, so the number in early 1942 probably was 8,000-9,000. That would allow for 12-13,000 refugees, or even fewer if the Einsatzgruppe A total is too

> *low. Indeed, in early 1946, long after most refugees had been free to return to Latvia, only 8,000 Jews lived in Latvia, of whom 3,400 were in Riga. As these included thousands of Soviet Jews, the number of returnees can hardly have exceeded 6,000. The death rate for refugees surely was no higher than that for deportees (1/3), so it is unlikely that more than 10,000 had fled in 1941."*[117]

The above argument rests on two dubious assumptions, namely 1) that the victim figures found in the *Einsatzgruppen* reports are to be taken as more or less reliable, and 2) that virtually all of the Jews residing in Latvia in 1946 declared themselves as such in the census. Nevertheless, Anders and Dubrovskis conclude that some 78,000 Latvian Jews remained under German control; of these some 70,000 were shot, 3,500 deported to Stutthof (near Danzig) in 1944, and 3,800 survived in Latvia in camps or in hiding (this makes for a total of 77,300, the remaining 700 being unaccounted for).[118] Yitzhak Arad on the other hand estimates the number of Latvian Jews remaining under German control at 74,000–75,000, implying a higher number of evacuees.[119] In his study *The Displacement of Population in Europe* from 1943 the demography professor E.M. Kulischer estimated the number of Jews evacuated from Latvia at some 15,000.[120]

There exist indications that the number of Jews who escaped or were evacuated from Latvia far exceeded 12,771. In its issue for January–February 1942 the Swedish-Jewish journal *Judisk Krönika* noted that

> *"According to Deutsche Zeitung im Ostland [an official German newspaper published in Riga] the Russians evacuated 30,000 Jews from Lithuania, 24,000 Jews from Latvia and 1,000 Jews from Estonia at the beginning of the German–Russian war."*[121]

If this information is correct, then there would have remained some (90,400 – 24,000 =) 66,400 Latvian Jews under German control, a figure lower than the Stahlecker estimate. Assuming, however, that the evacuation estimate reportedly given by the German newspaper was based on a subtraction of the estimated number of remaining Jews from the 1935 census figure, then the number of remaining Jews would be 69,479, i.e. virtually identical with the Stahlecker estimate.

As for the number of Jews deported to the Russian interior just prior to the outbreak of the war some witnesses mention figures considerably higher than 1,771. According to a book published in 1947 by Riga Jew Max Kaufmann some 5,000 Latvian Jews were deported by the Soviet authorities to the Russian interior on 14 June 1941.[122] Israeli Holocaust historian Dov Levin informs us that the number of people that the Soviets managed to arrest and deport amounted to 34,250. the nationalities of 20,000 of these forced deportees are known: 14,000 were Latvians, 5,000 Jews and the rest other minorities (mainly Poles).[123] If 25% of the identified deportees were Jews, then it seems justifiable to assume that this ratio applied also to the total number of deportees, which would mean that the number of Jews deported by the Soviets in June 1941 may have amounted to some (34,250 x 0.25 =) 8,562, rounded off downward to 8,500. The real number may have been lower but may also have been slightly higher: Levin mentions estimates of 10,000 or more.[124] The figure mentioned by Anders and Dubrovskis (1,771) possibly refers to the deportations on 14 June 1941 alone, although as Levin points out the deportations were carried out over a period of some weeks. It is clear that the Anders-Dubrovskis figure of 78,000 remaining Jews must be reduced by (8,500 - 1,771 =) 6,729 to 71,271.

Andrew Ezergailis speaks of a "major flight of Jews towards the interior of the Soviet Union" following the German attack on the Soviet Union, while noting that the estimates for the number of refugees to the USSR "vary from 10,000 to about 30,000". This uncertainty, Ezergailis explains, is due to the fact that to this date no documents have been found providing statistics on the evacuations.[125]

One must also consider the problem of the presence of Polish-Jewish refugees in Latvia. According to the Polish Government-in-Exile and the Hebrew Immigrant Aid Society (HIAS) some 30,000 Polish Jews fled to Lithuania, Latvia, Hungary and Romania following the German occupation of western Poland in 1939, of whom approximately 11,000 went to the bordering Lithuania.[126] Other sources put the number of refugees in the Vilnius region alone to some 14–15,000.[127] According to E.M. Kulischer some 2,000 Polish refugees found their way to Latvia; presumably the majority of these were Jews.[128] Due to the lack of more exact sources we will assume that 1,500 Polish Jews reached Latvia. If as in Lithuania 37–47% of the refugees then left the country before June 1941[129] there would have remained some 795–945 Polish Jews. As seen above, Anders and Dubrovskis conservatively estimate that 12,771 out of 90,400

Latvian Jews, i.e. 14% were deported or evacuated in June 1941. If this ratio applied also to the Polish-Jewish refugees then there would have been 684-813 left of them under German control, the median of which is 748, rounded off upward to 750. Based on the above considerations we may conclude that there lived at the utmost some 73,000 Jews in Latvia at the onset of the German occupation, which means that the Stahlecker estimate of 70,000 Jews is roughly correct. I will, however, adjust my working estimate of the number of Jews remaining behind in the provincial settlements from 14,900 to 17,900.

3.4. Consequences of the geographic distribution of the reported Jewish victims

Now, if only some 17,900 Jews remained behind in provincial Latvia at the beginning of the German occupation, and if all these Jews were indeed wiped out by units sorting under *Einsatzgruppe* A, then (35,238 - 17,900 =) 17,338 of the total given in the second Stahlecker Report must refer to the three cities of Riga, Daugavpils and Liepāja. As seen above, the same three cities at the onset of the occupation had a total of approximately 55,100 Jewish residents (approximately 34,600 Jews in Riga, some 14,000 in Daugavpils, and some 6,500 in Liepāja), while in early 1942 a documented (4,358 + 962 + 864) 6,184 of these remained in the same cities, a reduction of some (55,100 - 6,184 =) 48,916.

Since the figure of 17,338 cannot contain the early July shooting by *Einsatzkommando* 1b of 1,155 Jews in Daugavpils, the summer 1941 mass shooting by *EK* 3 of 9,012 Jews in the same city *as well as* the massacre of 11,034 Jews in the same city on 9 November, as reported by the second Stahlecker Report, in addition to the more than 2,000 Riga Jews reported shot (1,155 + 9,012 + 11,034 + 2,300 = 23,501) the only conclusion to be drawn from this statistical basis is that all three Latvian massacres mentioned in the Stahlecker Report (Riga/Rumbula, Liepāja, Daugavpils) must be considered as *not* counted in the second Stahlecker Report's total of 35,238. If added together, the victim figures of these three mass shootings mentioned by Stahlecker amount to 41,184, or 40,184 if subtracting 1,000 Reich Jews possibly included in the 27,800 Rumbula figure. Now, if we add these 40,184 to the 35,238 *Einsatzgruppe* A figure, the 500 reported pogrom victims and the documented number of 6,184 survivors we arrive at a total of 82,106, that is, nearly 10,000 above the number of Jews estimated to have remained in Latvia *in its entirety* at the beginning of the German occupation. Clearly the statistics of the Stahlecker Reports do not hold up.

The first Stahlecker Report contains another contradiction, as it states that 9,256 Jews had been executed in the *Gebietskommissariat* Dünaburg by *Einsatzgruppe* A forces up until 15 October 1941. Yet the number of victims of the Latvian shootings reported in the Jäger Report as carried out by a detachment of *EK* 3 in July–August 1941 (9,224), the shooting of 1,155 Daugavpils Jews by *EK* 1b in early July, and the execution of at least 80 Rēzekne Jews, likewise in early July, add up to 10,459. In addition to the figures found in the incident reports and the Jäger Report, more than 3,000 Rēzekne Jews are alleged to have been murdered by Latvian "self-defence units" in August 1941.[130] In another town in the *Gebietskommissariat*, Ludza, some 800 Jews are alleged to have been murdered on 17 August 1941.[131]

The final blow to the credibility of the Stahlecker statistics comes from a rarely reproduced draft of the infamous "coffin map" attached to the second Stahlecker Report.[132] The draft (Figure 4 below) consists of a more detailed map of the Baltic states and Belarus to which text and figures have been added in pencil. To the upper right is also found, likewise pencilled in, the table of executions from the same report (although with the countries in different order, starting with Estonia instead of Lithuania). There are some small but interesting discrepancies between the draft and the final version:

- The victim figures are not placed within stylized pictures of coffins.
- The Vilnius ghetto (with the figure 15,000 faintly visible to its right) is struck out in the draft but not in the final version. The ghetto of Švenčionys in south-eastern Lithuania is struck out neither in the draft nor in the final version (and also goes unmentioned in the report itself), despite the fact that it is documented to have housed 566 Jews in August 1942,[133] i.e. a considerably higher figure than was indicated for the Liepāja ghetto (300).
- The number of estimated remaining Jews in Weissruthenien was first written as 110,000, then struck out and replaced with the text found in the final version, which gives the figure as 128,000.
- The number of Jews remaining in Minsk is given as 18,000, whereas the final version carries no figure at all. In the report

itself it is stated that "about 18 00 Jews" ("*rund 18 00 Juden*") remained in the Minsk ghetto, excluding Reich Jews deported there.[134] Since four-digit numbers are written in this way neither in English nor in German it is clear that "18 00" should in fact read "18,000" as on the draft map. According to Yitzhak Arad, however, "[b]etween 45,000 and 46,000 Jews remained in the [Minsk] ghetto" at the beginning of December 1941,[135] whereas in March 1942 the Minsk ghetto, "the largest in Belorussia, had a population of about 49,000 Jews, including the 7,000 brought there from the Reich".[136] How was it possible for Stahlecker to underestimate the number of remaining Minsk Jews by 27,000–28,000?

- The number of Jews shot in the border area between Lithuania and Germany (East Prussia) – 5,502 – is struck out on the draft but not in the final version.
- The Liepāja ghetto is struck out in the draft but absent in the final version.
- Finally, and most importantly for us in this context, under the number of Jews executed in Latvia – 35,238, the same as in the final version– is written in smaller letters "*+ 28.000 (Höh. SS u. Pol.F.)*" (cf. Figure 4 b). This in turn appears to have been written over something else that was then erased. Moreover it is clear that the first digit in the 35,238 figure was initially a "2", which was then overwritten (rather than erased). In the table, on the other hand, "35 238" appears to be the original figure.

Figure 4: Draft of the "coffin map" from the second Stahlecker Report.[137]

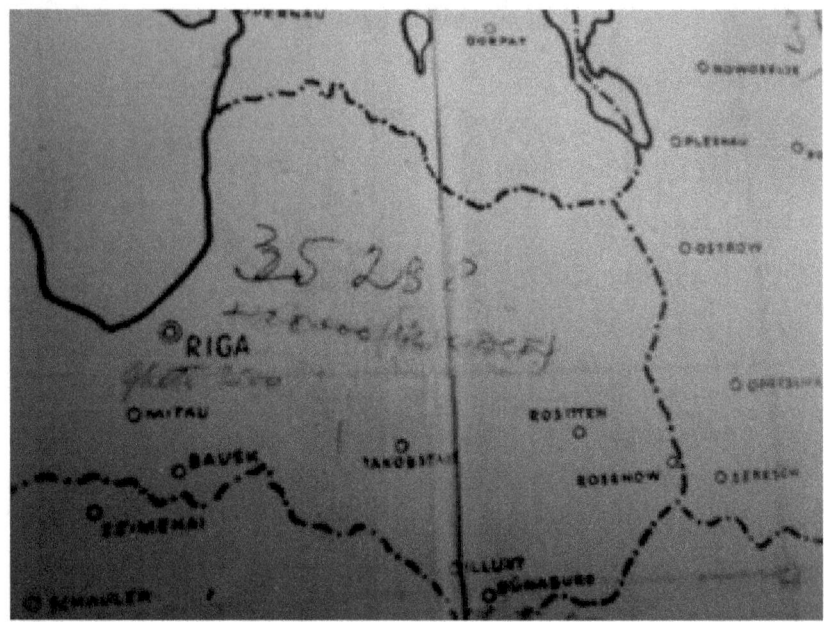

Illustration 4 b: Detail of the "coffin map" draft.

The final discrepancy provides us with a key to the Stahlecker statistics pertaining to the Jews of Latvia at the beginning of 1942. Their numbers and fates can accordingly be summed up thus:

Jews shot by *Einsatzgruppe* A	35,238
Jews shot by the *HSSPF*	28,000
Jews killed in pogrom	500
Jews remaining in ghettos	3,750
Total:	**67,488**

The total here is obviously very close to the number of Jews estimated by Stahlecker to have remained behind at the beginning of the occupation – 70,000. The words "+ *28.000 (Höh. SS u. Pol.F.)*" can only be taken to mean that the Rumbula Massacre (whose victim figure is given as 27,800 in the report) *alone* is ascribed to the Higher Leader of the Police and SS. From this follows that both of the two other major post-15-October mass shootings (in Dauvapils and Liepāja in November and December respectively) must fall under the account of *Einsatzgruppe* A. However, if we deduct the victim figures reported by Stahlecker for these two mass shootings from the *Einsatzgruppe* A total of executed Jews at the end of the report period we get (35,238 − 13,384 =) 21,854. But how then could *EG* A and their Latvian helpers have killed 30,025 Jews in Latvia up until 15 October 1941, as stated in the first Stahlecker Report, or "about 30,000 Jews" "up until October 1941" as stated in the second report?

The matter gets even more bizarre when we consider that the *Einsatzgruppe* A total for Lithuania indicated on the "coffin map" – 136,421 – is identical with the number of Jews executed by *EG* A *Einsatzkommando* 3 in Lithuania according to a telegram sent by Karl Jäger to the *EG* A headquarters in Riga on 9 February 1942,[138] which in turn is only slightly higher than the number of Jews listed in the Jäger Report as executed up until 1 December 1941 (135,318).[139] The total of executed Jews in the Jäger Report, however, includes not only 4,934 Reich Jews deported to Kaunas and 3,031 Belorussian Jews shot near Minsk, but also the already mentioned 9,224 Latvian Jews reportedly shot in Daugavpils, Dagda and Kraslava in July and August 1941. But if the Jewish victim figure found in the Jäger Report is contained in the 136,421 figure on the "coffin map", then these 9,224 Latvian Jews have consequently been erroneously counted among those executed in Lithuania. In turn this would mean that the second Stahlecker Report and the "coffin map" accounts for a total of (67,488 + 9,224 =) 76,712 Latvian Jews – considerably more than the 70,000 Jews estimated by Stahlecker to have been remained in Latvia at the onset of the German occupation. Now, one might argue that 76,712 is closer to our own estimate of some 73,000 Jews remaining in Latvia (including refugees), but if we instead consider the actual number of Jews remaining in the Latvian ghettos, rather than the number reported by Stahlecker, this would bring the total of accounted-for Jews up to 79,146 Jews, making for a remainder of some 6,000 Jews who simply should not be there.

The inevitable conclusion of the above examination is that the statistics found in the Stahlecker Reports are not reliable, but are rather to be understood as statistical fabrications, resulting from exaggerated numbers, bureaucratic confusion, or possibly even from willful falsification. This in turn raises the question: if the Stahlecker Reports present unreliable statistics on the mass killings of Baltic and Belorussian Jews, is it not then possible that at least some of the Jews reported as exterminated did in fact meet an altogether different fate?

To be continued.

Notes:

1. Cf. Herbert Tiedemann, "Babi Yar: Critical Questions and Comments", in Germar Rudolf (ed.), *Dissecting the Holocaust, The Growing Critique of "Truth" and "Memory"*, 2nd rev. ed., Theses & Dissertations Press, Chicago, 2003, pp. 501-528.
2. Cf. my article "The Maly Trostenets "Extermination Camp" – A Preliminary Historiographical Survey" published in two parts in Inconvenient History vol. 3 (2011) nos. 1 and 2 http://inconvenienthistory.com/archive/2011/volume_3/number_1/the_maly_trostenets_extermination_camp.php.
3. Geoffrey P. Megargee, Martin Dean (eds.), The United States Holocaust Memorial Muse.um Encyclopedia of Camps and Ghettos 1933–1945, Volume II: Ghettos in German-Occupied Eastern Europe, Part B, Indiana University Press, Bloomington (Ind.) 2012, pp. 1020–1021.
4. Bernhard Press, *The Murder of the Jews in Latvia 1941–1945*, Northwestern University Press, Evanston (Ill.) 2000, pp. 103–106.
5. Andrew Ezergailis, *The Holocaust in Latvia 1941–1944 – The Missing Center*, Historical Institute of Latvia/USHMM, Riga 1996, p. 241.
6. Andrew Ezergailis, Harold Otto, Gvido Augusts, *Nazi/Soviet Disinformation about the Holocaust in Nazi-Occupied Latvia*, Latvijas 50 Gadu Okupācijas Muzeja Fonds, Riga 2005, pp. 110–111.
7. *Contemporary Jewish Record*, vol. 5, no. 1 (February 1942), p. 77.
8. *Contemporary Jewish Record*, vol. 5, no. 2 (April 1942), p. 190.
9. *Contemporary Jewish Record*, vol. 5, no. 4 (August 1942), p. 422.
10. *Contemporary Jewish Record*, vol. 5, no. 6 (December 1942), p. 630.
11. It is further unclear what is meant by "second ghetto". Second to a previous one on the same location, or second to the Riga ghetto? In the latter case, it is odd, though not unthinkable, that the existence of the ghettos in the cities of Daugavpils and Liepāja would have escaped the attention of the CJR chroniclers.
12. *Contemporary Jewish Record*, vol. 6, no. 1 (February 1943), p. 67.
13. Andrej Angrick, Peter Klein, *The "Final Solution" in Riga. Exploitation and Annihilation, 1941–1944*, Berghahn Books, New York/Oxford 2009, p. 137.
14. Cf. map of the Riga ghetto in ibid., p. 217.
15. "Nazis Decide to Make Latvia 'Judenrein', Deport All Jews from Riga Ghetto", *JTA Daily News Bulletin*, 20 November 1942, p. 2.
16. *The Manchester Guardian,* 30 October 1942, p. 8.
17. Cf. A. Angrick, P. Klein, *The "Final Solution" in Riga*, op.cit., p. 219.
18. Ibid., p. 111.
19. *Contemporary Jewish Record*, vol. 6, no. 4 (August 1943), p. 413.
20. Quoted in Andrew Ezergailis (ed.), *Stockholm Documents. The German Occupation of Latvia 1941-1945. What Did America Know?*, Historical Institute of Latvia, Riga 2002, p. 472.
21. "Latvian Jewish woman who fled to Sweden reveals massacre of Riga Jews", 24 July 1944, p. 2.

22. Mats Deland, *Purgatorium. Sverige och andra världskrigets krigsförbrytare (Purgatory. Sweden and the War Criminals of World War II)*, Atlas, Stockholm 2010, p. 74, 77.
23. Ibid., pp. 78, 96.
24. *Soviet Government Statements on Nazi Atrocities*, Hutchinson & Co, London 1945, p. 60.
25. Statement of Gabriel Ziwjan, pp. 4–6. Hopper and Glass gives the archival source of this official English translation as: AJA, The World Jewish Congress Collection, Series H: Alphabetic Files, 1919–1981, Sub-Series 1: Alphabetical Files, A–Z, 1919, 1924–1929, 1931–1981, Box H 329, File 9, Switzerland, Warnings of Extermination of Jews, Baltic States, Statement of Ziwian, Gabriel, 1942. It is available in facsimile online: http://www.rumbula.org/Statement_of_Gabriel_Ziwjan.pdf
26. Ibid., page 2 of addendum on sources.
27. The letter c is pronounced as [ts] in Latvian.
28. Cf. http://en.wikipedia.org/wiki/Carnikava_municipality
29. A. Angrick, P. Klein, *The "Final Solution" in Riga*, op.cit., p. 132.
30. Bert Hoppe, Hildrun Glass (eds.), *Die Verfolgung und Ermordung der europäischen Juden durch das nationalsozialistische Deutschland 1933–1945*, Vol. 7: *Sowjetunion mit annektierten Gebieten I. Besetzte sowjetische Gebiete unter deutscher Militärverwaltung, Baltikum und Transnistrien*, Oldenbourg Verlag, Munich 2011, note 27 on p. 672.
31. Jürgen E. Kroeger, Eine baltische Illusion: Tagebuch eines Deutsch-Balten aus den Jahren 1939–1944, Nordland-Druck, Lüneburg 1973, p. 69. The passage reads in original: „Die Sicherheitspolizei hat heute unter tätiger Mithilfe lettischer Hinrichtungskommandos in der Gegend von Salaspilsungefähr 30 000 Juden ermordet, hauptsächlich Juden aus Wien und dem Altreich. Obschon die Aktion geheimhalten wurde, sickerte die grausige Wahrheit bald durch. Die Stadt liegt wie gelähmt da."
32. A. Ezergailis, *The Holocaust in Latvia 1941–1944*, op.cit., p. 262f.
33. Ibid., note 93 on p. 272.
34. J. E. Kroeger, Eine baltische Illusion, op.cit., p. 71. The passage reads in original: "Die Wahrheit ist schlimm! Eine Minderheit lettischer Rechtsextremisten hat unter Billigung und Führung der deutschen SS die Juden auf dem flachen Lande und in den Kreisstädten ausgerottet. Später sind von der SS mit lettischer Unterstützung beinah 100 000 zum Teil aus dem Altreich und Wien hierher evakuierte Juden in der Umgebung Rigas ermordet worden."
35. A. Ezergailis, *The Holocaust in Latvia 1941–1944*, op.cit., p. 262.
36. Latvija pod igom natsizma. Sbornik arkhivnykh dokumentov, Evropa, Moscow 2006, p. 10.
37. Ezergailis does not provide a source for this, but considering that Degenhardt stood trial in West Germany in the 1960s it seems most likely that the statement derives from him; cf. A. Angrick, P. Klein, *The "Final Solution" in Riga*, op.cit., p. 484.
38. A. Angrick, P. Klein, *The "Final Solution" in Riga*, op.cit., p.103.
39. Ibid., pp. 112–113.

40. Ibid., p. 219.
41. Ibid., p. 216, cf. also Avraham Tory, *Surviving the Holocaust. The Kovno Ghetto Diary*, Harvard University Press, Cambridge (MA)/London 1990, p. 69, 275–278.
42. A. Angrick, P. Klein, *The "Final Solution" in Riga*, op. cit., p. 153.
43. Ibid., p. 144.
44. Ibid., p. 155.
45. A. Ezergailis, *The Holocaust in Latvia 1941–1944*, op. cit., p. 258.
46. Cf. Max Michelson, *City of Life, City of Death. Memories of Riga*, University Press of Colorado, Boulder 2001, p. 107.
47. Ibid., pp. 111–112.
48. Ibid., p. 113.
49. Ibid., p. 140.
50. G. P. Megargee, M. Dean (eds.), *The United States Holocaust Memorial Museum Encyclopedia of Camps and Ghettos 1933–1945*, Vol. III, Part B, op.cit., p. 1020.
51. Max Kaufmann, *Churbn Lettland. The Destruction of the Jews of Latvia*, originally self-published in German, Munich 1947, online English edition: (http://www.jewsoflatvia.com/churbnlettland.pdf), p. 27.
52. A. Angrick, P. Klein, *The "Final Solution" in Riga*, op. cit., pp. 142–143.
53. NARA, T-175, Roll 234, p. 772.
54. NARA, T-175, Roll 234, p. 878.
55. Peter Klein (ed.), *Die Einsatzgruppen in der besetzten Sowjetunion 1941/42. Die Tätigkeits- und Lageberichte des Chefs der Sicherheitspolizei und des SD*, Edition Hentrich, Berlin 1997, p. 281.
56. NARA, T-175, Roll 234, p. 928.
57. PS-2273, IMT vol. XXX, pp. 73–74; RGVA, 500-4-92, pp. 57–59.
58. Nuremberg document 180-L, IMT vol. XXXVII, pp. 702–703.
59. For a map of the borders of these jurisdictions cf. http://en.wikipedia.org/wiki/Reichskommissariat_Ostland
60. Ibid., p. 688.
61. Ibid., p. 689.
62. Carlo Mattogno, Jürgen Graf, *Treblinka. Extermination Camp or Transit Camp?*, Theses & Dissertations Press, Chicago, 2004, pp. 208–209.
63. A. Angrick, P. Klein, *The "Final Solution" in Riga*, op.cit., p. 127, n. 81.
64. Katrin Reichelt, *Lettland unter deutscher Besatzung 1941–1944. Der lettische Anteil am Holocaust*, Metropol, Berlin 2011, p. 186.
65. See Table 4. In *Ereignismeldung* nr 24 from 16 July 1941 it is erroneously claimed that out of the 45,000 inhabitants of Daugavpils, 50% (i.e. 22,500) were Jews. It is hard to explain how the author of the *Ereignismeldung* could have made such a grossly exaggerated estimate; NARA, T 175 Roll 233, p. 181.
66. K. Reichelt, Lettland unter deutscher Besatzung 1941–1944, op.cit., p. 183.

67. Cf. Sidney Iwens, *How Dark the Heavens. 1400 Days in the Grip of Nazi Terror*, Shengold, New York 1990, p. 49. Holocaust historians Bernhard Press and Yitzhak Arad give widely divergent estimates for the original number of ghetto inmates – 7,000 and 16,000 respectively – but since the sources to these figures are far from clear the 14,000 figure must be regarded, for the time being, as the more reliable estimate; cf. Yitzhak Arad, *The Holocaust in the Soviet Union*, University of Nebraska Press, Lincoln 2009, p. 148; B. Press, *The Murder of the Jews in Latvia 1941–1945*, op.cit., p. 53.
68. Cf. reproduction of page 5 of the report online at: http://www.holocaust-history.org/works/jaeger-report/gif/img005.gif?size=-1
69. S. Iwens, *How Dark the Heavens*, op.cit., p. 50.
70. Ibid., pp. 49–50.
71. Ibid., p. 53.
72. Ibid., p. 57.
73. NARA, T-175, Roll 233, p. 182.
74. K. Reichelt, *Lettland unter deutscher Besatzung 1941–1944*, op.cit., p. 185.
75. Ibid., p. 184.
76. According to exterminationist historiography the massacre took place on 7–9 November 1941; cf. ibid, pp. 185–186.
77. Y. Arad, *The Holocaust in the Soviet Union*, op. cit., p. 149.
78. A. Angrick, P. Klein, *The "Final Solution" in Riga*, op. cit., p. 268.
79. K. Reichelt, *Lettland unter deutscher Besatzung 1941–1944*, op. cit., p. 186. Incredibly enough, Reichelt maintains that this estimate from *October 1941* is contradicted by the documents showing that the ghetto population in *December* that same year amounted to 962. In reality, of course, the October estimate contradicts the claim that 11,034 Daugavpils Jews were murdered in November.
80. Ibid., pp. 191–192.
81. Edward Anders, Juris Dubrovskis, "Who Died in the Holocaust? Recovering Names from Official Records", *Holocaust and Genocide Studies*, vol. 17, No. 1 (Spring 2003), p. 124.
82. K. Reichelt, Lettland unter deutscher Besatzung 1941–1944, op. cit., pp. 190–191.
83. Cf. http://wikimapia.org/5591391/lv/Rai%C5%86a-parks
84. *Liepāja*, http://www.liepajajews.org/LGhetto.pdf
85. K. Reichelt, Lettland unter deutscher Besatzung 1941–1944, op. cit., p. 194.
86. Y. Arad, *The Holocaust in the Soviet Union*, op. cit., p. 149.
87. K. Reichelt, *Lettland unter deutscher Besatzung 1941–1944*, op.cit., p. 191: "*In der Zeit vom 14. bis 17.12.41 wurden 2749 Juden evakuiert*". Reichelt states as her source "LVVA Riga, P-83, 1, 25, S. 50 (Tätigkeitsbericht des SS- und Polizeistandortsführers Libau vom 29. Dezember 1941)."

88. Edward Anders, Juris Dubrovskis, "Who Died in the Holocaust? Recovering Names from Official Records", *Holocaust and Genocide Studies*, vol. 17, No. 1 (Spring 2003) pp. 124–125.
89. Ibid., p. 125, 130.
90. Ibid., p. 117.
91. RGVA, 500-4-92, p. 184.
92. Cf. also IMT vol. XXXVII, p. 688: 4,500 had reportedly been killed during pogroms in Kaunas (Kauen), whereas another 500 had been killed in nearby towns.
93. While as stated above the Liepāja massacre in December 1941 is mentioned in an activity report of the SS and Police, the consensus among Holocaust historians appears to be that the mass shooting was carried out as part of the activity of *Einsatzkommando* 2, cf. the Ezergailis quote on the "Stahlecker method" in the first section of this article.
94. NARA, T 175 Roll 233, p. 92.
95. Ibid., p. 93.
96. NARA, T 175 Roll 233, p. 180.
97. Ibid., p. 182.
98. Ibid., p. 184.
99. NARA, T 175 Roll 233, p. 180.
100. Ibid.
101. NARA T 175 Roll 233, p. 403.
102. NARA T 175 Roll 233, p. 519.
103. NARA, T 175 Roll 233, p. 1077.
104. NARA, T 175 Roll 233, p. 1325.
105. Ibid.
106. Ibid., p. 1327.
107. NARA; T 175 Roll 234, p. 408.
108. Facsimile available online at: http://www.holocaust-history.org/works/jaeger-report/htm/intro000.htm
109. All census figures taken from *Strukturbereicht über das Ostland. Teil I: Ostland in Zahlen*, Riga 1942, p. 14. Available online at the website http://libx.bsu.edu On the German exonyms for the Latvian locations cf. http://en.wikipedia.org/wiki/List_of_German_exonyms_for_places_in_Latvia.
110. *Ostland in Zahlen* gives the German name as "Salis" but this is likely an error for Salisburg, as Salis is the German name of a river (Salaca in Latvian), not a locality.
111. *Holokausta izpēte Latvijā. Starptautisko konferenču materiāli, 2003. gada 12.–13. jūnijs, 24. oktobris, Rīga, un 2002.–2003. gada pētījumi par holokaustu Latvijā/The Holocaust research in Latvia. Materials of an International Conference 12–13 June 2003, Riga and 24 October 2003, Rīga and the Holocaust Studies in Latvia in 2002–2003* (Latvijas Vēsturnieku komisijas raksti 12. sējums/Symposium of the Commission of the Historians of Latvia, Volume 12), Latvijas vēstures institūta apgāds, Riga 2004.
112. *Holokausts Latvijā. Starptautiskās konferences materiāli, 2004. gada 3.– 4. jūnijs, Rīga, un 2004.–2005. gada pētījumi par holokaustu*

Latvijā/Holocaust in Latvia. Materials of an International Conference 3– 4 June 2004, Riga and the Holocaust Studies in Latvia in 2004–2005 (Latvijas Vēsturnieku komisijas raksti 18. sējums/Symposium of the Commission of the Historians of Latvia, Volume 18), Latvijas vēstures institūta apgāds, Riga 2006.
113. *Holokausta pētniecības problēmas Latvijā. 2006.–2007. gada pētījumi par holokaustu Latvijā un starptautiskās konferences materiāli, 2007. gada 6-7. novembris, Rīga/Problems of the Holocaust research in Latvia. The Holocaust Studies in Latvia in 2006–2007 and Proceedings of an International Conference 6–7 November 2007, Riga* (Latvijas Vēsturnieku komisijas raksti 23. sējums/Symposium of the Commission of the Historians of Latvia, Volume 23), Latvijas vēstures institūta apgāds, Riga 2008.
114. 29,602 Jews registered in the ghetto in October 1941 (see above) + some 5,000 Riga Jews killed in pogroms or shot by *EK*2 in July–September 1941 according to the *Ereignismeldungen*.
115. Mordechai Altshuler, *Soviet Jewry on the Eve of the Holocaust*, Centre for Research of East European Jewry/Ahva Press, Jerusalem 1998, p. 327.
116. Edward Anders, Juris Dubrovskis, "Fate of Latvian Jews 1941–1945: Recovering Names from Official Records", in: *Holokausta Izpētes Problemas Latvijā/The Issues of the Holocaust Research in Latvia*, Reports of an International Conference in Riga 16-17 October 2000, Latvijas vestures instituta apgads, Riga 2001, p. 50.
117. Ibid., p. 56.
118. Ibid., p. 50.
119. Y. Arad, T*he Holocaust in the Soviet Union*, op.cit., p. 525.
120. Eugene M. Kulischer, *The Displacement of Population in Europe*, International Labour Office, Montreal 1943, p. 64.
121. *Judisk Krönika*, Vol. 11 Nr 1 (January-February 1942), p. 12. The number of evacuees from Estonia is an underestimate; in reality some 3–4,000 Jews were evacuated from that country.
122. M. Kaufmann, *Churbn Lettland*, op. cit., p. 9.
123. Dov Levin, *Baltic Jews under the Soviets 1940-1946*, Centre for Research and Documentation of Eastern European Jewry, Jerusalem 1994, p. 100.
124. Ibid., p. 113, n. 15.
125. Andrew Ezergailis, Harold Otto, Gvido Augusts, *Nazi/Soviet Disinformation about the Holocaust in Nazi-Occupied Latvia*, Latvijas 50 Gadu Okupacijas Muzeja Fonds, Riga 2005, p. 113.
126. *American Jewish Year Book*, Vol. 42 (1940-1941), p. 598.
127. Y. Arad, T*he Holocaust in the Soviet Union*, op.cit., pp. 46-47.
128. E.M. Kulischer, *The Displacement of Population in Europe*, op. cit., p. 50.
129. Cf. Y. Arad, *The Holocaust in the Soviet Union*, op.cit., p. 47; Dov Levin, *The Lesser of Two Evils: Eastern European Jewry under Soviet rule, 1939-1941*, The Jewish Publication Society, Philadelphia/Jerusalem 1995, p. 200, 208; D. Levin, *Baltic Jews under the Soviets 1940–1946*, op.cit., comment to table on p. 129.

130. Cf. Geoffrey P. Megargee (ed.), *The United States Holocaust Memorial Museum Encyclopedia of Camps and Ghettos, 1933–1945: Ghettos in German-Occupied Eastern Europe*, vol. II, part B, Indiana University Press, Bloomington 2012, p. 1018.
131. http://www.jewishvirtuallibrary.org/jsource/judaica/ejud_0002_00 13_0_12842.html
132. Reproduced in negative in Nuremberg document 2273-PS, IMT vol. XXX, p. 77.
133. Christoph Dieckmann, *Deutsche Besatzungspolitik in Litauen 1941–1944*, Wallstein, Göttingen 2011, p. 1192.
134. 2273-PS, IMT vol. XXX, p. 78.
135. Y. Arad, *The Holocaust in the Soviet Union*, op. cit., p. 154.
136. Ibid., p. 251.
137. LVVA (Latvian State Historical Archives), P-1026-1-3, Bl. 351; reproduced in Hamburger Institut für Sozialforschung (ed.), *Verbrechen der Wehrmacht. Dimensionen des Vernichtungskrieges 1941–1944*, 2nd ed., Hamburger Edition, Hamburg 2002, p. 87.
138. RGVA 500-1-25/1, p. 170.
139. The Jäger Report lists the execution of a total of 2,028 non-Jews, mainly Lithuanian and Russian Communists.

And the War Came

Ralph Raico

The immediate origins of the 1914 war lie in the twisted politics of the Kingdom of Serbia.[1] In June 1903, Serbian army officers murdered their king and queen in the palace and threw their bodies out a window, at the same time massacring various royal relations, cabinet ministers, and members of the palace guards. It was an act that horrified and disgusted many in the civilized world. The military clique replaced the pro-Austrian Obrenović dynasty with the anti-Austrian Karađorđevićs. The new government pursued a pro-Russian, Pan-Slavist policy, and a network of secret societies sprang up, closely linked to the government, whose goal was the "liberation" of the Serb subjects of Austria (and Turkey), and perhaps the other South Slavs as well.

The man who became prime minister, Nicolas Pašić, aimed at the creation of a Greater Serbia, necessarily at the expense of Austria-Hungary. The Austrians felt, correctly, that the cession of their Serb-inhabited lands, and maybe even the lands inhabited by the other South Slavs, would set off the unraveling of the great multinational Empire. For Austria-Hungary, Serbian designs posed a mortal danger.

The Russian ambassador Hartwig worked closely with Pašić and cultivated connections with some of the secret societies. The upshot of the two Balkan Wars which he promoted was that Serbia more than doubled in size and threatened Austria-Hungary not only politically but militarily as well. Sazonov, the Russian Foreign Minister, wrote to Hartwig, "Serbia has only gone through the first stage of her historic road and for the attainment of her goal must still endure a terrible struggle in which her whole existence may be at stake." Sazonov went on, as indicated above, to direct Serbian expansion to the lands of Austria-Hungary, for which Serbia would have to wage "the future inevitable struggle."[2] The nationalist societies stepped up their activities, not only within Serbia, but also in the Austrian provinces of Bosnia and Herzegovina. The most radical of these groups was Union or Death, popularly known as the Black Hand. It was led by Colonel Dragutin Dimitrievic, called Apis, who also happened to be the head of Royal Serbian Military Intelligence. Apis was a veteran of the slaughter of his own king and queen in 1903, as well as of a number of other political murder plots. "He was quite possibly the foremost European expert in regicide of his time."[3] One of his close contacts was Colonel Artamonov, the Russian military attaché in Belgrade.

The venerable emperor of Austria and king of Hungary, Franz Josef, who had come to the throne in 1848, clearly had not much longer to live. His nephew and heir, Franz Ferdinand, was profoundly concerned by the wrenching ethnic problems of the Empire and sought their solution in some great structural reform, either in the direction of federalism for the various national groups, or else "trialism," the creation of a third, Slavic component of the Empire, alongside the Germans and the Magyars. Since such a concession would mean the ruin of any program for a Greater Serbia, Franz Ferdinand was a natural target for assassination by the Black Hand.[4]

In the spring of 1914, Serbian nationals who were agents of the Black Hand recruited a team of young Bosnian fanatics for the job. The youths were trained in Belgrade and provided with guns, bombs, guides (also Serbian nationals) to help them cross the border, and cyanide for after their mission was accomplished. Prime Minister Pašić learned of the plot, informed his cabinet, and made ineffectual attempts to halt it, including conveying a veiled, virtually meaningless warning to an Austrian official in Vienna. (It is also likely that the Russian attaché Artamonov knew of the plot.[5]) No clear message of the sort that might have prevented the assassination was forwarded to the Austrians. On June 28, 1914, the plot proved a brilliant success, as 19 year old Gavrilo Princip shot and killed Franz Ferdinand and his wife Sophie in the streets of Sarajevo.

In Serbia, Princip was instantly hailed as a hero, as he was also in post-World War I Yugoslavia, where the anniversary of the murders was celebrated as a national and religious holiday. A marble tablet was dedicated at the house in front of which the killings took place. It was inscribed: "On this historic spot, on 28 June 1914, Gavrilo Princip proclaimed freedom."[6] In his history of the First World War, Winston Churchill wrote of Princip that "he died in prison, and a monument erected in recent years by his fellow-countrymen records his infamy, and their own."[7]

Kaiser Wilhelm II(left) and Archduke Franz Ferdinand of Austria(right) in a car, 1912. The military airship "Parseval" (probably either PL 2/P. I or PL 4/M I) is on the left, and the Zeppelin on the right. This is an early example of photo fakery. Photographer Oscar Tellgmann added the airships to his photo. Bundesarchiv, Bild 136-B0435 / Tellgmann, Oscar / CC-BY-SA [Public domain or CC-BY-SA-3.0-de (http://creativecommons.org/licenses/by-sa/3.0/de/deed.en)], via Wikimedia Commons.

In Vienna, in that summer of 1914, the prevalent mood was much less Belgrade's celebration of the deed than Churchill's angry contempt. This atrocity was the sixth in less than four years and strong evidence of the worsening Serbian danger, leading the Austrians to conclude that the continued existence of an expansionist Serbia posed an unacceptable threat to the Habsburg monarchy. An ultimatum would be drawn up containing demands that Serbia would be compelled to reject, giving Austria an excuse to attack. In the end, Serbia would be destroyed, probably divided up among its neighbors (Austria, which did not care to have more disaffected South Slavs as subjects, would most likely abstain from the partition). Obviously, Russia might choose to intervene. However, this was a risk the Austrians were prepared to take, especially after they received a "blank check" from Kaiser Wilhelm to proceed with whatever measures they thought necessary. In the past, German support of Austria had forced the Russians to back down.

Scholars have now available to them the diary of Kurt Riezler, private secretary to the German Chancellor Bethmann Hollweg. From this and other documents it becomes clear that Bethmann Hollweg's position in the July crisis was a complex one. If Austria were to vanish as a power, Germany would be threatened by rampant Pan-Slavism supported by growing Russian power in the east and by French revanchism in the west. By prompting the Austrians to attack Serbia immediately, he hoped that the conflict would be localized and the Serbian menace nullified. The Chancellor, too, understood that the Central Powers were risking a continental war. But he believed that if Austria acted swiftly presenting Europe with "a rapid *fait accompli*," the war could be confined to the Balkans, and "the intervention of third parties [avoided] as much as possible." In this way, the German-Austrian alliance could emerge with a stunning political victory that might split the Entente and crack Germany's "encirclement."[8]

But the Austrians procrastinated, and the ultimatum was delivered to Serbia only on July 23. When Sazonov, in St. Petersburg, read it, he burst out: *"C'est la guerre européenne!"* – "It is the European war!" The Russians felt they could not leave Serbia once again in the lurch, after having failed to prevent the Austrian annexation of Bosnia-Herzegovina or to obtain a seaport for Serbia after the Second Balkan War. Sazonov told a cabinet meeting on July 24 that abandoning Serbia would mean betraying Russia's "historic mission" as the protector of the South Slavs, and also reduce Russia to the rank of a second-rate power.[9]

On July 25, the Russian leaders decided to institute what was known in their plans as "The period preparatory to war," the prelude to all-out mobilization. Directed against both of the Central Powers, this "set in train a whole succession of military measures along the Austrian and German frontiers."[10] Back in the 1920s, Sidney Fay had already cited the testimony of a Serbian military officer, who, in traveling from Germany to Russia on July 28, found no military measures underway on the German side of the border, while in Russian Poland "mobilization steps [were] being taken on a grand scale." "These secret 'preparatory measures,'" commented Fay, "enabled Russia, when war came, to surprise the world by the rapidity with which she poured her troops into East Prussia and Galicia."[11] In Paris, too, the military chiefs began taking preliminary steps to general mobilization as early as July 25.[12]

On July 28, Austria declared war on Serbia. The French ambassador in St. Petersburg, Maurice Paléologue, most likely with the support of Poincaré, urged the Russians on to intransigence and general mobilization. In any case, Poincaré had given the Russians their own "blank check" in 1912, when he assured them that "if Germany supported Austria [in the Balkans], France would march."[13] Following the (rather ineffectual) Austrian bombardment of Belgrade, the Tsar was finally persuaded on July 30 to authorize general mobilization, to the delight of the Russian generals (the decree was momentarily reversed, but then confirmed, finally). Nicholas II had no doubt as to what that meant: "Think of what awful responsibility you are advising me to take! Think of the thousands and thousands of men who will be sent to their deaths!"[14] In a very few years the Tsar himself, his family, and his servants would be shot to death by the Bolsheviks.

What had gone wrong? James Joll wrote, "The Austrians had believed that vigorous action against Serbia and a promise of German support would deter Russia; the Russians had believed that a show of strength against Austria would both check the Austrians and deter Germany. In both cases, the bluff had been called."[15] Russia – and, through its support of Russia, France – as well as Austria and Germany, was quite willing to risk war in July, 1914.

As the conflict appeared more and more inevitable, in all the capitals the generals clamored for their contingency plans to be put into play. The best-known was the Schlieffen Plan, drawn up some years before, which governed German strategy in case of a two-front war. It called for concentrating forces against France for a quick victory in the west, and then transporting the bulk of the army to the eastern front via the excellent German railway system, to meet and vanquish the slow-moving (it was assumed) Russians. Faced with Russian mobilization and the evident intention of attacking Austria, the Germans activated the Schlieffen Plan. It was, as Sazonov had cried out, the European War.[16]

On July 31, the French cabinet, acceding to the demand of the head of the army, General Joffre, authorized general mobilization. The next day, the German ambassador to St. Petersburg, Portalès, called on the Russian Foreign Minister. After asking him four times whether Russia would cancel mobilization and receiving each time a negative reply, Portalès presented Sazonov with Germany's declaration of war. The German ultimatum to France was a formality. On August 3, Germany declared war on France as well.[17]

The question of "war-guilt" has been endlessly agitated.[18] It can be stated with assurance that Fischer and his followers have in no way proven their case. That, for instance, Helmut Moltke, head of the German Army, like Conrad, his counterpart in Vienna, pressed for a preventive war has long been known. But both military chieftains were kept in check by their superiors. In any case, there is no evidence whatsoever that Germany in 1914 deliberately unleashed a European war which it had been preparing for years – no evidence in the diplomatic and internal political documents, in the military planning, in the activities of the intelligence agencies, or in the relations between the German and Austrian General Staffs.[19]

Karl Dietrich Erdmann, put the issue well:

> *"Peace could have been preserved in 1914, had Berchtold, Sazonov, Bethmann-Hollweg, Poincaré, [British Foreign Secretary] Grey, or one of the governments concerned, so sincerely wanted it that they were willing to sacrifice certain political ideas, traditions, and conceptions, which were not their own personal ones, but those of their peoples and their times."*[20]

This sober judgment throws light on the faulty assumptions of sympathizers with the Fischer approach. John W. Langdon, for instance, concedes that any Russian mobilization "would have required an escalatory response from Germany." He adds, however, that to expect Russia not to mobilize "when faced with an apparent

Austrian determination to undermine Serbian sovereignty and alter the Balkan power balance was to expect the impossible." Thus, Langdon exculpates Russia because Austria "seemed bent on a course of action clearly opposed to Russian interests in eastern Europe."[21] True enough – but Russia "seemed bent" on using Serbia to oppose Austrian interests (the Austrian interest in survival), and France "seemed bent" on giving full support to Russia, and so on. This is what historians meant when they spoke of shared responsibility for the onset of the First World War.

Britain still has to be accounted for. With the climax of the crisis, Prime Minister Asquith and Foreign Secretary Edward Grey were in a quandary. While the *Entente cordiale* was not a formal alliance, secret military conversations between the general staffs of the two nations had created certain expectations and even definite obligations. Yet, aside from high military circles and, of course, the First Lord of the Admiralty, Winston Churchill, no one in Britain was rabid for war. Luckily for the British leaders, the Germans came to their rescue. The success of the attack on France that was the linchpin of the Schlieffen Plan depended above all on speed. This could only be achieved, it was thought, by infringing the neutrality of Belgium. "The obligation to defend Belgian neutrality was incumbent on all the signatories to the 1839 treaty *acting collectively*, and this had been the view adopted by the [British] cabinet only a few days previously. But now Britain presented itself as Belgium's sole guarantor" (emphasis added).[22] Ignoring (or perhaps ignorant of) the crucial precondition of collective action among the guarantors, and with the felicity of expression customary among German statesmen of his time, Bethmann Hollweg labeled the Belgian neutrality treaty "a scrap of paper."[23] Grey, addressing the House of Commons, referred to the invasion of Belgium as "the direst crime that ever stained the pages of history."[24]

The violation of non-belligerent Belgium's territory, though deplorable, was scarcely unprecedented in the annals of great powers. In 1807, units of the British navy entered Copenhagen harbor, bombarded the city, and seized the Danish fleet. At the time, Britain was at peace with Denmark, which was a neutral in the Napoleonic wars. The British claimed that Napoleon was about to invade Denmark and seize the fleet himself. As they explained in a manifesto to the people of Copenhagen, Britain was acting not only for its own survival but for the freedom of all peoples.

As the German navy grew in strength, calls were heard in Britain "to Copenhagen" the German fleet, from Sir John Fischer, First Sea Lord, and even from Arthur Lee, First Lord of the Admiralty. They were rejected, and England took the path of outbuilding the Germans in the naval arms race. But the willingness of high British authorities to act without scruple on behalf of perceived vital national interests did not go unnoticed in Germany.[25] When the time came, the Germans acted harshly towards neutral Belgium, though sparing the Belgians lectures on the freedom of mankind. Ironically, by 1916, the king of Greece was protesting the seizure of Greek territories by the Allies; like Belgium, the neutrality of Corfu had been guaranteed by the powers. His protests went unheeded.[26]

The invasion of Belgium was merely a pretext for London.[27] This was clear to John Morley, as he witnessed the machinations of Grey and the war party in the cabinet. In the last act of authentic English liberalism, Lord Morley, biographer of Cobden and Gladstone and author of the tract, *On Compromise*, upholding moral principles in politics, handed in his resignation.[28]

Britain's entry into the war was crucial. In more ways than one, it sealed the fate of the Central Powers. Without Britain in the war, the United States would never have gone in.

Notes:

1. For this discussion, see especially Luigi Albertini, *The Origins of the War of 1914*, Isabella M. Massey, trans. (Westport, Conn: Greenwood, 1980 [1952]), 3 vols., Vol. 2, pp. 1-119; and Joachim Remak, *Sarajevo, the Story of a Political Murder*, (New York: Criterion, 1959) pp. 43-78 and passim.
2. Albertini, *Origins*, vol. 1, p. 486.
3. Remak, *Sarajevo*, p. 50.
4. Albertini, *Origins*, vol. 2, p. 17: "among Serb nationalists and the Southern Slavs who drew their inspiration from Belgrade he was regarded as their worst enemy."
5. Ibid., vol. 2, p. 86.
6. Ibid., vol. 2, p. 47 n. 2. A Yugoslav historian of the crime, Vladimir Dedijer, strongly sympathized with the assassins, who in his view committed an act of "tyrannicide," "for the common good, on the basis of the teachings of natural law." See his *The Road to Sarajevo* (New York: Simon & Schuster, 1966), p. 446.
7. Winston S. Churchill, *The World Crisis*, vol. 6 (New York: Charles Scribner's Sons, 1932), p. 54.

8. Konrad H. Jarausch, "The Illusion of Limited War: Chancellor Bethmann Hollweg's Calculated Risk, July 1914," *Central European History*, vol. 2, no. 1 (March 1969), pp. 60–61; L. C. F. Turner, *Origins of the First World War* (New York: Norton, 1970), p. 98; also Laurence Lafore, *The Long Fuse: An Interpretation of the Origins of World War I*, 2nd ed. (Prospect Heights, Ill.: Waveland Press, 1971), p. 217: "it was hoped and expected that no general European complications would follow, but if they did, Germany was prepared to face them."

9. Joachim Remak, *The Origins of World War I, 1871–1914*, 2nd ed. (Fort Worth, Tex.: Harcourt, Brace, 1995), p. 135.

10. L. C. F. Turner, "The Russian Mobilization in 1914," *Journal of Contemporary History*, vol. 3, no. 1 (January 1968), pp. 75–76.

11. Sidney B. Fay, *The Origins of the World War*, 2 vols. (New York: Free Press, 1966 [1928]), vol. 2, p. 321 n. 98.

12. L. C. F. Turner, "Russian Mobilization," *Journal of Contemporary History*, vol. 3, no. 1 (January 1968), p. 82. By 1914 the French general staff had grown optimistic about the outcome of a war with Germany. With the French army strengthened and Russian support guaranteed, in French military circles, as in German, "there was a sense that if war was to come to Europe, better now ... than later." Hew Strachan, *The First World War*, vol. 1, *To Arms* (Oxford: Oxford University Press, 2001), p. 93.

13. Albertini, *Origins*, vol. 2, pp. 587–89, vol. 3, pp. 80–85; Turner, *Origins*, p. 41.

14. Turner, "Russian Mobilization," pp. 85–86, Turner described this as "perhaps the most important decision taken in the history of Imperial Russia."

15. James Joll, *The Origins of the First World War*, 2nd ed. (Longman: London, 1992), p. 23, also pp. 125–26.

16. L. C. F. Turner, "The Significance of the Schlieffen Plan," in Paul M. Kennedy, ed., *The War Plans of the Great Powers, 1880–1914* (London: George Allen and Unwin, 1979), pp. 199–221.

17. S. L. A. Marshall, *World War I* (Boston: Houghton Mifflin, 1964), pp. 39–42

18. See Remak, *Origins*, pp. 132–41 for a fairly persuasive allocation of "national responsibility."

19. Egmont Zechlin, "July 1914: Reply to a Polemic," in H. W. Koch, ed., *The Origins of the First World War: Great Power Rivalries and German War Aims*, 2nd ed. (London: Macmillan, 1984), pp. 371–85. Geiss, for instance, in *German Foreign Policy 1871-1914*, (London: Routledge and Kegan Paul, 1975), pp. 142–45, wildly misinterpreted the meaning of the German "war council" of December 8, 1912, when he painted it as the initiation of the "plan" that was finally realized with Germany's "unleashing" of war in 1914. See Erwin Hölzle, *Die Entmachtung Europas: Das Experiment des Friedens vor und im Ersten Weltkrieg* (Göttingen: Musterschmidt, 1975), pp. 178–83; also H. W. Koch, ed., *The Origins of the First World War: Great Power Rivalries and German War Aims*, 2nd ed. (London: Macmillan, 1984), "Introduction," pp. 12–13; and Turner, *Origins*,

p. 49. See also the important article by Ulrich Trumpener, "War Premeditated? German Intelligence Operations in July 1914," *Central European History*, vol. 9, no. 1 (March 1976), pp. 58–85. Among Trumpener's findings are that there is no evidence of "any significant changes in the sleepy routine" of the German General Staff even after the German "blank check" to Austria, and that the actions of the German military chiefs until the last week of July suggest that, though war with Russia was considered a possibility, it was regarded as "not really all that likely" (Moltke, as well as the head of military intelligence, did not return to Berlin from their vacations until July 25).

20. Karl Dietrich Erdmann,"War Guilt 1914 Reconsidered: A Balance of New Research,"in Koch, ed., *The Origins of the First World War*, p. 369.

21. John W. Langdon, *July 1914: The Long Debate, 1918–1990* (New York: Berg, 1991), p. 181, emphasis in original.

22. Strachan, *The First World War. To Arms*, p. 97.

23. What Bethmann Hollweg actually told the British ambassador was somewhat less shocking: "Can this neutrality which we violate only out of necessity, fighting for our very existence ... really provide the reason for a world war? Compared to the disaster of such a holocaust does not the significance of this neutrality dwindle into a scrap of paper?" Jarausch, "The Illusion of Limited War," p. 71.

24. S. L. A. Marshall, *World War I* (Boston: Houghton Mifflin, 1964), p. 52.

25. Jonathan Steinberg, "The Copenhagen Complex," *Journal of Contemporary History*, vol. 1, no. 3 (July 1966), pp. 23–46.

26. H. C. Peterson, *Propaganda for War: The Campaign against American Neutrality, 1914–1917* (Norman, Okla.: University of Oklahoma Press, 1939), pp. 45–46.

27. Joll, *Origins*, p. 115, attributed Grey's lying to the public and to Parliament to the British democratic system, which "forces ministers to be devious and disingenuous." Joll added that more recent examples were Franklin Roosevelt in 1939–41 and Lyndon Johnson in the Vietnam War. A democratic leader "who is himself convinced that circumstances demand entry into a war, often has to conceal what he is doing from those who have elected him."

28. John Morley, *Memorandum on Resignation* (New York: Macmillan, 1928). In the discussions before the fateful decision was taken, Lord Morley challenged the cabinet: "Have you ever thought what will happen if Russia wins?" Tsarist Russia "will emerge pre-eminent in Europe." Lloyd George admitted that he had never thought of that.

This article is adapted from an essay in Chapter 1 of *Great Wars and Great Leaders: A Libertarian Rebuttal* © 2010 by the Ludwig von Mises Institute. Permission to reprint in whole or in part is hereby granted, provided full credit is given.

Unholy Pursuit: the Charles Zentai Case in Australia

Nigel Jackson

"Circumstantial evidence is a very tricky thing," answered Holmes thoughtfully; "it may seem to point very straight to one thing, but if you shift your own point of view a little, you may find it pointing in an equally uncompromising manner to something entirely different. It must be confessed, however, that the case looks exceedingly grave against the young man, and it is very possible that he is indeed the culprit."

The Boscombe Valley Mystery by Sir Arthur Conan Doyle

The Background

The current pursuit of alleged Nazi war criminals was enabled in Australia by the amendment of the War Crimes Act in 1988. Public pressure to enable such a campaign had been stimulated by various factors, including claims about the imminent deportation from Australia of an alleged Nazi war criminal, a Latvian named Konrad Kalejs, and a well-publicised Australian Broadcasting Corporation radio series produced by a collaboration between Mark Aarons (an ABC [Australian Broadcasting Corporation] producer and a longstanding associate of the Sydney communist community) and John Loftus (a disaffected former member of the US Office for Special Investigations).[1]

As Professor Robert Manne, a prominent Australian intellectual and a Jew, noted,[2] the issue thus raised became the subject of a government inquiry in 1986 under Mr Andrew Menzies, the resulting report being used as the basis of proposed new legislation in the form of an amendment to the 1945 legislation establishing a military tribunal to try Japanese war criminals. Menzies 'examined allegations against two hundred people who had allegedly committed war crimes and were living in Australia….. (he) put aside a number of allegations because they were too vague or because there was insufficient connection between the alleged events and the person concerned or the crime was not serious enough. His list was reduced to some seventy people.'[3] There is a reasonable presumption that Menzies was chosen for the job because he could be depended upon to produce a report consonant with the Australian Government's wishes; and it was convenient that he had a surname comforting to Australian conservatives because of the famous Liberal prime minister, Sir Robert Menzies. In my view the Menzies Report failed to find adequate justification for the holding of the desired trials. It relied on the tainted precedent of the Nuremberg and other post-World War Two trials, and on popular opinions.

Manne bravely pointed out that 'the momentum' for the campaign 'seems to have been generated by... the Office of Special Investigations, the Simon Wiesenthal Centre and the World Jewish Congress.'[4] In short, there was no demand for the campaign from the Australian people themselves.

After an intense debate in the nation's public forums, during which the proposed legislation was opposed by many of Australia's judges and lawyers, the amendment was made law by the federal Parliament, since it enjoyed the support of the then Government, led by Australian Labour Party prime minister Bob Hawke, which had a majority in both the House of Representatives and the Senate.

This decision went against the advice in 1961 of the then Acting Minister for External Affairs, Sir Garfield Barwick QC, to the effect that the time had come to close the chapter on war crimes relating to World War Two.[5] It also went against the joint decision in 1963 by the Australian Government and the opposition that, legally speaking, the question of Nazi war crimes should be drawn to a close.[6]

The Hawke government seemed over-zealous in its devotion to the cause. Thus, in 1987, well before the amendment bill had been passed in the Parliament, the man who became head of the nation's war crimes unit, Robert F. Greenwood QC, was travelling overseas to negotiate agreements about the provision of evidence by the Soviet Union and the communist governments in Hungary and Yugoslavia![7]

A challenge to the legislation was later made in the Australian High Court.[8] It was narrowly lost in August 1991 by a 4-3 decision. This enabled cases to be brought against three suspects. Ivan Polyukhovich went on trial on 28 October of that year and was found not guilty in May 1993. The charges against Heinrich Wagner were later withdrawn 'because of ill health'. A third case against Mikolay Berezowsky was withdrawn because there was 'insufficient evidence for a trial.'[9] The farcical nature of some stages in these legal proceedings was exemplified by an incident during the first stages of the prosecution of Berezowsky. "A 78 year-old witness was asked to identify the accused. Instead of doing so, the witness confidently put his glasses on and pointed to a 76 year-old Texan lawyer, Mr Robert Caswell, who was seated in the public gallery about ten yards from Berezowsky!"[10]

No wonder, then, that one of the public protesters against these trials had been, in November 1991, Sir Walter Crocker, a former Lieutenant Governor of South Australia for nine years and, before that, an Australian ambassador for nearly twenty years. Sir Walter issued an important statement at the time, in which he said, *inter alia*: 'Our Federal Government, in spite of including a number of men of undoubted integrity and ability, has agreed to the trial [of Polyukhovich] through giving in to the pressures of a lobby that represents very few Australians and no Australian interests, but which is buttressed with great wealth, with exceptional self-centred persistence, and with ruthless cleverness. A connected lobby has been operating with similar effects in England and France. Its propaganda, accepted by large segments of the mass media, has confused and misled Australians, even those normally well informed.

> *"...This and related trials are not driven by justice but by hatred and revenge..... The events took place half a century ago. The nature of evidence available is dubious. That is why the great majority of names on the lobby's original lists have, on legal advice, been dropped by the Government..... The accused committed no crimes in Australia during their years here..... The accused committed no crimes against Australians anywhere..... The spirit of hatred and revenge unleashed by the trials can poison and destabilise nations as well as persons."*[11]

The campaign had ended in fiasco. Its promoters then turned to a second strategy. In 1988 Professor Manne had commented that one way of dealing with alleged Nazi war criminals would be deportation to the Soviet Union. 'This,' he said, 'would be legally proper in a sense, but would mean the impossibility of a fair trial and their death. For the reasons given by Senator Cooney, this is impossible.'[12]

Despite this, the relevant lobby, apparently determined to ensure that Australia played its part in their scheme, turned in subsequent years to the different approach of extradition. Australian justice had proved itself to be too protective of the rights of those accused. It seemed better, then, to turn to the US model. Get the suspects deported to some Eastern European nation where the style of justice was rather different and successful prosecutions thus more likely. To facilitate this, over the next two decades Australian extradition law was changed and agreements for extradition signed with various relevant nations. The attack was then renewed in Australia. Some of the suspects, like Kalejs, died before they could be deported. But Charles Zentai has lived on into his nineties and is now the prime target. At the time of writing (31 July 2012) his case is before the High Court. If he loses it, the Australian Government will have the final say over whether or not he should be deported to Hungary. It is time to turn to his story.

The Accusations

The chief pursuer of Charles Zentai is Dr. Efraim Zuroff, director of the Jerusalem-based Simon Wiesenthal Centre. He provided a summary of the case against Zentai in 2007.[13] Zuroff explained that the Centre had launched 'Operation Last Chance', a final attempt to bring Nazi war criminals to justice, in Hungary on 13 July 2004. Zuroff explained how this project, which included the offering of money for information, brought attention to Zentai: 'Local Holocaust scholar Laszlo Karsai sent me a letter from Adam Balazs, an elderly Holocaust survivor living in Budapest, with about two dozen yellowing pages that clearly were copies of witness statements from 1948. According to Karsai's cover letter, Adam Balazs had "a lot of first-hand documents proving that his brother Peter Balazs was killed by Karoly [later Charles] Zentai.

> *'What emerged from the testimonies was that in the fall of 1944, Karoly Zentai, an officer in the Hungarian Army serving in Budapest, would frequently go on manhunts for Jews, who were taken to his army barracks where they were severely beaten. On 8 November 1944 Zentai, while riding in a streetcar, identified 18-year-old Peter Balazs as a Jew who was not wearing the requisite yellow star. He forced Peter Balazs off the streetcar and took him to his barracks at Arena Street 51. There, together with two fellow-officers accomplices, Bela Mader and Lajos Nagy, he beat the Jewish teenager to death. Later, together with the latter, he weighted the body down with rocks and threw it into the Danube River. After the war, Mader was sentenced to life imprisonment and Nagy to death for war crimes; and, in the course of the*

latter's trial, Zentai's role in the murder of Peter Balazs was revealed."

Chief pursuer of Charles Zentai is Efraim Zuroff, director of the Simon Wiesenthal Centre (2007). Arikb at the Hebrew language Wikipedia [GFDL (http://www.gnu.org/copyleft/fdl.html) or CC-BY-SA-3.0 (http://creativecommons.org/licenses/by-sa/3.0/)], from Wikimedia Commons

Further information of the case against Zentai comes from Gyorgy Vamos.[14] This commentator stated that he had spent several months sifting through the surviving records of the Budapest People's Court.[15]

Vamos wrote: "In the autumn of 1944 the army unit in which Karoly Zentai was a junior officer was housed at 51 Arena Avenue. After the Hungarian equivalent of the Nazi Party, the Arrow Cross, assumed power in October of that year, Budapest's residents lived in terror. Jews who ventured on to the streets risked their lives. Members of the army and the Arrow Cross stopped people on a whim and demanded that they prove their identity. Those whose papers were not considered to be in order were detained by army units and taken to the Arena Avenue barracks, where – under the guise of interrogation - they were beaten mercilessly."

After the war, several witnesses testified that in early November 1944 a young man was beaten to death at the barracks. Peter Balazs, a young Jewish man, had been drafted for forced-labour service in April 1944, but did not show up at the appointed place and time. Instead he lived in Budapest using false (Christian) identity papers. On 8 November 1944 he left home and disappeared.

> *"Peter's father, Dezso, a lawyer from the outlying suburb of Budafok, subsequently spoke to one of the witnesses who claimed that a young man had been killed by the army at around this time. In April 1948 Dezso Balazs officially accused Karoly Zentai of involvement in his son's murder....."*
>
> *"Dezso Balazs [testified]: 'Zentai knew that my son visited the Union Construction Workers and that he took part in the resistance movement. He mentioned a number of times to his fellow officers that he would like to get hold of my son.'"*

Vamos listed a number of others who testified against Zentai before the People's Court in 1948. These included Janos Mahr (a soldier in the unit), although there is some doubt as to whether or not he specifically implicated Zentai. Others were Nagy, Mader, Miklos Polonyi (another unit member), Imre Zoltan (a Jewish forced-labourer) and Sergeant Jozsef Monori (who stated that he arranged the transport to the Danube for the murderers and the body).

More light on the case against Zentai was cast by David Weber of the Australian Broadcasting Corporation in 2010.[16] Weber explained how the Soviet Army 'was driving across Hungary' at the time, 'crushing German resistance. By November, the Soviets were in the suburbs of the capital. The transport unit [Zentai's] was ordered out of the city, possibly as a means to save Hungarian troops, their families and their equipment from obliteration.....

> *"After the war, the regime in Hungary set about charging and convicting those who'd persecuted or killed Jewish people....."*
>
> *"Statements from Mader and Nagy reportedly prompted the Hungarian authorities to ask for Zentai – then in the American zone in Germany – to be sent back..... It's not known why Zentai was not extradited to Hungary then..... There's no evidence that Zentai knew of the request from Hungary, or of the accusations against him..... Zentai has never directly been accused of being a member of the Nazi Party or any Hungarian affiliate."*

Vamos pointed out that, when Mader and Nagy were called to account for the killing, no proof of their alleged action was found. Presumably this means that the body was never found.

In summary, Zentai stands charged with a specific act of murder, understood as a war crime in the overall context of the Holocaust, and with other non-specified acts of violence against Jews.

Without at this stage considering the veracity or otherwise of the case against Zentai, we can note that it is credible and makes sense; and we can feel sympathy and admiration for a father and a brother who may well have laboured hard and sincerely to obtain what they believed was justice in connection with their lost relative.

The Proceedings

In 2005 the Hungarian Government sought to have Zentai extradited from Australia to Hungary. In March of that year a Hungarian military tribunal issued an international warrant for Zentai's arrest. Australian Justice Minister Chris Ellison, a member of the then Liberal-National Coalition government, signed the request.[17] On 8 July Zentai was arrested by the Australian Federal Police to await an extradition hearing.[18]

In 2006 Perth magistrate Wayne Tarr rejected an attempt by Zentai to alter his bail conditions for reasons of poor health. A Federal Court bid to have the extradition quashed was scheduled to be heard on 28 July of that year.[19] On 29 July *The Australian* reported on a joint challenge by Zentai and another litigant fighting extradition to Ireland over fraud charges. 'Lawyers for Zentai claimed that magistrates do not have the constitutional power to hear extradition applications. Barrister Dr Steven Churches argued that magistrates had no standing in international law and were not legally equipped under the Constitution to make decisions on behalf of the Commonwealth of Australia.'[20] On 12 September Judge Antony Siopis of the Federal Court ruled that Zentai must face an extradition hearing in Perth Magistrates Court on 22 September, when a hearing date could be set.[21]

Zentai and his co-litigant appealed the decision of Judge Siopis to the full bench of the Federal Court. Zentai's lawyers argued that his health was too poor to justify extradition. They said that the role of hearing extraditions was not the responsibility of a magistrate because the state government did not assent to it. The republics of Ireland and Hungary claimed that magistrates do have the right to hear extradition proceedings because their posts make them *persona designata*. On 16 April 2007 Zentai's appeal was dismissed, the result being announced by Justice Brian Tamberlin. [22]

The High Court on 3 September granted Zentai special leave to appeal to it. Earlier he had failed to avoid extradition proceedings while his appeal went to the High Court. Prosecutor Pauline Cust had argued that the warrant for Zentai's arrest had been issued in 2005 and that proceedings should no longer be delayed. Magistrate Graeme Calder agreed and adjourned the matter until 7 August. However, on 25 September Perth magistrate Steven Heath put off until February 2008 a decision on Zentai's extradition hearing date, pending the result of his High Court challenge.[23]

The challenge was lost on 23 April 2008 by a majority of six to one. Zentai on this occasion had been joined with two other litigants. The trio had argued that extradition law was invalid because it involved a 'constitutionally impermissible' attempt by the Commonwealth to impose a duty upon magistrates as holders of a statutory office. But the High Court found the law did not impose a duty on magistrates. 'It conferred a power which, under the Crimes Act, the state magistrates were not obliged to accept.' Zentai's extradition case was now to be heard in court in Perth on 12 August.[24]

The date was later changed to 18 August, on which date Zentai was to face a three-day extradition hearing before Magistrate Barbara Lane. If she decided Zentai should be extradited, his only avenue of appeal would be to the ALP Government's Home Affairs Minister Bob Debus. There were several grounds on which the minister could prevent an extradition, including health or humanitarian issues.[25] Michael Corboy SC, acting for Hungary, told the court on 18 August that the extradition was an administrative process and that the Federal Attorney General would make the final decision.[26] Zentai's lawyers told the magistrate that the legislation under which their client had been charged was not valid at the time of the alleged offence. Zentai had been charged under the wrong legislation. Grant Donaldson SC said that, although the 1878 Hungarian Criminal Code was valid at the time, Zentai had been arrested under legislation that did not come into effect until 1945, a year after the alleged offence.
Commonwealth prosecutor Michael Corboy SC said that, under

extradition proceedings, the magistrate was not permitted to delve into foreign law. He said that whether the legislation was valid was a matter for the Federal Attorney General.[27]

In August 2008 Magistrate Barbara Lane ruled that Zentai had satisfied administrative requirements for extradition. The alleged crime must be punishable by more than one year in prison, it must be an offence under the laws of both countries, and the charges must not be politically motivated. [These were the criteria for extradition according to a bilateral treaty signed by Australia and Hungary in 1997.][28]

Zentai appealed against this ruling to the Federal Court. On 30 March 2009 Federal Court Judge John Gilmour ruled that Zentai was eligible for extradition and that Magistrate Barbara Lane had been correct to rule that he could be sent to Hungary. In response to the argument that the extradition could not proceed because the charge Zentai was facing was not an offence at the time it was allegedly committed, Grant Donaldson SC had replied that under the extradition treaty between Hungary and Australia, the law could be applied retrospectively.[29]

Zentai decided to appeal to the full bench of the Federal Court. On 8 October 2009 he lost this appeal, but was granted a stay of fourteen days on the execution of the extradition warrant.[30] Zentai's legal team now had to consider whether to seek leave to appeal to the High Court. According to Ernie Steiner, his son, Zentai had already faced legal bills of more than $200,000. The final say on Zentai's surrender would now be made by Home Affairs Minister Brendan O'Connor, to whom Zentai's family had already made lengthy submissions.[31] Zentai decided not to seek leave to appeal to the High Court and surrendered himself to the Australian Federal Police and imprisonment.[32] On 12 November 2009 the Australian Government approved Zentai's extradition to Hungary, making this the first case in which that government had approved of extraditing any Nazi suspect.[33] O'Connor confirmed that the Government would not intervene to overturn the Federal Court ruling that Zentai could be extradited. Subject to any legal challenge, Hungarian authorities had two months to arrange the extradition. Zentai had spent the past three weeks in gaol. O'Connor said that the decision to approve extradition was not an indication of Zentai's guilt or innocence. 'It was about deciding whether or not Zentai should be surrendered to Hungary in accordance with Australia's extradition legislation and its international obligations,' [34] Zentai's lawyers had argued that he should not be extradited because of his ill health, because he would not receive a fair trial and because witness statements were tainted. [35]

Zentai decided to appeal the Australian Government's decision to the Federal Court. Hungary stated that it would wait until all Zentai's appeals were exhausted before taking any further steps on the extradition. Zentai was granted bail on 16 December 2009, ending two months in custody, during which he was locked up for fifteen hours minimum each day.[36]

Early in 2010 there came the dramatic news that a leading Perth barrister, Malcolm McCusker QC, had taken up Zentai's fight for no fee. 'His first task will be to argue to the Federal Court for access to the unedited documents on which Home Affairs Minister Brendan O'Connor based his November 2009 extradition ruling in the case.' The Minister's office had told Zentai the departmental documents could not be completely released due to legal professional privilege. Zentai's legal team had only an edited version of the sixty-page document. 'We need to at least know what the reason was behind the Minister's decision,' said McCusker. 'They're refusing to give it to us... so much for open government!' McCusker said that grounds for appeal could be that there is no basis to extradite for questioning, and that it would be unfair because there were no living witnesses who could testify.[37]

In February Zentai asked the Australian Human Rights Commission to help stop the extradition. His lawyer wanted the Commission to intervene in the coming legal challenge to be heard in the Federal Court in late March.[38] In asking the Commission President, Catherine Branson, to intervene, lawyer Denis Barich argued that the Zentai case qualified as a discrimination and human rights issue because of the need of Hungary to ensure it could provide for a fair trial. The Commission could investigate whether any trial might be jeopardised by the absence of any relevant witnesses and whether a trial could also be prejudiced by Zentai's political leanings or nationality. The application also questioned whether possible coercion or torture were grounds for investigating statements made to Hungarian authorities in the late 1940's which could be used against Zentai. Barich said that the Commission could assist the courts and help Zentai pay for his fight against extradition. Barich sought the Commission's intervention on the basis that 'the applicant is a pensioner without legal aid who is not in a financial position to afford the numerous human rights documents and authorities that the case requires.'[39]

During the appeal hearing the Government lawyer, Jeremy Allanson SC, insisted that O'Connor's decision was in accordance with Australia's extradition treaty with Hungary. 'This is a matter of international obligation. It's a matter of Australia being consistent with the treaty.' Zentai was appealing to the Court to either quash O'Connor's decision or refer his case back to the Minister so that discretionary factors such as his nationality and age could be considered. Allanson responded that O'Connor had already been told [before making his decision] of these matters and that Zentai was an Australian citizen with a 'meaningful connection' to Australia. [Zentai had migrated to Australia in 1950.][40]

At this point Zentai experienced a dramatic change of fortune. On 2 July he won his appeal. Federal Court Judge Neil McKerracher found that Zentai was not liable for extradition and that it was beyond O'Connor's jurisdiction to make the order. The Judge said the Minister had failed to consider whether it would be 'oppressive and incompatible with humanitarian considerations' to extradite Zentai, given his age, ill health and the potential severity of the punishment.[41] The Judge also found that war crime was not a 'qualifying extradition offence.'[42] Additional findings concerned the unreliability of the allegations against him, the difficulty in obtaining a conviction and the fact that Zentai had not actually been formally accused or charged with a crime.[43]

The Australian Government indicated that it would need time to decide whether there were legal grounds for appealing Judge McKerracher's decision. Some months went by and on 10 December 2010 the Judge noted that if no appeal had been received by 24 January 2011, Zentai should be considered a free man and released from bail. He also awarded costs to Zentai related to his 2 July decision.

Many of the minority of Australians who had followed this case were no doubt hopeful that reason and justice had finally prevailed. However, on 4 January 2011 O'Connor did launch an appeal.[44] McCusker, now an Australian of the Year nominee, said that he was appalled by the Government's determination to extradite one of its own citizens for unfounded war crime allegations. He pointed out that in the past the Commonwealth Director of Public Prosecutions had looked at all the evidence and determined there was no case to be answered. 'You have to question... what's motivating the Government to do this.' [45]

There was a two-day hearing of the appeal before Interstate Federal Court judges Anthony North, Christopher Jessup and Anthony Besanko on 16 and 17 May 2011. Zentai could not appear in court after suffering a stroke. (He had also suffered a stroke in 2010.) [46] Peter Johnston, a lawyer for Zentai, stated that O'Connor might have been misled by false information when he approved the extradition. In fact, Zentai's change of family name from Steiner to Zentai had occurred when Zentai was only thirteen. Zentai's legal team also claimed that the Hungarian authorities appeared to have no live witnesses for cross-examination in any case that might be taken against Zentai, this meaning that a fair trial was impossible. However, Government lawyer Stephen Lloyd said that those authorities had given an assurance that any trial would be fair and that it was not a safe assumption they had no witnesses. 'Hungarian authorities have their own material... they don't have to tell us.' He said it was clear that criminal proceedings were under way in Hungary against Zentai and that it was not just a preliminary investigation, as Judge McKerracher had concluded. [This, however, appears to have marked a change of position made very recently by Hungary, presumably to give them a better chance of obtaining the extradition.] Lloyd added that the Hungarian authorities did not have to send officers to Australia to question Zentai, as they "wanted to execute their own criminal procedures as they see fit." 47

Throughout this protracted legal process of over six years, Zentai had always denied pulling Peter Balazs from a tram in Budapest and in taking part in the beating that led to his death. [48]

On 16 August 2011 the Federal Court judges announced that they upheld parts of the challenge but dismissed most of the arguments. Peter Johnston, acting for Zentai, said that O'Connor now must determine what constituted a 'war crime' before the case could continue. Zentai could lodge a further appeal in the High Court. A spokeswoman from O'Connor's office noted that the Court had in fact upheld two of the three grounds on which the Government had appealed. The one matter it did not agree with was that the offence should come under Australia and Hungary's extradition agreement.[49]

Zentai's case is currently, as of 31 July, before the High Court. On 28 March 2012 the Government told the court that it should be allowed to extradite Zentai to Hungary, despite war crimes not being an offence in Hungary at the time of the alleged actions. Zentai's counsel, Geoffrey Kennett SC, said that if Zentai could have been charged with murder under 1944 law, that offence should have been listed on the extradition warrant.[50]

As a postscript, the following information about proceedings in Hungary after World War Two may be noted.

Bela Mader was extradited to Hungary by the American Army in 1945. On 21 March 1946 he was sentenced to forced labour for life, but was released in September 1956. Lajos Nagy was accused when he returned from captivity in Russia in mid-1947. He was sentenced to death on 26 February 1948 for several crimes, including Balazs's murder, but this was later commuted to forced labour for life. Nagy left Hungary at the end of 1956.[51] The anti-communist uprising in Hungary of 1956 appears to have had favourable repercussions for both men. On 21 April 1948 the public prosecutor requested that the Budapest People's Court issue an arrest warrant for Zentai, alleging his involvement in war crimes and stating that he was in the American zone of Germany. The court issued the warrant on 29 April and requested that the Minister of Justice arrange Zentai's extradition. On 20 May the ministry announced that this had been undertaken through diplomatic channels, but the extradition never occurred. It is not known why.[52]

The Case against Zentai

The case against Zentai appears to rest almost, if not entirely, upon documentary evidence, most of it coming from the communist-run People's Court in 1948. 'Evidence hidden in long-forgotten archives in Budapest indicts Zentai as the sole surviving suspect in this killing [of Peter Balazs].'[53] Vamos points out that the information Dezso Balazs had acquired 'was detailed, right down to the presence of six Jewish forced labourers at the barracks.'[54] Vamos also addresses the claim by Zentai that he had already left Budapest the day before on 7 November 1944: "This is unlikely, as a soldier usually leaves his unit only if he is transferred or goes absent without leave. Zentai has not claimed that either situation applied..... Unit member Sandor Lippkai stated that they left some time between 10 and 15 November.

According to yet another, Laszlo Moricz, the unit moved to Hanta on 11 November."⁵⁵

The various witness statements appear largely, if not wholly, to support each other. Vamos reports: 'Some of the witnesses in the Mader and Nagy cases served in their unit, while others were Jews they had arrested. The testimonies coincide in some areas, and in others are complementary. They demonstrate that the unit regularly patrolled Budapest, checking people's identities and arresting and beating suspects.'⁵⁶

Vamos brings forward a number of the key testimonies, as follows. In February 1948 another unit member, Miklos Polonyi, testified that... Nagy had boasted about the operations..... 'He also mentioned that one person, whom they had beaten to death, had been thrown into the Danube. He said he had someone helping him: Zentai.'..... In 1947 Nagy recalled a 17 or 18 year-old Jewish boy who had been brought in by Zentai and who was the son of a lawyer or physician from Budafok..... Mader, the unit's commanding officer, made two statements about the Balazs killing, the first on 22 March 1948: 'As far as I know... Zentai, too, had an active role in the case of the young man who was beaten to death..... when I arrived at the office and this young man was already lying dying on the floor, Zentai was present together with Nagy, and he was checking the dying man's pulse... it was Zentai who told me that he had arrested this young man in the street and had brought him to the barracks.' Subsequently Mader claimed that he had gone home to his family at around 4pm on that day. 'Of the company offcers only Zentai stayed on..... I returned to the barracks only at 11pm..... Zentai and Nagy were also there..... I then caught sight of a man who was lying on the floor and rattled.'

Imre Zoltan, a forced labourer, recalled being taken... to the unit's office, where Mader, Nagy and Zentai were present..... according to his account, Mader called the rattling sounds of the dying man 'music'..... Sergeant Jozsef Monori stated that 'Nagy and Zentai brought out a dead body..... During the ride [to the Danube] they discussed that they shouldn't have hit the boy as hard as they had..... they took the dead body and threw it in the Danube.' Janos Mahr identified 'the young man who had been brought in and who had been maltreated by Nagy and Mader' as Peter Balazs. Mahr's statement includes Zentai's name in several places, but wherever the name appears, the letter X has been repeatedly typed over it. Vamos thinks this may mean that Zentai's name was mentioned at Mahr's interrogation, but that Mahr did not remember him.[57]

Zuroff has claimed that 'witnesses' will prove that Zentai was in Budapest at the relevant time.[58]

Aarons has asserted in an opinion article in *The Australian* that 'the case against Zentai… indicates that he took part in the systematic persecution of Jews….. *The Australian*'s investigation of Zentai in 2005 uncovered evidence that he had been involved in systematically rounding up and torturing Jews. The evidence included the testimony of witness Jakob Mermelstein.'[59]

Overall it is my view that a *prima facie* case does exist against Zentai. There is a reasonable degree of probability, but not certainty, that it is true.

The Case for Zentai

There are two senses in which one can refer to the case for Zentai. The first concerns whether or not he is innocent of the charges that have been levelled against him. The second concerns whether or not he should be extradited to Hungary and required to face a trial there. In my view it is impossible at this date to determine beyond all doubt whether Zentai is or is not guilty. No court, whether in Australia or Hungary, can do that. Too long a period has elapsed since the alleged actions; and there is inadequate opportunity for full and complete research into documents and questioning of witnesses. From the point of view of British and Australian law, however, he must be granted the presumption of innocence. His pursuers appear to be so convinced that he is guilty that they overlook a number of important aspects of the present situation.

There are many arguments against the proposal that he be extradited to face trial. Taken as a whole they seem to me to amount to an overwhelming case that he should be released from custody and allowed to pass his remaining years in Perth, in freedom, and with his family around him. If he really is guilty, then the matter should now be left in the hands of the Almighty.

Zentai, now ninety, is too old for it to be ethically right and humane to place him on trial, especially considering the complex nature of the issues, the fact that he would be removed from his family and their support and the fact that the trial would occur in a language he has not used as his first language for many decades. Critics might argue: at what age, then, do we draw the line? I am inclined to suggest that retiring age might be a good yardstick, particularly if we take it to be seventy rather than the sixty-five nominated by Bismarck, because of the increased life expectancy that people now have compared to a century ago.

People are fairly frail at eighty, very frail at ninety. Nonagenarians do not have the nervous strength and resilience to cope with protracted legal proceedings.

Zentai's health is also poor. In 2007 it was reported that he had become 'too frail to prepare his meals' and had 'been admitted to hospital twice in the past month with heart problems' according to his children. He was said to be unsteady on his feet.[60] In 2009 he was reported to suffer from 'an irregular heart condition called symptomatic paroxysmal atrial fibrillation'.[61] In 2011 the news came that he had had a second stroke on 13 May, having had an earlier one in 2010.[62] Some doubt must remain about the exact state of Zentai's health, as it is reasonable to suppose that he and his family would tend to paint as black a picture as possible. However, from what has been reported so far, a very strong presumption exists that it would be seriously inhumane to send a man as old as this for trial, given he has ill health.

Just as the most serious evidence against Zentai is witness statements from communist-run courts in Hungary in 1947 and 1948, so the most important argument in his favour is that such statements may be tainted and thus unable to be fairly relied upon. Vamos touched briefly on this in his article: 'The witness testimonies relating to the case should be treated with care. Evaluating statements made sixty years ago to the police, the Department of Military Politics and the People's Court is complex – not least because most witnesses are now dead. Also there were unusual circumstances in the Hungary of the late 1940's, where the communist-dominated government placed considerable store on "social justice" – and established special procedures in which emotions played a significant part. Furthermore, the interrogators, investigators and prosecutors were largely under communist control. They were frequently manipulated for party-political purposes.'[63] Concerning certain testimony by Nagy, Vamos notes that this witness 'was already imprisoned and awaiting trial.

Subsequently, Nagy stated that he had given his testimony in accordance with the interrogator's wishes, because he wanted to get away and had been promised contact with his family.'⁶⁴

In its edition of 14-15 May 2005 *The Australian* claimed that it was publishing documents which established that Zentai 'was living in Budapest' at the time of the alleged murder. However, close scrutiny of the reproduced material showed that it merely tended to indicate that he was in Hungary until March 1945.

One of the most profound political commentators in Australia in the second half of the Twentieth Century was the Catholic anti-communist B. A. Santamaria, president of the National Civic Council, a man so highly respected in conservative quarters that the then prime minister, John Howard, made a special trip to his deathbed in 1998. Santamaria, during the controversy over 'Nazi war crimes' in the 1980's and 1990's was emphatic that evidence emanating from the Soviet Union or its satellites, one of which was Hungary, could not and should not be trusted in any trials.

Count Nikolai Tolstoy in 1988 asserted that 'the validation of evidence emanating from the Soviet Union requires not merely authentication of specific documents or assessment of the reliability of individual witnesses, but also a deep understanding of Soviet history and government such as is possessed by few jurists.'⁶⁵

Manne was even more scathing about communist jurisprudence: 'Soviet rules of procedure….. have included threats to witnesses….. defense counsels have had their cross-examinations severely curtailed by the Soviet procurator in charge of proceedings….. the atmosphere… is said to be intimidatory towards witnesses….. witnesses have been prompted by the Soviet procurator in giving answers to critical questions….. [there is at times] no means available for defense counsel to check the identity of witnesses….. [as regards] documents… on several occasions courts have been presented with photocopies and not originals for testing….. forensic experts for the defense have not been allowed to conduct full investigations on the documents….. access to Soviet archives has been refused. The Soviet Union routinely passes on only the documentary evidence it chooses….. KGB forgery [involves]….. an unending production of disinformation documents.'⁶⁶

Shortly after World War Two, in 1948, a British jurist (and former member of the British Union of Fascists), F. J. P. Veale, published a profound study of the war crimes controversy, *Advance to Barbarism*. This, together with his subsequent book, *Crimes Discreetly Veiled*, was republished by the Institute for Historical Review in the USA in 1979 as *The Veale File* in two volumes. Veale pointed out that at the Nuremberg Trials 'according to the Russian judge, General Nikitchenko, the only duty of the court would be to rubberstamp the decision of the politicians at the Yalta Conference that the prisoners were guilty.'[67] Veale stressed that Marxist philosophy, as practised in the U.S.S.R., led to a practice fundamentally opposed to the traditional justice of Britain and other Christian nations. 'In a political trial in Soviet Russia, the judges and the prosecuting counsel together form a team..... The speeches for the prosecution are political manifestoes, designed to justify the action of the government in instituting proceedings and are directed... to the outside public.'[68] Veale quoted F. Beck and V. Godin (*Russian Purge*, Hurst & Blackett, London, 1951): 'The authors, themselves prominent Soviet citizens who were victims of the Great Purge of 1936-1938 but escaped with their lives, express surprise that the delusion should persist in the West that, in Soviet Russia, there exists any necessary connection between a man's arrest and any particular offence alleged against him.'[69]

As to the capacity of communist governments to produce false or tainted evidence for political purposes, another authority is Chapman Pincher, who published a whole book on the topic in 1985.[70] In his introduction Pincher wrote: 'To Western politicians war is the continuation of politics by other means. To the Politburo, with its ideological compulsion to invert reality as free societies see it – which is what I call the "upside-down ploy" – politics is the continuation of war by other means. These other means, now known in the Soviet jargon as "active measures", form the major subject of this book. They comprise sophisticated techniques of deception, disinformation, forgery, blackmail, subversion, penetration and manipulation, the insidious use of agents of influence, the organisation of mass demonstrations with the promotion of violence and other criminal acts and even military violations. The scale on which this underhand offensive is being relentlessly pursued in the Politburo's game-plan against countries of the free world... is far greater and much more menacing than is generally appreciated, especially as so little is being done to combat it.'[71]

What if the whole story about Peter Balazs being snatched from a tram, beaten, tortured and killed at the Arena Utca barracks, his body then being dumped in the Danube, was from the start a fabrication made in a communist-dominated state, in an atmosphere of post-war political hysteria, for purposes of revenge? What if the US legation was correct in 1948 in not handing Zentai over to face pseudo-justice in an effectively Soviet-controlled state? What if Balazs's father was simply in error in believing the story of his son's murder? What if all eleven witnesses were lying at the trial of Nagy, some for political propaganda purposes and others to ingratiate themselves with the communist government? Hundreds of respectable publications, including novels by Arthur Koestler, George Orwell and Alexander Solzhenitsyn, have testified to the corruption of justice under communism.

Moreover, some of the ancient testimony is favourable to Zentai. His military commander, Mader, on one occasion blamed a fellow soldier, not him. 'In a translated transcript of Mader's interrogation at Budapest's military political office on 15 November 1945, Mader points the finger of blame for Balazs's [murder] at only one person, Nagy.' This transcript was discovered in a Hungarian government archive by Zentai's son, Ernie Steiner.[72] As a correspondent in an online discussion noted, 'the evidence is very old and was taken from suspicious witnesses who may have been trying to displace their guilt on the absent Zentai.'[73] And Zentai's lawyer, Denis Barich, stated on 22 October 2009 that witness statements against him by two of his former army colleagues who were convicted over Balazs's death… were probably obtained under coercion and were tainted. 'Maybe these soldiers were tortured and they were fearing for their own lives, maybe they were pointing the finger at somebody else.'[74] Zentai's son also raised the possibility that Zentai may have been implicated in those testimonies 'as payback for having given evidence against a superior officer who had deserted.' He may have been a scapegoat.[75]

This leads to the key question of whether or not a fair trial is now possible. A number of factors suggest that it is not.

In 2010 McCusker argued that another ground of appeal for Zentai was that any trial would be unfair, 'because there are no living witnesses who can testify', which struck him as 'pretty dangerous'.[76] The result of the trial of alleged Canadian war criminal Imre Finta, which ended on 25 May 1990, supports this position. Douglas Christie, the successful defense barrister, had this to say in his introduction to Keltie Zubko's account of that case: 'The Finta case demonstrated that a careful examination of survivors' testimony reveals a wealth of contradictions casting serious doubt on the whole story….. Cross examinations remain the only real weapon for the defense in these cases. This is so because all the mechanisms of investigation are in the hands of the prosecution, not to mention enormous money to do it all. In Israel or in Hungary, the state simply assisted the prosecution for years before the trial. They were not obliged to assist the defense at all by the agreement negotiated with Canada by which access to Archives and to all records was assured…. My opponents know that fearless cross examination within the existing bounds of the law, allows the defense to level all those unfair advantages of the Crown. It is a skill which only comes with experience, only possessed by a few lawyers, and then only when they are unafraid and at their best.'[77]

Zentai's lawyer Denis Barich has claimed that cross examination is an enshrined right in the International Covenant on Civil and Political Rights. 'Potentially, if Australia does extradite Zentai under these circumstances, [it] could be in breach of the covenant, which is serious.'[78]

That witness statements in such cases are unreliable has been shown in other cases, notably those of Frank Walus and John Demjanjuk. In 2005 *The Australian* published a story about the collapse of what it then called 'the last big war crimes trial in Germany'.[79] A German judge had released 88 year-old Ladislav Niznansky on the grounds that there was 'insufficient evidence to convict him'. The witnesses were too aged; their memories too erratic; their testimony broke down under cross examination; the paper trail was inconclusive; and evidence might have been manipulated by communist authorities after World War Two to falsely incriminate Niznansky because of his resolute anti-communism.

In 2008 Hungarian military prosecutor Tibor Acs 'conceded there were no living witnesses to the brutal beating of Balazs.'[80] His body was never recovered. No proof of the alleged crimes of Nagy and Mader was found. All this means that a strong element of doubt hangs over the whole tale. Zentai was entitled to a fair trial, if one could be staged, in 1948. However, there is a strong presumption that the reason he was not surrendered to the Hungarian authorities is that the US officials had no confidence that he would get a fair trial under the communists.

Another reason a fair trial of Zentai cannot now be provided in Hungary is the unequal contest that would be involved. Extremely aged, frail and with little energy, he would face opponents (the international Jewish lobby) vastly more wealthy and able to unduly influence governments. In 2009 Zentai stated that Hungary 'was far from a democratic country' and that he was worried about the quality of treatment and representation he could expect there.'[81] In 2010 *The Australian* reported on internal dissent in Hungary.[82] 'In Hungary, anti-establishment attitudes sky-rocketed from 12% to 46% of the population between 2003 and last year because of striking dissatisfaction with political institutions and democracy itself.' (The data came from the Political Capital Institute.) In 2010 McCusker argued that Zentai's life would be threatened if he were detained in the 'deplorable' conditions of a Hungarian prison.[83] This fear would appear to be justified, in view of Italy's treatment of Canadian extradited 'Nazi war criminal Michael Seifert.[84] Two recent pieces of news cast further doubt on whether a fair trial could occur in this nation at this time. The first was the imminent visit of the Hungarian prime minister to Israel. The second was the arrest in Budapest of a 97 year-old man, Laszlo Csatary, on a war crimes charge.[85]

On 2 March 2009 Zentai passed a polygraph test conducted by Gavin Wilson from Australian Polygraph Services. In interviews, Wilson expressed 'no doubt' that Zentai was telling him the truth.[86]

There is some doubt about when Zentai left Budapest in 1944. He claims he departed on 7 November. Other unit members have stated that the unit departed on 8 November, 11 November and sometime between 10 and 15 November. With such confusion, it seems doubtful that Zentai can be proved incorrect at this stage. In any case, testimony exists in support of Zentai's claim. In 2005 *The Australian* reported that Julia Nikoletti, 90 year-old sister of Zentai, had provided 'a rare first-hand account that places him sixty kilometers away from the scene of the crime around the time it was committed.'[87] Mrs Nikoletti had provided a signed statement to Australian Justice Minister Chris Ellison, saying that she and Zentai left Budapest for Hanta, sixty kilometers west of the capital, with his military transport unit in the first few days of November 1944. She added that the other two soldiers who were later gaoled for crimes, including Balazs's murder, stayed in Budapest and travelled to Hanta by bus two days later. Unlike Zentai, she could not remember the exact date she and he left Budapest. In 2009 *The Australian* reported Mrs Nikoletti's death.[88] She would no longer be available as a witness for Zentai. Her death 'left just one known witness who could verify Zentai's claim that he led a convoy out of Budapest on 7 November 1944….. That witness – octogenarian Stefi Fonyodi of Budafok, Hungary – has revealed that she cannot remember the date on which she left Budapest with Zentai….. Both women backed Zentai's claim that the two fellow soldiers later convicted of Balazs's murder… stayed behind.' It might be argued that Nikoletti was family, so that her testimony could be biased; but her admission that she could not name the date suggests it may well be the truth. At any rate, overall, there is serious doubt as to whether Zentai was in Budapest at the time of the alleged murder; and it seems doubtful that certainty can now be obtained either way.

Zuroff appears to be too ready to treat the People's Court of communist-dominated Hungary in 1947-1948 as 'a court of law' without conceding the legitimate doubts about such 'justice', and he also seems to be too easily confident of the documentation, stating that it is 'reliable', but not explaining why.[89]

Not only is there no evidence that Zentai was a Nazi, but it is also clear that he did not hide after leaving Hungary and entered both Germany and later Australia by fully legal means. He then lived in Australia under his own name for more than fifty years.[90] That looks like the behaviour of an innocent man. Moreover, the Zentai family have produced correspondence that shows that the Hungarian Government knew where Zentai was living in Perth for several decades after his arrival in Australia. No extradition requests were made during this time.[91] This implies, though it does not prove, that Zentai had a clean record in Hungary's eyes during that period.

It has been reported that an elderly Sydney man who was at the Budapest barracks in 1944 has provided a statement saying he remembers Mader and Nagy being involved in the murder, but not Zentai.[92]

The legality of Hungary's request for extradition is also in doubt. "Zentai's lawyers today argued that the nominated offence of a war crime was not an offence in Hungary in 1944, and they questioned whether it could qualify as an extraditory offence."[93]

The Hungarian authorities have not explained why they could not question Zentai in Australia under the treaty on criminal cooperation.⁹⁴ In 2009 a letter from the Leader of the Military Panel in Hungary, Dr Bela Varga, confirmed 'there is no criminal proceeding at present' against Zentai, and said he was only wanted for questioning 'in the interest of the investigation'.⁹⁵ As noted above, the Hungarian authorities seem to have changed from this position later, when it appeared that it might cause the request for extradition to be denied. Such inconsistency calls into question the impartiality of these authorities.

It can be seen that during the past seven years Zentai has had to fight in a limited context, possibly to his disadvantage. His son, Ernie Steiner, has pointed this out: 'We were always involved in these really narrow arguments relating to the conditions of extradition and the definitions and so forth. For the last four years that was the only avenue open to my father.'⁹⁶

It seems clear to me that, taking all these factors into consideration, the case against approval of the extradition of Zentai to Hungary is now overwhelming, and that any informed, impartial and reasonable observer will agree.

The Significance of This Pursuit

The pursuit of Zentai and, more generally, the campaign in many countries during the last three decades to 'bring to justice' alleged 'Nazi war criminals', raise many significant issues.

One is the question of the bias in favour of the accusers of the major mass media. There is much evidence to suggest that the 'fourth estate' has actively assisted the pursuers, while offering no balancing assistance to the defendants. For example, the three major Melbourne newspapers during the past seven years have published a number of opinion articles hostile to Zentai,⁹⁷ but none favourable to him. *The Australian* has published editorials suggesting that it could well be correct to extradite Zentai⁹⁸ and indeed that he should be extradited.⁹⁹ Zuroff himself has provided an account of media assistance for the campaign: 'Now the question was whether Zentai was still alive and healthy enough to stand trial. I enlisted the help of a sympathetic Australian investigative journalist for the task..... his [Zentai's]health had still to be verified. For this task, we teamed up with Channel Nine News in Australia which sent a team to film Zentai without his knowledge.'¹⁰⁰ In 2005 a journalist for *The Australian* reported that evidence against Zentai had been 'uncovered and translated' by the newspaper.[101]

In 2007 *The Australian* stated that it had 'unearthed' six witness statements against Zentai in June 2005.[102] In 2008 I wrote to each editor of the three major newspapers read in Melbourne pleading for greater coverage of Zentai's side of the story[103], but none of them replied and subsequent events showed that my appeal had clearly fallen on deaf ears.

The Australian did occasionally publish letters by me sympathetic to Zentai. Very few if any letters from that standpoint appeared in *The Age* or the *Herald Sun*. A strong presumption exists that *The Australian* and Zentai's pursuers worked in tandem throughout this period, while the other two papers minimised coverage of the case. By regularly reporting on developments in the struggle in the way it did, *The Australian*, in particular, gave the impression that such a political phenomenon was an entirely normal and acceptable matter, rather than something morally atrocious. It perhaps habituated readers to accepting the abnormal as normal – on the principle 'What I say three times is true!'.

In 1955, while studying modern European history in my penultimate year of secondary education, I read the following sentence about events in France after Napoleon Bonaparte had escaped from exile on the island of Elba and was returning to Paris at the beginning of his last hundred days of liberty: 'Ere long Louis XVIII was in flight, while the French newspapers underwent a rapid change of tone – "the scoundrel Bonaparte" becoming first "Napoleon", then finally "our great and beloved Emperor".' This supine knuckling under to political power was, I thought at the time, morally unimpressive, to say the least; but one suspects that today's mass media are tarred with the same brush, which makes the struggle for justice and freedom all that much harder.

Another significance of the belated campaign to punish Nazi war criminals found in Australia is the impression given that the pursuers are seeking a scalp or seeking Australia's humble submission beneath the yoke. For example, Aarons complained in 2005 that Australia 'is the only Western country that took a significant number of Nazis but which has had no success at all in any type of prosecution.'[104] In 2007 *The Australian* reported on dissatisfaction in certain Jewish heads about Australia's action in this context: 'The Simon Wiesenthal

Centre, which is dedicated to finding suspected World War II criminals and helping to prosecute them, gave Australia a fail mark in its annual worldwide report last year. The centre has been highly critical of Australia for failing to track down and prosecute "at least several hundred" Nazi war criminals believed to have found refuge here. "Australia remains the only Western country of refuge which admitted at least several hundred Nazi war criminals and collaborators, which has hereto failed to take successful legal action against a single one," Dr Zuroff reported in 2005. "Numerous attempts have been made… to convince the Australian authorities to adopt civil remedies – denaturalisation and/or deportation – to deal with Holocaust perpetrators in the country, but the Government has refused to do so."'[105] Actually it is not so much that Australian governments have been unco-operative, as that Australian law, based in the Constitution and British legal tradition, whose integrity is matched by few other legal systems in the world, has offered high quality protection to persons accused.

It is in this context that we should understand the constant refrain that 'if Zentai is sent back to Hungary, he will become the first accused war criminal to be extradited by Australia.'[106]

In 2009 Zuroff commented: 'It's fairly clear this will be the last opportunity Australia will have to take successful legal action against a war criminal from World War II.'[107] In 2010 he continued the refrain: 'This means Australia has totally failed on the Nazi war crimes issue.'[108] 'Efraim Zuroff… said if the Commonwealth did not appeal, a serious injustice would occur. "Australia until now has given a perfect example of how not to achieve justice, how to allow all sorts of legal technicalities to prevent someone who is accused of the worst crime imaginable to escape being brought to trial."'[109]

A touch of passion can be seen in his exaggerated description of the alleged crime. The problem with this aspect of the Zentai case and the 'Nazi war crimes' campaign generally is that a presumption exists that the pursuits are more about the imposition of Jewish power on nations and the insistence that all must toe the line, rather than just about justice. They then appear as requirements of Jewish political propaganda and power-seeking, rather than purely ethical activities.

A third important significance of the Zentai case and associated phenomena is that it seems to have exposed a rather unprincipled willingness of Australian governments to assist the campaign rather than do everything in their power to protect the legitimate interests of their own citizens. Are these governments, like the major mass media, secretly subject to a Jewish *imperium in imperio*? On 18 January 2005 the Attorney-General, Phillip Ruddock, representing the then Coalition Liberal-National government, confirmed that Australia had an extradition treaty with Hungary, but then added: 'In fact we've just signed an extradition treaty with Latvia which given the sources of allegations in relation to war crimes, we are increasingly covering the field with relevant treaties for mutual co-operation in investigating matters for extradition.'[110] Did his poor English on air reflect a secret unease?

The 1989 amendment of the War Crimes Act was followed by a further amendment to remove the requirement, where extradition is sought by a foreign country, of proof of a prima facie case that a relevant offence has been committed. Distinguished barrister Dr. I. C. F. Spry QC was one critic of that change, which he described as 'regrettable'.[111]

In 2009 Zentai's son, Ernie Steiner, raised a very pertinent question: 'When you read the Minister's statement and he places such emphasis on Australia's international obligations at the expense of protecting an Australian citizen, I understand how political this decision is.'[112] A presumption exists that, in order to avoid opprobrium for engaging in manifestly inhumane and unjust behaviour (enabling such an extradition), Australian governments have sought to shelter behind extradition treaties and international covenants which they themselves signed in the first place. It appears as a convenient shedding of responsibility.

In 2010 David Weber pointed to further apparent failure of the Australian Government to protect its own: 'Zentai has said he's quite willing to answer questions in Australia if Hungary were to send people to speak to him. There's no evidence that any Australian minister has attempted to facilitate this, preferring to let the extradition process "run its course"..... It seems the Federal Government has been quite willing to allow an Australian citizen to spend his life savings battling a case that could have, at any time, been halted by the minister responsible.'[113] And McCusker had this to say: 'You look at all that [the finding by the Commonwealth Director of Public Prosecutions that Zentai had no case to answer] and say what are you doing extraditing to a Hungarian prison for purposes of interrogation an Australian citizen who's been such for half a century..... You have to question, as an Australian citizen and taxpayer, what's motivating the Government to do this?'[114] As long ago as 1988 the distinguished Catholic political commentator B. A. Santamaria noted that the Australian Government of the day, the Hawke government, had 'accepted the view that all evidence, including Soviet evidence, should be equally admissible' and pointed out how the record of NKVD and KGB behaviour made such a position morally and practically unacceptable.[115]

In their actions over the last twenty-five years or so in this context, Australian governments do not seem to have been truly representing their own constituency. A very strong presumption exists that they have proved obsequious to undue Jewish influence.

Another aspect of the case is that it may be tending to make easier in the future extraditions of Australian citizens for ideological and/or political reasons, rather than purely as a matter of justice. As noted earlier in this essay, one of the grounds barring extradition from Australia would be if it were sought 'for political reasons'. The Zentai team, judging by news coverage, do not seem to have tried to use this point as a defense; but a strong case can be made that the pursuit of Zentai is tainted by extra-judicial agendas. Moreover, one can foresee that in the future, when the supply of 'Nazis' runs out, the pursuers might adjust their aim on to so-called 'Holocaust deniers' (in accordance with UNO resolutions) or other 'politically incorrect' persons. The Australian media do not seem to have chosen to investigate this aspect of the Zentai case.

It can be argued also that the extradition of Zentai would constitute a grave moral blot on the honour and integrity of Australia. Indeed, from the time in 1986 when I first heard the news of the extradition of an 86 year-old man, Arturo Artukovich, to Yugoslavia, to face 'war crimes' charges – under a communist government! – I immediately thought of the horror with which the ancient Greek tragedians viewed evil and impious acts and the conviction they expressed that all such behaviour must sooner or later be expiated, whether willingly or not. This is another aspect of the Zentai case which the major media have chosen not to explore.

As noted above, there is good reason to question whether the allegedly 'democratic' Australian governments have really been acting in a truly representative manner in facilitating this manhunt. In an unpublished email to the *Herald Sun* in 2007 I endeavoured to make this point: 'It is not "the country" of Hungary that "wants to try Charles Zentai" ('Alleged war crim loses bid'), although the Hungarian Government may officially have claimed such. We can be sure that the vast majority of Hungarians – and of Australians… - have no desire whatever for such a farcical show trial.'[116]

Yet another significant aspect of the Zentai case is the extraordinary silence about it from ordinary Australians and, especially the intellectual elite of our nation, including civil libertarians. Of course, it is possible that the major media have suppressed letters and articles submitted on his behalf, but that is not the full explanation. During the period 1986 to 1993, when Robert Greenwood's Special Investigations Unit was closed down, there were quite a number of intellectuals and others who published statements in defense of those accused. Spokesmen from the communities of those born in Eastern European nations then under communist rule were prominent in this; but from 2005 there has hardly been a voice raised to defend Zentai's interests. This moral apathy does not bode well for freedom in the Australia of the future. One has the impression that many intellectuals are willing to defend justice and free speech, while making sure at the same time that nothing they write or say could in any way be construed as 'anti-Semitic'. What does this say about the true political condition of Australia?

The question of what other agendas are being served by the pursuits also needs to be considered. In 2008 the Jewish former editor of *The Age*, Michael Gawenda, wrote in an opinion article that the campaign to bring Zentai to justice was 'as much about recognition of what was done as about delivering justice'. He saw Zentai's crime as being 'part of the annihilation of millions of Jews during World War II'.[117] In 2011 there was a report of Zuroff, 'the world's chief Nazi hunter', touching down in Western Australia 'to educate the community over the importance of never forgetting the Holocaust' and help 'bring closure to victims of the Holocaust'. Obviously referring to the Zentai case, he stated: 'Ninety-nine per cent of the people who committed the crimes of the Holocaust are normative people. They did not commit murder before the Holocaust, before World War II, they did not commit murder after World War II.'[118] In its editorial on 13 June 2005, titled 'Ellison must send Zentai to Hungary', *The Australian* began its argument by stating: 'The Holocaust is the defining atrocity of the 20th Century', a rather peculiar assertion.

It seems clear that promotion of the Holocaust dogma is one of the chief motivations of the campaign to 'bring to justice' alleged 'Nazi war criminals'. This is used as a justification of the obviously selective nature of the whole operation, other 'war criminals' being left alone. Part of an unpublished letter I sent to *The Australian* on 13 June in response to its editorial read as follows: 'That *The Australian* is itself biased in this great issue is suggested by your clichéd opening that 'the Holocaust is the defining atrocity of the 20th Century' (a curiously vague statement), which needs to be related to your complete refusal to publish the news of the deportation of Holocaust revisionist Ernst Zundel from Canada to Germany in March. An alleged historical event which is not allowed to be openly discussed from all points of view in the public forums is immediately open to grave doubt; and this is more so when its challengers are judicially punished and official silence about their punishment has become the order of the day. Everything in the Zentai case smacks of conspiracy and manipulation by a semi-secret Establishment for which you are acting as publicity agent.'[119]

This touches on an international issue of the gravest import. It is a commonplace now to note that one can, in Western nations, engage in adverse criticism of Christianity and Islam, Jesus and Mohammed, without fear of incurring legal proceedings and the status of social pariah. It is not so with the Holocaust dogma. This appears to be virtually proof positive that these nations, including Australia, already live under a semi-tyranny imposed by an *imperium in imperio*. Unfortunately, Zentai's defense team could not raise matters such as this in their struggle to protect their client, partly because of their irrelevance to legalities about extradition, but also partly because they would not have been responded to fairly and might have excited odium towards Zentai.

Yet another aspect of the Zentai case is the apparent refusal, or inability, of his pursuers to consider the legal and moral objections to their campaign. This is typified by a report that Zuroff in 2010 said that Zentai's age was irrelevant and the notion that he would be treated harshly in Hungary was ludicrous.[120] I have not seen any admission by the pursuers in the press that findings of post-war communist courts are inherently untrustworthy.

Yet another aspect of the Zentai case is the suggestion that a kind of blackmail may be being applied to Australia (and perhaps Hungary) in the matter. In 2009 a Monash University law school senior lecturer,

Gideon Boas, a strong advocate of war crimes trials generally, stated: 'We're [Australia] going to start to be perceived internationally, if not internally, as being a country that's not serious about prosecuting war crimes.'[121] Boas, presumably a Jew, is a former senior legal officer at the International Criminal Tribunal for the former Yugoslavia. *The Age* has published articles by him in favour of war crimes trials.[122] Remarks such as that of Boas make one wonder about other possible threats that may have been made to governments behind the scenes.

Another aspect of the Zentai controversy is the relative lack of discussion in the press of the political conditions in Hungary in 1944, the context in which the alleged murder of Balazs took place. Ever since 1933 the nations of eastern Europe had lived in a lose-lose situation where they had a choice of acquiescence to Soviet tyranny or Nazi tyranny. Naturally there were good persons in both camps, those choosing the Soviet, those choosing Hitler. Neutrality was an ideal, but not an option. Jews, in general, were likely to prefer the Soviet, partly because communism had always attracted politically idealistic Jews and partly because of Nazi anti-Semitism. Thus in 1944 anti-Soviet Hungarians would have tended to see Jews not so much as a persecuted minority as a dangerous sub-group of enemies – and not without some justification. David Irving in his history of the 1956 Hungarian revolt, *Uprising*, explained how he had been surprised to find that many of the rebels saw themselves as freeing Hungary from Jewish, rather than merely communist, domination. In this context a point raised by Santamaria is worth quoting: 'What happened in Romania [in 1939-1941], also occupied by the Soviet forces, is detailed from a Jewish source by the Chief Rabbi of Romania, Alexandre Safran. In a *Times Literary Supplement* (8 July 1988) review of Safran's work (*Resisting the Storm: Romania 1940-47*), Jessica Douglas-Home writes: "His narrative – which is neither bitter nor vengeful – also sets the destruction of Romanian Judaism in the context of the wider assault on such democracy as pre-war Romania possessed; begun by the Nazis, it was subsequently carried on by a tiny handful of communists, 1,100 to be precise – directed from Moscow. For Safran there was both pain and paradox in the fact that 900 of the 1,100 were lapsed Jews."[123]

It is legitimate to wonder exactly what were the political affiliations of Dezso Balazs and his sons, as well as the nature of their actions in those critical months in 1944 as invasion by the Soviet Russians came closer and closer. It would also be interesting to see clearly what kind of pressures Zentai and his fellow soldiers in the Hungarian Army were under. Possibly facts helpful to Zentai's defense might emerge; but now it is probably too late to find out.

One final point concerns the very legitimacy – or lawfulness – of war crimes trials generally. This point was raised in 1970 by Laurens van der Post, who had been a prisoner of the Japanese in the Dutch East Indies and who owed his life to the dropping of the atom bombs on Hiroshima and Nagasaki. Despite the sufferings he had incurred, van der Post wrote: 'I myself was utterly opposed to any form of war trials. I refused to collaborate with the officers of the various war crimes tribunals that were set up in the Far East. There seemed to me something unreal, if not utterly false, about a process that made men like the War Crimes Investigators from Europe, who had not suffered under the Japanese, more bitter and vengeful about our suffering than we were ourselves.

> 'There seemed in this to be the seeds of the great, classic and fateful evasions of the human spirit which, I believe, both in the collective and in the individual sense, have been responsible for most of the major tragedies of recorded life and time and are increasingly so in the tragedies that confront us in the world today.
>
> 'I refer to the tendencies in men to blame their own misfortunes and those of their cultures on others; to exercise judgement they need for themselves on the lives of others; to search for a villain to explain everything that goes wrong in their private and collective courses.....
>
> 'I felt strongly that, if war had had any justification at all, it was only in the sense that, at its end, it should leave victors and vanquished free for a moment from the destructive aspects of their past.....
>
> 'It was as if war today were a bitter form of penance for all our inadequate yesterdays. Once this terrible penance had been paid, my own experience suggested, it re-established men in a brief state of innocence which, if seized with imagination, could enable us to build better than before. To go looking for particular persons and societies to blame and punish at the end of war seemed to me to throw men back into the negative aspects of the past from which they had been trying to escape, and to deprive them of the opportunity they had so bitterly earned in order to begin afresh.....
>
> 'Far from being an instrument of redemption, which is punishment's only moral justification, it is an increasingly self-

> *defeating weapon in the hands of dangerously one-sided men.....
> Forgiveness, my prison experience had taught me, was not mere
> religious sentimentality; it was as fundamental a law of the
> human spirit as the law of gravity..... if one broke this law of
> forgiveness, one inflicted a mortal wound on one's spirit.*'[124]

In his monumental study of war-crimes trials, Veale noted how in the Tokyo trials in 1947-48 the Indian representative, Mr. Justice Rahabinode Pal, delivered a 1900-page dissenting judgement in which he laid down that 'the farce of a trial of vanquished leaders by the victors was itself an offence against humanity' and was therefore in itself a war crime.[125]

In 1988 I struggled in vain to have this point of view properly and fully discussed in the major newspapers and other public forums in Australia. In 2012 I cannot help wondering if the main reason for the proliferation in recent years of war crimes trials under the International Criminal Court or other international tribunals is not arranged in order to ensure that when a world government (desired by certain elites) is in place, anyone leading a revolt against that tyranny will know that, if defeated, he will face a war-crimes tribunal and condign punishment. There may be a wolf in sheep's clothing in this development.

Sherlock Holmes was right in his comments quoted as the epigraph to this essay. Eighteen-year-old James McCarthy looked just as clearly guilty from the initial evidence as Charles Zentai looks from the evidence of the People's Court of Budapest in 1947-48; but close investigation revealed that McCarthy was completely innocent. Perhaps Zentai is too. And it is far too late to arrange a fair trial for him. Let us hope that Australia eventually sets him free, preferring not to risk unjust punishment of an innocent man rather than gain the plaudits of a powerful minority lobby and associated benefits.

Epilogue

Shortly after the above account was completed, *The Age* on 16 August 2012 reported a High Court decision critical to Zentai's fate.[126] 'The full Federal Court said last year that the government could not decide to surrender Mr Zentai for an offence that was not a crime under Hungarian law when it allegedly occurred. The High Court upheld the decision by a 5-1 majority yesterday.' *The Age* noted that the judgement 'which ruled on a technical argument... brings to an end another episode in a long history of failed extradition bids.' It quoted Professor Ivan Shearer, author of *Extradition in International Law*, as saying that 'all of the other attempted extraditions of alleged war criminals have fallen foul of some or other procedural rule..... If Hungary had made its request on the basis of an alleged "murder", and not a "war crime" claim, the extradition might have been successful.'

Next day *The Age* discussed the decision in an editorial headed 'Zentai ruling joins litany of failure'. It wrote: 'The judgement... brings into uncomfortable focus Australia's lack of success both in extraditing other accused war criminals and securing war crimes prosecutions in domestic courts..... Australia has been anything but proactive when it comes to acting on war-crimes allegations against migrants who entered the country during the Cold War period and also in recent years.'

It seems a reasonable presumption to state that *The Age* was disappointed by the decision.

Only one reader's letter was published on the matter.[127] The writer misrepresented the High Court by asserting that 'it takes the view that in 1944 there was no such thing as a war crime.' He provided no reason for his opposition to the decision, but suggested some hypothetical implications of it.

As soon as the High Court decision was known I asked *The Age* opinion editor if she would be interested in a piece by me on the case and she said she would willingly consider it. Unfortunately, in the end, it was not accepted. I publish it here to show what sort of commentary on the Zentai story did *not* appear at this stage in Melbourne's leading newspaper. It is titled 'Zentai case decision a credit for Australian law' and subtitled 'Important principles of justice have been upheld'.

Now that the High Court has ruled that Charles Zentai is not to be extradited to face a war crimes charge in Hungary, it is time to consider the significance of his case, as it has unfolded during the past seven years. The question of whether justice has or has not been fully done in this matter will probably never be resolved. The world will never know for certain whether Zentai did or did not participate in an unlawful beating to death of Jewish teenager Peter Balazs in 1944, or whether he engaged in other unjustifiable acts of brutal harassment of Jewish Hungarians while a Hungarian army officer. His family members naturally proclaim his innocence and no doubt believe in it; but they cannot be taken by others to know that with complete certainty. Efraim Zuroff and his colleagues in the Simon Wiesenthal Centre remain equally convinced that Zentai is guilty. Thanks to the father and brother of Balazs, who struggled for many years to ensure appropriate punishment for the man they believed to be one of his murderers, the Centre brought forward a credible case, based on testimony by a number of witnesses, both soldiers in Zentai's wartime unit, and Jewish forced labourers then under their supervision.

While Zuroff and others are entitled to be disappointed, it is not so clear that they are right to condemn either the Australian Government or the Australian justice system for failure to ensure that right has been done. Rather, the contrary seems to be the case. It is a very serious matter for a national government to surrender one of its citizens to another nation to face judicial proceedings. Thus great care has to be taken before allowing that surrender. This point is made in Section 65 of the High Court ruling, which notes that "it is well settled that the Executive requires the authority of statute to surrender a person for extradition and that the power cannot be exercised except in accordance with the laws which prescribe in detail the precautions to be taken to prevent unwarrantable interference with individual liberty." What this reminds us is that, far from the Zentai case having been "mired in the courts" ('Stunned as "war crime" ordeal ends, 16/8), it stands now on record as a fine example of the scrupulous ways in which our legal tradition operates to protect ordinary citizens, weak and vulnerable as they often are, from administrative error or wrongdoing.

There are other reasons for feeling glad, not sad, about the High Court decision. In the first place it appears clearly to have indirectly protected, if not directly upheld, Zentai's right to the presumption of innocence. By contrast, his pursuers seem too readily to have acted on a presumption of his guilt.

The principle of the presumption of innocence goes hand in hand with another cardinal principle of Australian justice, which is that an accused shall have a fair trial. For many reasons it has always been very doubtful that Zentai would have enjoyed a fair trial, once extradited. Too many doubts exist about the integrity of the allegations against him, which were made in the infamous People's Court of Budapest, a communist institution operating in a period (1947-48) of post-war hysteria and recrimination. Indeed, the witness statements against him may have been obtained by torture. An Australian court is unlikely to have given credence to such evidence, but such is not so clear about a Hungarian military tribunal (which Zentai was to have faced), given the facts that Hungary chose to seek extradition on that basis and has recently arrested a man of 97, Laszlo Csatary, to face analogous charges. Moreover, documents necessary for Zentai's defense may have been lost or corrupted, and his accusers and other witnesses he may have needed are dead, so that cross examination, an essential for justice, would not have been possible.

There is another reason why we should feel glad about Zentai's victory. It would have been a moral atrocity to send overseas for such a trial a man so old and frail. We should remember the wisdom of the Greek tragedians of ancient Athens who showed, in the dramas about Electra and Orestes, that a search for justice can easily be corrupted into impious acts (as when they killed their own mother) motivated by blind revenge. Perhaps Laurens van der Post was correct in the postscript of his 1970 book *Night of the New Moon* that war crimes trials are in fact an ethically mistaken institution and that a spirit of mercy and forgiveness is better and in the interests of humanity and future generations, once wars have been concluded.

Our national newspaper, *The Australian*, provided a more extensive and even-handed coverage of the High Court decision. On 16 August it published a front page news story, which included the comment that Australia's hunt for alleged Nazi war criminals since 1987 has cost 'tens of millions of dollars'. Efraim Zuroff was reported as saying that it was 'a terrible day for survivors of the Holocaust'. *The Australian* also published on 16 August a human interest report of the reactions of Zentai and his son, a comment by its Legal Affairs Editor, Chris Merritt, about the 'dreadful decision' and a full page news story by Paige Taylor and Nicolas Perpitch under the heading 'War crime case is halted'.

This last item noted that none of Zentai's accusers was alive and that there were doubts about the 'communist-controlled' courts of Budapest. An important statement was included by Mark Ierace, a former prosecutor at the UN International Criminal Tribunal for the former Yugoslavia. Ierace said: 'It seems the Australian Government's attitude in the Zentai case, to extradite regardless of the human rights issue of a fair trial, is prompted by a fear of being seen internationally as soft on suspected war criminals. If so, this is quite misguided..... It seems the only evidence against him were the confessions of two men tried in the 1950's for the crime, in which they named Mr Zentai as a co-offender. Both men resiled from their confessions, claiming they had been extracted under torture. The police station where they were questioned was notorious at the time for such practices..... Any trial in Hungary, or anywhere else in the Western world for that matter, would have been a sham.'

A week later *The Australian* published an opinion article by Efraim Zuroff entitled 'The case that broke the heart of a Nazi hunter'.[128] This included a rather remarkable appeal for the reader's sympathy, as follows. 'Another reason for the issue becoming personal was the active efforts of the Zentai children to prevent their father's extradition. All of a sudden, I found myself pitted against them in the fight for public opinion, with the odds heavily against me. They were an ostensibly normal Australian family trying to save their elderly father from prosecution for a crime committed decades ago in a foreign country, where they claimed he would not get a fair trial. They were present at all the proceedings and always easily available to the local media.'

In response to this account I sent an email to the paper's Letters Editor as follows: 'Efraim Zuroff believes "the odds were heavily against him" in his attempt to have Charles Zentai extradited to Hungary to face "Nazi war crimes" charges. However, during the seven years involved (2005-2012) I do not recall seeing a single opinion piece favourable to Zentai's cause published in any of the three major newspapers read in Melbourne. By contrast, all three papers published opinion pieces favourable to his pursuers. *The Australian*, in particular, mentioned more than once that its own research had turned up evidence against Zentai, this leading to the impression that the paper was giving assistance to his opponents. Zuroff is correct that good coverage was given to the views and research of Zentai's own family, but these could easily be discounted as "biased by blood". Little or no effort was made to publicise the views of other Australians opposed to Zentai's extradition and the belated campaign of the "Nazi hunter".' Unfortunately *The Australian* did not publish this response.

Zuroff on 23 August also wrote, disingenuously I believe, that in the minds of Zentai's children he 'was responsible for the predicament the family faced', whereas 'of course, it was Hungary that had asked for Zentai's extradition.' That nation's request, surely, was only made as a result of strong inducement or pressure exerted by international Jewish agencies. It is most unlikely that the majority of Hungarians were behind it or even in favour of it.

The Australian did publish on 24 August one response to Zuroff – a letter by Robin Linke headed 'Nazi witch hunt'. It forms a good epitaph for the case: 'Efraim Zuroff's justification in pursuing Charles Zentai for alleged war crimes is flawed. After 70 years there is no way a court of law could find Zentai guilty beyond reasonable doubt. Despite millions of dollars spent over several decades not a single person has been successfully prosecuted. The passage of time long ago turned the pursuit of alleged Nazi war criminals into a witch hunt.'

Theoretically Hungary could submit to Australia a new request for Zentai's extradition, replacing the charge 'war crime' with 'murder'. Legal opinion is that, if so, such a request might be successful. It is to be hoped that Hungary will have the common humanity and good sense not to do that.

Notes:

1. Robert Manne, 'A Case against the War Crimes Act', in *The Report of the Symposium on the Proposed War Crimes Legislation in Australia*, Captive Nations Council of Victoria, Melbourne, 1988, p 6.
2. Ibid, pp 6-7.
3. Tom Sherman, 'The Government's Position on the Bill', in *The Report of the Symposium on the Proposed War Crimes Legislation in Australia*, Captive Nations Council of Victoria, Melbourne, 1988, pp 14-15. (Sherman was deputy secretary of the Federal Attorney General's Department.)
4. Manne, op.cit., p 7.
5. Sherman, op.cit., p 14.
6. Manne, op.cit., p 9.
7. Anthony Endrey QC, 'The Overzealous Nazi Hunter', in *Hungarian Observer*, Victoria, April 1988, pp 4-5.
8. The highest court holding jurisdiction in Australia. (The hierarchy of courts involved in the Charles Zentai case, in ascending order, is as follows: (i) The State Magistrates Court exercising federal jurisdiction; (ii) the Federal Court on appeal from (i); the Full Federal Court on appeal from (ii); and the High Court on appeal from (iii).)
9. 'SA Man Being Investigated for Alleged War Crimes', *On Target*, The Australian League of Rights, Vol. 35, No. 29, Melbourne, 30 July 1999.

10. *On Target*, Vol. 28, No. 25, 10 July 1992.
11. 'Former lieutenant-governor of South Australia issues press release on war crimes trials', *On Target*, The Australian League of Rights, Melbourne, Vol. 27, No. 44, 15 November 1991.
12. Robert Manne, 'Discussion', in *The Report of the Symposium on the Proposed War Crimes Legislation in Australia*, Captive Nations Council of Victoria, Melbourne, 1988, p 36. (Senator Cooney, an ALP senator, had said during the symposium: 'The trouble with extradition is that those you send back tend to end up dead. I do not want anybody I have associated with to go back to their death. I cannot support this approach.' See p 27.)
13. Dr. Efraim Zuroff, 'Zentai Case', in *Shalom Magazine*, No. 48, September 2007, online.
14. Gyorgy Vamos, 'Murder on Arena Avenue: is Charles Zentai Guilty?', in *The Monthly*, No. 43, March 2009, online,
15. This is the name of the communist court that was operative in Hungary during 1947 and 1948.
16. David Weber, 'Zentai case tossed in the too-hard basket', *The Drum*, Australian Broadcasting Corporation, 8 July 2010, online.
17. Zuroff, op.cit., p 3.
18. Wikipedia article on Zentai, accessed 6 July 2012.
19. *The Australian*, 21 June 2006. (There are three major newspapers read in the author's home town of Melbourne – *The Age*, the *Herald Sun* and *The Australian*, the latter being Australia's only national paper. Coverage of the Zentai case has been much more frequent in *The Australian* than in the other two dailies.)
20. *The Australian, 29-30 July 2006*. (Australia has a federal constitution, inaugurated in 1901, whereby the Australian Government holds and exercises certain powers, while the states and territories hold and exercise other powers.)
21. *The Australian*, 13 September 2006. (Perth is the capital of the state of Western Australia. It is Zentai's home city.)
22. Wikipedia, op.cit. and reports in *The Australian* on 14 February and 17 April 2007.
23. *Herald Sun*, 31 May 2007; *The Australian*, 4 September 2007 and 26 September 2007.
24. *The Age*, 24 April 2008; the *Herald Sun*, 24 April 2008.
25. *The Australian*, 18 August 2008.
26. *The Age*, 19 August 2008.
27. *The Australian*, 19 August 2008.
28. Naomi Levin, *Jewish News* online at Fightdemback, 1 September 2008.
29. *The Australian*, 31 March 2009.
30. *The Age*, 9 October 2009.
31. *The Australian*, 9 October 2009.
32. *The Australian*, 23 October 2009.
33. *Wikipedia* entry on Charles Zentai, consulted on 6 July 2012.
34. *The Age*, 13 November 2009.
35. *The Australian*, 13 November 2009.

36. Tanalee Smith, Australian Associated Press, online, 13 November 2009; *The Australian*, 17 December 2009.
37. *The Australian*, 12 January 2010.
38. *The Age*, 24 February 2010.
39. Warwick Stanley, Australian Associated Press, online, 23 February 2010.
40. *The Australian*, 29 April 2010.
41. *The Australian*, 3-4 July 2010.
42. *The Age*, 3 July 2010.
43. David Weber, op.cit.
44. *Wikipedia,* article on Charles Zentai, consulted on 4 July 2012.
45. *Perth Now*, online, 25 January 2011.
46. *Perth Now*, online, 16 May 2011.
47. Lloyd Jones, *Perth Now*, online, 17 May 2011.
48. *The Australian*, 17 May 2011.
49. *Herald Sun*, 17 August 2011; 'Extradition saga in Charles Zentai case continues', *News.com.au*, Australian Associated Press, online, 16 August 2011.
50. *The Age*, 29 March 2012.
51. Vamos, op.cit., pp 3-4.
52. Ibid., p 7.
53. Ibid., p 1.
54. Ibid, p 3.
55. Ibid, p 3.
57. Ibid, pp 4-6.
58. 'Zentai case raises serious questions', editorial in *The Australian*, 17 May 2005.
59. Mark Aarons, 'No refuge for war criminals', *The Australian*, 25 April 2008.
60. 'War crime accused "too frail"', *The Australian*, 14 February 2007.
61. 'Zentai in prison as minister ponders', *The Australian*, 23 October 2009.
62. *Perth Now*, online, 16 May 2011.
63. Vamos, op.cit., pp 1-2.
64. Ibid., p 5.
65. Nikolai Tolstoy, foreword in *The Report of the Symposium on the Proposed War Crimes Legislation in Australia*, Captive Nations Council of Victoria, Melbourne, 1988, p 4.
66. Manne, op.cit., pp 10-12.
67. F.J.P.Veale, *The Veale File*, Institute for Historical Review, USA, Vol. 1, p 31.
68. Ibid, p 229.
69. Ibid., p 230.
70. Chapman Pincher, *The Secret Offensive*, Sidgwick and Jackson, London, 1985.
71. Ibid, p 2.
72. 'Testimony "clears" Zentai's name', *The Australian*, 1 October 2007.
73. Tomas Melicharek, online, 19 June 2008.

74. 'Zentai in prison as minister ponders', *The Australian*, 23 October 2009.
75. 'Accused war criminal's extradition fight fails', *The Australian*, 13 September 2006; 'Alleged war criminal beat teenager to death, court told', *The Age*, 19 August 2008.
76. 'Barrister takes on Zentai case for free', *The Australian*, 12 January 2010.
77. In Keltie Zubko, *The Path of Legal Warfare*, subtitled 'Imre Finta's Trial for War Crimes', Veritas, Western Australia, 1991, pp 2-3.
78. In Debbie Guest, 'Nazi era's cold case', *The* Australian, 3 November 2009.
79. 'Nazi officer acquitted of wartime mass murder', *The Australian*, 21 December 2005.
80. 'Evidence "strong" on war charges', *The Australian*, 25 April 2008.
81. 'Zentai in prison as minister ponders', *The Australian*, 23 October 2009.
82. 'Hungarian far right grows', *The Australian*, 19 February 2010.
83. 'Zentai ruling wrong: QC', *The Australian*, 28 April 2010.
84. Douglas Christie described Seifert's condition in prison on 5 July 2010: 'The temperature in Mr. Seifert's cell was approximately 35 degrees Celsius, with one small fan producing very little effect and an open window about eight feet above the floor, with no screen and thus mosquitoes were free to come in and out of the cell. Mr. Seifert, at present, suffers severe infections of his lower legs. Dr. Cariello assures me this is chronic, but two years ago I was well aware that Mr. Seifert could walk and did not have infections as he has now...... His toes are all infected; one nail having either fallen off or been torn off. His feet are bleeding and emitting pus or evidence of bleeding and weeping infection up to the knees. He had, in an endeavour to staunch the bleeding and flow of infected material, wrapped his leg in paper, since there were no bandages provided and no evidence of antibiotic prescriptions or topical ointment. He has psoriasis, or had, when he went to Italy, and this appears to have been untreated to a large degree.' In *Friends of Freedom*, Newsletter for the supporters of the Canadian Free Speech League, Victoria, Canada, July 2010. Seifert died fairly soon after this report.
85. 'Nazi suspect arrested', *The Age*, 19 July 2012.
86. *Wikipedia* article on Charles Zentai, consulted on 6 July 2012.
87. *The Australian*, 4 October 2005.
88. 'Setback for accused war criminal', *The Australian*, 16 February 2009.
89. Zuroff, op.cit, p 2.
90. Tomas Melicharek, op.cit.
91. David Weber, op.cit.
92. Ibid.
93. Joseph Sapienza, *WAtoday*, online, 26 August 2009.
94. *Wikipedia*, article on Charles Zentai, 6 July 2012.
95. Joseph Sapienza, op.cit.
96. In Karlis Salna, 'Zentai to challenge extradition decision', Australian Associated Press, *News.com.au*, online, 12 November 2009.
97. For example: - Christopher Bantick, 'A shadow cast over us', *Herald Sun*, 29 October 2007; Mark Aarons, 'No refuge for war criminals', *The*

Australian, April 25 2008; Alan Howe, 'All aboard? Not quite.', *Herald Sun*, 2 August 2008; Michael Gawenda, 'War crimes should be punished – no matter how long it takes', *The Age*, 28 August 2008; Alan Howe, 'No use-by date for evil', *Herald Sun*, 12 October 2009.
98. 'Zentai case raises serious questions', *The* Australian, 17 May 2005.
99. 'Ellison must send Zentai to Hungary', *The Australian*, 13 June 2005.
100..Zuroff, op.cit., p 3.
101..Paige Taylor, 'Warrant of war accused revealed', *The Australian*, 9 June 2005.
102.'Testimony' "clears" Zentai's name', *The Australian*, 1 October 2007.
103.On 2 September 2008 I sent letters to Bruce Guthrie, editor of the *Herald Sun*, Paul Ramadge, editor of *The Age* and Paul Whittaker, editor of *The Australian*. Each letter appealed to the editor concerned to allow publication of the case in favour of disallowing Zentai's extradition to Hungary.
104. In *The Australian*, 18 May 2005.
105. 'Zentai case document "worthless"', *The Australian*, 3 October 2007.
106. 'Zentai could be extradited this week', *The Australian*, 18 August 2008.
107. 'War accused loses appeal', *The Australian*, 9 October 2009.
108. 'Court overrules Zentai extradition order', *The Australian*, 3-4 July 2010.
109. 'Zentai wants answers on extradition appeal', *The Australian*, 11-12 December 2010.
110. On Channel Nine, the transcript having been provided by his department.
111. Dr. I. C. F. Spry QC, 'Legal Notes: The Kalejs Case: An Inappropriate Pursuit', in *National Observer*, Council for the National Interest, No. 44, Autumn 2000, pp 61-66.
112. 'Zentai to challenge extradition decision', *News.com.au*, online, Australian Associated Press, 12 November 2009.
113. David Weber, op.cit.
114. Malcolm McCusker QC, in 'Zentai extradition is "appalling" – Aussie of the Year contender McCusker', *Perth Now*, online, 25 January 2011.
115. B. A. Santamaria, 'War crimes trials open Pandora's Box', *News Weekly*, Melbourne, 12 October 1988.
116.Author's email to the *Herald Sun* in response to its news report on 17 April 2007.
117. 'War crimes should be punished – no matter how long it takes', *The Age*, 31 August 2008.
118. WA News, *WA Today.com.au*, online, 20 June 2011.
119. The author sent letters of protest to *The Australian*, *The Age* and the *Herald Sun* as soon as he learned of Zundel's deportation to Germany. None were published and for several months not a word about the deportation was published in the three newspapers. The author on 28 March 2005 wrote a 3,226-word essay about the deportation and the media silence about it and sent it to *Quadrant*, one of Australia's most prestigious literary and cultural periodicals. Despite his enclosing a stamped, self-addressed envelope for

return of the MSS if it was rejected, he heard nothing for over two months. A query led to the simple reply that the MSS would not be used. It appeared that *Quadrant* had joined the syndicate of silence.

120. 'Zentai ruling needs scrutiny, says Smith', *The Age*, 3 July 2010, online.
121. In a news report by Debbie Guest, 'Nazi era's cold case', *The Australian*, 3 November 2009.
122. For example, 'Laws give wriggle room to war criminals', *The Age*, 27 February 2010.
123. B. A. Santamaria, op.cit.
124. Laurens van der Post, Postscript, in *Night of the New Moon*, Random House, USA, 1970.
125. Veale, op. cit., p 254.
126. 'Stunned as "war crime" ordeal ends', *The Age*, 16 August 2012.
127. Thomas Mautner, 'High Court owes us an explanation', *The Age*, 20 August 2012.
128. Efraim Zuroff, 'The case that broke the heart of a Nazi hunter', *The Australian*, 23 August 2012.

Why They Said There Were Gas Chambers—or, Sing for Your Life!

Jett Rucker

They all said it, didn't they? Or all of those testifying under oath anyway, no? Or nobody said there *weren't* any, did they? Certainly not under oath, eh? The weight of testimonial evidence in support of the existence and use of gas chambers in German wartime concentration camps seems to be as overwhelming as it could possibly be given that no one actually killed in a gas chamber could testify to having suffered that fate. For that, of course, we have the bodies. Or, at least the ashes, bones and teeth. Or, at least the steep declines in the "Jewish" populations of European countries and worldwide.[1]

Testimony to the effect that there were no gas chambers, in any case, seems to be entirely lacking from the records of dozens of trials of people accused of having taken part in one way or another in the operation of "death camps," or the process of rounding people up and sending them to those camps. It *is* hard to prove a negative, and just as hard to "observe" it. There are, to be sure, occasional accounts of camp experience that somehow omit reports of gas chambers. And there are even those veterans such as Paul Rassinier who claim[2] that their passages through multiple camps left them unpersuaded that such things existed, at least in the places he experienced. But these are so few and far between that they constitute the exceptions that prove the rule: that the Germans designed, installed, and operated gas chambers for killing people (the first ever, anywhere) in their infamous camps of World War II. Quite aside from their frequency (and certitude), their actual *consistency* provides that "convergence of evidence" whose "moral certainty" buttresses laws throughout Europe, and Israel, that provide jail terms for those who publicly express doubt as to any detail of the narrative.

The tsunami of "eyewitness reports" of this industrialization of murder constitutes a veritable "perfect storm" of evidence to confirm in the minds of all within the reach of Western media and educational systems the unassailable truth of the gas-chamber story. It is, indeed, a storm so very perfect as to require what in evolutionary theory is known as "intelligent design." This, despite the fact that no gas chamber for killing people with a capacity above two (both victims strapped into their chairs) has ever been suggested, much less known to have existed, before or since.

Rudolf Höss after his capture by the British. In a letter to his wife (11 April 1947) he wrote, "Most of the terrible and horrible things that took place there I learned only during this investigation and during the trial itself." [Public domain], via Wikimedia Commons

The story had its beginnings, of course, before the facts—facts, indeed, that never did occur, not in German-controlled areas nor anywhere else, if only because of the numerous physical impossibilities or impracticalities involved. The earliest "reports" came via Polish agents who had, in some cases, actually visited or been imprisoned in concentration camps on Polish territory, by clandestine radio transmissions to the Polish government-in-exile in

London[3]. These initially entailed mass killings by an improbable panoply of exotic means including electroshock, steam, engine exhausts, "gas vans," and eventually the potentially lethal insecticide, Zyklon-B. The passage of time and the penetration of evidence-based inquiry have ineluctably eroded away the electroshock and steam mythologies, and are doing so to Diesel exhaust (which isn't toxic), and "gas vans" (lack of evidence, and practicality), but the accounts alleging carbon monoxide (expensively available in low concentrations in the exhaust from gasoline engines) and Zyklon-B (unlikely on a dozen scores, including high time requirements for the processing of "batches" of killings) march on with nary a hitch, so compelling are the interests whose defense absolutely requires *some* credible vehicle with which to promote the tragedy of the mass injustice that befell the racial foes cited in National Socialist ideological rantings.

How, then, did this incredible (literally) groundswell of testimony arise, if, as growing numbers of revisionists now assert, "No one was gassed" ("*Niemand wurde vergast*," in a language in which it is forbidden to publish such notions)? The facts of the matter lie somewhere between the "groundswell" and a nefarious conspiracy by some obscure Star Chamber to deceive the future masses of the world.

But that groundswell is not entirely composed of victims (actual and self-styled) of the infamous camps. Involved also are various parties opposed, under more, or less, desperate circumstances, to the expansionist regime that controlled Germany from 1933 to 1945. It starts, of course, with the first victims, the Poles. But it doesn't hit high gear until those Polish opponents of German rule are joined by the Soviet behemoth to the east, the one that after the war overthrew and subsumed the Polish polity and erected a simulacrum of it as the vehicle of its suzerainty over the people and territory of Poland, that only fell in 1989.

But the Soviets were not the only victorious power involved—far from it. Fired by a hard core of Jewish vengeance-seekers (as was the Soviet Union) were also recently occupied France, bombed Great Britain, and that distant, but Jewish-suffused behemoth, the United States—the four powers, in fact, that divided the former Germany into pieces occupied by each of them, not counting the large pieces sundered and parceled out to Poland and Czechoslovakia as their permanent territories. These powers, and their agendas, became literally the law of the land that once was Germany, and the features of that law reflected the inconceivably violent circumstances under which it had gained its supremacy over the people and territory of hapless Germany.

Under this "law," then, proceeded the "trials" of those apprehended on suspicion of having caused or abetted the recent unpleasantness that had arisen among the various governments, and racial/religious groups, and armies, involved.[4]

This "law" governed all the land, and all the people on the land, and all the food, and even the water and shelter, that constituted the rump Germany that remained after the pre-war entity so known had been suitably divided among the neighboring powers that had ended up on the winning side of World War II. On this land was not only the decimated population that survived the bombing campaigns, the starvation, the disease, the ravagement of desperate, defensive combat, and the depredations of post-war prisoner-of-war camps, but also hundreds of thousands of various refugees including concentration-camp veterans and those fleeing, for many reasons, the Communist hegemony that even then was clearly arising in the east. The previous residents were "Germans." The rest were "displaced persons" (DPs). In this witches' brew of inchoate masses clinging desperately to whatever vestiges of life they could claw hold of to survive to the next day, arose the victorious Allies' enterprise to visit "justice" upon those upon whom blame for the past five years of suffering and destruction could be fixed.

The process, though not orchestrated "from above" by some sort of vengeful divinity, worked as though so ordained. Jews, perhaps understandably, manned the vise that closed over that portion of the surviving German populace who could credibly be branded as perpetrators of either the alleged genocide or of the "aggressive war" that had so impinged upon the territorial prerogatives of the victors at the outset. All the prosecuting powers recruited from their populations those who might be: (a) in some way versed in legal procedures; and (b) able to speak German, and translate it into some other language (French, English, or Russian).

What group could form this cadre, but those who, born and raised in Germany, had escaped or otherwise left it because of their membership in a group disfavored (with increasing severity as the war progressed to its disastrous conclusion) by the National Socialist regime of Germany? Their spirit of vengeance was fired not only by the misfortunes (if any) they had experienced, but further by the worse misfortunes (as they understood them) of their co-racialists who had remained behind after they themselves had effected their fortuitous exits. Indeed, it seems inescapable that some of these avenging angels may even have felt some guilt arising from the contrast between their own fates and those imputed to their *mischpoche* who had remained behind. Perhaps they (thought they) had parents to avenge, or grandparents, or uncles, or . . . other family members, and only the most-scathing sorts of vengeance could expiate their own sins of having abandoned these relatives to their actual or supposed fates.

In any case, a horrific "Catch-22" arose in the prosecution of "war criminals" in occupied Germany after the War. Participants in the Recent Unpleasantness (of concentration camps) were divided up into two groups: Victims, and Accuseds. Victims were, for the most part, Jews, or people who could pass themselves off as Jews. With the returning Jewish-emigrant prosecutors, these formed the opposing "jaws" between which suspected Germans were easily and relentlessly crushed.

Accuseds (the term "defendants" was not used) were for the most part Germans, or other nationalities from which the Germans recruited guards and other such helpmates. There was some "leakage" between these categories, as some Jews were identified (though not prosecuted) as vigorous collaborators in the Nazis' nefarious schemes, and a good few Gentile Germans, such as Seventh-Day Adventists, were identified as victims in the wartime control schemes of the National Socialists.

But matters seemed to sort themselves out, mostly along ethnic lines. It was, in the most lethal form imaginable, a swearing contest. The winners of this contest included many like Elie Wiesel, recipient of a Nobel Prize and many other trophies for the prosecution he pursues even to this present day.

And in this contest, a certain kind of swearer seemed, ineluctably, to gain sway over the proceedings. This was the swearer who affirmed the legend, dating all the way back to clandestine broadcasts of 1942 from Polish resistance fighters, that the Germans had invented, designed, built, and successfully deployed, an entirely new technology for mass murder, the gas chamber—and this employing the crudest and most unlikely of vehicles, that of either the cyanide-based insecticide Zyklon-B, or of carbon monoxide produced, variously, by gasoline engines or even cylinders clearly marked CO_2 (carbon dioxide, a totally non-toxic gas).

The support for these notions was considerable—even compelling—and compelled. First, perhaps, was the surrounding conditions in Germany at the time "witnesses" were recruited to provide their damning tales for the proceedings then underway.

The land, it might be said, was starving. Food, and warmth, and shelter, were to be found in only one place: the hands of the conquering Allies. These alone could provide the necessaries of survival; all else was cold, and hunger, and fatal exposure.

But this precious Allies-monopolized sustenance could be had, at a price that many were able, by hook or by crook, to pay: testimony as to German atrocities. This did not by any means require actual *experience* of said atrocities. It only required an awareness of what the dominant thrust of desired testimony already was and a credible account supporting the "witness's" presence at or even just near the places where they were said to have occurred. And this, in turn, was available, perhaps for a price, from those conspicuous, well-fed and otherwise comfortable denizens of the enviable living that was provided for "witnesses" able to provide testimony of the desired sort. An "industry"—the first "Holocaust Industry"—was born.

Opportunists, not to mention those intent on mere survival, naturally piled on, including, no doubt, many who were "Jews" merely for the occasion, if it buttressed the particular testimony that they had managed to concoct. A testifying contest ensued, in which Allied prosecutors enjoyed the luxury of selecting those who by various means legitimate and otherwise managed to proffer the most-damning testimony with which to convict the many accuseds then held in the Allies' well-populated prisons.

These "witnesses," no doubt, included Jews, and included people who had endured the hardships of labor camps—even people who were both. But whatever these witnesses were or were not, they contrived to present barely credible tales of the depredations of "the Germans" upon their own and other persons, and while they were engaged in this activity, they received from the Allies good food, good clothing, and good shelter such as not even the surrounding native population were in most cases able to enjoy. And such incentives, no doubt, goaded them continually to provide testimony that satisfied their Allied benefactors—for one more winter, if for nothing more.

Such "witnesses" were not sworn to any truth, not on a Bible, nor on any tract pertaining to their actual or pretended beliefs. They were likewise immune, in effect, against any sort of charge of perjury. If a tribunal happened to discount their testimony, and mete out against the accused(s) some sentence a bit short of what might have been implied as appropriate by the testimony provided, that was the end of it. No witness in any of the post-war atrocity trials was ever even threatened with any such sanctions as those arising from perjury.

The accuseds, for their part, were subject to strictures that cut very much in the opposite direction. To begin with, they were barred from arguing against the alleged crimes having even been committed—the defense of corpus delicti (body missing) was denied them by a "judicial notice" the tribunals took to the effect that a practice of deliberate genocide had been pursued by the nation into which the accuseds had been born, and in whose service they took part, whether willingly or through conscription.[5]

Further to the "judicial notice" that the tribunals took regarding who was guilty of what, and why, was a blanket allegation of "constructive conspiracy," in which any person who took any part in any function of any suspected camp or other such operation was held to be guilty of the alleged genocidal enterprise, even if he were able somehow to *prove* actual unawareness of the enterprise, and entirely aside from whether his duties entailed killing, sustaining, or having nothing whatsoever directly to do with the putative victims.[6]

Finally, a defense provided for the powerless underlings who constitute upwards of ninety percent of the muscle of every army or otherwise violence-based suasive force, the defense of "orders from above" was likewise arbitrarily suspended for the accuseds, though after the tribunals, it was hastily restored to the codes by which subordinates in the triumphant armed forces might defend themselves in tribunals as yet unestablished. No matter if you faced discipline, transfer to the dreaded Eastern Front, being broken in rank, or even the firing squad for insubordination, if you followed (or could not prove you refused to follow) those orders to do things of which you were accused, you were guilty.

This left only two recourses to accuseds who hoped to attain a prison sentence instead of a quick trip to the gallows, both recourses having similar effects. The first was, to confirm, amplify, and extend the overall tales of atrocity and genocide. Doing this was hoped, and was seen, to garner at least some degree of leniency on the part of the prosecution, whose goal was, after all, the incrimination of an entire nation, and not just of whatever hapless accused might occupy the dock at any particular moment. So, many accuseds, from Rudolf Höss[7] on down, took up this gambit as a desperate attempt to appease their inquisitors, quite like defendants in proceedings throughout history in which the verdict, if not the sentence, was quite foregone.

The second recourse was even more potent, but accordingly more demanding in terms of testimonial content: one could, given sufficient information and guile, accuse some *other* of the crimes of which one stood accused oneself. It was preferable, of course, to name some other accused who was within the reach of the prosecutors, and if one could somehow arrange the cooperation of victim-witnesses, this enabled the inquisitors to at least appear to be casting their damning nets so much the wider.[8]

Obviously, both of these techniques of self-defense broadened and deepened the channels in which the original lie ran—all the product of the efforts of accused perpetrators to avoid bearing themselves the brunt of the victors' wrath—and of the vengeful refugees from, and of self-styled victims of, the racial policies of the vanquished. Thus did policies of ethnic cleansing and industrial enslavement become transmogrified in the eyes of later generations, by way of "judicial" testimony, into a gruesome, hideous program of torture and extermination that quite boggled the minds of all who heard of it.

Is that such a great leap, after all? Morally, it bridges the chasm that would seem to lie between racial and national survival, on the one hand, and inhuman hubris and cruelty on the other. But in tangible terms, the two in a retrospect beclouded by war can barely be distinguished one from another.

The only thing imaginable that could forever cement this critical, moral distinction—a distinction that forever damns the perpetrators and all their descendants in time, and ennobles their innocent victims and their issue forever, would be ... gas chambers.

Notes:

1. An interesting discussion of the population effects appeared in *Smith's Report* for February 2010 (No. 169) in N. Joseph Potts's "Fighting Hatred, One Lie at a Time."
2. Paul Rassinier. *The Holocaust Story and the Lies of Ulysses*. Institute for Historical Review, Newport Beach, Cal., 1978.
3. The best review of the development of the Holocaust Narrative is the subject of Part 1 of *The Gas Chamber of Sherlock Holmes*, by Samuel Crowell, Nine-Banded Books, Charleston, W. Va., 2011.
4. An unforgettable account of the inner workings of these war-crimes trials is the subject of *Innocent at Dachau*, by Joseph Halow, Institute for Historical Review, Newport Beach, Cal., 1993.
5. Article 21, Constitution of the International Military Tribunal, at http://avalon.law.yale.edu/imt/imtconst.asp.
6. The last line of Article 6 of the Constitution of the International Military Tribunal reads (emphasis mine): "Leaders, organizers, instigators *and accomplices* participating in the formulation or execution of a common plan or conspiracy to commit any of the foregoing crimes are responsible for all acts performed by any persons in execution of such plan." The term "accomplices" was relied upon to indict virtually any person present at, or otherwise involved in supporting, concentration camps who was not an actual detainee.
7. Höss was the commandant of Auschwitz. He is the putative author of *Commandant of Auschwitz*, Weidenfeld & Nicolson, London, 1959. This book contains details (many of which have since been disproven) of atrocities at Auschwitz which Höss claimed to have witnessed and/or ordered.
8. Perhaps the greatest example of this is *KZ Auschwitz—Reminiscences of Pery Broad—SS Man in Auschwitz Concentration Camp*, Panstwowe Muzeum Oswiecim, Oswiecim, Poland, 1965, which SS Unterscharführer Pery Broad wrote while defending against charges in the Frankfurt Auschwitz Trials. His success in this endeavor may be gauged against his sentence: four years of imprisonment, or about the same as Germar Rudolf served for the crime of investigating and reporting allegations such as Broad's.

From the Memoirs of a German Soldier: Auschwitz, Buchenwald and Alfred Hitchcock's First Horror Movie

Nemo Anonymous

1. Auschwitz-Birkenau as Seen through the Eyes of a Recuperating Trooper

I was a tank soldier, a member of a unit consisting of 70 Panther tanks which was pulled out of the Normandy invasion-opposition front and transferred to the Eastern front in mid-June 1944. By countless attacks by day and by night, we broke the enemy ring around Vilna and halted the advance of the Red Army against East Prussia. We also saw action in the Narew and Weichsel salients, and in October of 1944 we repulsed the hordes of Russian tanks moving toward Warsaw. By the middle of November, my company consisted of a mere three tanks. At that time an armored unit moved into our sector of the front to which we were allowed to attach our three remaining *Panzers*.

For almost six months we were constantly engaged in combat, both day and night, fighting under the worst supply situation imaginable. More than half of my comrades were killed, and those still alive looked terrible. We were nothing but skin and bones, with deeply lined faces and pale waxy complexions, indescribably filthy and infested with lice. For months we had been wearing the same uniforms and underwear, completely soaked with oil and sweat. The relentless overexertion had visibly frayed the nerves of many of my comrades. We were thankful to have survived the countless battles and overjoyed when we got the prospect of a little recuperation with a chance to catch up on our sleep. We left our section of the front and were transported by truck to the concentration camp at Birkenau. Approaching our destination, we saw columns of concentration-camp laborers wearing brown uniforms and engaged in constructing fallback defensive positions. Toward evening we arrived at Camp Birkenau.

Ostfront-Süd, Panzer V "Panther" Ausf. A.; PK 695 Bundesarchiv, Bild 101I-244-2321-34 / Waidelich / CC-BY-SA [CC-BY-SA-3.0-de (http://creativecommons.org/licenses/by-sa/3.0/de/deed.en)], via Wikimedia Commons

The camp seemed to have been mostly evacuated, administered by the "Todt" Organization (major construction firm) using a large number of convicts. In addition to us, there were several other small groups from dissolved front-line units in camp. We three tank crews were assigned a barracks but not yet allowed to enter it. Four prisoners were assigned to us as orderlies; they led us to the shower installations. Our uniforms, underwear and blankets had to be deloused. The orderlies were horrified at the sight of our filthy rags. After bathing we were dusted with delousing powder and issued new underwear and overalls, along with two new blankets each. Finally we were allowed to enter our barracks; then we went to the mess hall to eat. After six months, finally getting a good hot meal, two warm blankets and being allowed to sleep in a bed, seemed too good to be true. After two days we got our cleaned and deloused uniforms back.

Several days later an SS sergeant approached us and requested that we take charge of supplies for his armored unit and deliver them to the front. We were to go to Auschwitz and pick up submachine guns, ammunition, smoke signal devices, blankets and other items for the combat squadron of our SS *Panzer* comrades. We drove there next day, but some of the items were not in stock and so we had to wait several days. We were quartered in the transit barracks. Every day we went to the warehouse with our requisition forms until finally we had everything on the list.

Included on the list were 50 blankets, which were stored in a building two stories high. This building had a central passageway with four tiers of wooden shelves on the right and left, part of which were filled with blankets. When I entered the building I could not see anyone but I heard voices coming from behind the bales of blankets. When I announced myself with a loud "hallo!" someone up above asked what I wanted. I replied that I wanted 50 blankets whereupon the unseen voice told me to count out fifty and take them away. When I replied that this was their job, four dark figures climbed down from the top bales of blankets, where they had been playing cards. Then they very ceremoniously counted out 50 blankets and loaded them onto our lorry while offering to sell us foreign cigarettes, chewing gum, cookies and wrist watches. The prisoners explained that they were allowed to receive Red Cross packages every month, and the camp was regularly inspected by the Red Cross.

On another occasion I observed six loafing prisoners pushing a small cart containing two bales of hair from the railroad dock to the camp. (During the War, barbers were required to collect human hair and turn it in, since hair was a raw material for the manufacture of felt boots.) I became really angry as I watched the lazy tempo of these prisoners, goofing off and smoking cigarettes. After all, I had just spent six months in constant combat, day and night, under the most severe exertion and deprivation imaginable. Half of my comrades had been killed while these jailbirds were having an easy time of it. This seemed unjust, incomprehensible! My comrades, filled with indignation, expressed the same sentiments.

After three days we finally received all the requested material and drove to the front with our supplies. I had the impression that Auschwitz was a huge supply depot for the Eastern Front, with additional buildings used for production and repair. While there we spoke with a large number of prisoners, but no one mentioned anything about gassings or cremations. We departed Auschwitz with the disquieting impression that the prisoners there had a much easier time of it than the front-line soldiers in their daily duty.

2. A Train of Cattle Cars near Buchenwald

On June 6, 1945 I was released by the Americans and transported from the POW camp near Hof to Weimar, which I had designated as my home. I spent several days with the family of a comrade named Rauf, who had been a radio operator in my last tank crew. Since I was a native of East Prussia and could not return home, I was hoping to find work and lodging with a master craftsman.

During the day Weimar was populated by concentration-camp inmates from Buchenwald, who were identified by a red triangle on their clothing. I conversed with a large number of them, and they were in good physical condition. During the day they participated in political studies for several hours, returning to camp by 10 o'clock. They were waiting for their official release papers so that they could file claims for compensation. Among others, I met the orderly of Ernst Thälmann, whose official duties had been to wait on the Communist leader. He described how Thälmann had been killed next to the railroad tracks during an air raid. The official version was that the Nazis had murdered him. The orderly complained that the political prisoners had too many special privileges and were not required to work.

Since I was well supplied with American cigarettes I went into the Buchenwald Camp several times in order to exchange them for underwear, shirts and socks.

After a few days an inmate told me that the wife of the last commandant, a pretty blonde woman, had been raped countless times, all day long, by the American guard detachment. When she lodged a complaint, someone started the rumor that she had lampshades made from human skin. Other inmates disputed the story, describing it as disgusting atrocity propaganda invented to cover the crimes of her guards.

The streets of Weimar were patrolled by German auxiliary police appointed by the Americans. They wore Wehrmacht uniforms that had been dyed blue and they carried wooden clubs on their belts. I recognized one of these policemen as a resident of my home town who had been convicted of raping little girls. But when I greeted him as a hometown acquaintance, he denied being from there and pretended not to know me. I looked for work everywhere in Weimar without success, so I decided to go to Erfurt in search of employment. I also wanted to visit relatives there.

On a sunny day in mid-June 1945, I hopped on a freight train and went to Erfurt. The train stopped about a kilometer and a half before the station, so I shouldered my rucksack and began walking toward the station. I soon noticed a freight train of about 20 cattle cars sitting on a side track. A foul odor was coming from that direction. As I came closer I saw hands protruding from ventilation holes and heard sounds of moaning, so I crossed several tracks and approached the cattle cars. The people inside noticed me and began crying "Water, comrade, water!" Then I reached the train and recognized the terrible stench of feces and rotting corpses. The sliding doors and ventilation holes were crisscrossed with barbed wire securely nailed. Urine and partially dried feces oozed from under the sliding doors and between the boards.

I experienced a feeling of helplessness in a completely unexpected situation. In vain I looked about for a water hydrant used to fill the locomotive boilers. In the cattle cars they continued crying for water and saying that there were many corpses inside, people who had been dead for many days. I felt I had to do something but I was completely helpless. I took a few green apples from my knapsack, stuck them in my uniform jacket, and climbed up to a ventilation hole so that I could push them through the barbed wire. Suddenly an American guard began yelling and yanked me down from the cattle car. Another guard came and began jabbing me with his bayonet. Both guards hustled me out through the station entrance, where they let me go. I spent that night in a burned out lorry with another released Wehrmacht soldier, whom I told about our comrades in the cattle cars. Hoping to free the prisoners with an iron bar, we crept over to the rail yard, but our mission was impossible since the train was guarded by doubled sentries with dogs.

Alfred Hitchcock was persuaded by Sidney Bernstein to leave Hollywood to assist on project "F3080." F3080 was the name given to a project to compile a documentary film on German atrocities. The project originated in February 1945 in the Psychological Warfare Division of SHAEF (Supreme Headquarters Allied Expeditionary Force). Hitchcock was recorded expressing his primary concern that "we should try to prevent people thinking that any of this was faked." By Studio publicity still. Connormah at en.wikipedia [Public domain], from Wikimedia Commons

3. Hitchcock: The Great Simplifier

In 1977, during a visit to New York and Cape May, I recounted the story of the trainload of dying German prisoners to two former US officers. They had both been stationed in Heidelberg shortly after the war and they knew all about it. They agreed that the cattle cars were filled with captured German soldiers who were infected with typhus and dysentery. They were in fact unwitting extras in a movie being made by Alfred Hitchcock, the Hollywood horror-film specialist. He had been awarded a contract to make a movie about concentration camps for the Nuremberg tribunal. At night the dead prisoners would be unloaded at Buchenwald, Dachau and other concentration camps by those who were still alive. Hitchcock would then film them, depicting the heaps of corpses as victims of German atrocities. A large number of corpses were dumped at Buchenwald at night, and next day the citizens of Weimar were forced to walk past the heaps of rotting corpses and smell the sickening stench. Some of them actually believed the American propaganda, that the corpses had been concentration-camp inmates. It was all filmed as part of Hitchcock's movie. Afterwards the corpses were shoved into mass graves in the vicinity. That too was part of the script. This is the explanation that the two former officers of the US Army gave me concerning the trainload of dying German prisoners that I witnessed on June 16, 1945.

I certify that my testimony is a true account of what I myself have personally seen and experienced.

[The name and address of the US officer has been removed for his privacy and safety. The name and address of the author is on file with *Vrij Historisch Onderzoek* magazine, Postbus 46, B-2600 Berchem 1, Flanders in Belgium. —Ed.]

Translated by James M. Damon.

Smoking Crematory Chimney at Auschwitz: A Correction

Robert Bartec

Eyewitnesses of the Auschwitz-Birkenau camp have frequently testified that thick smoke belched out of the chimneys of the four crematories of that camp. One classic example is the testimony of former Auschwitz inmate Arnold Friedman. While being cross-examined about his experiences at Auschwitz, Friedman stated during the first Zündel trial in 1985:[1]

> *"There was smoke belching from the crematoria, and it gave us a constant smell – the crematoria being close enough and low enough for the smoke to be dispersed through the camp rather than go straight up."*

The paintings by former Auschwitz inmate David Olère, who claims to have lived in one of the Birkenau crematories for almost two years, give an artistic rendering of the general theme that pervades Auschwitz survivor statements. See for example his drawing "Inmates Hauling a Wagon Loaded with Victims' Belongings", where thick smoke can be seen rising from two crematory chimneys in the background.[2]

Also according to witness statements, the Birkenau crematories are said to have been in basically uninterrupted operation from May 1944 into the late summer of 1944, when the Nazis are said to have exterminated up to half a million Jews from Hungary and up to 70,000 Jews from the Lodz Ghetto.

At the same time, Allied reconnaissance aircraft took several air photos of the camp. Hence, if the witnesses' claims were true, we would expect to see thick smoke emanating from at least some of the crematory chimneys on at least some of these photos. In his trail-blazing work on air photo evidence about the Holocaust – or rather the lack thereof – John C. Ball has reproduced several of these reconnaissance photos which had been released to the public by that time. He posited that none of them shows any smoke-emitting crematory chimneys.[3]

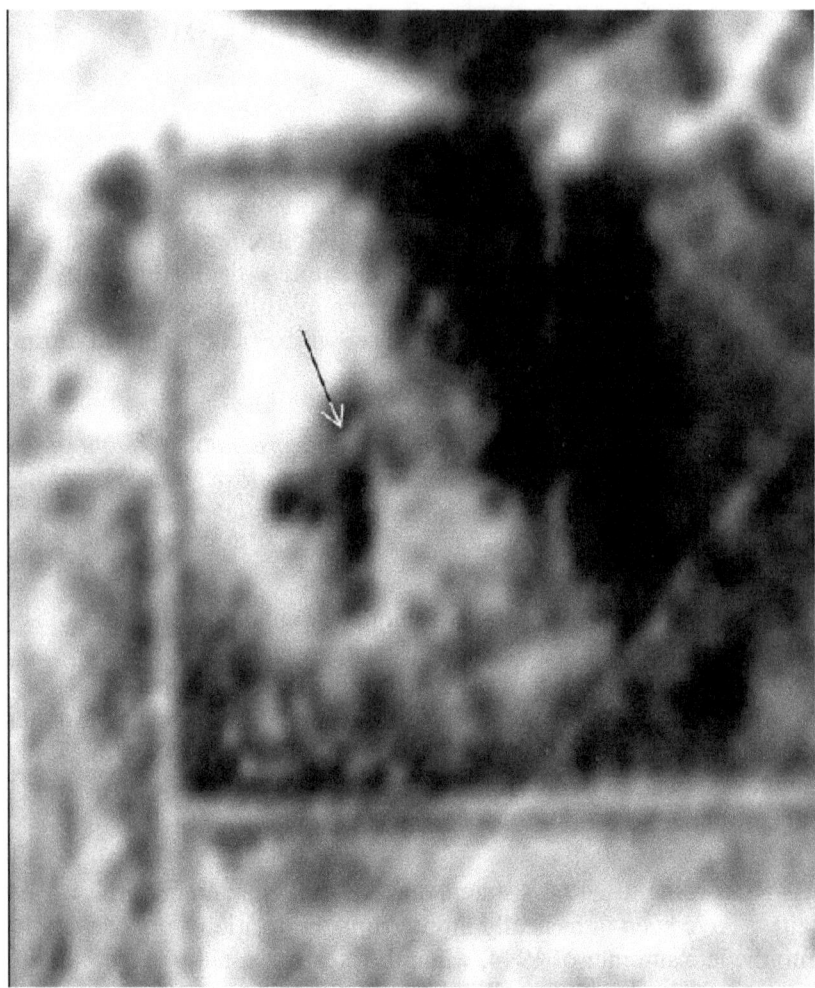

Ill. 1: Carlo Mattogno's Doc. 35 with his arrow allegedly pointing to smoke rising from the chimney of Crematory III at Auschwitz-Birkenau. Note the multitude of scratches on that photo running parallel to this line. Click to view the second image which shows the same location, but taken from the photo of August 23.

However, in his impressive 2005 work on open-air incinerations at Auschwitz, Carlo Mattogno hypothesized that one air photo taken by a Canadian reconnaissance airplane on August 20, 1944, over the Birkenau camp "shows a dense column of smoke rising in a spiral from the chimney of crematorium III." See Illustration 1.[4]

Ill. 2: A section enlargement of the air photo of Aug. 20, 1944, showing Crematory III and its vicinity.

Although I do not wish to argue here that coke-fired crematory chimneys of that era did not emit smoke, I will show in the following that Mattogno's air photo evidence is flawed. In fact, what is visible on that particular air photo is not smoke from a chimney, as Mattogno claimed (see my Ill. 1), but rather a defect in the photograph.

As can be seen on the Aug. 20 photo, there are several slanted lines crossing the photo, which are probably mere streaks caused during some step of the film's processing/storing. One of these slanted lines happens to run across Crematory III, causing a bright smudge which appears to be smoke. Lots of these smudges can be seen in other parts of the photo as well, especially in contrast with the almost black ground in the right-hand part of the photo. I have highlighted some of these scratches in a GIF image, see Ill. 2. The photo has a few of the parallel scratches marked with thin red lines. As the reader can easily see, there are many more scratches. In fact, the entire photo is covered with them. These lines are not visible on the Aug. 23 photo, which is of a much better quality.[5]

To support my assertion, I wish to make a few additional points:

1. The actual chimney is located roughly in the center of the side wing of the crematory building, which extends towardsthe left on the photo. Yet the bright, hence thickest part of the alleged "smoke" is located on the roof of the building's main wing, some 10 meters away from the actual chimney location. There is no bright smudge above the chimney itself. I posit that it is quite impossible for a coke-fired crematory to emit smoke in occasional spurts, leading in this instance to its most conspicuous visibility some 10 m away from the source. The smoke should actually be more visible closer to the source rather than not visible at all.

2. Smoke rising from a chimney always produces a conical shape (or a triangle on a 2D projection = photo), which widens with increasing distance from the source. But if we take an even closer look at the image, Ill. 3, it turns out this "smoke" appears to be tapering down with increasing distance from the chimney. Real smoke behaves differently: It is thick and focused at the source, but thins out and widens in the distance. To prove that point, see the actual smoke cone rising from the yard of Crematory V, see Ill. 3.

This brings up my final point.

3. The wind direction on this photo is from the south to north as shown by the real smoke coming from the yard of Crematory V, but this alleged "smoke" coming from Crematory III has a direction from southeast to northwest, parallel to all the other streaks. See the arrows on Ill. 3.

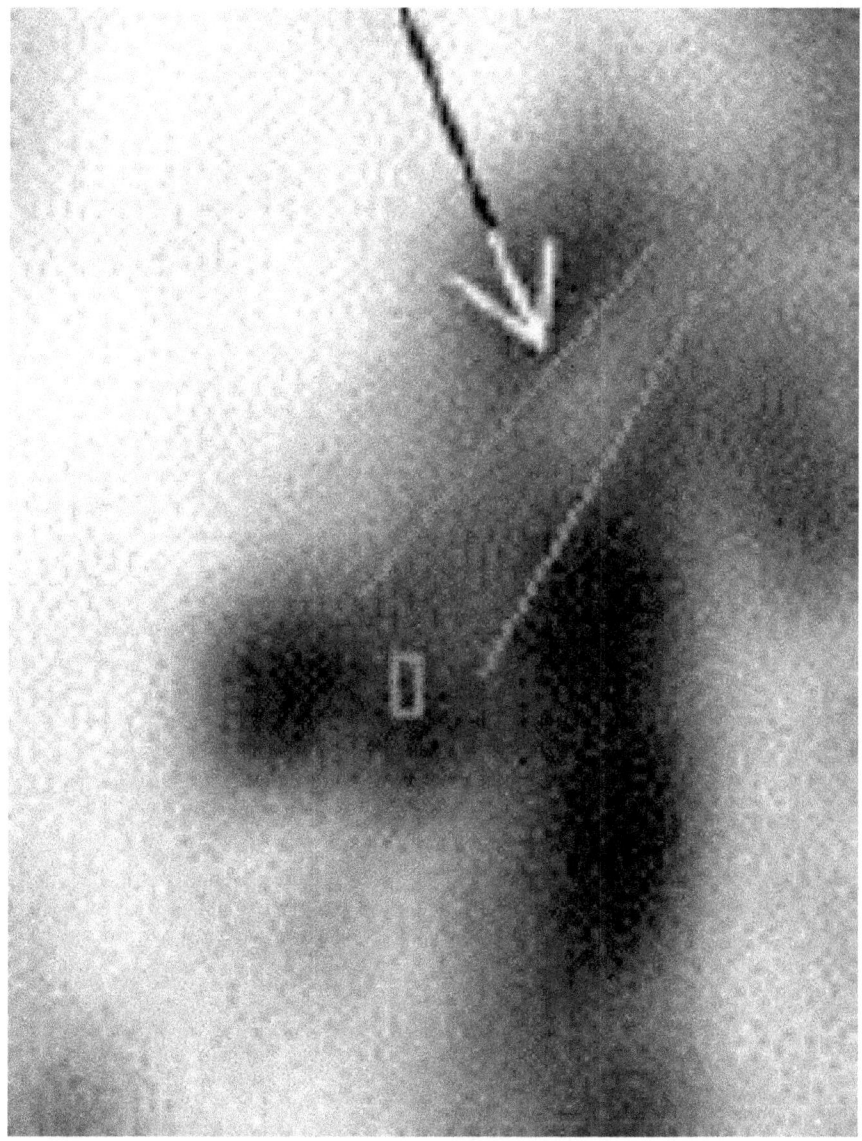

Ill. 3: Further enlargement of the air photo of Aug. 20, 1944, showing only Crematory III. The conical shape of the grey shade over this building is highlighted with gray lines. The gray rectangle denotes the rough position of the chimney.

My conclusion is therefore that this is only an error/artifact on the photo, since the entire photo is covered by these slanted streaks in the same direction as the one marked by a red arrow over Crematory III.

One of these streaks anomalously produced the illusion of smoke rising from that chimney.

Ill. 4: Mattogno's Doc. 34, from which his Doc. 35 was taken (my Ill. 1): The direction of the alleged smoke rising from Crematory III (short dark gray arrow to the left) is from southeast to northwest, whereas the direction of the smoke rising from the yard of Crematory V is roughly from south to north (long dark gray arrow, center top).[6]

Hence, as of this day there is not a single known air photo of Auschwitz-Birkenau showing smoke coming out of any of the crematories. Yet there are several showing smoke billowing from a limited area in the yard of Crematory V, as for instance also on the one shot three days later, on Aug. 23, 1944, and on one taken on July 8 of that year. Aerial photography does not support witness statements of profusely smoking crematory chimneys at Auschwitz-Birkenau. In fact, the absence of smoke in these photographs suggests just the opposite.

Notes:

1. District Court of Ontario. Between: Her Majesty the Queen and Ernst Zündel. Before: The Honourable Judge H.R. Locke and Jury (verbal record of the "first Zündel" trial of 1985), p. 315; similar on pp. 326, 344, 347; cf. Michael Hoffmann, *The Great Holocaust Trial*, 3rd ed., Wiswell Ruffin House, Dresden, N.Y., 1995, pp. 45-47.
2. To see more of Olères's artwork, http://fcit.usf.edu/holocaust/resource/gallery/olere.htm.
3. John C. Ball, *Air Photo Evidence*, publ. by author, Delta, B.C., 1992, esp. pp. 64f.
4. Carlo Mattogno, *Auschwitz: Open Air Incinerations*, Theses & Dissertations Press, Chicago 2005, p. 64, referring to Doc. 34f. on pp. 115f. Note: the photo enlargement on p. 116 incorrectly refers back to Doc. 31; it should be Doc. 34.
5. Ibid., Doc. 36, p. 117.
6. Ibid., Docs. 33 & 38, p. 114, 119.

REVIEW

In the Garden of Beasts

by Erik Larson. Crown Publishing Group, New York, 2011, 448 pp.

Ezra MacVie

By June 1933, the "Nazis"—a new word in the world's lexicon—had held power in Germany for almost six months, and were not expected to last, unlikely characters as virtually all of them were. The American ambassador to Germany had left his post shortly after Franklin D. Roosevelt's inauguration, and filling this post turned out to be a minor problem for the new president, because no one in the diplomatic establishment wanted it. Roosevelt had to "beat the bushes" with unwonted vigor to find an emissary. So finally, he secured assent to man the post from a candidate from very far outside the usual "farm" of blue-blooded New England WASPs from whom ambassadors to such important countries normally were recruited. Roosevelt picked a historian—a North Carolinian by birth, specialist in Southern history and biographer of Woodrow Wilson—who at that time chaired the History Department at the University of Chicago, to dive with his whole family into the seething cauldron that Germany turned out to be during the ensuing four-and-a-half years.

And this mild-mannered Southern historian, with some well-justified trepidation, did just that, to the enduring benefit of those who in later years seek understanding of just who was doing what to whom in that place and those times, and why, and how. William E. Dodd, "yeoman historian" though he was deservedly styled by his biographer, never published a memoir of his 1933-1937 service in Berlin, but his daughter Martha, who with his wife and son accompanied Ambassador Dodd to his European posting, wrote memoirs, and novels, from which much can be gleaned concerning the view an American might gain of events in the same times and places. And Dodd himself, of course, left a trove of dispatches to the US State Department that serve very well as a chronicle of his own perception of events, and after his retirement and return to America, Dodd availed himself of a "pulpit" from which to declaim messages that he felt must be conveyed after his service and the undoubtedly unique perspectives it afforded him.

William E. Dodd and family arrive in Hamburg, Germany in 1933. Public Domain. Library of Congress

But this book is not about Dodd, nor by any means entirely even him and his active and interesting family members. And it is of course not by Dodd, having been written some sixty years after his death. It is, rather, by a best-selling author of "novelized history," and this book itself enjoyed many weeks at the very top of the *New York Times's* Bestseller (Non-Fiction) list, making it perhaps the most-successful book yet reviewed in *Inconvenient History*. For anyone interested in history, revisionist or otherwise, it offers a wealth of impressions and experiences from times and places today much freighted with meaning in terms of subsequent events—including, of course, "events" celebrated primarily in propaganda and mythology since pressed into the service of national and ideological agendas in the present day.

According to Author Erik Larson, and I do not doubt him on this score, Dodd came away from his four-and-a-half years of representing the US government in Berlin with a loathing and fear of the new masters of Germany that built slowly from his arrival as an open-minded historian who had developed a love of German culture, the German language, and perhaps even German people from his student days in Leipzig before the First World War. Dodd was not only fluent in German, he had actually written a biography of Thomas Jefferson *in German* during his long and distinguished academic career that preceded his appointment. He was, in fact, a dissenting revisionist in his own right: at a time when an unbiased posture toward the behavior of the Confederate rebels spelled an early and ignominious end to the career of any academic, Dodd specialized in just such an illuminating perspective, and ultimately reaped success from this audacity. Harry Elmer Barnes would have found a kindred soul in this scholar of history. Dodd's views on blame in the First World War are not reviewed in this book, but I suspect they may have been such as Dodd may have found it most-politic to keep to himself, busy as he was with War between the States revisionism.

The book by no means limits itself to Dodd's own experiences, but excurds freely into experiences of his very-active daughter, Martha, with various (attractive, young) men, and even on some occasions into observations that the author has drawn directly from authoritative history, where it serves to provide context to what the main "characters" of this account undergo in their own rights. The end product of this style is an account that is notably more-engaging than conventional history, and affords the more intrepid sort of history aficionado the opportunity to extract understanding at a level that is simply unavailable to those holding to more-rigorous standards of historical exposition and inference. Readers respecting only "established facts" might do well to pass this book up; those seeking levels of experience transcending what can be objectively supported in accounts rendered by one person about yet another person(s) they never even met, on the other hand, may find Larson's confection highly rewarding. It is, assuredly, neither fiction nor non-fiction.

At the end of this slowly and magnificently building story, Ambassador Dodd returns to the United States a changed man. Upon his initial posting, it appeared as though Dodd planned to return to the appointment he held at the time in the History Department of the University of Chicago. Oddly, the narrative quite neglects this expectation, possibly because after four-and-a-half years, Dodd had attained an age at which retirement was much to be expected, at least at the time: 68. Or perhaps the death of his wife less than a year after his return affected his career decisions.

Be all this as it may, after his return to the US at the end of 1937, Dodd took up a "career" as a clarion to alert Americans to the "threat" Nazism—by then firmly established in indefinite control of the government of Germany—posed to America, and indeed to "mankind" in general. Both before and after the death of his lifelong mate, also named Martha, he maintained a schedule of appearances before groups across the United States that must have been punishing indeed for a man of his years. A cynic such as myself is tempted to infer some level of financial need in the enterprise, but that might be mere projection on the part of a person whose own success at providing for his material needs can at best be labeled no better than "marginal."

Dodd delivered himself of a scathing peroration against his (official) German hosts as early as his landing at New York on his final return to his homeland in early 1938. It was filmed and recorded in videos that are still today to be found on YouTube. He was by that time a "private citizen" of the United States by a matter of no more than a few days, and his subsequent agitation against the holders of governmental power in Germany of the times occasioned several heated complaints delivered to the US State Department by Dodd's former hosts. These complaints were all dismissed with a refrain to be heard even to the present day that America is a land of "free speech," in which anyone (no longer a governmental official) may espouse any view he might choose without interference from the government. Of course, this policy, to the extent it is still respected in the United States, continues to arouse frustration, bafflement, and suspicion on the part of persons not accustomed by experience to the compliance with such a principle.

Dodd's imprecations against the by-then-surprisingly durable masters of Germany seemed to rise in pitch and ferocity during the almost three years he pursued his new calling before his death in 1940. It is easy to imagine that this might have been prompted by his desire for a hearing—bearers of not-terribly-bad news can experience difficulty in gaining attention, as others, such as William Randolph Hearst, experienced (and overcame). Larson reports that Dodd frequently addressed Jewish groups on the subject, inviting speculation on the part of suspicious persons such as this reviewer as to who his paymasters might have been. By June 10, 1938, he was telling the Harvard Club, in a speech, that Hitler's intentions were "to kill them all," meaning the Jews at least of Germany, and perhaps of Europe. Dodd's later mental acuity also comes in for some telling criticism according to Larson's account, especially in the recording of his Consul General throughout his Berlin tour, George Messersmith. Messersmith noted, a couple of years before Dodd's death, an "organic decline" in the intellect of his former boss. What is called senility would be neither notable nor culpable in a person in that era who had attained the advanced age that Dodd had.

In the end, the cataclysmic war that Dodd foretold came to pass, as what in retrospect appears in the case of the US very much a self-fulfilling prophecy, not unlike other wars and human events of popular impetus in general.

Author Larson gently toes the lines that are clearly marked out for anyone venturing to publish a book in the present day on the history covered in his narrative. But, especially in view of those lines (to be toed) and the grave consequences awaiting anyone who does not deftly and persuasively honor them, the remaining tale, as a product of its own times, is compelling and quite possibly informative if decoded according to the cyphers that prevail in the times of its publication.

Embedded in its pages is a veritable bonus romantic novel covering the exploits of Dodd's 27-year-old daughter Martha, a woman of conspicuous "sexual appetite," that might clutter the history involved if it did not involve partners who embodied so much historical value in their own rights. Just one example is Rudolf Diehls, the first head of the GeStaPo, who survived not only the Second World War, but the witch trials of Nuremberg that came in its train.

A fascinating read, for devotees of revisionist and mainstream viewpoints alike.

www.ingramcontent.com/pod-product-compliance
Lightning Source LLC
Chambersburg PA
CBHW060103170426
43198CB00010B/752